Secrets of
GREATNESS

Untold Stories of Passed Sports Icons

Andy Purvis

Thank you so much!

Andy Purvis

xulon
PRESS

Editorial Reviews

Andy, the depth of your exposure to so many "greats" in the world of sports is amazing. Your research on these people has to have been a daunting task. With a couple of exceptions, the stories from the world of baseball made me laugh the most, although the football narratives really held my interest. No surprise there. Regardless of the reader's special interest in any particular sport, he will be drawn to the intimate portrayals of each and every story. No sugarcoating. Good job, Andy.

Ron Harms
College Football Hall of Fame Coach

Having been involved in baseball for over 65 years, the last 20 as an associate scout with the Houston Astros, I can now relax in my recliner and read the best sports stories ever written, thanks to my good friend, Andy Purvis. Keep them coming, Andy.

Pat Dwyer
Baseball Scout, Houston Astros and Brainchild of the RBI program for kids

I have always been fascinated with the story telling of Mr. Purvis. His ability to capture the reader's attention and paint a vivid picture is unlike any other. Cheers to you, and write on!

Victor Betancourt
Owner and Operator of V-Fit Training Centers

This book refreshes my memory and educates me on sports figures, famous and not so famous, that have passed on from this life with the passage of time. It emphasizes their great athletic accomplishments and returns us to the joys we received in our past days. I highly recommend its purchase to all sports fans as an enjoyable read and reminder of the satisfaction we have received from our association with these greats.

Sandy Clark
Baseball Fan and Fine Fisherman

Andy, your books are an enjoyable and informative read. They are insightful, truthful, and sometimes humorous. Your ability to look in-depth at each player and see the best in each of them is remarkable. You are a bridge between athlete and reader, making sure the story is correctly told. As athletes use their gifts in their chosen sport, you use your gifts each time you put pen to paper, to make sure the spirit of greatness in each athlete is captured. I am grateful to call you friend, and even more grateful for the authenticity of your literary works and character.

Bobby Smith
Two-time AFL Champion running back, Buffalo Bills

What pleasure I've received in my life by my interest in sports. Andy Purvis has enlarged that rich reward for me by revisiting these great athletes. His latest book is a real page turner.
What fun!

Jack Richmond
Chairman Emeritus of San Antonio Pizza Huts

With the knowledge of a historian and the love of a sports fan, Andy has a wonderful way with words, and his sense of humor and pathos make his essays a joy to read. Andy Purvis gave me my first foray into sports talk radio. A profound "thank you" to him and my heartfelt congratulations on his 20 years on the air!

Henry "Tiger" Hernandez
Radio Show Host

Andy Purvis continues to enthrall with his magical spell of weaving words into more than just sports stories, but also enhancing lives. Thank You Andy for sharing your gift with the world. The world needs to discover more of your talent. Next!

Rick Geiter
ABC-KIII TV

This book brought back so many great memories of the life of my favorite sports heroes during my childhood. I also listened to nightly play-by-play on my transistor radio. I followed the Cleveland Indians, and it was great to relive those exciting years, especially 1948. Thanks to Andy Purvis for making me feel young again. Now I'm giving this book to my 12-year-old grandson to read, so he can also learn about these great heroes of the past.

Wilson Perrin, DDS

Andy has a way with words that allows the casual reader to gain some remarkable insights into the lives of many of our greatest sports heroes. He enhances many of these stories with anecdotes from his own personal experiences with these stars, which enables you to have a unique perspective into their lives.

Sean Murphy
Vice President & General Manager of Andrews Distributing Company

These are all great books and they make excellent gifts. They made me think of many players that may have been forgotten.

Dave Sullivan
Friend and former Business Associate

What I really enjoy about Andy's books is that they are not all facts or statistics, but instead intimate short stories about the amazing athletes and coaches of our time. Myself, I have not met many of the legends he shares stories about. However, his short stories honoring our lost heroes bring them to life one more time. I get to see the personal side, a side I never knew or heard on ESPN or any other media.

Mark Dannhoff
Texas A&M Corpus Christi Islanders Men's Basketball Coach

To all who enjoy sports and sports history, Andy's books are the essential read. Having owned and read all of his books, I have not been disappointed in any of them. Andy has the unparalleled ability for the research he puts into each story. I can only describe his writing style as "smooth," like a Bluebell vanilla milkshake, something to savor from start to finish. I am proud to count Andy as a friend and look forward to his future books.

Marty Robinson
Hardball Fan

I have read all but the last book in the "Greatness Series" and I believe them to be the most informative, easiest reading, and most entertaining stories about true sports heroes. I'm not an avid reader, but your short-story style and sparkling wit keeps even me focused on the finish line. Thanks for your heartfelt dedication to capturing not only the statistics, but the heart and soul of these heroes. Keep writing and God Bless!

Dick Hermann
My Basketball Partner

Reading an Andy Purvis book is a walk through our own childhood. His insightful thoughts and little-known facts about our past heroes keep one glued to every word of every story. I can't count the times I have said "Wow, I didn't know that." Always a great read, I can't wait for the next story!

Chris Wicker
Just Another Weekend Warrior

Andy, your books are a hit!!! I have been a fan of your books since the first one you sent me years ago. I have enjoyed them so much that I can reread them. Your newest books are easy reading, full of history and interesting fun facts on sports greats that will help keep them in our sports talk. You have made your books enjoyable for all, not just sports fans. Thank you for putting their stories to paper for all to share. You keep writing and I will keep reading and sharing with others. Great Job on your writing!

Russ & Bev Ansley
Business Associate and Friend

Andy Purvis has a remarkable way of reaching into the lives of great athletes and sharing not only their accomplishments, but also the character and motivations that have made them great. Through his books, Andy's gift as a writer and heart of a hero has invited me to consider the best in others while accepting that like me, my heroes are human.

Michael Doane
Interim Pastor of Island Presbyterian Church

ALSO BY ANDY PURVIS

Until Next Wednesday
We'll See You at the Park
Copyright © 1998

Buy Me Some Peanuts...
Copyright © 1999

Love, Laughter & Cornbread
Copyright © 2001

Upon Further Review
Copyright © 2009

In the Company of Greatness
Copyright © 2010

Remembered Greatness
Copyright © 2012

Greatness Continued
Copyright © 2014

DEDICATION

This book is dedicated to to my four grandchildren: Sarah Bennett, Matt, Hannah and Nathan James and my two great-grandchildren, Jack and Caroline James. I am so proud of all of you and love you more than you will ever know.

CONTENTS

CONTENTS

FOREWORD

I was pleased and honored when I was asked to write the foreword to Andy Purvis' latest book. To my way of thinking this, his fourth book in the Greatness series, comes as close to perfection as anyone I've ever known as a writer, human being and friend. His devotion to his family and his sunny disposition keeps all of us who know him feeling bright and happy. Everyone who knows him has the same great respect for him that I do. Although there are many forms of friendship, some of which may vary from place to place, he has the characteristics which are present in any type of friendship. These characteristics include affection, sympathy, empathy, honesty, altruism, mutual understanding and compassion, enjoyment of each other's company, trust, and the ability to be oneself, express one's feelings, and make mistakes without fear of judgment from the friend. Andy Purvis is a true friend.

Andy's intimate knowledge of sports and sports personalities serves him well in these accounts of those who join us from the great beyond. Whether he writes of an individual or a sport, he brings these to us as if we are sitting around the table in one of Corpus Christi's favorite bistros.

I believe Andy would rather write than do anything else. He is, as most successful authors are, much disciplined and simply enjoys writing. Many aspiring authors enjoy the idea of writing, not the hard work itself, but Andy appears to thrive on the hard work, and works much harder than we might suppose. Writing is his passion.

As readers emotions move us; we want to experience emotion while reading. I believe all of the 63 stories in this book will make you feel emotions and you will love them.

Dotson Lewis
College Football Officiating Hall of Fame
Corpus Christi, Texas

PREFACE

All new things begin and end with a story. Quite frankly, our stories are gifts. In the traditional Japanese Tea Ceremony, it is believed that every human encounter is a singular occasion which can never occur again in exactly the same way. The great secret to storytelling is that memories are about now, not about then. We are all a collection of our memories. By listening to others share their memories; they make us feel now, in the present. That's why history is so important because it's about us and how we see ourselves. We can take history and learn from it. Things that matter often are attached to faith, children, science, and nature. I believe this to also be true about sports. Still, all of us need to be connected to one another. All of us have these complicated secret stories we need to tell.

I've been this close to some of the greatest athletes in the world. The greatest reality show is sports. Why, because it matters to us, the fans, and to them, the athletes. Babe Ruth once said, "It's hard to beat a person who never gives up." Rivalry and conflict make us wonder how we will be tested, how far we are willing to go to win. The lessons we learn in these games repeat themselves over and over in our lives. Every player from any sport is insecure. The pressure to succeed is great.

Your own mind is always your toughest opponent. Since the time we were six or seven years old, we have been built to be a part of a team. We were taught that the team is important. We shared as a team in the glory of winning and in the pain of losing. Along the way, we rooted for our teammates, because we all wanted to win. We do the same with our heroes in world of sports. My goal is to show you with my words who these people were. We can keep our heroes alive even though their physical body is gone. You can keep them alive by keeping their spirit alive, by keeping their beliefs and thoughts alive. What would they say, how would they react, the things you believed in them; just keep those alive and they stay alive. As long as we remember them, these people live.

There is a big difference between routine and commitment. Lots of people do the same things everyday, but few commit to the process. These athletes greatness lie in those commitments and they give us, the fans, moments to remember. Those moments never fade and we wait until the right time to close our eyes so they can come out and play once more.

This is my 20th year in sports talk radio and the fourth book of my "Greatness Series." They are all available without a prescription. Inside <u>Secrets of Greatness</u> you will find inspirational stories of some of the best of the best from the world of sports. Their names ring across time and most hang in the halls of fame of their chosen profession. Athletes like Ernie Banks, Frank Gifford, Calvin Peete, Yogi Berra, Buddy Baker, Kenny Stabler, "Hurricane" Carter, Meadowlark Lemon and Moses Malone remind us of better days from our past. Coaches like Chuck Noll, Dean Smith, Allie Sherman, Don Zimmer, Guy Lewis and Jack Ramsey left us way too early. We long to hear the familiar voices of announcers like Milo Hamilton, Jerry Coleman and Gene Elston. So pull up a chair, crack open this book and let me take you back to a time where "team" mattered most. I promise you will feel better after reading. Don't forget to checkout my website, www.purvisbooks.com.

BLACK BEAUTY

Action is the loudest and clearest statement of what people can do when they know they can. His ability to play the "hot corner" and then switch to the first sack was uncanny. It was as if he could see into the future. In my opinion, first base is the most underrated defensive position on the field. First basemen are involved in the majority of the plays and instrumental in saving errors. "He was the best defensive first baseman I have ever seen," said Red Sox vice president-emeritus and team historian, Dick Bresciani. His mantra was "Play as hard as you can and respect your opponent. Meanwhile, catch everything you can within reach and knock the cover off the ball." You never looked for reasons to take this guy out of the lineup; you looked for reasons to keep him in. He owned a smile that would melt chocolate and a great sense of humor; but at times, he could be as cold-blooded as an icebox. He once told a reporter that the necklace he wore around his neck was made out of second basemen teeth. Boy, could he blister a fastball; some say he could hit .300 with a pool cue. He hit baseballs like Floyd Patterson hits a chin. Maybe he had a coupon for all-you-can-eat fastballs. No doubt he could shrink a ballpark with one swing of his bat. Everyone knew that if you threw it in the wrong place you were going to need another baseball. When greatness meets class, there you have George "Boomer" Scott.

George Charles "Boomer" Scott Jr., was born early on the morning of March 23, 1944. He was a farm kid, dug up from a town named Greenville, Mississippi. He was the youngest of three children. His father George Sr. picked cotton for a living, but died before George turned three years old. Scott had no choice but to follow in his dad's footsteps and was picking cotton himself by the age of nine. "That's all we knew. Nothing could have been worse than getting up at four in the morning and waiting for a truck to pick you up to go pick and chop cotton from six in the morning until six in the afternoon." said Scott. When he was able to find the time, he did play Little League baseball and was once dismissed from the league for being too good. All he had done was hit two or three home runs per game over a six-game stretch. Coleman High School coaches could not wait for George to attend. But there was trouble on the horizon. There is a little-known story that George actually quit high school as a freshman. He decided to take a job to help his mother financially. When word got around that one of Greenville's best athletes had left school, a local bottling plant offered George a deal where he could work for them and return to school fulltime. This break would allow Scott to not only help support his family, but also to blossom into a great all-around athlete. They gave him the chance to become the Boomer.

While at Coleman, Scott excelled in baseball, basketball, and football. Interestingly, he was the starting quarterback and power forward for the Mississippi State Championship teams in football and basketball. George chose baseball instead of the other two sports because he could no longer stand watching his mom work three jobs to make ends meet. "I didn't have the mind that I could go to college and see my mother struggle for another four or five years," said Scott.

George Scott was discovered by Ed Scott (no relationship) of the Red Sox. He was actually signed by Milt Bolling, who was white, as African-Americans were not allowed at that time by the Red Sox brass to negotiate deals with players. George signed straight out of high school on May 28, 1962, as an amateur free agent. George was 18 years of age, received $8,000, and was a little overwhelmed. By the age of 22, Scott had worked his way through the Boston farm system with a stop in Pittsfield with the Double-A Eastern League team for the Red Sox. While there, in 1965, he became the League's Triple Crown winner. Scott flourished under Minor League Manager Eddie Popowski. Scott was one of the very first black players promoted as an everyday-position player for Boston.

Big George made his Major League debut on April 12, 1966, as a third baseman. He did not get off to a good start at the plate. It was either feast or famine for Scott. In his first season, Scott led the American League in two categories; strikeouts with 152 and grounding into double plays (25), but when he did connect, they traveled high and deep and gone. In fact, Scott led the American League three times in grounding into double plays (1966,'74,'75). He hit so many ground balls to the shortstop they started calling him "six-to-three." Interestingly, he became the last Red Sox rookie to start and play in all 162 games. He also started in the 1966 All-Star Game. Offensively, Scott ended the 1966 season with 27 home runs and recorded 90 RBI's. It was enough to reward him the American League Rookie of the Year Award.

At 6'2" tall and weighing over 250 pounds, his arms looked like the masts of a pirate ship. George Scott loved food, especially potatoes, baked, mashed, sweet potatoes, and just taters; you know "taters," those long home runs that left the playing field off Scott's bat, 271 times during his career. That's what he called his home runs, taters. In fact, that's how he got his nickname, "Boomer." Seems that Red Sox teammate Joe Foy claimed that the balls made a booming sound off Scott's bat when hit. Boston Globe writer Bud Collins heard the nickname and referred to Scott as "Boomer" in print, and the rest is history. Just ask Yankees' Hall-of-Fame pitcher, Whitey Ford. On April

26, 1966, it was Ford, "The Chairman of the Board," who threw the pitch that rookie George Scott promptly parked in the third deck of old Yankee Stadium. It was estimated to have traveled over 500 feet. "I love my home runs just like my taters," said Scott.

The most unlikely quality about George Scott was that for a big guy he could really move well and more importantly, catch. Whether he was playing third base or first, nothing got by him. George Scott could pick groundballs like a chicken picks up corn. George nicknamed his glove "Black Beauty" for obvious reasons. Watching George field hot grounders or dig out low throws was a thing of beauty. Along the way, he made fans gasp, teammates exhale relief, and collected eight Gold Glove Awards. George Scott without a glove was like Brooklyn without the Dodgers.

"He was the best first baseman I ever played with," said Red Sox pitcher, Bill Lee. "We were playing the Oakland A's at Fenway and I was on the mound. Bert Campaneris laid a bunt down the first baseline. I stumbled off the mound, grabbed the ball, my body now horizontal to the ground to make the throw. The ball actually bounced between Campaneris's legs, and Scott had to move to the coaching box side of first base to make the catch for the putout. It was the greatest play I had ever seen," said Lee.

Scott also wore a batting helmet while playing in the field, like Dick Allen and later John Olerud. Scott claimed he had been hit several times while on the road in the Minor Leagues, by fans who threw hard objects from their seats. I remember seeing George Scott chase pitcher Dennis Martinez into centerfield after being thrown at in a game against Baltimore.

George Scott is still the Red Sox all-time leader in games played at first base, with 988. In his 14-year career, Scott played in 2,034 games, batted .268, while clubbing 271 home runs, and recorded 1051 RBI's. He was great friends with teammates, Tony Conigliaro, Bill Lee, Reggie Smith,

Rico Petrocelli, and Carl Yastrzemski. Scott hit over 20 home runs six different times in his career. He played in one World Series (1967), spent six seasons playing both first and third base during the same season, and was an All Star in 1966, 1975 and 1977. His two best years at the plate occurred in 1967 when he batted .303 for Boston and in 1973 where he hit .306 for the Milwaukee Brewers. He had been traded on October 10, 1971, to the Brewers. In 1975, while still in Milwaukee, Scott almost won the Triple Crown. He lead the American League in home runs with (36) and RBI's (109), but fell short by batting only .285. Major League Baseball Commissioner, Bud Selig, said, "He was my first $100,000 player."

Scott was traded back to the Red Sox on December 6, 1976, and was later traded again in 1979, to the Kansas City Royals. While in Kansas City, he disappeared faster than the big kid in a dodge ball game. Months later, Scott was traded to the New York Yankees. Scott's final game occurred on September 27, 1979, as a Yankee. He was 35 years of age and looking forward to staying in the game he loved so much as a coach or manager. But, it was not to be.

The George Scott we all knew really died inside years ago, from a phone call that never came. He died from bitterness and anguish brought on by being overlooked after his playing days. Scott wanted desperately to stay in baseball. It was all he had. He felt passed over by the Red Sox and Major League Baseball. He had wanted to be a coach, a manager; even an instructor would have been okay. Forgiveness does not change the past, but it does enlarge the future. Scott had a run-in with Red Sox Manager Dick Williams early on in his career, and he remained haunted by that experience. Scott was finally somewhat recognized in 2006, when he was inducted into the Boston Red Sox Hall of Fame. As if being punished, he was joined by none other than Dick Williams that same year. George recalled years later that no one from the team including teammates or management came to his table that night at dinner, to congratulate him. Scott did not bother to attend the Red Sox 100th year anniversary celebration, even though he was invited. In fairness, Scott did manage in the Mexican Leagues for awhile and also managed for a few independent leagues, but nothing after that.

Scott left us suddenly, without warning, on a Sunday. *Sports Collectors Digest* claimed he died in a drowning accident. The date will be recorded as July 28, 2013. He was 69 years of age and was laid to rest in Lakewood Cemetery located in Greenville, Mississippi. George raised three sons: Dion, George III and Brian. His grandson, Deion Williams, played shortstop at Redan High School in Georgia and was selected by the Washington Nationals in the 2011 draft. He now pitches for the Auburn Doubleday's, a Class-A team in the New York-Penn League.

George Scott was a proud black man who revealed very little about himself, about how he had become a diabetic. He was angry, embarrassed, and had declared bankruptcy. Scott died while living in the home he had built for his mother, in Greenville, Mississippi, after the 1967 World Series. Some might say that George Scott had done the impossible. Like most poorly educated men born in the Deep South, Scott was not considered very smart; but if you took the time to watch and listen to this God-fearing man, his wisdom spoke volumes. The Boston Red Sox honored George Scott with a moment of silence before their July 27th Monday night game with the Tampa Bay Rays.

George Scott hit 154 of his 271 career home runs at Fenway. George was home cooking, and everybody loves home cooking.

MOTORMOUTH

This guy was a ball hawk that caught everything, including falling baseballs. He was so fast he was in scoring position when standing in the on-deck circle. As an outfielder, he got to everything he was supposed to. Nothing fell in the outfield grass but, perhaps, raindrops. He practiced until his legs "melted" from overuse, played shallow, and counted his steps to the warning track. He was Mr. "Web Gem" before ESPN's night-time segment on "Baseball Tonight." He was what they called a "gap to gap" player, a wizard with the leather. He played quickly, roamed centerfield with flair, and would hold his glove to his chest like a newborn baby, as he trotted off the field when the inning ended. Watching a game with this guy was not just a day at the park, it was grad school for the game of baseball. You can't read a book and learn how to play baseball. You need to play the game and watch the game being played. You should be able to walk into any park with the scoreboard covered up and know which team is winning just by watching how they are playing. He could play anywhere, because he just knew how to play baseball. He could leap like a spawning salmon, and he would fall on a grenade to save his team a run. There is an old story about a doctor who asked a young fellow what he dreamed about at night. The fellow answers, "playing baseball." The doctor then asked, "Don't you ever dream about anything else?" "Of course not," says the fellow, "then I would miss my turn at bat." That was Paul Blair. His teammates referred to him as a deodorant player, because he made every stinky thing on his team smell better.

Blair also loved to talk, and he could be crafty like a dealer of Three Card Monty. This guy was not the teammate you wanted to sit beside on a plane ride from Baltimore to Seattle, because he just would not shut up. He talked so much I was afraid his teammates might have to hood him like a falcon so they could get some sleep. He was, however, referred to by many as a walking, talking history lesson involving Major League baseball.

Paul L.D. Blair was born in Cushing, Oklahoma, on February 1, 1944. A 1969 article in *Sport Magazine* explained that the L.D. did not stand for anything. In his neighborhood, you couldn't sling a cat around over your head without hitting a church. His family eventually moved to Los Angeles, California. In 1961, Paul graduated from Manual Arts High School and proclaimed to be a Dodgers fan, mainly because of Jackie Robinson. Blair had grown up on 52nd Street, just a short walk from L.A. Coliseum. He also enjoyed watching Duke Snider and Carl Furillo. A fine athlete, Paul lettered in three sports, the high jump in track and field, basketball, and of course baseball. At the age of 17, Paul was invited to a Dodgers' tryout camp. Paul went 3-for-5 at the plate, with a home run, but his glove work lacked finesse. The Dodgers never called him back. Paul's feelings ran deep and now he had been hurt by the Dodgers. Now his dream became beating the Dodgers in their park for a World Series title. Fortunately for Paul, the New York Mets disagreed with the Dodgers and offered him a contract.

Floyd "Babe" Herman signed 17-year-old Paul Blair on July 20, 1961, for the New York Mets. As an amateur free-agent shortstop, Blair received $2,000. Blair told an interesting story about when he reported to the Mets, they told the players to lineup at their positions. "Seven guys went to the shortstop position and six to second base," said Blair. "But only one went to right field and knew I could throw better than him and run better than him. So, I ran out to right and played there. Then the centerfielder got hurt, so I moved to center." It would be the beginning of a wonderful career. In 1962, he was sent to Santa Barbara of the California League, where he hit .228 with 147 strikeouts. Those results prompted the Mets to leave Blair unprotected and the Baltimore Orioles drafted him in the 1962 first-year draft. The Orioles sent Blair to their farm club in Elmira, New York. At the age of 20, Blair appeared in his first Major League game on September, 9, 1964, as a pinch runner. The Mets lost that day, 4-3 to the Washington Senators.

Blair also met his first wife, Evelyn Cohen, in Elmira. They married on the baseball diamond, on April 15, 1964. They had two children, a son Terry, born September 23, 1965, and a daughter Paula, born May 29, 1968.

Before the 1965 season began, Blair completed a six-month tour of duty with the Army Reserve at Fort Jackson, South Carolina. Guess what his duties were; you guessed it, communication specialist. He more than likely talked his way through the reserves. Blair and his wife moved into a Baltimore apartment located in a black neighborhood known as Beacon Hill. They would join two other black players for the Orioles, Frank Robinson and Sam Bowen. Brooks Robinson would make sure he invited Frank, Paul and Sam to join him and "Boog" Powell for postgame food and drinks. Blair was scared to death of snakes. Teammate Moe Drabowsky would purchase live snakes from a pet store and hide them in Blair's uniform and gloves.

Blair opened the 1965 season in centerfield for the Baltimore Orioles. Manager Hank Bauer liked his speed but thought Blair played too shallow to be effective. Earl Weaver, Blair's second manager, loved Blair's abilities. Weaver believed that saving a run was as good as scoring a run, but playing shallow was a concern. One day Weaver aired out Blair in front of the team in the dugout, after a line drive had been hit over Blair's head. So, Blair stood on the warning track the next inning and would not move. Luckily no balls were hit his way. When Paul returned to the dugout, Weaver was waiting for him again. Blair had already won several Gold Gloves by this time so Weaver said, "Play where you want."

Pitching and defense became the motto of Baltimore. Weaver called it "The Oriole Way." "We don't make mistakes that cause us to lose a game," said Weaver. The Oriole Way would lead Baltimore to the 1966 World Series. In 1966, Blair hit a respectable .277 and helped the Orioles win the World Series over the Los Angeles Dodgers in a four-game sweep. In Game Three of that Series, Blair hit a 430-foot home run over the bull pen for the only run of the game. While rounding the bases, Blair grinned so wide he could have swallowed his own ears. Oriole's pitcher, Wally Bunker, would benefit from a 1-0 shutout. Blair had become the third player to win a World Series game on a home run, 1-0. Only Casey Stengel of the 1923 New York Giants and Tommy Henrich of the 1949 New York Yankees had done the same. In Game Four, Blair climbed the centerfield fence, robbing Dodgers' Jim Lefebvre of an eighth-inning home run to protect Orioles pitcher, Dave McNally's 1-0 shutout. Baltimore became the first non-New York American League team to win a World Series since 1948. Blair's play had made the difference in two of the four games.

In 1967, Blair hit a career high .293 with eleven home runs and 64 RBI's. Blair also hit a league high, 12 triples. Later that same year, Blair broke his ankle playing winter ball in Puerto Rico. Still, he recovered in time and played 141 games in 1968, but batted only .211. In 1969, Weaver batted Blair second behind Don Buford, and Paul responded by hitting .285 with a career-high 26 home runs and 76 RBI's. His Orioles won the pennant again. Blair also scored 102 runs and became the first player to record five hits in a single post-season game. Blair went 5 for 6 on October 6, 1969, against the Minnesota Twins. The Orioles would later lose to the "Miracle Mets" in the 1969 World Series. In Game Three of that Series, Paul Blair became the first batter ever to face a "fireballer' from Texas. They called him Nolan Ryan. It turned out that Game Three of the 1969 World Series is the only game in which Ryan would pitch, during his entire career. He never got back to a World Series. Blair sent a line drive to the outfield that was caught by a diving Tommy Agee.

On May 31, 1970, Blair was hit in the face by a ball thrown by California Angels' pitcher Ken Tatum. Paul had to be carried off the field. He had suffered a broken nose. Blair did recover and returned to the line-up three weeks later. The 1970 Orioles would meet Pete Rose, Joe Morgan, Johnny Bench, George Foster and the rest of the "Big Red Machine" from Cincinnati, for all the marbles. The Orioles would defeat the Reds, as Blair batted .474 by hitting safely nine times in a five-game World Series. It is still a Major League record. What most people remember about that Series is the glove work by Brooks Robinson, who would be selected the MVP of the Series.

In 1971, Blair attempted to learn how to switch hit, but he later gave it up. In 1972, his average slipped to .233. He was afraid at the plate and, being a fastball hitter he stood a little too close to home plate. He sought advice from a psychiatrist, Dr. Jacob H. Conn, and received hypnosis therapy, which restored his confidence in his ability to avoid inside pitches. Over the next two weeks, he hit .522. He ended the season at a respectable .280.

On August 26, 1973, his hitting continued. Blair hit a rare inside-the-park grand-slam home run off Paul Splittorff of the Kansas City Royals. On September 3, 1973, Blair again hit a three-run, inside-the-park home run against John Curtis. In 1974, Blair led the American League with 477 put-outs from centerfield. In 1975 and 1976, his batting average dropped again, and he was traded to the New York

Yankees on January 20, 1977, as a reserve outfielder.

On June 18, 1977, Blair became involved in one of the most talked-about happenings in baseball that year. The Yankees were at Fenway Park playing the Boston Red Sox, when Jim Rice hit a fly ball to right field. Yankees' right-fielder, Reggie Jackson, appeared to be nonchalant in his attempt to catch the ball, and it dropped in front of him for a base hit. In the Yankee dugout stood a seething Billy Martin, the Yankees' manager, who refused anything but the best effort from all his players. Martin immediately signaled for Paul Blair to go to right field and replace Jackson. Reggie was dumbfounded, and the look on his face was priceless. As Reggie approached the bench with his mouth open and his arms flailing, he challenged Martin physically for showing him up. It took Elston Howard and Yogi Berra to step in between the two to keep them from coming to blows. Of course, the cameras caught all the action. Interestingly, both Jim Rice and Reggie Jackson would end up in the Baseball Hall of Fame.

Blair would be a part of two more World Series' titles for the Yankees, in 1977 and 1978. Blair was released in 1979 by the Yankees and signed with The Cincinnati Reds. He returned briefly to the Yankees before being released again in July of 1980. His last at-bat occurred on June 20, 1980. Blair accepted a position as outfield instructor for the Yankees in 1981. He was then named Head Baseball Coach at Fordham University in August of 1982, and coached the 1983 season. You could find him in Houston, Texas, with the Astros in 1985 as an instructor. The Astros became his last stop in professional baseball.

My friend Bill Lee once said, "Some of us just love playing baseball." In 1989, Blair, at the age of 45, played 17 games with the Senior Professional Baseball Association. He was a member of the Gold Coast Suns. Blair began to spend time coaching high-school baseball and operating a baseball camp. He did become the head baseball coach at Coppin

State University, from 1998 to 2002.

Defensively, Blair may have been as good as Willie Mays or Ken Griffey, Jr. I have never seen anyone but Blair bounce a baseball off the grass before a game. He was testing the firmness of the turf. No one will forget how he catapulted his body head-first, with throws from the outfield. He twice led the league with put-outs and threw out 104 base runners during his career. "When you talk about the greatest defensive centerfielders, he was right in the mix," said Don Buford. "He could really go get it." Paul Blair was inducted into the Orioles' Hall of Fame in 1984.

Paul Blair participated in 52 post-season games during his 17 seasons. His teams won nine of the 13 post-season series. Paul won four rings in six World Series and received votes for the American League MVP in four separate seasons. When Blair retired, his eight Gold Gloves were still the record for outfielders. This record has since been passed by Ken Griffey, Jr. Blair's .987 fielding percentage is outstanding, as he had just 57 errors in 4,462 chances. Blair batted .250 for his career, during a time in baseball when the league only averaged .254.

On May 30, 1992, I met Paul Blair at the Astrodome in Houston, Texas, before the Upper Deck "Heroes of the Game." George Scott, Freddie Patek, Amos Otis, Tom Tresh, Andy Etchebarren, Jose Cruz, Tony Oliva, Mark Fidrych, Joe Niekro, Roger Metzger, and many others were present. Blair loved the Old Timers' Games and participated in every one he could.

Paul's son, Terry, died in December of 1994 from complications of a blood clot in his leg. "Cardic arrest" was written on the official autopsy. He was being treated with blood thinners. Terry was but 29 years old. No one should lose a child. Paul Blair was beside himself.

On December 26, 2013, Paul Blair collapsed and lost consciousness while bowling at AMF Pikesville Lanes, located in Maryland. After a 911 call, he was transported to

Mount Sinai Hospital located in Baltimore, where he died of a heart attack. The baseball gods had slid a called third strike past him for his final out, greatness from days gone by. Blair was but 69 years old. Gloria, his second wife of 42 years, told *The Baltimore Sun* that Paul had played a round of golf with friends earlier in the day, on that Thursday morning. Blair rolled a couple of balls during a practice round and then sat down. He told a friend that he felt "funny" and then collapsed. Blair had suffered an earlier heart attack on December 23, 2009. A stent was inserted and he had returned home in time for Christmas, that year.

Paul Blair spent 17 seasons in the game of baseball and played in 1,947 games. He was known for taunting hitters by playing shallow and then running down long fly balls. Blair spent years counting his steps to the warning track, finding the hidden sprinkler heads and testing the padding on the centerfield walls. He wore #6 and loved every minute he was on the field. He was considered a good-luck charm, as his teams won continuously. Paul spent 13 of the 17 seasons with his beloved Orioles. Blair played on an Oriole team built on strong defense and pitching. Paul was surrounded by stars, yet his picture most likely would end up on the cover of Baltimore's yearbook, program or World Series program. His batting average of .250 with 134 home runs does not reflect his timely hitting skills. Paul recorded 1,513 hits, 620 RBI's and stole 171 bases. He won eight Gold Gloves, in 1967 and 1969-1975. Blair took the field in six World Series, winning two in Baltimore, in 1966 and 1970, and two with the New York Yankees, in 1977 and 1978. Blair also participated in two All-Star Games, 1969 and 1973.

As for his nickname "Motormouth," he earned it. "He was that way, he never stopped talking and it wasn't always about baseball. I figured with all the Gold Gloves he had won, it gave him the right to talk," said teammate Al Bumby. "Everybody loved him." Hall of Fame outfielder Frank

Robinson said, "He loved to talk. I think he probably tried to talk when he was sleeping. He kept you loose. On and off the field, he'd be yakking, yakking in the dugout. He was a tremendous outfielder. I never saw Blair run into a wall. He knew where the wall was at all times." Ken Singleton attended Blair's funeral and said, "He never had a wasted step. He was smooth as silk and made all the plays in centerfield. They don't hand out Gold Gloves for nothing and when you have eight of them, there is a reason."

Vince Lombardi once said, "Once you've won their hearts, they will follow you anywhere." Paul Blair was never alone. If they play ball in Heaven, I know he's in centerfield.

American Original

C. J. Lewis once wrote, "Humility is not thinking less of yourself; it's thinking about yourself less." I can find no other statement truer about this guy. He hated to talk about himself. He had a great laugh, was beloved by the public, very likeable, and loved baseball. Some said he was just another ballplayer, as common as a sidewalk, but how untrue. He owned a compact swing that was totally efficient, and could roll out of bed and hit line drives for RBI's. It has been said that Yankee fans will cheer the worst baseball player on the planet if he can hit. This fellow never hit .400, but it sure seemed that way. He played during a time when, for seven months a year, baseball players were considered gods in wool uniforms, and the other five months they sold cars, life insurance, and hardware. From second base, the ball would come out of his hand so easily, over the top with poise. An error by the home team would most likely be described in the next day's newspaper as, "Coleman would have caught it." Hall-of-Fame catcher Bill Dickey once said about Jerry Coleman, "He was the smoothest second baseman I ever saw. You couldn't take Coleman out of a play. He got rid of the ball so quickly. You couldn't get a shot at him. First the ball was gone; then he was gone." He was also very fast of foot, dirt in motion; he could cover the Louisiana Purchase in about ten seconds. His bat was attracted to leather; if you left the ball out over the plate, he would send it back to you a little faster than it had arrived. Most Jerry Coleman hits never got higher than a ten-foot ladder. Here is my story of an American original.

Gerald Frances "Jerry" Coleman was born on September 14, 1924, in San Jose, California. At the age of ten, Coleman met Charlie Silvera and Bobby Brown on the ball fields of San Francisco. These three would become local stars and eventually play with each other in the Yankees farm systems. Jerry was a fine athlete who attended Lowell High School and was offered a college scholarship to play baseball and basketball at the University of Southern California (USC). All that changed during Jerry's senior year, when the Japanese bombed Pearl Harbor in December of 1941. Instead of going to USC, Jerry decided to take the Yankees' Minor League offer and joined their Class-D team in Wellsville, New York. At 17, Jerry Coleman joined the Yankees.

Jerry was an instant hit, batting .304 in 83 games. Even though he got off to a great start, Jerry knew that he was simply waiting until he turned 18 to join the Marines. He wanted to be a pilot in the Marines and he thought it best to fight for his country. Coleman enlisted in September of 1942. Jerry would become a Marine bomber pilot in the Pacific Theater of World War II. He flew 57 combat missions in the Solomon Islands and the Philippines.

Even though he had missed four seasons, Jerry returned from the war in 1946 and promptly reported to the Yankees' Spring Training camp. Jerry Coleman joined the Newark Bears as a shortstop, but was switched to second base because the Yanks already had Phil Rizzuto at shortstop. He was glad to get out of the lumber business, meaning he had sat on the bench so long he had splinters. In 1948, Jerry was the last player cut at the end of Spring Training. During that season, Bears' Manager Bill Skiff had convinced Coleman to do three things to get better: Give up smoking, lift weights to gain weight and strength, and choke up on the bat about three or four inches. This was good advice, as Coleman had no idea that during his career, he would be challenged by the likes of Billy Martin, Gil McDougald, and eventually Bobby Richardson. "I also learned a lot from Yankee coach, Frank Crosetti," said Coleman. He spent three seasons in the Minors before arriving in New York City for good.

At the beginning of the 1949 season, George "Snuffy" Stirnweiss had been the Yankees' second baseman, but Coleman won the job. Snuffy had good speed but not much power. Casey liked the tall rookie named Jerry Coleman. Casey loved Jerry's accuracy and smooth overhand throws. Stengel also liked the way Coleman wore his uniform. "Instead of putting the pants way down, which some do, he rolls his pants tight over the knees, which shows all them nice baseball stockings. The umpires are less likely to call low strikes on a player which wears his pants like that, which made him harder to pitch to. And this kid's a fighter, soft-spoken and so forth, but he can be vicious to a pitcher," sprouted Casey. Coleman responded, "First of all, about the pants. I didn't wear 'em the way I did to shrink the strike zone. The truth is, when I wore them longer I could feel fabric against my knee and that was inhibiting. Rolled up they felt comfortable and I believed I could run better."

Jerry's first Major League game occurred on April 20, 1949. To his credit, the pennant-winning hit was delivered by Coleman on the final day of the regular season. The results of his first season speak for themselves. Jerry Coleman was named the Associated Press Rookie of the Year in 1949. The vastness of Yankee Stadium and the sheer number of fans in the seats scared him at first. It took some time for him to get used to the excitement. Coleman was also excited that he was getting to play with his childhood hero, Joe DiMaggio. He would play in 128 games his rookie season and hit a respectable .275 during the regular season and .250 against the Brooklyn Dodgers in the World Series. "Casey was tough to play for," said Coleman. "If you didn't perform, he would get you out of the lineup."

In 1950, Coleman hit a career-high .287 and set a new Yankee record for double plays by a second baseman, with 137. Casey Stengel's comment to the press about Coleman was, "The best second baseman I ever saw on the double play." He also recorded six home runs and batted in 69 RBI's. Can you say All-Star team? Coleman also played a tremendous role in the Yankees' World Series sweep of the Philadelphia Phillies' "Whiz Kids." He hit .286, scored two runs, and collected a Series-high three RBI's. For his effort, he was presented the Babe Ruth Award as the World Series' Most Valuable Player.

Coleman got hurt in June of 1951 and missed 25 games. He started off well in 1952, but was recalled into service for the Korean conflict. Rookie Billy Martin was riding the pine for the Yanks when the best second baseman, Jerry Coleman, was called up by the U. S. Marines. There Jerry would fly another 120 missions and was promoted to the rank of Lieutenant Colonel. He was discharged from Korea in September of 1953 and returned home. He was 28 years old but, unfortunately, he was not the same player. He had become somewhat injury prone. You got the feeling that if he got the hiccups he could snap his spine. On April 22, 1955, Jerry missed 3 ½ months with a broken collar bone that had been shattered into 20 pieces. Then on July 20 of the same year, he was "beaned" by Chicago White Sox pitcher Harry Byrd, which left him with a concussion. Coleman would finish his career as a utility infielder in 1956 and 1957. His last regular season game occurred on September 29, 1957. He did go out with a bang, by hitting .364 against the Milwaukee Braves during the 1957 World Series. At 33 years old, he was finished. "The Colonel" had played in parts of nine seasons from 1949 to 1957, with the Yanks. He had played in six World Series contests with the Yankees, while winning four rings (1949, '50,'51, and '56). His career lifetime average was .263. He recorded 558 hits and 217 RBI's. His highest salary was $19,000 a year.

My pal Bill "Spaceman" Lee once said, "You don't work baseball, you play it." Jerry Coleman was too high-strung to understand that concept. "The game was never fun for me, but it was satisfying. The satisfaction came from winning. I always played with lots of intensity," said Jerry. "Numbers were not important to me." "Jerry was the best double-play second baseman I ever saw. The ball never hit his glove. It was just deflected to first," said Joe Collins.

In 1958, Dan Topping offered Coleman a front office job with the Yankees as the Assistant Farm Director. Jerry accepted and spent five years in that capacity. Jerry was asked by his friend, Howard Cosell, if he would consider broadcasting. In 1960, Jerry began working with CBS Radio "Game of the Week," calling games, and eventually joined the Yankees' broadcast team of Phil Rizzuto and Joe Garagiola, in 1963. Coleman could be seen on WPIX-TV and heard on WCBS Radio. Coleman's 1967 call of Mickey Mantle's 500th home run was a classic. It went like this: "Here's the payoff pitch...This is it! There it goes! It's out of here!" He would stay with CBS for 22 seasons and for seven years (1963-1969) with the Yankees. In 1970, Jerry headed back to California and took a job broadcasting California Angels' games. He would leave in 1972 to take the San Diego Padres' broadcasting job. In 1980, Jerry was asked to manage the Padres. It did not turn out well, as the Padres finished dead last in the National League West with a 73-89 record. He gladly went back up top to the radio booth in 1981. There, with partners Ted Leitner and Andy Masur, he stayed until 2013. Along the way Coleman became known for his "Colemanisms." He could be heard using his signature calls of "Oh Doctor!" "The best goes on!" "The natives are getting restless!" and "You can hang a star on that baby!" My favorite flub was "Willie McCovery swings and misses and its fouled back." It was pure Jerry Coleman. Jerry always claimed his favorite player to cover was Tony Gwynn. He was one of the most underrated baseball broadcasters in the game.

There is a story that can now be told. It was recalled by Coleman's longtime Padres radio partner, Ted Leitner. "Jerry made me promise I would never tell this story," said Ted. "Those guys who fought in the war didn't often share their experiences as they had lost so many of their pals and the pain became too great. This is the story Jerry shared with me, said Leitner. "We were on a bombing run in Korea and there was no moon out that night. It was perfect for a raid. I later noticed that it was unusually dark and decided to draw back my canopy and take a look. The force of the wind entering the cockpit blew off my headset. Then I saw that my windshield was covered in oil. My Corsair Jet was leaking oil from the engine. Now I had no way to transmit my dilemma, but I could see out the side of my plane well enough to follow the squadron. I realized that my chances of getting back to the base alive were not good. I'm a Marine; I decided to continue and delivered my bombs on the target as ordered and turned for home. I almost made it back but was forced to crash land. My aircraft ended up upside down with me hanging from my seat. I managed to cut myself loose to save my life."

In the HBO made-for-TV mini-series, *Band of Brothers*, one of the characters plays the real life story of Major Dick Winters, a leader of Easy Company, 101st Airborne. In an interview, Dick Winters tells us about a letter he received from one of his soldiers named Mike Ranney. "My grandson asked me the other day, 'Were you a hero in the war, Grandpa?' wrote Ranney. Mike answered, "No, but I served in a company of heroes.'" Jerry Coleman helped win four World-Series Championships for the New York Yankees and one World War for the United States as a Marine, and he would not let you call him a hero. Jerry Coleman flew hundreds of bombing missions, earning two Distinguished Flying Crosses, 13 Air Medals, and three Navy citations. He retired from the United States Marine Corp at the rank of Lieutenant Colonel. As far as I'm concerned, his middle name should have been "Hero." Jerry Coleman was a highly-decorated United States Marine fighter pilot of two wars, the 1949 Major League Baseball American League Rookie-of-the-Year at second base, a World Series MVP and All-Star in 1950, a Hall-of-Fame broadcaster, and an American treasure. I was graduating from high school at 18 and he was flying bombing missions overseas. "The guys who didn't come back...they were the real heroes," said Coleman.

Coleman spent close to 70 years in Major League Baseball and was elected to the San Diego Padres' Hall of Fame in 2001. In 2005, Jerry Coleman was given the Ford C. Frick Award of the National Baseball Hall of Fame, for broadcasting excellence. Coleman is one of five Frick Award winners who also played in the Major Leagues before going into broadcasting. The other four are: Joe Garagiola, Tony Kubek, Tim McCarver, and Bob Uecker. During the fall of the 2007, Jerry was inducted into the National Radio Hall of Fame as a Sports Broadcaster, the United States Marine Corp Hall of Fame, and also the International Aerospace Hall of Fame. Jerry Coleman attended the New York Yankees' Old-Timers' Day event in 2013.

I once saw Jerry Coleman at what was then called Jack Murphy Stadium, at that time, a multi-purpose stadium used for baseball, Pro football, and college football, located in San Diego, California. The Houston Astros were in town playing the Padres. I was there on a business trip and decided to catch a game. As my cab pulled up to the entrance, Jerry Coleman was entering the building in front of me. I called out, "Hey Jerry," and he turned toward me with a face built for smiling. We nodded toward each other. That's it, a nod, but the nod said it all. It was all that was required. I was disappointed I didn't get to shake his hand, but glad to have seen him in person.

Jerry Coleman left us too soon on Sunday January 5, 2014.

He was 89 years old. He is survived by his wife Maggie and two daughters. Jerry had been in and out of the hospital for about a month after suffering a terrible head injury during a fall at home. This was an accident and Jerry died at Scripps Hospital from complications of his head injury. Even at 89 years of age, Jerry was not a feeble old man. He walked his eleven-year-old German Shepard named Gus every morning at 5AM. Jerry knew everybody and everybody knew Jerry. He always made his way around the clubhouse with his cup of coffee and a hotdog stuck on the end of a fork to say hello. Jerry loved hotdogs. He never said "no" to fans when they stopped him for a picture or an autograph. Coleman felt that one of the drawbacks of the modern day player was his unwillingness to play when hurt. Jerry felt that the intensity for playing the game had diminished.

On September 15, 2012, the San Diego Padres unveiled a statue at Petco Park, in Jerry Coleman's honor. It stands 7' 5" high. It is one of two statues, the other being Tony Gwynn. Four F-18 fighter-and-attack aircraft performed a flyover during the event. "I started getting tears in my eyes when I started thinking about the past. I couldn't find a better place to spend my final days than in San Diego," said Coleman. As the news of Jerry's death got out in San Diego, hundreds of baseball fans visited Coleman's statue outside Petco Park, to pay their respects. "When I think of Padres baseball, I will always think of Jerry Coleman," said Tony Gwynn.

"My family was deeply saddened to learn of the passing of Jerry Coleman," said Hal Steinbrenner. "First and foremost, he was an American hero whose service to this country is his laying legacy. He was also a great Yankee, a true ambassador for baseball, and someone whose imprint on the game will be felt for generations. On behalf of the entire New York Yankees organization, we send our deepest condolences to the Coleman family."

Abraham Lincoln once said, "It's not the years in your

life, it's the life in your years." As for Jerry Coleman's life, as far as I'm concerned, you can hang a star on that baby!

LEADING BY EXAMPLE

Maya Angelou once wrote, "I've learned that people will forget what you said, people will forget what you did, but people will never forget how you made them feel." She was talking about guys like this. He was considered quiet, unselfish, and as genuine as one could be. He thought of himself as nobody special; just an ordinary man, but of course that was a deception. By good fortune or by design, it had fallen on him to play the hero's part. This guy could bring thousands of fans to their feet with a smile, a dribble of the ball, or by simply running onto the court. Tall and narrow like an old phone booth, he measured half way between six and seven feet tall, but rebounded like he was eight feet tall. He played at a time when one-handed set shots, soaring hook shots with his back to the basket, and open court steals would rule the game. He could also raise his level of performance at will and could guard you to death. You could see his shoulders rise and then sag as he breathed away his nerves at the free throw line. Very few players would take the college basketball world by storm like this guy. Leading by example not only inspired people to feel good but would place his name permanently in the record books.

He played during the time of Clyde Lovellette of Kansas and Johnny "Red" Kerr of Illinois. Holy Cross had Bob Cousy and Duke had Dick Groat. And don't forget about a freshman by the name of Bob Pettit who played for LSU. Coach Chuck Daley used to ask his players, "What do you do when the play breaks down?" If Tom Gola was in the lineup the answer was easy, get the ball to him. Gola, a soft-spoken leader, just saw the game differently than most. It has been said that ego is the killer of potential. Gola, a guy who smiled at the future, owned a large dose of athleticism and no ego. In fact, some thought him as square as a checker board. He became a 20-20 guy every night; he never disappointed. In the game of basketball, only teams are successful. He could be unemotional and possessed no flash. His coach, Obie O'Brian, once said, "I've never met an iceberg like him." Tom Gola understood that you let your offense hurt your defense with bad shots and turnovers.

Thomas Joseph "Tom" Gola was born on January 13, 1933. Tom was the oldest of seven children (three boys, four girls) reared by Helen and Ike Gola of Philadelphia, Pennsylvania. His dad was a policeman from Polish descent who shortened the original family name from Galinsky to Gola. Both of his parents were less than six feet tall, yet by his sophomore year in high school Tom stood 6' 5" tall. Before he discovered basketball, Tom loved reading comic books and playing the harmonica. He grew up in an Olney row house located in north Philadelphia. By 1950, Tom had already been a star basketball player for a few years, as he had led his eighth grade school team to a State and National Schoolboy title under coach "Lefty" Huber. In the late forties and early fifties, you had to climb a flight of outdoor steps to enter Incarnation of Our Lord Parish. Near the base of those steps was a sunken doorway that led to a cold, dank basement gymnasium. Not very well lit, the top of the backboards touched the ceiling leaving some shots almost impossible to make. It was "down there" that Tom Gola learned to play basketball. Father Joseph Betz introduced Gola to the game of basketball as a fifth grader. He would become one of the most accomplished high-school basketball players in Philadelphia history.

Gola's teams won titles at every level from CYO (Catholic Youth Organization) League, the Catholic High School League, the NIT (National Invitational Tournament), and NCAA (National Collegiate Association of Athletics) championships while at La Salle, and an NBA (National Basketball Association) championship with the Philadelphia Warriors. "When I was growing up, you whispered the name Tom Gola. He was like a saint," said Wilt Chamberlain. If you made a list of Philadelphia sports icons, Tom Gola would be near the top. Among those giants representing the City of Brotherly Love, you would find the names Wilt Chamberlain, Harry Kalas, Joe Frazier, Julius Erving, Chuck Bednarik, John Chaney, Paul Arizin, Eddie George, Mike Piazza, Kobe Bryant, and of course Tom Gola.

In 1947, Tom attended La Salle High School, a member of the Philadelphia Catholic League, where he excelled in several sports. He starred on the track team as a miler, half-miler, and shot-putter. Gola, set a new Catholic League scoring record every year he played, ended his career with 2,222 points, and won the Catholic League's top-player award. The Public League Award went to John Caney, the future basketball coach at Temple. Scouts from as many as 60 colleges could be found sitting in the stands of a La Salle High School game. Gola would visit several college campuses including Adolph Rupp at Kentucky and Everett Case at N.C. State. Temple coach, Josh Cody, even offered scholarships to Gola and five or six of his high school teammates if Tom would attend Temple University. West Point offered to waive their long-standing 6' 4" height restriction if he would sign with Army. In 1951, Gola, a devout Catholic, chose to stay close to home and picked La Salle University, a school with less than 1,000 students. Under Gola's leadership, La Salle posted a win-loss record of 102-19 during his four years. Gola averaged 20.9 points and 18.7 rebounds per game.

At the end of the 1951-52 seasons, 19,000 basketball

crazies crammed into Madison Square Garden for the National Invitational Tournament (NIT) final between La Salle of Philadelphia and University of Dayton. The crowd cheered so loudly at Gola's introduction that the dust flew off the back of my television. The Explorers of La Salle (25-7) won 75-64 with the aid of 6' 6" freshman, Tom Gola's 22 points. As a freshman, Gola had averaged 15 points and 15 rebounds a game. It was only the beginning.

In 1953-54, Adolph Rupp's Kentucky Wildcats were the favorites to win it all. This was the first year 24 teams were selected to play in the National Collegiate Athletic Association Tournament. This NCAA Tournament title game was the first to be nationally televised. The tournament was getting bigger and better than ever. La Salle needed Tom Gola and a late run to beat Fordham 76-74 in their first game. Gola, wearing gold shorts and the #15, scored 28. Then La Salle hung on against N.C. State 88-81, as Gola scored 26 points and pulled down 26 rebounds. Gola scored 22 points against Navy in a 64-48 win and gathered 24 boards. The semi-final game against Penn State was a cakewalk with La Salle winning 69-54. La Salle would meet Bradley for all the marbles in college basketball. Bradley was no stranger to playoff basketball and held a one-point advantage at halftime, 43-42. La Salle switched from man-to-man defense to a zone defense in the second half. It made all the difference as La Salle, led by Gola's 19 points, won easily 92-76, and Gola received the MVP trophy for the tournament. La Salle had become the 1954 NCAA Champions and Gola, the 1954 College Player of the Year.

The 1954-55 seasons produced one of the greatest basketball players of all time, The University of San Francisco's Bill Russell. His style of play would revolutionize the college game and later the professional game. Russell's game was born of defense. Simply put, Russell became the best shot blocker and rebounder in the game. Having a guard by the name of K.C. Jones to get the ball to Russell didn't hurt either. As the NCAA Tournament evolved, Gola and La Salle beat Iowa 76-73 in their semi-finals and were looking to win back-to-back titles. The Dons of San Francisco stood in the doorway. The Dons beat the University of Colorado 62-50 behind Russell's 24 points to earn the right to play La Salle. Of course the title game was billed as a showdown between Russell and Gola, but that match-up never materialized. San Francisco coach, Phil Woolpert, chose to place K.C. Jones on Gola. The Dons held a nine-point lead at halftime and won 77-63 behind Russell's 23 points. But the key had been K.C. Jones, who not only scored 24 points but held Gola to 16. The La Salle Explorers would finish second in the nation behind the Dons.

The future of college basketball looked bright and then, in 1956, Wilt Chamberlain enrolled at the University of Kansas, Lenny Rosenbluth would lead the University of North Carolina by Kansas in the NCAA Finals to an unbeaten season, and a fellow by the name of Elgin Baylor would place the University of Seattle on the basketball map. The year 1958 would unfold as the names of Jerry West and Oscar Robertson would become household words, and the game and its players just kept getting better.

Gola was a perfect example of a kid who taught himself the complete game. He was not considered a leaper. Yet, while in college, at his height he played center in two separate years, and led the nation in rebounding. It has been 59 years since Gola left La Salle; and I still find it amazing that with all the great players, no one has eclipsed his NCAA record for rebounds. To this day Gola still holds the NCAA record for total rebounds with 2,201. His coach, Ken Loeffler, said, "I've never seen any one player control a game by himself the way he does." Gola was selected a four-time All-District player, a four-time All-State player and a four-time All-American, and remains only one of two players (Joe Holup of George Washington University) in Division-I college basketball history to score more than 2,000 points

(2,461) and pull down more than 2,000 rebounds. La Salle was part of the Big Five Conference which consisted of Temple, La Salle, Villanova, St. Joseph, and the University of Pennsylvania. Gola was inducted into the La Salle Hall of Athletes in 1961 and the Big Five Hall of Fame in 1986. His #15 was retired by La Salle.

Tom Gola would transition to the tallest starting guard in the NBA. He credited the offense that Coach Loeffler ran at La Salle. "At La Salle we played a five-man weave. Anybody could bring the ball up and we all had places to go on the court. We had nobody sitting in the pivot and the middle was always open to drives if you got by your man. So, that's how I learned how to handle the basketball, how to shoot from the outside, and eventually how to play guard for eleven years in the NBA," said Gola.

His NBA years were also stellar. Chosen in 1955 by the Warriors as a territorial draft pick, Gola, now wearing #6, concentrated on his defense and passing skills, while allowing stars Neil Johnson and Paul Arizin to score. Gola signed with the Warriors for 11,500 dollars a year plus a $6,000 signing bonus. The Warriors would win the 1956 NBA Championship. By 1959, Johnson had retired and Philadelphia had added Goliath to their team. His name was Wilt Chamberlain. They would return to the NBA Finals that year but lose to the Boston Celtics. During his eleven-year career with the Philadelphia Warriors (1955-1962) and New York Knicks (1962-1966), he was chosen a five-time All-Star. Why play for the Knicks? In 1962, the Warriors moved from Philadelphia to San Francisco. Gola did not want to move so far away from home and asked to be traded. The Knicks became the logically choice. As a point guard, he could do it all. Imagine him as "Magic" Johnson before Magic. Tom Gola scored 7,871 points, while pulling down 5,417 rebounds. He also dished out 2,962 assists and was an important piece of the 1956 NBA Champions. Tom Gola and Arnie Ferrin are the only two players to win an

NIT, NCAA, and NBA title. Arnie played with the Utah Utes and the Minneapolis Lakers.

In 1966, after his playing career had ended, Gola was elected to the Pennsylvania House of Representatives. He did return to La Salle and coached his alma mater for two years, starting in 1968. The 1968-69 La Salle team was considered the best in Big Five history. Their record stood at 23-1 with a No. 2 national ranking behind only UCLA, but they were ineligible for postseason play due to previous NCAA violations. La Salle finished 14-12 in Gola's second year as head coach. Gola became Philadelphia's city comptroller in 1970 and was forced to step down as coach due to time restraints. By 1980 you could find Gola involved in the Ronald Reagan presidential race, where he became the Philadelphia chairman of campaign funds. After Reagan's win, Gola was appointed as regional administrator of U.S. Department of Housing and Urban Development. Gola took a run at the mayor's job in 1982, but without GOP backing, he finished third in a three-man race. Gola would return to his insurance business.

In 1998, La Salle refurbished their on-campus arena known as the Hayman Center and renamed their arena after their star athlete. Gola is considered to be one of the best college basketball players of all time and a true folk hero. UCLA coach John Wooden once called him the "greatest all-around basketball player" he had ever seen. Tom Gola, died on January 26, 2014. He had been convalescing at St. Joseph Minor located in Meadowbrook, Pennsylvania. Gola had suffered from a head injury sustained in a fall from a Philadelphia curb in July of 2003. He was but 81 years of age. He is survived by his wife Carolina, whom he married in 1955. They had one son, Thomas, and two granddaughters.

The Naismith Memorial Basketball Hall of Fame received Tom Gola on April 26, 1976. On April 24, 1989, Tom Gola became one of seven to be inducted into the Philadelphia

Basketball Hall of Fame. The other six were Wilt Chamberlain, Paul Arizin, Harry Litwack, Zack Clayton, Eddie Gottlieb, and Charles Cooper. In 2002, Madison Square Garden held their 50th Anniversary Holiday Festival to honor the five greatest basketball players ever to play at MSG: Bill Bradley of Princeton, Oscar Robertson of Cincinnati, Chris Mullin of St. Johns, Kareem Abdul-Jabbar of UCLA, and Tom Gola of La Salle were the chosen ones.

Albert Einstein once said, "Logic gets you from A to B. Imagination will take you everywhere." I can't imagine Philadelphia basketball without Tom Gola.

THE BEST DAY OF THE WEEK

Alfred Hitchcock once said, "There is no terror in the bang, only in the anticipation of it." Fans sat forward in their seats when he stepped into the batters' box. The bang was expected. This fellow was one of a kind. He was tall, good-looking and well spoken, a "Pretty Boy" Floyd look-alike if there ever was one. If he had never played baseball, if you had never heard his name and you passed him on the sidewalk one day, you'd turn around and look. Besides being able to beat a baseball out of shape, he didn't want to be *just* an all-star; he wanted to be an all-the-time-star. He knew a secret that just being good was the enemy of being great. Giving this guy a bat was like giving Ivanhoe a sword, the outlaw Josey Wales a pistol, or Mick Jagger a microphone. Something electrifying was about to happen. He owned what the locals in Pittsburgh called "light tower power." Writers of his day called his home runs "Moon Shots;" I like to refer to them as "The Big Fly."

He became an icon of the batters' box and the broadcast booth. This guy wasn't as good as they said he was; he was better. He was bigger than life, became a legendary baseball announcer, and could read a get-well card and make you giggle. Anytime Ralph Kiner spoke about baseball it became the best day of the week.

Ralph Kiner provided a wonderful link to the past through his words spoken in the present. He had an incredible memory that reached as far back as the dead-ball era and owned an unlimited supply of baseball knowledge.

Only Kiner could talk about Paul Waner and Zack Wheat with authority. Kiner spoke about Ebbets field and Forbes field like it was yesterday. Heck, he was a Met before there was a Shea Stadium. Kiner was as comfortable among his Hollywood pals like Bing Crosby, Frank Sinatra, Liz Taylor, and Janet Leigh, as he was in the clubhouse or behind a microphone. It has even been reported that he dated Marilyn Monroe, Esther Williams, and Ava Gardner.

Ralph McPherran Kiner was born on October 27, 1922, in the copper mining town of Santa Rita, New Mexico. Ralph's father, a baker by trade, died when Ralph was four years old. His mother, Beatrice, a nurse during World War I in France, moved them to Alhambra, California. He was their only child. There, Ralph grew up playing sandlot ball. At the age of 17, Ralph was introduced to "Babe" Ruth by "Babe" Herman. Later Ruth would mention Kiner as someone who could possibly break his single-season home-run record. In 1941, after graduating from Alhambra High School, Kiner signed with the Pittsburgh Pirates as an amateur free agent by scout Dan Crowley. His signing bonus was 3,000 dollars with the Pirates. Ralph was given #43 and spent two years in the minor leagues, before joining the fight during World War II. Kiner became a Navy pilot and served in the Pacific Theater searching for Japanese submarines.

In the 1930's and 40's most athletes played baseball or boxed because you could not make enough money to live on playing basketball or football. "My only dream was to be a ballplayer," said Ralph.

For ten years, from 1946 to 1955, Ralph Kiner took his turns at the plate for three different teams: the Pittsburgh Pirates (1946-53), Chicago Cubs 1953-54), and the Cleveland Indians (1954). Some said he could hit home runs Monday through Monday. While there, he hit 369 satellites, more than any other player over a ten-year career, into the afternoon air for home runs. This mediocre outfielder became one of the game's greatest right-handed sluggers. Just think how many he could have hit if he had not had issues with his back. "Hard work beats talent," said Kiner.

While with the Pirates, Ralph Kiner was introduced to Elizabeth Taylor by Pittsburgh Pirates' owner, Bing Crosby. Bing, Comedian Lou Costello, and Ralph played golf together. Ralph escorted Liz to the 1949 movie premier of "Twelve O'clock High," starring Gregory Peck. The premier was held at Grauman's Chinese Theater. Kiner did not have a chauffeur and his car ended up being parked in an empty lot. He and Liz had to walk to his car, there was no second date. Kiner also dated actress Janet Leigh and played himself in a 1951 movie entitled "Angels in the Outfield," shot at Forbes Field in Pittsburgh. Eventually Kiner would marry Nancy Chaffee, a professional tennis star. Together they had three children.

Kiner tells a funny story about meeting actress Jamie Lee Curtis, daughter of Janet Leigh. When he introduced himself as a ball player and now announcer who had once dated her mom, Jamie jumped up and hugged him while yelling, "Daddy, I've been searching for you all my life." "Of course it was a joke," said Ralph, "but I was still surprised."

Ralph Kiner, now wearing #4, debuted as an outfielder for the Pirates on April 12, 1946. With an upper-cut swing, he proceeded to hit 23 home runs, but he also led the National League in strikeouts, with 109. In 1947, the Pirates convinced future Hall-of-Famer, Hank Greenberg, to join the Pittsburgh club. Greenberg would show up in the afternoon before a night game in Pittsburgh and work on his hitting, and would help Kiner and others who showed up. He roomed with Kiner, teaching him the mechanics of hitting and polishing him for stardom. Greenberg also hit behind Kiner in the lineup, protecting him, making sure he got better pitches to hit. And hit them he did. Kiner's batting average rose to .313 while hitting 51 home runs in

1947, and he also lowered his strikeouts to 81. Greenberg hit 25 home runs, in what would be his final year in baseball. They also became friends, and later Greenberg was Kiner's best man at his first wedding.

Kiner tells a great story of batting against the great Satchel Paige in a barnstorming game. In his first at bat, Kiner hits a home run to leftfield off Satchel. Paige calls his catcher out to the mound and tells him to let him know when that guy comes up to bat again. Later in the game, Kiner comes to bat and the catcher lets Satchel know. So, Paige begins to talk in rhymes as he pitches. He first says, "A pea at the knee," as the first pitch is called a low strike. Then Satchel says, "A taste at the waist," as the second strike passes Kiner waist high for strike two. Then Paige says, "It gets better at the letters," as Kiner is called out on three pitches. "I never swung the bat," said Ralph.

While in Pittsburgh, Kiner benefited greatly from the teachings of Billy Meyer and the great Honus Wagner. Originally the left field wall at Forbes stood 365' away from home plate. Pittsburgh helped both hitters by moving in the left field wall at Forbes Field and placing the bullpen behind it. What originally started out as Greenberg Gardens turned into Kiner's Korner, as Ralph followed his first two seasons of 23 and 51 home runs with 40, 54, 47, 42, 37, and 35. Ralph Kiner was a star when this country needed a star. Kiner's 54 home runs hit in 1949 were just two short of Hack Wilson's then-National League record of 56 home runs hit in 1930. Kiner's 54 home runs were the highest total hit in the Major Leagues from 1939 to 1960, and the highest National League total from 1931 to 1997. Interestingly, Hank Aaron, Willie Mays, Ernie Banks, Mike Schmidt, or Willie McCovey never hit more than 54 home runs in a season; and they all hit 500 or more home runs during their career.

In 1949, his ability to clout home runs at a record pace did not go unnoticed, and Ralph began to receive death threats.

As the home runs piled up that season, Kiner received a letter in the mail that said he would be shot if he broke Babe Ruth's single-season home run record. He could save his own life if he were to place a certain amount of money in a bag and leave it in a cab. Kiner made GM, Branch Rickey, aware and Rickey notified the FBI. A Ralph Kiner look-alike placed a bag of fake money with a honing device, in the specified cab. No one showed up to take the money. "During the game, no one would sit next to me, while I was on the bench," laughed Ralph. The FBI eventually caught the boy. He was a visiting team's batboy who had lost a bet. Rickey spoke in the boy's favor at the trial, and he did not have to do any time.

With the Pirates, Kiner won or tied the National League home-run crown in each of his first seven years and became the first National League player to hit 50 home runs in a season *twice*. His home run totals of 40 or more for five consecutive years (1947 to 1951) tied Babe Ruth. Kiner was also among baseball's highest paid players. In 1952, Pittsburgh finished their year with a 42-112 win-loss record, despite Kiner leading the League again in home runs. "I was making 90,000 dollars a year," said Kiner "and Rickey wanted to cut my salary by 25%. I said 'I would play for the same amount.'" Pirates' General Manager, Branch Rickey, was reported as answering Kiner this way. "Son, how did we finish?" Kiner responded, "We finished last." Rickey, "We can finish last without you." On June 4, 1953, after 41 games, Kiner was traded to the Chicago Cubs.

The Cubs were dreadful, also. With the Chicago Cubs, Kiner became part of an outfield known as the "Quicksand Kids." This outfield consisting of Frank Baumholtz, Hank Sauer and Ralph Kiner, never lost any speed, because they never had any to begin with. It was like watching a sundial; it was as if they were running in quicksand. Kiner hit 22 home runs for the Cubs in 1954.

By 1955, an old friend named Hank Greenberg had put

together a pretty good team as the General Manager of the Cleveland Indians. Greenberg negotiated a trade for Ralph Kiner on November 16, 1954. Ralph, now wearing #9, played in only 113 games that season for Cleveland and hit a career low of 18 home runs. The Indians finished second that year to the New York Yankees. It would be the closest Kiner would ever come to playing in a World Series. A bad back forced his retirement at the end of the 1955 season. His last at-bat occurred on September, 25, 1955. He was but 32 years of age.

Next stop for Ralph was the manager's position with the Minor League team known as the San Diego Padres. Kiner spent five years in San Diego (1956-1960).

"After I resigned from the Padres, I went to Spring Training looking for a new job and was offered three: broadcast for the Cincinnati Reds or Chicago White Sox with Bob Elston, or become a nightly TV sportscaster. Kiner chose the White Sox job. Kiner spent one year in the broadcast booth with the 1961 Chicago White Sox, before heading to Queens, New York, and joining the new 1962 expansion team known as the New York Mets.

From 1962 until last year, Ralph Kiner spoke baseball to Mets fans every summer. Kiner was as permanent as taxes. "No one expected much from the Mets and they got what they expected," said Kiner. His broadcast partners, Lindsey Nelson and Bob Murphy, were by his side until Nelson left in 1978. Murphy retired in 2003. Kiner outlasted them both. He also broadcast with Tim McCarver on WWOR for sixteen seasons. Every Father's Day, Ralph would wish all the dads a happy birthday; it was part of Ralph's way of being funny. He smoked a big cigar in the booth. He could also be straight with you without being mean. His insight about hitting was flawless, and his humor was under-appreciated. The Mets' first year was a disaster, as they won 44 games while losing 120, still the record for losses in a single season. Ralph said, "Losing to the Mets that first year was like drowning in three inches of water; it was not supposed to happen." Ralph was also known for his mistakes with names. He called his broadcast partner, Tim McCarver, "Tim MacArthur;" Gary Carter became "Gary Cooper," and he even once called himself "Ralph Korner." He also said, "If Casey Stengel were alive today, he'd be spinning in his grave." My favorite Kiner mistake was when he said "The Mets have gotten their leadoff hitter on base only once this inning."

Ralph developed a popular post-game interview segment with current players, called "Kiner's Korner." "In 1962, Casey Stengel was my first guest," said Ralph. "I was afraid he would start talking and never stop. Interestingly, Casey finished the interview right on time and thanked me for the time, then got up and walked off the set. He was still wired for sound and pulled the entire set down behind him," laughed Ralph. "It was a conspicuous start."

I met Ralph Kiner in 1994, two years before he suffered a bout with Bell's palsy. He signed my Louisville Slugger bat with his name burned into the barrel. He also wrote "HOF 1975." He was a proud man. Although our meeting was brief, I will remember the vice-like grip from his handshake.

Ralph Kiner was more than a home-run hitter. At 6' 2" tall and weighing 195 pounds, Ralph led the National League three times in walks 1949, 1951, and 1952. In 1949, Ralph also led the League in RBI's with 127. He was selected to participate in the All-Star Game for six straight years (1948-1953). The 1950 All-Star Game played at Chicago's White Sox Comiskey Park, experienced the power of Ralph Kiner in more ways than one. In the first inning, Ralph unleashed a line drive that was caught by Ted Williams as he ran toward the left field wall. Ted fractured his elbow running into that wall. In the ninth inning with the National League behind 3-2, Kiner hit a game-tying home run to send the game into extra innings. The National League eventually won 4-3 on a home run by "Red" Schoendienst in the fourteenth inning.

This was the first time a National League team had won an All-Star Game in an American League park.

Like most baseball players, Ralph was superstitious. He never stepped on a white line on the field of play. "It didn't help or hurt me," said Kiner. "I just didn't want to take any chances." Ralph went to the plate 5,205 times and only struck out 749 times, recorded 1,015 RBI's and finished with a .279 batting average and a .398 on-base percentage for his career. "Underrated" is a word that comes to mind, when I think of Kiner. I loved his analysis, "Home run hitters drive Cadillac's, singles hitters drive Fords."

During the season of 2013, Kiner would occasionally join Gary Cohen, Keith Hernandez, and Ron Darling, in the Mets' television booth. Things felt different at Citi Field when Kiner was in the house. There he would weave his magic by sharing baseball stories from the past about this great game, with a memory that remained accurate and intact. There is no other announcer alive that can claim to have seen their team play every year that they had been in existence. Ralph Kiner had been the voice and conscience of the New York Mets for 51 years. Only Ralph could exclaim "That ball is going, going, gone, goodbye."

Ralph Kiner left us on a Thursday, February 6, 2014. He was at home in Rancho Mirage, California, surrounded by family. He died of natural causes at the age of 91. He was never afraid of dying, but he was afraid of losing. After 72 years in the game of baseball, his body just gave out. He suffered from the effects of a stroke, which occurred some ten years ago and from Bell's palsy (1996) which slurred his speech and limited his time behind the Mets microphone to just a few games, in 2013. At 91 years of age, he was the oldest announcer in Major League Baseball. He left behind five kids and twelve grandkids.

In 1975, Ralph Kiner was elected on his last ballot, to the Baseball Museum Hall of Fame. He may as well have had Dangerfield written on the back of his jersey, because he certainly got no respect. They thought he was just a home-run hitter. His total reflected 75.41% of the votes counted. Kiner would be the only inductee that year. Kiner made it a point to travel to Cooperstown, New York, and attend every induction, until his death. He was also elected to the New York Mets Hall of Fame in 1984, followed by the retiring of his #4 by the Pittsburgh Pirates in 1987. On Saturday, July 14, 2007, Yogi Berra, Bob Feller, Tom Seaver, Ernie Harwell, and others, joined Kiner on the field for "Ralph Kiner Night" at Shea Stadium. Together, they honored his legacy. The Mets' TV booth at Citi Park is named after Kiner.

The Mets never built a statue of Kiner; why build a statue when you have the real thing? They had Ralph. And like so many of our treasured institutions, the Mets never rid themselves of Kiner. They kept him until the end. Will they build him a statue now? Probably, but nothing will take his place. Maybe the Mets will honor all three: Kiner, Murphy, and Nelson with one statue. Ralph does have a statue standing at Almansor Park, California, where he grew into a man. I have often thought that as we get older, the future looks a little darker and the past gets brighter. Ralph Kiner brought buckets of sunshine to the park every day. I will not forget him.

MAKING DREAMS COME TRUE

Ralph Waldo Emerson once said, "Do not go where the path may lead, go instead where there is no path, and leave a trail." You've all heard the words "game changer." Well, this guy has been as instrumental in forwarding the game of baseball, as "Candy" Cummings was when he invented the curveball. And oh, what a trail he did leave. Some claim he changed the game forever. I had never seen the words "orthopedic surgeon" used in a sports article until he came along. This fellow brought sports medicine out of the dark ages and into the future. Like most pioneers, his job was to change lives and solve problems. Not only did he save many careers, but we the fans benefitted from his work and still do. Many a great pitcher retired early because there was no medical procedure to put their shoulders and elbows back together. Now it has been estimated that more than a third of today's current pitchers have gone under his knife. Handing this fellow a scalpel was like giving Arnold Palmer a putter, game over. "I wanted to help people heal," said Jobe. That's exactly what he did. Dr. Frank Jobe made dreams come true.

Frank Wilson Jobe was born in Greensboro, North Carolina, on July 16, 1925. He grew up a country boy with a slight southern twang. After graduating from Collegedale Academy located in Collegedale, Tennessee, in 1943, he was drafted into the United States Army. He would report to Camp Barkeley. There he became a medical staff sergeant in the 101st Airborne Division. "I got drafted right at 18," said Jobe. "I was healthy, and we didn't have many of those left. All the strong men had already gone to war." Jobe's job would take him to the front lines. After landing in Normandy by glider, he would eventually be captured during the Siege of Bastogne, while fighting in the Battle of the Bulge. After he escaped, his job was to collect the medical supplies being delivered by gliders and deliver them on to the front. He would be confronted by danger on a daily basis. Jobe earned several medals, including the Bronze Star for bravery, the Glider Badge and the Combat Medical Badge. By the end of the war, Jobe had gotten to meet many of the Army doctors. When asked what he was going to do after the war, he did not have an answer. One doctor suggested he go to medical school so that's exactly what he did. Jobe first enrolled at Southern Missionary College, also located in Collegedale, and then headed west where he completed his bachelor's degree at La Sierra University in Riverside, California. He then enrolled on the GI Bill at Loma Linda University, located near Los Angeles. He would receive his MD in 1956 and become a family practice doctor. After three years of general practice, he completed a residency in orthopedic surgery at the Los Angeles County Hospital.

He began to consult with the Los Angeles Dodgers in 1964. It was there that he met his future business partner, Dr. Robert Kerlan, who specialized in sports medicine. In 1965, together they would form the Kerlan-Jobe Orthopedic Clinic. Jobe then joined the Dodgers' medical staff in 1968 and stayed for over 40 years.

A distinguished-looking gentleman with wire-rimmed glasses, his office was full of books, as you would expect from a doctor who was about to devise a revolutionary procedure. Jobe was not 100% convinced the procedure would work and remembers asking Tommy John if he had some other plan to support his family if it didn't. "He knew my wife was pregnant," said John.

Tommy John had logged over 2,000 innings, while winning

124 games for the Los Angeles Dodgers. That right arm had taken him from a small town in Indiana to the bright lights of Hollywood. John had just left a game early with a 13-3 record and an arm that was killing him. He was given the standard treatment at that time: rest for a month. After a month, he still couldn't throw. During Jobe's evaluation, he told John there might be a chance to put his elbow back together, but there was no guarantee. "Let's do it," said John. Jobe: "Those three words changed baseball." As far as baseball is concerned, Dr. Frank Jobe went about changing water into wine. The operation performed on Tommy John on September 25, 1974, achieved breakthrough results. John was 31 years of age.

The surgery itself was fairly simple. Jobe would remove the Palmaris tendon located in the wrist that really serves no purpose. It is often used in surgeries, and removing it has no effect on the function of the wrist. After opening John's arm, Jobe drilled a couple of holes through the elbow bones and looped the Palmaris tendon through a couple of times, in figures of eight, locking it in with anchors. The surgery is done almost identically today. In a few months, John was up and beginning to throw. But then a setback occurred. John began having pain, which required Jobe to go back in. The issue was the ulnar nerve, which we refer to as the "funny bone." This nerve had become trapped inside scar tissue and was causing the pain. That procedure removed all the pain. John missed the entire 1975 season. "I didn't do any more surgeries for two years to see how John came out, and then I started doing a few more. At that time, I thought I shouldn't do this on anyone that's going to be a pitcher, due to the year of rehab," said Jobe. Tommy John went on to pitch another 14 years in the Major Leagues, winning an additional 164 games after the surgery. He also never missed a start after the surgery. In fact, he won 20 or more games in three different seasons and was elected to three more All-Star games. John retired in 1989 at the age of 46. Brett Strom, currant pitching coach for the Houston Astros, was the second pitcher to have Tommy John surgery.

Ah, you think the story is over now. Not by a long shot. In 1990, Jobe performed major reconstructive surgery on the shoulder of Dodgers' pitcher Orel Hershiser. Again, the surgery he used was "cutting edge" and the first of its kind. Jobe pioneered a new procedure that reduced the amount of trauma suffered by the shoulder tissue when throwing a baseball over handed. The procedure allowed Hershiser to continue his career. This procedure continues to be used today.

Jobe then created what is now known as the "Jobe exercises." This is a series of ten motions that pitchers use to help stave off rotator-cuff problems with their shoulders. "The shoulder is far harder to put back together," said Jobe. "So, prevention is even more important."

Imagine not being able to see Matt Harvey, Billy Wagner, Joe Nathan, Chris Carpenter, Stephen Strasburg, Adam Wainwright or Anibal Sanchez pitch. Did you know that in 1992, a young kid pitching in the low minors of the Yankees system, named Mariano Rivera, damaged his ulnar collateral ligament, and that baseball's all-time saves leader had his elbow repaired by Jobe? Over 1,000 pitchers have had their careers saved or extended by the Tommy John surgery. They all owe Frank Jobe a place in their will. Should there be a medical wing in the Baseball Hall of Fame? How about a section for contributions to the game of baseball that moved the game forward? Marvin Miller and Frank Jobe would surely qualify. The first Tommy John patient to be inducted into the Baseball Hall of Fame will more than likely be Atlanta Braves' pitcher, John Smoltz; who is eligible for the Class of 2015. How appropriate it would be to have the Jobe's families receive a Hall-of-Fame plaque at the same time. Jobe was honored for his work by the National Baseball Hall of Fame, in August of 2012, by HOF President Jeff Idelson.

"Frank Jobe was the leading contributor and developer of baseball medicine. Without his contributions both clinically and scientifically, none of us would be where we are today. The careers he has saved are a landmark that probably will never be duplicated," said Dr. James Andrews.

In an article written by Jorge L. Ortiz, he writes, "It seems like every year I'm doing more and more (Tommy John surgeries), so from my standpoint it's an epidemic," said Dr. James Andrews, the noted orthopedic surgeon who has become the go-to doctor for Major Leaguers with elbow problems. This procedure has become as common as a groundball out to the shortstop. At this writing, sixteen Major League pitchers have needed this surgery since the beginning of Spring Training this year. Last year, 2013, the total was 19 elbow surgeries. The average number of surgeries the last ten years had been around ten, but that number sky-rocketed to 36 in 2012. According to records, most elbow injuries occur in June, not April or May. "You have more guys throwing in the mid to high nineties than ever before. That speed comes with the expense of tendons and ligaments," said Dr. Andrews. "Even with proper mechanics; the muscles get stronger, but not the ligaments and tendons." The fact is they do not get as much blood as the muscles. So, clubs have no choice but to stockpile additional arms in their Minor League system. As recently as the 1980's, teams would carry only nine to ten pitchers on a 25-man roster. Now, it is normal to have as many as fourteen.

"Baseball lost a great man, and Tommy John lost a great friend," said former Dodger, Tommy John. "There are a lot of pitchers in baseball who should celebrate his life and what he did for the game of baseball. My deepest condolences and prayers go out to Beverly and the entire family. He's going to be missed." Tommy John went on to establish the "Let's do it" foundation. John is asked quite often to show his scar. It's about eight inches long and faded by time.

"Year around pitching is not how you strengthen your arm," said John. "Your arm needs to rest."

Jobe received three honorary doctorates, two in the United States and one in Japan. He authored over 140 medical publications, wrote 30 book chapters, and edited seven books on his specialty.

Jobe was the emeritus physician for the PGA Tour. Jobe also supervised medical treatment for the California Angels, the Los Angeles Rams and the Los Angles Lakers, and eventually worked with the Anaheim Ducks and Los Angeles Kings.

Frank Jobe left us on March 6, 2014. He was 88 years of age and living with his wife Beverly in Santa Monica, California. They had four sons together which provided eight grandchildren. He had undergone a coronary bypass in 2002 and had a defibrillator implanted in 2010.

Baseball owner Bill Veeck once said, "Tradition is the albatross around the neck of progress." Shouldn't we rename this procedure "The Frank Jobe Surgery?"

HANDS DOWN

Abraham Lincoln once said, "Nearly all men can stand adversity but if you really want to test his character, give him power." This guy passed the test with flying colors. He was a trusted advisor, used a common-sense approach and was a good looking man. If he had run for President, he could have won. He was old school, grew up at a time where you didn't talk about yourself. If you were good enough, someone else did that for you. Some claimed he swore once, but quickly felt ashamed. He was also accused of being stubborn and a bit outspoken at times. He believed that most football games were lost, not won. He was smart, could be influential, and it seemed like he could see ahead of everyone else. This fellow understood that no one has ever made him self great by showing how small someone else is. He looked like your newspaper boy, but he was a tough customer to deal with when it came to his team. You see, he was an owner and, just because he made it look easy, doesn't mean it was. This guy had a higher annual income than Bolivia. If he had a dollar for every time he had heard that; no wait, he did! Who knew that wise Ralph Wilson would become the conscience of the NFL? Ralph Wilson may have been one of the best owners in all of professional sports, "Hands down!"

"You didn't need a contract with Ralph Wilson," said former General Manager Bill Polian. "His word was his bond." Ralph Cookerly Wilson, Jr., was born on October 17, 1918, in Columbus, Ohio. His family moved to

Michigan where Wilson would grow up in the Motor City known as Detroit. His father, Ralph Wilson, Sr., was a salesman, and his Mother, Edith, claimed she was the first women in the State of Michigan to own a driver's license. Ralph graduated from the University of Virginia and then the University of Michigan Law School. Ralph then joined the U.S. Navy and served his country in both the Atlantic and Pacific Theaters. When he returned home, he joined his dad in the insurance business. Wilson later owned and operated several radio and television stations, along with a construction and trucking company. He also dabbled in oil and gas. He eventually founded Ralph Wilson Industries.

Wilson attended his first professional football in 1935, Chicago Bears vs. Detroit Lions. He fell in love with the game. Ralph later purchased a minority share of the Detroit Lions. All his friends thought he was nuts but in fact, it was this purchase that put his name on the map as a potential new owner years later, when the AFL was formed. "I called Ralph," said Lamar Hunt. "We needed an eighth franchise to balance the new league."

"Count me in with Buffalo," said Ralph Wilson. "Lamar had given me a choice of several cities, and I chose Buffalo." Wilson was the last member to join "The Foolish Club," the label given to a group of eight individuals who sought to create their own professional football league in the face of the monster known as the National Football League. On October 28, 1959, the Buffalo Bills were born. The initial price for a chance to lose tons of money was $25,000. Wilson chose the name Bills after a previous team in the area that had played in the All-American Football Conference from 1946-1949. Ralph has been the only owner of this team since their inception. Early success by Coach Lou Saban and some of the Bills' great players from the early days included "Cookie" Gilchrist, Jack Kemp, and Hall-of-Famers, Billy Shaw and O.J. Simpson. Ralph Wilson would become a national institution in Western New York, like

Secrets of Greatness

Yellowstone Park.

The Bills originally played in a run-down stadium known as War Memorial Stadium. It was built in 1937, and the players referred to it as "The Rockpile." Still, regardless of the stadium situation, fans came early to see their team warm up. War Memorial was in disrepair and seated only 46,204 fans. The new AFL-NFL merger required a stadium that seated at least 50,000. Rich Stadium was built in 1973, in Orchard Park, a suburb of Buffalo, New York. Fans numbering 80,020 were stacked inside of Rich Stadium like cords of wood, to watch a game. Not bad for what most consider a small market team. Rich Stadium was renamed in 1998, Ralph Wilson Stadium.

In November of 1963, after the announcement of President Kennedy's assassination, out of respect, Ralph Wilson successfully swayed his fellow owners to cancel all of the AFL football games to be played that Sunday. It was the right decision. Just ask NFL Commissioner, Pete Rozell, who admitted until his dying day, that he had made a mistake by allowing the NFL to continue.

The Bills faired well early, as they won two American Football Conference Championships back-to-back in 1964 and 1965. The 1990's also belonged to the Buffalo Bills of the American Football Conference (AFC). Wilson's teams were always geared to win, not develop. With great players like Jim Kelly, Thurman Thomas, André Reed and Bruce Smith, they played their way to four straight Super Bowls from 1990-1993, only to lose all four times. Their nemeses were the New York Giants, Washington Redskins, and the Dallas Cowboys, twice. I believe that the Buffalo Bills will be remembered a lot longer for qualifying for four straight Super Bowls, even though they lost all four, than for perhaps winning just one Super Bowl like the New Orleans Saints.

I read where Ralph Wilson would show up at practice and catch passes. These were his boys as far as he was concerned; he had fathered three daughters. "He wasn't

72

my boss, he was my friend," said former Bills coach, Marv Levy. One of my favorite sports quotations of all time was said by Coach Levy right before one of the Bills' Super Bowl games. "Where would you rather be than right here, right now?" asked Levy. What a powerful statement. Wilson also insisted on sitting in the owner's box, to the far left, by himself, while watching his Bills play at home. Even if he was entertaining friends, he did not want to be disturbed.

Shane Nelson, my friend, my radio mentor, and a local kid from Mathis, Texas, grew up with a dream to play professional football. After high school, Shane played at Blinn Junior College where he would later be chosen a Junior College Football All-American at linebacker. After he had finished his college eligibility at Baylor, he signed with the Buffalo Bills after turning down a chance with the Dallas Cowboys. He wanted to play right away. In 1977, while with Buffalo, not only did Nelson become captain of the team, but he led the team and NFL in tackles, his rookie season. Shane, along with fellow linebacker, Jim Haslett, and nose tackle, Freddie Smerlas, would become known as "The Bermuda Triangle." John Facenda, the voice of NFL Films, would proclaim, "The Bermuda Triangle of the Buffalo Bills was where running backs entered, but did not leave." Shane spent six years with the Buffalo Bills before he retired after suffering a terrible knee injury. He made a comeback in 1983 and signed with the San Diego Chargers. A torn Achilles tendon would eventually end his career. In Buffalo, Nelson played for Chuck Knox and Jim Ringo. His coach in San Diego was none other than Don Coryell.

Shane eventually moved back home after his NFL career and asked me to join him as his radio partner in 1992, which I gladly did. This would allow me to speak with Reggie McKenzie, Conrad Dobler, Billy Ray Smith, Jr., Gil Byrd, Bobby Chandler and many others. I asked Shane some questions about his boss, Ralph Wilson. "He was very consistent with his genuine acts of kindness toward his players' health, their family and their life away from football," said Nelson. "In 2001, I took my family to Buffalo for the Bills' alumni weekend. All the Bills were invited back. Ralph Wilson and Dan Rooney (Pittsburgh Steelers) were known as owners who cared about the history of their teams and the players that played for them," said Nelson. I asked how visible Wilson was to the team. "Ralph Wilson was not only present quite a bit during practice, but he also traveled with the team. He was there during pregame meals and check-in at the hotels on the road. He was so proud of his guys," said Shane.

Ralph Wilson was the only owner of the Buffalo Bills and a 33rd degree Scottish Rites Freemason. He was inducted into the Greater Buffalo Sports Hall Of Fame, in 1992. On August 8, 2009, ESPN's Chris Berman took the podium in Canton, Ohio, as Ralph Wilson's presenter into the Pro Football Hall of Fame. Ralph would be joined by another great Buffalo Bills' player, defensive end, Bruce Smith. Also included in this class were Rod Woodson, Randall McDaniel, Bob Hayes, and Derrick Thomas. It was quite a class. In 2011, several NFL owners were honored for their service in World War II. The World War II Museum awarded "Bud" Adams (Oilers-Titans), William Clay Ford, Sr. (Lions), Tom Benson (Saints), Alex Spanos (Chargers), and Ralph Wilson (Bills), the American Spirit Award.

According the *Forbes Magazine,* The Buffalo Bills' current net worth is valued at 870 million. Not bad for the original investment of 25,000 dollars. The club is ranked 30th of the 32 NFL teams, in value. Ralph also had another love that had nothing to do with his family or football, thoroughbred horse racing. He was not only a breeder, but an owner of fine horses in the United States and France. No wonder they call horse racing the "Sport of Kings." Ralph Wilson could have easily qualified as a king of life.

Before he died, Wilson made sure the Bills would stay in Buffalo, at Ralph Wilson Stadium, for at least the next six years, as he extended the lease by ten years. The new lease began on 2013 with a buyout option in 2019. For now, the franchise will remain in Mary Wilson's name, Ralph's wife. There could be an eventual sale of the franchise according to Marc Ganis, President of Sports Corp, a consulting firm which brokered the new lease.

Ralph Wilson died on Tuesday, March 25, 2014, at his home in Grosse Point, Michigan. He was 95 years old. Ralph had been receiving in-home hospice care for several years, as his health continued to deteriorate from a fall that occurred at home in July of 2011. He underwent hip surgery and became wheelchair bound. Ralph then suffered from an infection, in August and September of 2012. He had not attended a Buffalo Bills game since 2010. He was the oldest owner in the NFL when he died.

The NFL owners' meetings were underway in Orlando, Florida, when the news came of Wilson's death. In accordance with Wilson's wishes, NFL Commissioner Roger Goodell cleared the room so that only owners were present and told them the news of Wilson's passing.

Wilson always believed that true happiness is doing what you love with the people you love. He believed that you can get divorced from your wife but if you recruit and sign a player, they are your family for life. Ten or twenty years later and they get in trouble; you're still the one they will turn to.

On Saturday April 5, they traveled from all corners of the country. Former players, employees and thousands of fans came to celebrate Ralph Wilson's life. The team's practice facility was awash with photos, trophies and souvenirs as they paid their last respects to Wilson. Ralph's Pro Football Hall-of-Fame gold jacket hung next to the two AFL Championship trophies. Frank Sinatra music echoed in the background, as Mary Wilson was on hand to greet and sign autographs. It was grey and cloudy, a good day for some football; Ralph would have approved.

Buddha once wrote, "We are shaped by our thoughts; we

become what we think. When the mind is pure, joy follows like a shadow that never leaves." As long as they play the game of football, Ralph Wilson will continue to cast a shadow of goodness across this sport. As my pal Shane Nelson said when I called him, "Man Andy, we lost a good one today."

SWEET LOU

Teddy Roosevelt once said, "Believe you can and you're halfway there." He was tall and thin with a smile that breaks hearts. He jumped up and down like a jack-in-the-box. This fellow could leap so high you wondered which part of his body would hit the rim first. In fact, he actually hit his head on the backboard, in the middle of a 1964 game against Purdue University. The lick required stitches to close the wound. He scored 36 points that night, with 24 of those points being scored after the stitches. He was born with desire and a basketball in his hands. He was sneaky quick; he could have invented the drive-by. This guy could go "Yosemite Sam" on you and moved around on his toes like Sugar Ray Leonard. When someone is in constant motion, it's hard to get a clear look at them. In the early days of professional basketball, at 6'5", 210 pounds, he was referred to as a swingman. Today, he would be a perfect shooting guard. This guy could take a team that made more turnovers than a bakery and make enough sweet icing to cover a four-tier cake. He could play anywhere, because he just knew how to play. On a good day, he could become an F18 with a basketball, deploying his 3-point bombs all around you. He was the kind of player to whom you would continue to feed the ball. When this guy got dialed in, you could forget about it. He could light up a scoreboard faster than a cash register at Walmart and could scream like Little Richard. His middle name should have been "zone buster." Crowds cheered so loud for him that the dust flew off the back of my TV when he scored. All he had to do was see the rim, and it went in. For him, the magic of round ball was just a bounce pass away. When you prepared to guard "Sweet Lou" Hudson, you added prayer to your list of things to do before game time.

Louis Clyde Hudson was born in Greensboro, North Carolina, on July 11, 1944. Like most great athletes, Lou starred in several sports, but basketball would be his ticket to stardom. "I grew up playing in the back yard like every other kid," said Hudson. Lou attended and graduated from an all-black high school by the name of James B. Dudley, in 1963. Lou was one of the top basketball players in the State of North Carolina. Many African American kids, who attended all-black high schools in North Carolina before they became segregated, headed north to continue to play basketball. Walt Bellemy from New Bern, North Carolina, became the first African American to play at the University of Indiana. Hudson was recruited by the University of North Carolina A&T, then coached by Cal Irvin. According to an interview with the *Charlotte Observer* in 2009, when Coach Irvin found out that Lou had received a scholarship offer from the University of Minnesota, he told Lou, "Take this opportunity to play in the big time." "He told me I was good enough," said Lou. I spoke with my good friend, Cy Alexander, who is now the head coach at the University of North Carolina A&T. Cy said, "Hudson had a much better career by going to Minnesota. He would have been a great player anywhere he played, but he received more exposure in the Big Ten Conference than he would have here at North Carolina A&T. Lou was one of the best shooters alive."

Lou attended Minnesota from 1963-66 and played for Head Coach, John Kundla. In 1965, Lou, the kid with the silky-smooth jump shot was selected to the All-Big-Ten Team, as a guard. He would also be selected an All-American that year. "I've always played with great guards who controlled the ball. Archie Clark and I were together at Minnesota," said Hudson. Lou averaged 24.8 points per game and 10.7 rebounds. His Gophers finished second in the Big Ten Conference. The following year, Lou would break a bone in his shooting hand and was forced to wear a cast on his right wrist, most of the year. Still, he averaged 19.0 points and 7.5 rebounds per game, while shooting a lot of his shots with his left hand. Lou finished his college career with 1,329 points scored, while playing in 65 games. Hudson was one of the first of three African Americans to play for Minnesota.

"I always wanted to be like Elgin Baylor," said Lou. Hudson was chosen with the fourth pick of the first round of the 1966 NBA draft, by the St. Louis Hawks. That same year, he was also drafted by the NFL's Dallas Cowboys even though he did not play football in college. Lou debuted with the St. Louis Hawks on October 15, 1966. As an NBA rookie, #23 Lou Hudson, played very well and averaged 18.4 points per game. Lou made the NBA All-Rookie team in 1967. He did miss a part of the 1967-1968 season to serve in the U. S. Army. The Hawks moved to Atlanta in 1968, and Lou scored the first basket for Atlanta on October 15, 1968. As a kid, watching the Atlanta Hawks play in the seventies was like looking at an old photo album from North Carolina. Both Lou Hudson and Walt Bellamy were born in the Tar Heel state; as "Pistol Pete" Maravich lived in Raleigh, while his dad, Press, coached at N.C. State. These three did not win a title together, but they did have a heck of a team. Hudson led his Atlanta Hawks team to the 1970 Western Division Championship. The backcourt of Hudson teamed with Lenny Wilkins at first, and later Pete Maravich was something to watch.

From 1969-1974, Lou Hudson was an NBA All-Star six years in a row. Hudson was known for jumping straight up in the air with his right elbow tucked close to his side and the ball resting on his fingertips. He would release the ball high over his head and make the words "jump shot" a part of basketball's jargon. He shot 50% or better from the field, four times in his career.

Hudson was traded on September 30, 1977, and played his last two NBA seasons with the Los Angeles Lakers. During the 1978-79 seasons, Lou shot an incredible 51.7% from the floor, unheard of in today's game. Hudson played in the NBA for 13 seasons (1966-1979). At the time he retired, Lou had scored 17,980 points, placing him twelfth on the all-time scoring list. Lou also snagged 3,926 rebounds and shelled out 2,432 assists. On November 10, 1969, Hudson scored a career high 57 points against the Chicago Bulls. The Atlanta Hawks retired his #23.

After his basketball career, Lou moved to Park City, Utah. There he started a recreation program that he named "The Growth League." This program was designed to teach life skills to kids through the game of basketball. "They spend an hour in the classroom and an hour in the gym," said Hudson. In 1993, Lou was elected to Park City's City Council. Hudson's #14 was retired by the University of Minnesota on March 5, 1994, with Lou in attendance. Lou was inducted into the North Carolina Sports Hall of Fame in 1988. In 2002, Lou Hudson was inducted into the Georgia Sports Hall of Fame. In 2003, Hudson was named Humanitarian of the Year by retired NBA players. He was also selected for the Atlanta Sports Hall of Fame in 2007.

Hudson suffered a major stroke in February of 2005, while skiing on the slopes in Park City. Lou would be confined to a wheelchair the rest of his days. He would later be transported back to Atlanta, Georgia, where he was placed in hospice care. Sweet Lou Hudson died on a Friday, April 11, 2014. He was 69 years of age and claimed he could still shoot. Lou left behind his wife, Mardi, and one daughter, Adrienne. Lou also had a son from a previous marriage, Louis Jr., who died in 1996 from a blot clot.

"Young people today don't know how good Lou Hudson

really was," said Hall-of-Famer Dominique Wilkins. "He was a hell of a player. The guy could score with the best in history. He was a phenomenal basketball player. He should be a Hall-of-Famer and it's amazing to me he's not. He was one of the best shooting guards and that's a fact. You go back and look at his career and look at the numbers and see what he did, you will understand." Some people pursue happiness while others create it. That, my friend, was Lou Hudson!

Throwing Hands

I once asked an applicant in an interview, "What would you say are your greatest strengths?" The fellow answered, "My arms and back." Obviously being physical was important to him, just like the guy I will describe to you here. In the world of professional boxing you have to grow up fast, as the forecast usually calls for a daily beat-down. You have to put your body through pain by endless hours of running and training before you can deliver the pain to another. You could be full of dreams or beaten hopeless in a matter of minutes. He was naturally mean-spirited and not the kind of guy you would list as your emergency contact. In the ring he was like poison ivy, he just wouldn't go away. This guy wasn't afraid of dying, he was afraid of losing. He was baldheaded and shorter than a Greg Popovich answer. He owned a pair of heavy hands that hung from the lightning bolts that were attached to his sides. The rest of us call them arms. This fellow didn't throw jabs, he threw haymakers. In the sport of boxing you don't have to move a lot, just enough to make your opponent miss. He was born to the fight game and would have had no issue with them removing the three knock-down rule. This guy didn't compete because he wanted to; he competed because he had to. He would challenge his opponent's courage, bloody their nose, leave welts under their eyes and eventually put them to sleep. They simply had no answers for his combinations. Most of them left the ring looking like they had fallen on their car keys. Throwing hands was what this guy did best.

In sports the eyes tell you the truth, especially in boxing. Just look into their eyes and you can see if they really want to be there. Rubin Carter understood that the two things we control in life are attitude and effort. He won his first ten out of eleven fights, so he didn't need to worry about taking the subway home late at night. In the beginning, he was good; so good his future was sure to include long limousines and expensive champagne.

Rubin Carter came into this world on May 6, 1937. Rubin was number four of seven children born to his parents in Clifton, New Jersey. His middle name should have been "trouble" as trouble found him quickly in 1951. Some thought he grew up on the corner of Violent and Defiant, and he was black. He also had a slight speech impediment. At the young age of 14, he lead the state in burglaries and was placed in the Jamesburg Home for Boys, a reformatory school for troubled youth, after being arrested and convicted of assault and battery. Carter escaped in 1954 and joined the Army "on the sly," at 17 years of age. He was off to Fort Jackson, South Carolina, for a three-year enlistment instead of back to prison. After his training was completed Carter's division was transferred to West Germany. It was there that he began to box.

In May of 1956, Carter's past caught up with him and he received an "Undesirable" discharge from the Army for not completing his three-year enlistment. He was arrested immediately after he returned to New Jersey for his earlier escape and was made to serve an additional nine months, five of which he served in Annandale Prison. His reputation was such that anytime a crime was committed, he became a suspect. An angry Carter was arrested again shortly after being released. This time he had committed assault and robbery of an elderly woman. After pleading guilty, he was sentenced to East Jersey State Prison in Avenel, New Jersey. He spent the next four years in their maximum-security facility.

By the time Carter turned 24, he had spent almost four years in a reformatory school and four years in prison. This dude was so bad, his picture hung on every Post Office wall in New Jersey. Needless to say, it wasn't a very good start. Rubin was released from prison in September of 1961, and he turned professional. At 5'8" tall and weighing 155 pounds he was much shorter than an average middleweight boxer. Carter shaved his head and went to work in the gym to hone his skills. His goal was to hit the other guy so often that he would think he as surrounded. His natural aggressiveness and endless punching power overwhelmed most of his opponents. He won 20 of his first 24 fights.

In the early 1960's, Carter fought most of his early bouts in New Jersey and Pennsylvania. His success would take him worldwide to London, England, Johannesburg, South Africa, and Paris, France. He also fought in Honolulu, Hawaii. My dad, a huge boxing fan, allowed me to stay up late and watch the "Gillette Friday Night Fights" with him. It was then that I discovered Rubin Carter. Rubin fought at Madison Square Garden eleven times during his career. My dad and I watched Carter defeat George Benton by split decision on May 25, 1963. *The Ring* magazine listed George Benton as one of the top-ten middleweights in all of professional boxing. Benton would later retire and join Lou Duva as a trainer of many World Champions. I later met and had lunch with George Benton and his cut man, Ace Marotta, in Corpus Christi, Texas. George was there for an Evander Holyfield fight.

Joey Archer lost to Carter by split decision on October 25, 1963. On December 20, 1963, at the Pittsburgh Civic Arena, Carter stunned future World Champion Emile Griffith with two booming right-hand knockdowns. The fight was stopped by the referee, 2:13 seconds into the first round. Carter had scored a technical knockout for the win. Jimmy Ellis was beaten by Rubin in a unanimous decision on February 28, 1964. Carter, now ranked third by *The Ring* magazine, also fought Joey Giardello on December 14, 1964, at the Philadelphia Convention Hall, for the WBC/WBA World Middleweight title. Carter staggered Giardello in the 4th round, but could not follow up. Giardello responded in the 5th round to win on a unanimous decision.

Carter then lost to Dick Tiger on May 20, 1965 at the Garden. Carter was knocked down three times by Tiger before the fight was stopped. After that fight, Carter described the results of the fight this way: "The worst beating that I took in my life inside or outside the ring." A fighter can get old between rounds. It's a level of unconsciousness while standing. It's called an "adrenaline dump." They just give the other guy whatever they have left. It's like being in a gun battle and running out of ammunition.

Rubin Carter fought often: twelve times in 1962, six times in 1963 and nine times in 1965. It was as if he knew his time would be short. He entered the ring a total of 40 times, winning 27 fights, and 19 by knockout, and lost 12. He also had one draw. Carter flaunted his success. He joked about killing policemen in a 1964 *Saturday Evening Post* story and rode around in his black Eldorado Cadillac with his name stenciled in silver above each headlight. Even with a 27-12-1 record, the police considered him more of a suspect than contender.

And then! On June 17, 1966, two males entered the Lafayette Bar and Grill located at East 18th Street in Patterson, New Jersey. It was approximately 2:30 PM when the shooting started. Bartender James Oliver and patron Fred Nauyoks were killed instantly. Female patron Hazel Tanis died a month later from her wounds. She had been shot in the throat, stomach; intestine, spleen and left lung, and her left arm had been shattered from shotgun pellets. A fourth customer, Willie Marins, survived but lost the sight of one eye from the shotgun blast. Both Tanis and Marins told police that the shooters had been black males.

Convicted thieves, Alfredo Bello and Arthur Bradley

arrived on the scene shortly after the shooting. Bello claimed he was an eyewitness. He described two black males, one with a shotgun and the other with a pistol fleeing the crime scene and getting into a white car. Shortly thereafter, based on this information, the New Jersey police stopped a white dodge being driven by Carter. Rubin and his friend John Artis were taken back to the scene, questioned and released. Neither of them was identified by Bello as the shooters. There were no fingerprints taken at the scene and the police did not conduct a paraffin test for gunshot residue. During a search, there was a .32 caliber handgun found under the passenger's front seat in the white Dodge, along with a shotgun in the trunk, but that info was not logged into the records until a week had passed after the shooting. Both Carter and Artis had alibis, but were arrested a month later based on the testimony of Bello and now Bradley. Under questioning, Bello revealed that Bradley had been with him that night. Both men "now" claim they recognized Carter and Artis as the murderers. With little or no physical evidence found at the scene and no eyewitness identification, Carter and Artis were still arrested and indicted. Carter received a double life sentence and Artis a single life sentence. Artis was later paroled in 1981.

I'm in no way letting the sloppy police work off the hook. There appeared to have been a rush to judgment on their part; but I'm saying, if you go into the jungle often enough, eventually the tiger will get you. Carter's past criminal record surely played a part in the police efforts to solve this murder quickly.

Carter was convicted twice in 1967 and 1976. The second conviction was overturned. Carter spent most of his time in prison in solitary confinement because he refused to follow the prison rules. He would not wear the prison clothes (stripes) and refused to eat the prison food. He wouldn't work. "Because I was not guilty," said Carter, "I refused to act like a guilty person."

In November of 1988, at the age of 48, Rubin Carter was set free for the first time in almost twenty years. United States District Judge Haddon Lee Sarokin wrote that Carter's prosecution had been "Predicated upon an appeal to racism rather than reason, and concealment rather than disclosure." And that "The prosecution's case rested on racial stereotypes, fear and prejudices."

Carter became a motivational speaker after moving to Toronto. From 1993 until 2005, Carter served as the Executive Director of the Association in Defense of the Wrongfully Convicted. His partner, Win Wahrer, was a co-founder of this group. Carter would later receive two honorary doctorates for his efforts. Rubin Carter's autobiography was published in 1975, by Warner Books. It was entitled The Sixteenth Round. Singer songwriter Bob Dylan read his book and wrote the song "Hurricane" later that same year. This song claimed that Carter was innocent. Dylan's words rang out:

> "So, that's the story of Hurricane.
> A man the authorities came to blame.
> For something that he never done,
> Put in a prison cell, but one time
> He could have been the champion of
> the world."

Dylan performed that song at a concert in Trenton State Prison, while Carter was incarcerated there. There is no doubt that Rubin Carter became the most well-known wrongfully-convicted person worldwide. Even Muhammad Ali spoke on Carter's behalf. Actor Denzel Washington, who played Carter in the 1999 Movie *The Hurricane*, said when he heard about Rubin's death, "God Bless Rubin Carter and his tireless fight to ensure justice for all." Washington won a Golden Globe for his portrayal of Carter, even though the movie was criticized for not revealing Carter's criminal past before the shooting. Rubin Carter also received an Honorary Championship Title belt from the World Boxing Commission in 1993.

Rubin Carter died in his sleep on Easter Sunday, April 20, 2014. He was living in his adopted hometown of Toronto, Ontario. Rubin was 76. He had been battling prostate cancer since being diagnosed in March of 2012. Longtime friend, John Artis, lived with and cared for Carter until the end. Carter was cremated with most of his remains sprinkled in the ocean of Cape Cod. Some of his ashes were given to two of his sisters yet he remained estranged from most of his family. I believe Carter became more famous for his wrongful conviction than he ever would have as a boxer.

Charlie Chaplin once said, "My only enemy is time." How true; especially if you have 19 years of it taken away from you. For most of us, our past does not define us; it's what we do now that matters. But, sometimes the worst scars are not the ones we can see. For a time, his aggressive whirlwind punching power in the ring earned him his nickname, "Hurricane." But for almost twenty years, everybody else knew him as a convicted killer, by the name of Rubin Carter.

KING OF THE FLAT TOP

William Feather once said, "Success seems to be largely a matter of hanging on after others have let go." This guy became the best relief pitcher in the National Football League. As a professional quarterback, he participated in 255 games during 21 seasons, for six different teams. He was passed around like a stale bag of chips. He was traded so much he never got to send out for dry cleaning. You got the feeling this guy was sitting on a ledge six stories high outside his hotel room, but how untrue. A blue-collar guy, he outlasted his critics. He was a quiet fellow except when he laughed, and then he sounded like an electrical storm. As the years went by, he began to look like an unmade bed and reminded you of the old guy at the YMCA pulling on his knee brace and rubbing Ben-Gay on his shoulder. He owned a face without a name and loved being recognized, especially when he stepped in and got the job done. He was simply the other quarterback, solid as they come, always prepared and a great team player. You can get bumped into more times at Kmart during a blue light special than some backup quarterbacks do in an entire season. But football is not about if we will get hurt; it's about when and how bad. A season-ending shoulder injury occurred in October of 1964.

"Earl was an intelligent quarterback who's won a lot of ballgames for me," said Don Shula. Hall-of-Fame quarterback George Blanda once said, "No one dreams about being a backup quarterback." That may be true unless you're Earl Morrall, the perfect backup quarterback. Earl Morrall was king of the flat-top; you could almost land a plane on his head. He was perhaps the greatest backup quarterback in NFL history.

He was named Earl Edwin Morrall on May 17, 1934. Muskegon, Michigan became his hometown and he grew to 6'1" tall and weighed 205 pounds. That's a fairly good size for a quarterback. Earl led his Muskegon High School to the Michigan State High School Championship in 1951. His success set off fireworks between Michigan, Michigan State and the Notre Dame recruiters. The competition for his services became so ferocious that his high school principal complained that Earl's grades began to suffer.

Morrall chose the Michigan State Spartans, where he played three seasons becoming a consensus All-American and led his 9-1 Spartans over the U.C.L.A. Bruins in the 1956 Rose Bowl. As we find in most great athletes, they usually played more than one sport, and that was the case for Morrall. Earl also played shortstop and third base for the Spartans baseball team and was a part of their 1954 College Baseball World Series team. He received several offers to play baseball professionally, but chose professional football as his career. Earl Morrall's name was called by the San Francisco 49ers with the second pick of the 1956 NFL draft. He was given the #15 which he would wear his entire career. The Pittsburgh Steelers had the first pick and chose Colorado State quarterback, Gary Glick. Detroit, with the third pick, took Howard "Hopalong" Cassidy, a halfback from Ohio State.

Morrall and offensive guard Mike Sandusky would be traded the following year (1957) to the Pittsburgh Steelers, who were completely unhappy with Gary Glick. Besides, the 49ers had a pretty good quarterback by the name of Y.A. Tittle, which made Morrall expendable. The 49ers received linebacker Marv Matuszak and two future first-round draft picks from Pittsburgh. The Steelers had two young quarterbacks by the names of Len Dawson and Jack Kemp, which they couldn't count on. So they went after Morrall. In 1958, Earl threw seven interceptions in his first two games. The Steelers then traded Morrall to the Detroit Lions for quarterback Bobby Layne. Morrall would stay with the Lions for seven years, and he threw for 2,600 yards and 24 touchdowns in 1963. While in Detroit, he mostly backed up Tobin Rote and Milt Plum. Then he suffered a shoulder injury. There's a great story told by Detroit offensive guard John Gordy. Morrall said to a reporter before a game with the 49ers that defensive tackle Leo Nomellini was over the hill. "I gave out a big yell when I read what Earl said. I told Morrall if you think he's over the hill, you go play against him," said Gordy. With no front teeth and eyes that appeared crossed, Nomellini was a raving maniac trying to get to Earl that day.

In 1965, Earl was pulled like a loose tooth. Morrall was on the move again and eventually was traded to the New York Football Giants on August 30th. Y.A. Tittle retired from the Giants at the end of the 1964 season. With Morrall's shoulder healed, Earl put up 2,446 yards and recorded 22 touchdowns for a rebuilding Giants team. In 1967, Fran Tarkenton joined the Giants and on August 25, 1968, Earl was again traded. This time to the Baltimore Colts, who had quarterback Johnny Unitas as their starter. As luck would have it, Unitas incurred an elbow injury in the 1968 final exhibition game, and Morrall became the Baltimore starter. Under Earl's leadership the Colts won 13 of 14 games, and he led the NFL in touchdown passes, with 26, and threw for 2,909 yards. Earl and the Colts then added two more playoff wins on their way to Super Bowl III against Joe Namath's New York Jets. The Baltimore Colts were favored by 21 points.

In a shocker, the upstart AFL Jets upset the NFL Colts, 16-7. Morrall had thrown three crucial interceptions. The clincher was a second-quarter interception over the middle while receiver Jimmy Orr stood in the end zone, wide open, waving his hands in the air. The Colt fans were so devastated by the loss to the Jets; they had to take a number to jump off the bridge. In 1968, Earl Morrall would go from the playgrounds of Michigan to the cover of *Sports Illustrated*. He also received the 1968 NFL's Most Valuable Player Award. Interestingly, two years later during Super Bowl V, Morrall would again replace an injured Unitas to lead the Colts to a 16-13 win over the Dallas Cowboys. The difference was a 32-yard field goal by Colts' kicker Jim O'Brien with time running out.

On April 25, 1972, Morrall was claimed off waivers for $100 by the Miami Dolphins. Dolphins' head coach Don Shula had been Morrall's coach in Baltimore and trusted Earl. "I wanted to pick Earl up as an insurance policy," said Don Shula. "I had to talk owner Joe Robbie into doing it, because Earl was making 90,000 dollars a year. I wanted to claim him off waivers, and Robbie said, 'Pay 90,000 for a backup! Are you out of your mind?'" It would prove to be an incredibly smart decision. On October 15, 1972, against the San Diego Chargers, starting Miami quarterback Bob Griese injured his ankle. In comes 38-year-old Earl Morrall, the perfect backup. Morrall's teammates called him "old man" and placed a rocking chair in front of his locker. Everyone else had a folding chair. He would proceed to start for the Dolphins in 11 out of 17 games that season and helped this squad become the only undefeated team in NFL history. After beating the Cleveland Browns in their first playoff game, Morrall struggled against the Pittsburgh Steelers in the AFC Championship game and was pulled and replaced by Bob Griese. "It was one of the toughest decisions I have ever had to make," said Shula. "But I chose Griese to start the Super Bowl, as he was my quarterback going into the season and my quarterback for the future." Here's an interesting footnote to the Miami Dolphins 1972 season. A season ticket cost but $77.00.

The Dolphins would continue undefeated and won Super Bowl VII, beating the Washington Redskins 14-7. The Dolphins, primarily a running team with Larry Csonka and Mercury Morris, finished 17-0. "There would not have been a perfect season without Earl Morrall," said Bob Griese. Morrall's play in 1972 did not go unnoticed, as he received the very first NFL Comeback-Player-of-the-Year Award and was also chosen the American Football Conference Player-of-the-Year. He was the perfect backup quarterback for the perfect season. The Dolphins would win Super Bowl VIII the following season by whipping the Minnesota Vikings, 24-7. Earl would announce his retirement four years later on May 2, 1977. He was 42 years old. In his 21 NFL seasons, Earl Morrall had played in three Super Bowls, completed 1,379 passes for 20,809 yards, and recorded 161 touchdowns and 148 interceptions.

One of my favorite stories that included Earl Morrall was told by the great Colts' tight end, John Mackey. It had been said that quarterback Johnny Unitas was so accurate that if he threw you a pass in your gut, it meant catch the football and go down, because you were about to get hit. If he threw it up and out over your head, it meant you were wide open and you needed to turn and run under it, catch it, and score. If he threw it wide of you, it meant you needed to lay out for the catch or knock it down to keep it from being intercepted. So, when back-up quarterback Earl Morrall took over in a game for an injured Unitas and threw a pass up and out to tight end John Mackey, Mackey said, "I got hit so hard my teeth hurt."

"So I've always said Unitas, Griese and Dan Marino are in the Hall of Fame, and Earl is in my own personal Hall of Fame," said Don Shula. Earl Morrall was inducted into the Michigan State Athletics Hall of Fame in 1992. Earl attended Miami's 40th team reunion in 2012 and was inducted into the Dolphins' Walk of Fame.

Morrall became the quarterback coach for the University

of Miami in 1979. His work with talents like Jim Kelly, Bernie Kosar and Vinny Testaverde showed that he was not only a fine quarterback, but also a very good teacher.

In 1969, Earl Morrall wrote his autobiography entitled <u>In the Pocket: My Life as a Quarterback</u>. You can find it for less than $4.00 on Amazon.com, in hardback. In 1989, Earl tried his hand at politics and served some time on the Davie, Florida City Council before becoming the town's Mayor.

Two-time NFL All-Pro, Earl Morrall, died on Friday, April 25, 2014, exactly 42 years to the day after he had been acquired from the Colts by the Dolphins. He had struggled with poor health for several years, while living in Naples, Florida. Recently Earl had been moved into his son Matthew's home, located in Fort Lauderdale. His cause of death has been listed as complications from Parkinson's disease. Earl was survived by his wife, Jane, five children and nine grandchildren.

Earl Morrall is not in the NFL Hall of Fame, but I would challenge you to find another quarterback whose career intertwined with names like Tittle, Dawson, Kemp, Layne, Plum, Rote, Tarkenton, Unitas, Namath and Griese. His coaching career would connect him to Kelly, Testaverde and Kosar. When you discuss great moments and games from the 1960's and 1970's, it doesn't take very long before you get to the name Morrall.

NFL Hall of Fame coach Paul Brown once said, "If you win say nothing. If you lose say less." That was the essence of Earl Morrall.

DR. JACK

When thinking about this particular coach, I am reminded of World War I General "Black Jack" Pershing, who once sent a message back to his superiors from the frontlines in France. It read, "My center is giving away! My right is being pushed back! And my left is wavering! The situation is excellent! I shall attack!" Attack was this coach's specialty. This fellow reminded me of George Pickett at Gettysburg before his charge. He was one of those coaches who believed in stretching the flooring and destroying the rim. I can see him now in my mind, red coat, checkered bell-bottom pants, down on one knee, hands clasped together, and almost baldheaded. He could have been Abraham in tennis shoes. Before every game on the blackboard he wrote three words: run, run, run. His high-tempo offense was copied by coaches like Paul Westhead, who played for him at St. Joe, and Pat Riley of the Los Angeles Lakers. His teams didn't beat you with the give-and-go; they beat you with their endurance and their minds. He brought one of the finest, most inventive and resourceful minds to the game of basketball.

This fellow excelled at friendship and, as long as he was tied to the game of basketball as a player, coach or analyst, he was at home. He owned a big personality and a laugh like "Times Square." He moved in circles that included "Red" Holtzman and "Red" Auerbach. He believed that as a coach it was always good to know what you don't know. He understood that one of the toughest things to do in the game of basketball was to keep your opponent out of the paint. Therefore he became a master of the zone defense. We are a lot like magnets; we attract others who are our reflections. If we appear friendly then most others will seem to also be friendly. He was a master of the moment. His teams emptied themselves in front of their fans. He valued what he called an "assist of the imagination."

John T. "Jack" Ramsey was born on February 21, 1925, in the "City of Brotherly Love," Philadelphia, Pennsylvania. He spent his childhood in Connecticut, where his dad was in the mortgage and loan business. The Ramsey family later returned to the area where he was born, and Jack graduated from Upper Darby High School in 1942.

At the age of eleven, Jack's childhood hero was a baseball player by the name of Burgess "Whitey" Whitehead, a poor-hitting second baseman for the New York Giants. Whitehead, a one time member of the 1934 World Champion St. Louis Cardinals, was a great friend and teammate of "Dizzy" Dean's. Burgess was traded to the New York Giants in 1936, and became an All-Star for the second time in 1937. The New York Giants would win the National League Pennant in both 1936 and 1937. Born in Tarboro, North Carolina, about twenty miles from where I grew up, Whitehead died of a heart attack in 1993. He was the last living member of the St. Louis Cardinals' "Gashouse Gang" of 1934. In 1981, Burgess Whitehead was inducted into the North Carolina Sports Hall of Fame. Jack Ramsey had wanted to be a baseball player, but he couldn't hit the ball hard enough to score Usain Bolt from third base.

Jack entered St. Joseph College after being allowed to work out privately in St. Joseph's Prep gym for Hawks' coach Bill Ferguson. St. Joe offered Ramsey a full scholarship to play basketball. His college education was interrupted by World War II. Ramsey spent three years as a U. S. Navy frogman, planting explosives in the Pacific Ocean. "I learned how important physical conditioning is," said Ramsey. Working with explosives, you also learn how to stay focused and deal with stress. Jack would return to get his degree in education and become the captain of Bill Ferguson's St. Joe Hawks. His mother had wanted him to become a doctor, but basketball kept getting in the way.

After graduation Ramsey played some semi-pro ball for Sunbury and Harrisburg, in the old eastern Pennsylvania Basketball League, before becoming a head coach in high school. Ramsey proved to be a fiery competitor and very detail-oriented. His teams at St. James High School in Chester and Mount Pleasant High School in Wilmington played well. His record over three seasons at Mount Pleasant was 40-18.

In 1949, Jack earned a doctorate in education from the University of Pennsylvania. In 1955, St. Joe's Coach, John McMenamin, retired. Ramsey began coaching at Saint Joseph College that year, six years after high school. Ramsey's first team played in the NIT (National Invitational Tournament). Ramsey coached for eleven years (1955-1966) at St. Joe in Philadelphia, posting a 234-72 win-loss record, leading the Hawks to the NCAA Tournament seven times and the 1961 Final Four. St. Joe lost to Ohio State but beat Utah for third place, 127-120, in four overtimes. Their 1961 Final Four appearance was vacated when three players from St. Joe (John Egan, Frank Majewski and Vince Kempton) were implicated in a point-shaving scandal. Ramsey's teams won 75% of his games at St. Joseph. They would also achieve a #3 ranking nationally, in 1963.

In 1966, Coach Alex Hannum departed. The Philadelphia 76ers asked Jack Ramsey to be their general manager. "The team was ready made and I did not sign any new players," said Jack. This team consisted of Wilt Chamberlain, Hal Greer, Wally Jones, Chet Walker, Gary Costello, and their sixth man was Billy Cunningham. The 76ers finished the season with a 68-13 win-loss record and beat the dreaded Celtics, who had won the last eight years in a row, for the

(1967-1968) NBA Championship. The following year, Jack left the front office to become the coach. Wilt wanted to be a player-coach and asked Ramsey about the possibility. As Ramsey took his time contemplating the idea, Wilt changed his mind. When asked years later why he traded Wilt Chamberlain before the 1968-69 season, he responded. "I never traded Wilt; he traded himself." Ramsey coached the 76ers from 1968-1972. During his four seasons as head coach, Philadelphia participated in three playoffs.

Ramsey joined the Buffalo Braves in 1972, their third year of existence. He had a very young group of players and ended up changing nine players by the end of his second year as head coach. In 1976, after four seasons and three playoff berths, he left Buffalo for Portland, Oregon.

For ten seasons (1976-1986), Jack's Trailblazers made the playoffs every year but one. With stars like Lionel Hollins, Maurice Lucas and Bill Walton, Ramsey was able to get his teams out and run, forcing the action and doing his part in helping create the origin of "Rip City." Announcer Bill Schonely used that phrase when describing a long shot by Portland's Jim Barnett. It stuck. The basketball we were watching was straight from the streets of Philadelphia. Ramsey explained his success by talking about one of his players more than the others. "Bill Walton had a great basketball mind. He was hungry to win," said Ramsey.

In the locker room, after the Portland Trailblazers had beaten the Philadelphia 76ers 109-107, for the 1977 NBA Championship, Ramsey was asked by a reporter about his starting center. "I've never coached a better player, I've never coached a better competitor, and I've never coached a better person than Bill Walton," said Jack Ramsey.

For all the good decisions Ramsey had made during his career, he will also be remembered as the coach who passed on Jordan. Portland had the second pick in the 1984 NBA draft and chose 7' 2" Kentucky center, Sam Bowie, and passed on Michael Jordan. Yes, that Michael Jordan. "I needed a center," said Jack when questioned. Bowie's career was very brief while Jordan and his Chicago Bulls won six NBA titles. Ramsey also coached the Indiana Pacers for two seasons (1986-1988).

Jack Ramsey coached and lived by the following principle. You are accountable for your situation, good or bad, successful or unsuccessful, happy or sad, fair or unfair, you are responsible. That is how it is! You see, most of us believe we work hard every day. The truth is we don't. We work until we find a comfortable level and then we try to hold onto that! We never achieve breakthrough results. We never get really tested. We get caught up in being a bit better than yesterday or business as usual. The fact is, we settle. Jack Ramsey would not allow you to settle. NBA Hall-of-Fame center, Bill Walton, once said, "He taught me more about myself and basketball than anyone," and this was a guy who played for John Wooden. "We loved Jack Ramsey," said Walton. "His stare got results."

I was at the 1992 Final Four in San Antonio, Texas, when Dr. Jack Ramsey was introduced as one of the newest members of the Naismith Basketball Hall of Fame. He would be inducted later that spring on May 11, 1992.

There are not vary many words left for me to use that haven't already been written about Dr. Jack Ramsey, but I can tell you how I felt when I met him in 1993, at the NBA All-Star Jam, held that year in Salt Lake City, Utah. My friend and fellow Pizza Hut Franchisee, Mike Patranella, had made the trip with me. Mike and I had made it a habit of attending big-time sporting events such as Super Bowls, World Series Games and NBA Finals. It was February 18th, cold and snowing, when we left our hotel for the event. Dr. Jack was with then-fellow-coach, Don Nelson, when I approached. I waited until they were through talking and said, "Hello." Dr. Jack turned and smiled as if he had known me for years. We shook hands, exchanged pleasantries, and he gave me his autograph. He was relaxed, kind and never stopped smiling. Nelson, on the other hand, looked bothered and stood with his hands in his pockets. Mike and I had a blast that weekend and especially enjoyed the Legends Game with "Hot Rod" Hundley, Zelmo Batty and Artis Gilmore. That was the last year the legends played during the NBA Jam. We collected many autographs including one particular signature that remains unique. We met James Jordan, Michael Jordan's dad and received his autograph. Little did anyone know that he would be assaulted in his car and killed in July of that summer? He had been wearing a Chicago Bulls NBA Championship ring given to him by his son. It was stolen.

Ramsey's success made him a household name. He would write several books including: <u>Pressure Basketball</u>, <u>Dr. Jack's Leadership Lessons Learned From a Lifetime in Basketball</u> and <u>The Coach's Art</u>. In his last book, Ramsey wrote, "What is this game that runs through my mind? It is a ballet, a graceful sweep and flow of patterned movement, counterpointed by daring and imaginative flights of solitary brilliance." Jack Ramsey also developed some fine coaches, most of whom had played for him. Jim Lyman, Paul Westhead, Matt Goukas Jr., and Jack McKinney all had some success in basketball. In 1996, Ramsey would be elected one of the top ten coaches in NBA history.

David Stern chose Jack Ramsey to spread the word about basketball to the world. Ramsey's assignment was to travel the globe teaching and promoting the NBA. He would soon be referred to as "Mr. Clinic." Ramsey began broadcasting for the Philadelphia 76ers and Miami Heat before becoming an analyst for ESPN and ESPN Radio. He worked with Mike Tirico on television and Jim Durham on radio. He spent 21 years in coaching and 25 years as a basketball analyst. In 2009, St. Joseph named its new basketball facility the Ramsey Basketball Center, after their most famous coach. Ramsey's professional teams won 864 games, while losing 783.

"From his coaching tenure to his broadcast work, Dr. Jack left an incredible mark on every facet of our game and on every person he came in contact with, including me," said NBA commissioner, Adam Silver.

The man who invented "Blazermania" died in his sleep on Sunday, April 28, 2014. He was living in Naples, Florida, and had celebrated 89 great years of life. "The game lost a giant," said Pat Riley. Dr. Jack had fought melanoma cancer since 2004. Dr. Jack maintained a home in Ocean City, New Jersey, all his life, regardless of where he was coaching. He loved swimming in the ocean and jogging on the beach. Ramsey competed in 20 triathlons and worked out daily, well into his eighties. He was a devout Catholic and his players swore he had a unique spiritual aura all around him. Jack's NBA teams reached the playoffs 16 times in his 21 coaching seasons. At the end, he was surrounded by his sons, Chris and John, daughters Sharon, Carolyn and Susan, 13 grandchildren and four great grandchildren. His wife Jean passed away earlier in 2010 from Alzheimer's disease. Norman Vincent Peale once wrote, "Believe in yourself. Have faith in your abilities. Without humble but reasonable confidence in your own powers, you cannot be successful or happy." Jack Ramsey was both.

GOOD CHIN

Have you ever been in a situation where you wished you had chosen door number two? This guy's whole life was like that. He had always been there, in the shadows, preparing for his turn. He didn't have any money. His pre-fight meal was KFC. In the beginning, he fought against fighters who were so bad that the only thing they broke was a sweat. Fighters with names like Herman Calhoun, Clarence Riley and Arley Seifer; they all found themselves on the canvas looking up as the referee counted them out. A fine boxer with quick hands, his shoulders were big and broad, as if they were still hanging on a hanger. He had no problem hitting his opponents with everything but his tool box. They called him an ear, nose and throat guy, because that's where he hit most of his opponents. This fellow surrounded his opponents like Grant at Vicksburg. He was a meat and potatoes man and when he hit you, the crowd went OHHH! The greatest gift his father ever gave him was that he believed in him. A God-fearing man, he was always looking for that sweet spot between good and evil. His Bible was his fortress. He often wondered what had happened to respect and dignity. He spent most of his career as the betting underdog, fighting on the undercard of Cassius Clay. Keeping one's temper is a priceless attribute for a boxer. A skilled tactician, he always remained calm and even-keeled during a bout.

He fought thirteen times at Freedom Hall, where the smell of hotdogs, cigars and mustard were embedded in the concrete. It was located in his hometown of Louisville, Kentucky. Fighters are as superstitious as any other athletes, and he was no different. In fact, I once read where Marvin Hagler would not eat the food he was brought while training for "Sugar Ray" Leonard. He switched food with his trainer. This fellow was a good-looking guy. His friend, Muhammad Ali, always said, "Look at me, I'm so pretty." His response, "Anybody would look pretty if the only two people he stood next to were Howard Cosell and Joe Frazier." Whitney Young, Jr. once said, "It is better to be prepared for an opportunity and not have one, than to have an opportunity and not be prepared." Even though he had served as Ali's sparring partner, this fellow prepared his whole life to step into the spotlight. He was somewhat overshadowed, but maintained his pride. Fighting often, he spent his time learning how to accept an occasional loss without being defeated. Ask any athlete. Most of their wins feel the same; it's the tough losses that haunt them. His chosen profession was a rock fight, and he was in it to win it. Thank goodness Jimmy Ellis had a good chin.

James Albert "Jimmy" Ellis was born February 24, 1940, in the hometown of Cassius Clay, Louisville, Kentucky. Jimmy was one of ten children born to Pastor Ellis. He worked in a cement factory as a teenager, sang in his father's church choir, and became a devout Christian. His favorite boxer was the great Joe Louis. Ellis was drawn to boxing while watching one of his friends, Donnie Hall, box a kid from the neighborhood named Cassius Clay, on a local television show called "Tomorrow's Champions." Ellis thought he could do better and followed Hall to Louisville's Columbia Gym, where local kids were trained by a police officer named Joe Martin. Ellis proved worthy as he recorded a win-loss record of 59-7 as an amateur. Jimmy would be crowned a Gold Glove Champion. He did box Clay on two occasions as an amateur, with Clay winning the first bout and Ellis winning the second. In 1961, Jimmy Ellis turned professional as a middleweight.

Ellis was initially trained by Bud Bruner and won 15 of his first 20 bouts, six by knockout. His five losses came at the hands of some pretty fair opponents. George Benton, Rubin "Hurricane" Carter, Don Fullmer, Henry Hank and top contender, Holly Mims, all defeated Ellis. Ellis would redeem himself with a win over Mims in a rematch. In 1964, several things happened. Jimmy's friend, Cassius Clay, knocked out Sonny Liston to win the Heavyweight Championship, Clay then changed his name to Muhammad Ali, and Jimmy Ellis petitioned Angelo Dundee, Ali's trainer, to handle his career. In a letter, Ellis, now fighting as a 190-pound heavyweight, asked Dundee to be his trainer and manager. Dundee agreed and Ellis became a sparring partner for Ali. Ellis also fought on several of Ali's undercards, winning six of his first eight fights with Dundee. Ellis, being tall and naturally athletic, had continuing problems trying to maintain a lower weight, therefore he moved up to the heavyweight class. By 1966, Ellis was on his way to stardom.

In 1966, Ali was stripped of his world title because he refused to enter the military. Therefore, that left a vacant title for the World Boxing Association (WBA). They decided to conduct an eight-man tournament with the best heavyweight contenders. Ellis was ranked eighth in the world and received an invitation. Interestingly, Joe Frazier, who was ranked second by the WBA decided not to participate. He instead fought Buster Mathis for the vacant New York State Athletic Commission World Heavyweight Championship, and won by knockout in the eleventh round.

Jimmy Ellis drew Leotis Martin for his first foe. The referee stopped the fight on cuts in the ninth round, as Ellis pummeled Martin's face into a bloody mess. Ellis met Oscar Bonavena in the second fight. Jimmy was declared the winner by unanimous decision, after flooring Bonavena in the third round with a right hand and again in the ninth round by a powerful left hook. This win advanced Ellis to the tournament finals. Ellis fought Jerry Quarry on April 27, 1968, in Oakland, California. Reporters described the fight as "extremely cautious" by both fighters. Jimmy Ellis won on a 15-round split decision to become the new WBA Heavyweight Champion.

Ellis defended his title only once against Floyd Patterson in Stockholm, Sweden, on September 14, 1968. Patterson broke Ellis's nose in the second round, but the time-tested Dundee was able to buy his fighter some time while stopping the bleeding. This fight had but one judge, the referee, who awarded the controversial win to Ellis. Including the *New York Times*, many fans disagreed with the results. Ellis would take the next 17 months off, as one fight after another fell through.

On February 16, 1970, Ellis and Joe Frazier took center stage at Madison Square Garden, for the purpose of unifying the World Heavyweight Championship. Frazier was undefeated and a heavy betting favorite in Vegas. Frazier simply proved to be too overpowering for Ellis. Jimmy, who had never been knocked down, went to the canvas twice in the fourth round, to a superior foe. Angelo Dundee, Ellis' trainer, always looked after his fighters and threw in the towel before the start of round five. Jimmy could not continue. It would be the first knockout loss by Ellis, in his career.

Ellis recuperated and then won his next three fights, placing himself in position to fight his friend and old sparring partner, Muhammad Ali. Ali's conviction of draft evasion had been overturned by the Supreme Court. Dundee, who was also Ali's trainer, chose to work in Jimmy's corner. Ellis needed all the help he could get, and Dundee's share of the purse would be bigger. It was one of the few fights in Ali's career in which Dundee was not in his corner. Harry Wiley worked Ali's corner. The fight was held on July 26, 1971, at the Astrodome, located in Houston, Texas. The first three rounds went well for Ellis, until he was stunned by an Ali right hand in the fourth round. Ellis stayed upright but the blow took away his stamina. "The right hand hurt me so bad I couldn't really fight my best after that," said Ellis. Even though Ellis was never knocked down, the referee finally stopped the fight at 2:10 of the twelfth round and awarded the fight to Ali.

Ellis won his next eight fights after the loss to Ali, but he never really fought the same. On June 18, 1973, Ellis got into a slugfest with big Ernie Shavers, who had won 44 of his 46 bouts, with 43 knockouts. Ellis dominated the fight right from the start and hurt Shaver with a chopping right hand to the jaw that backed him into the corner. Ellis closed in and battered a stunned Shaver. When the referee separated the fighters, Shavers retaliated with a right hand uppercut to the chin that floored Ellis. The fight was stopped. The time was 2:39 in the first round. Ellis and the crowd were stunned at the results. Jimmy Ellis disappeared faster than a drive-in movie. It was the beginning of the end for Ellis.

Ellis won only one of his next six fights. He lost decisions to Ron Lyle, Joe Bugner and Larry Middleton. He also lost again to Joe Frazier in a rematch, when the fight was stopped by Dundee in the ninth round.

Ellis retired at the age of 35, after suffering an eye injury while training. This injury would leave him partially blind in his left eye. After recovery, he began to train other boxers. His last fight occurred on Tuesday, May 6, 1975. Jimmy was 74 years old. His final record stands at 40-12-1 with 24 knockouts. Jimmy Ellis later worked for Louisville Parks Development from 1984-2003.

Complications from dementia claimed Jimmy's life on May 6, 2014. He died in the Baptist Hospital in Louisville Kentucky. Jimmy had been diagnosed over a decade ago, and he advanced to the point where he knew no one. Until the end, he insisted his wife Mary, who had died 12 years earlier in 2006, was still alive. Although he personally disliked the "sparring partner" tag, he and Ali remained true friends all of his life. Jimmy believed he had proved himself a worthy opponent. He left behind six kids and a brother who had also boxed for the U.S. in the 1964 Olympics.

Albert Einstein once said, "There are only two ways to live your life. One is as though nothing is a miracle. The other is as though everything is a miracle. All Jimmy Ellis ever wanted to be was a good fighter and a good man. I'd say he was both, a miracle indeed.

NOT BAD FOR A .235 HITTER

Sometimes we walk under the sun and stars so much we forget that they are there. That's how I felt about this guy. He was always there, somewhere, and played everywhere, kind of like a travel agent with a baseball bat. He was so old he may have been an original member of the Knothole Gang. To him, baseball was slipping a fresh piece of gum through the fence to your brother during the game. He owned a circus wink, could drown you with his laughter and, with a huge chaw in his left cheek, he told stories in bunches. Were all the stories true? Who knows; he outlived most everyone who would know the truth. At 5' 9" tall and weighing 170 pounds, you would think the pitcher could knock the bat out of his hands, but not so.

This guy was a strong little dude. He received the nickname "Popeye" because of his huge forearms. All that was missing were the anchor tattoos. They invented the words "grizzled veteran" for guys like this. He met "Babe" Ruth when he played in American Legion ball. He played "with" Jackie Robinson and "for" Casey Stengel. He threw "out" Yogi Berra at first base during the 1955 World Series and, in 1957; he campaigned with "Pee Wee" Reece to keep the Dodgers in Brooklyn. In 1978, you could find him in the Red Sox dugout taking pointers from Ted Williams. You just naturally gravitate toward guys like this. Anyone who ever saw him will never forget that face. That was baseball that face. Someone once said his voice could be used as the sound track of baseball history. He was referred to as passionate, a throwback, and a national treasure. He wanted to win so badly, at times you could see the veins popping out of his skin. He would do anything to help his team win. If they had a bus, he would gladly drive it. He loved being at the park. He just never seemed quite comfortable anywhere else, except for at home or at the race track. Yet, he believed that none of us were bigger than the game. Not bad for a .235 hitter.

As a player, he was a fine utility infielder who even caught 33 games at the end of his career. "Zim" debuted for the Brooklyn Dodgers on July 2, 1954. My pal and Zimmer's Dodger teammate, Bart Shirley, told me that Zimmer would challenge anyone to a fight. "No one could believe he had come back from being hit in the head," said Shirley. It has been said, "Zim played baseball like someone charging a machine gun nest." He was a two-time All-Star in games played in 1961. Zimmer played for five different Major League clubs (Brooklyn-Los Angeles Dodgers, Chicago Cubs, New York Mets, Cincinnati Reds and Washington Senators), not counting the Toei Flyers of Japan and several teams in Mexico, Puerto Rico and Cuba. Don played for twelve seasons in 1,095 games. He compiled 773 hits, 91 home runs, 352 RBI's, 45 stolen bases and a .235 batting average. His last at-bat occurred on October 2, 1965, with the Washington Senators. As a player, Zimmer was a part of two World Series teams (1955 and 1959), both with the Dodgers. On September, 24, 1957, it was fitting that it was Don Zimmer who scooped up a ground ball and threw over to first baseman Gil Hodges for the final out of the last Dodgers home game at Ebbets Field. They outscored the Pittsburgh Pirates that day, 2-0. They would play in Los Angeles the following year.

As a coach, Zimmer was a part of eight different clubs over 43 years. Those clubs are as follows: Montreal Expos, San Diego Padres, Boston Red Sox (twice), New York Yankees (three times), Chicago Cubs, San Francisco Giants,

Colorado Rockies and the Tampa Bay Rays. As a bench coach, he may have led the league in information. He was like a bloodhound and nothing got by him. He always got to the park hours in advance and would cry at the drop of a hat when done a kindness. "His stories and experiences were amazing," said Derek Jeter. "And he was good to me and my family." Jeter would always take Zimmer's hat off and rub his head for good luck, before going up to the plate. Don was a coach under some of the best managers like Billy Martin, Gene Mauch and Joe Torre. He coached on the staff of 12 playoff teams and seven pennant winners. Zimmer was also a part of four World Series teams (1996, 1998-2000) all with the New York Yankees.

As a manager, he plodded to the mound as if he hated it. "I didn't manage by the book, because I never read the book," said Zimmer. That may have been his biggest regret. He loved being aggressive, hit and run, squeeze and steal. He was good at reading players and he understood that to win a war you have to sometimes start a war. "If they hit one of us, they hit all of us," he would say. Zimmer managed thirteen years with four different clubs: San Diego Padres, Boston Red Sox, Texas Rangers and Chicago Cubs. Zimmer was named the 1989 National League Manager of the Year, while managing the Chicago Cubs. He won 906 games and recorded a winning percentage of .508 as a manager. Don managed four 90-plus win seasons, but never managed a pennant winner. Don Zimmer was living proof that for every bad guy there were several good guys. "Nobody loved being in the game more than Don Zimmer," said Tim Kurkjian. Being connected with Zim, made others feel safe. He was old school, a baseball lifer. Did anyone love baseball more than Don Zimmer? I doubt it.

Donald William Zimmer was born January 17, 1931, in his beloved hometown of Cincinnati, Ohio. As the quarterback for the football team, a guard on the basketball team and the shortstop for the Ohio State Champion baseball team, Don became famous at Western Hills High School. In 1947, the American Legion team Don played on won the World Championship in California. The coach took the boys on a Hollywood tour where they met and took pictures with Lana Turner and Clark Gable. In 1949, he signed at the age of 18, as an amateur free-agent shortstop with the Brooklyn Dodgers. He began his career with the Dodgers' team in the Class-D Eastern Shore League. He was earning $150 a month and his dad was sending him an extra $50 more for food. By 1950, he was tearing up the PONY League, while leading the entire league in home runs (23), runs scored (146), as well as in put-outs and assists. On August 16, 1951, he married his lovely wife, "Soot," at Dunn Field, located in Elmira, New York, during a doubleheader between games, at home plate, baseball style. Her real name was Carol Jean and her nickname Soot was loosely translated in German meaning "Sweetie Pie." They had met when she asked him to join her on a hayride when they were juniors in high school. From that day until now, Soot has kept a scrapbook filled with Zimmer's sporting exploits. There are clippings from more than 10,500 games played in hundreds of ballparks across the land. On the first scrapbook cover it says 1945-1949. Each trip to the World Series has its own album. There are now a total of 70 scrapbooks and photo albums. Don played for the Single-A Elmira Pioneers in 1951, and the Double-A Mobile Bears in 1952.

Don Zimmer spent 66 years in the game, longer than anyone else. He once said, "Every paycheck I have ever gotten came from baseball." That's quite a statement considering he was told at the age of 22 that his career was over. On July 7, 1953, while Zimmer was playing for the Triple-A American Association St. Paul Saints, he was hit in the head with a pitch thrown by Jim Kirk. Zim was unconscious for 13 days. In one scrapbook there are pictures of Zimmer lying in a hospital bed recovering. Finally, after spending a total of 31 days in the hospital and after losing 42 pounds, he left the hospital holding his wife's hand while he walked. He whispered, "On a good day, I could make it 50 yards." Initially, his vision had been blurred and he had trouble speaking. They had to drill four holes in his skull to relieve the pressure and surgically inserted four tantalum metal corkscrew-shaped buttons. It has been widely reported that Zimmer had a steel plate in his head. This rumor was false. When asked about it, Zimmer said, "When people brought up the steel plate, I just said 'yeah, sure!'" After sitting out the rest of that year he came back and played the following season for the 1954 Brooklyn Dodgers. "Pitchers still threw at me when I came back," he said. "They wanted to see if I still had courage."

At 83 years old, Don Zimmer was a baseball man. It's a little boy's game that is all about the team and protecting their teammates. In this game, retaliation is required. No one messes with the game; if so, it requires revenge. One way to retaliate is to throw at someone. It has been called the "bean ball" or the "brush back" pitch. Negro League pitcher, Satchel Paige, referred to this pitch as the "bowtie pitch," as he placed his hand underneath his chin. Pitchers who wield these rockets are referred to as "headhunters." Texas legends Nolan Ryan and Roger Clemens were known as headhunters. These altercations more than likely lead to charging the mound, fist fights, and bench-clearing brawls.

Most of you baseball fans should remember the "dust up" when Nolan Ryan hit Chicago White Sox third baseman, Robin Ventura, with a pitch on August 4, 1993. Ventura made the fatal mistake of charging the mound and attacking Nolan. Ryan countered by placing Ventura in a good-old-country-boy Texas headlock and started to batter away on Robin's noggin. There is no telling how many of those photos Ryan has signed since then for his fans. Then there was "The Katy Rocket," Roger Clemens, who made all the headlines in the sports pages when he hit New York Mets catcher Mike Piazza in the head, during the 2000 season.

Piazza later wrote in his autobiography, <u>The Longshot</u>, "Clemens scared me so bad; I started taking karate lessons in case we had another confrontation."

In some sports, you get fined for leaving the bench during a fight. In baseball, you lose your status among your teammates for not joining in the ruckus. Several players' careers have been cut short by being hit while batting. Hall-of-Famers Mickey Cochrane, Lou Boudreau, and Kirby Puckett all had to leave the game they loved, shortly after being hit. Other fine players like Pete Reiser, Tony Conigliaro, and Dickie Thon all left the game far too early, after being hit in the head or face.

Only one player has died after being hit in the head by a pitched ball. His name was Ray Chapman, a shortstop for the Cleveland Indians. Chapman was hit by submarine pitcher and a known headhunter, named Carl Mays, of the New York Yankees. The game was being played at the Pologrounds, home of the New York Giants, as Yankee Stadium was not yet finished being built. August 16, 1920, was a fog-infested day, with drizzle. Eye witnesses said Chapman never saw the ball or attempted to move out of the way. It has been estimated that a pitch thrown at 90 mph gives the batter four-tenths of a second to determine the speed and location of a pitched ball. The sound of the ball hitting Chapman in the temple provided a loud crack, and the ball rolled back to Mays on the mound. Mays picked up the ball and threw it to Wally Pipp at first base, thinking the ball may have hit Chapman's bat. Ray took two steps toward first and then fell, blood gushing from his left ear. The umpire yelled for a doctor and they finally got Chapman to his feet, but he fell again before he could leave the field. At this point, he required a stretcher. Ray Chapman died 12 hours later, which was early the next day. It took 36 years before players were required to wear hard batting helmets. Baseballs are now routinely thrown out of the game with the slightest smudge of dirt or nicks. The idea is to keep them as white as possible to help players to see the ball in flight.

Don Zimmer was one of the lucky ones. In fact, he was "beaned" again in 1956, when a fastball broke his cheekbone in Cincinnati. This second beaning led the Major Leagues to adopt batting helmets for safety when players were at-bat. Phil Rizzuto of the New York Yankees was the first to use this helmet.

In 1955, the Brooklyn Dodgers won their only World Series Championship over their arch nemesis, the New York Yankees. Zimmer was ecstatic. Don was fifth on the team after hitting 15 home runs that year in just 88 games. There is a photo in Soot's scrapbooks of Don, wearing his baggy wool uniform, with teammates Jackie Robinson, Roy Campanella and Pee Wee Reese, celebrating their victory. Her favorite headline stated: "Players to receive $9,684 each." They used that money as a down payment for the house they built on Treasure Island, Florida, where they lived together for 50 years. Don started three games in that 1955 World series. He had two hits in nine at-bats. He moved with the club to Los Angeles at the end of the 1957 season, but was traded to the Chicago Cubs in 1960, for three players and $25,000 in cash. After the 1961 season, Zimmer was picked up by the New York Mets in baseball's expansion draft. On April 11, 1962, Zimmer was the starting third baseman for the Mets. Don got to model the first-ever Mets uniform. The 1962 New York Mets lost a record 120 games that first season, under Casey Stengel. This reminded me of one of my favorite quotations by Casey, who once said, "The only thing worse than a Mets game that year was a double-header." In May of 1962, after starting the season 4-for-52, they traded Zimmer to the Cincinnati Reds for two players. He returned briefly to the Los Angeles Dodgers in 1963 before being purchased by the Washington Senators in June of that year. Don was released after the 1965 season and headed to Japan to play for the 1966 Toei Flyers of the

Nippon Professional Baseball League.

Don Zimmer never mastered the art of managing a pitching staff. Even though his Red Sox team won 90 or more games three years in a row, he is remembered more for the 1978 collapse of Boston. The Red Sox led the American League by as many as 14 games in August only to see their lead reduced to four games by September. The New York Yankees forced a one-game playoff on October 2, 1978. A Bucky Dent home run over the Green Monster sealed the deal for the Yanks' pennant and Zimmer's career as the Red Sox manager. It would become known as "The Boston Massacre." In all fairness, The Red Sox pitching staff was a little different. With guys like Ferguson Jenkins, Bill "Spaceman" Lee and Bernie Carbo, the Red Sox formed a group called "The Loyal Order of the Buffalo Heads" whose sole purpose was to second-guess Don Zimmer. They even nicknamed Zimmer "The designated Gerbil." Zim hated it and his dislike for Lee grew to the point where the team thought Zimmer pitched rookie Bobby Sprowl instead of Lee, in the decisive last game. Sprowl never made it out of the first inning. It was reported that Carl Yastrzemski begged Zimmer to start Bill Lee instead, as Lee had beaten the Yankees in 12 of his last 17 starts against them.

There are many wonderful stories about Zimmer. Here are a few of my favorites. I met Zim and Joe Torre briefly before a game in Tampa, at Dunedin Park, the Minor League Park for the Toronto Blue Jays. They were walking by the fence and I said "hello." They stopped and shook my hand. They were close and had been referred to as "Fire and Ice."

In 1959, Zimmer bet Duke Snider he couldn't throw a ball out of the L.A. Coliseum from home plate. Duke ended up hurting his arm and Manager Walter Alston was none too happy. In fact, Zimmer got fined by General Manager, "Buzzie" Bavasi. The funny part came when Alston went looking for Don. "Zimmer hid in a locker inside the dressing room so Alston couldn't find him," laughed Snider.

"He cried in the locker room after we lost to San Francisco Giants," said Chicago Cubs pitcher, Rick Sutcliffe. "You guys have no idea what you have done for me and my family," said Zimmer. "The folks in Boston thought I was the dumbest manager that ever lived. My family couldn't even go to the games."

Zimmer had the ability to laugh at himself. One year while Zimmer was managing the Chicago Cubs he wondered into the exercise room and leaned against a piece of equipment. The equipment gave way and down went Zimmer, out cold. When he comes too the trainer is there and he holds up two fingers and asked Don, "How many fingers do I have?" Zim says, "Two." The trainer then asked, "What are your kid's names?" "Tom and Donna," answered Zimmer. The trainer then asked, "What is the name of our President?" "Ah that's a trick question," said Zimmer. "I didn't know that before I fell."

In 1996, Zimmer joined the Yankees as Joe Torre's bench coach. Zimmer was hit by a foul ball off the bat of Yankees' second baseman Chuck Knoblauch, when he was the bench coach for Joe Torre and the New York Yankees. The next game, Zimmer showed up wearing a WWII Army helmet with the letters "NY" painted on the front and the name "ZIM" stenciled on the side. In 1999, Zim filled in for Joe while Torre recuperated from prostate cancer, and guided the club to a 21-15 win-loss record. Zimmer increased his uniform number each year he remained in the game. Don was to wear #66 this year with the Tampa Bay Rays. When Don joined the Rays, Soot went out and bought scrapbook number seventy. It would be the last. With Don in the hospital at the beginning of the season, Ray's third base coach, Tim Foley, wore the #66 as a tribute to Zim. Joe Torre and Don Zimmer had a very special relationship. They won four world championships in eight years together on the Yankee bench. Torre never made a decision without asking Zim's advice. Torre tells a story about writing down some team rules before their first season together. "I handed them to Zim for a first look," said Joe. "When he got to the part about team travel, he hesitated. 'Ties?' he asked. I decided to relax and only require that everyone wear sport coats. I later found out that Zim didn't know how to tie a tie. Soot, his wife of 63 years, would do it for him before he left home, but the return trips would have been an issue," said Torre.

There is a wonderful story told about Zimmer when he was with the New York Yankees. Owner George Steinbrenner called a meeting after a tough loss at home. After everyone gets in the room, George says, "If there is anyone in this room that believes he's doing all he can to help us win a ballgame, he can leave right now." Don Zimmer got up and left. Don's wife, Soot, was used to waiting quite awhile during meetings like this. She thought Don had been fired.

"He was as sensitive as he was a competitor," said Joe Torre. "Just ask Pedro Martinez." During the 2003 playoffs, Don Zimmer had charged Pedro in a heated game between the Red Sox and Yankees. As he approached Pedro Martinez, Pedro side-stepped Zimmer, grabbed him by the shoulders, and spun him to the ground. Zim was helped up and left the park in an ambulance only to return the following day, unhurt and with an apology. Zimmer was fined $5,000 by Major League Baseball.

Current Manager Joe Girardi said, "Zim liked to have fun. I saw Zim dance on a table after we came from behind and won a game. The table broke and snapped and down came Zim."

Zimmer loved the horse and dog tracks almost as much as baseball. You could find him, Duke Snider and Johnny Podres at either Suffolk or Wonderland Park during Spring Training. One of his best friends was Jim Leland. They talked on the phone at least once every day and loved going to Tampa Bay Downs to bet the horses. He also bet on college football.

Don started kidney dialysis in May of 2008 and then, in December, he suffered a stroke which affected his speech for a week or so. He underwent open heart surgery on April 16, 2014. The baseball gods slipped a called third strike by Don Zimmer on Wednesday, June 4, 2014. Don died from kidney and heart problems. He lived with his wife, Soot, in Seminole, Florida, and is survived by his son, Thomas, and a daughter, Donna, along with four grandchildren.

Don Zimmer wrote two books, <u>Zim: A Baseball Life</u> and <u>The Zen of Zim</u>. He was the last former Brooklyn Dodger to still be serving on the field in some capacity. He may have been born in a dugout. In his book <u>The Zen of Zim,</u> written with the help of Bill Madden, Zimmer said, "All I've ever been is a simple baseball man, but it's never ceased to amaze me how so many, far more accomplished people I've met in this life, wanted to be one, too."

Before Thursday night's Rays' home game against the Marlins, the team held a moment of silence for Zimmer who had passed away the day before. Don's son, Tom Zimmer, thanked everyone for their prayers. Tom, a San Francisco Giants' scout, noted how lucky his dad felt being a part of the great game of baseball for 66 years. There is also a local connection with Tom Zimmer who managed the Victoria Rosebuds in 1977. The Rosebuds were in the same Lone Star League with the Corpus Christi Barracudas. In 1971, Tom had been drafted by the St. Louis Cardinals organization. Tom played catcher and second base in the Gulf Coast League.

Vince Scully is the last chapter of the old Brooklyn Dodgers. This one man parade, with a snazzy coat and tie, works alone while reminding us of Jackie, "Pee Wee," Zimmer and "The Duke" as we watch Kershaw, Kemp and Puig. When Scully heard about Don's passing he said, "All I can tell you—when you say Don Zimmer, anybody who knew him will smile. He was the most beloved Dodger amongst his teammates."

Monday April 6, 2015, was Opening Day for the Tampa Bay Rays at Tropicana Field. Buck Showalter and the Orioles were in town. The Rays retired Don Zimmer's jersey. His #66 now hangs at the top of Tropicana Field for all time. His wife Soot and their kids were all present. She will have a few new items to place in her seventh and final scrap book for Zim.

The Heavens must have needed a bench coach; he was a delight.

CHEESE AT THE KNEES

This World Series at-bat lasted for over seven minutes and became one of baseball's most famous post-season contests. In from the bullpen trotted a 21-year-old rookie flame-thrower, who had already beaten tremendous odds in his personal life just to be wearing a Los Angeles Dodgers uniform. This reliever's job was to protect a one-run lead, with two men on base, and one out in the ninth inning of Game Two, of the 1978 World Series. Waiting at home plate was the captain and catcher of the New York Yankees, Thurman Munson. Munson hit a floater to right field which was caught for out number two. Up next, waiting with confidence, was Reggie Jackson, a ten-year veteran fastball hitter, who could time a jet airplane. "I didn't come to New York to be a star, I brought my star with me," said Reggie. Jackson, the future Hall-of-Fame slugger, stepped into the batter's box. He had the previous year before hit three consecutive home runs off three different pitchers in Game Six against these same Dodgers, to clinch the 1977 World Series title. The kid on the mound did what he does best; he proceeded to fill up the strike zone with nine consecutive 95-plus mph fastballs. Giving this guy a baseball and glove was like handing Billy the Kid a handgun and bullets, something amazing was about to happen. This guy threw so hard he made the ball feel hot. Some suggested his fastball may have been allergic to wooden bats and fast enough to become invisible. Reggie knew what was coming and still he couldn't put the ball in play. The count got to 3-2 on Jackson, before he swung violently and missed, ending the game. The Dodgers won Game Two, 4-3.

Reggie Jackson shouted obscenities towards the Dodgers' bench as he walked back to the Yanks' dugout. Reggie swore the kid's two-seam fastball changed lanes. "Against this guy, you just pick a zone and hope for the best," said Jackson afterwards. Bob Welch, the kid, said after the game, "I just threw him some cheese at the knees." To be fair to Jackson and New York, the Yankees won the next four games and the 1978 World Series title. Reggie Jackson recorded a hit off Welch in Game Four, and also hit a home run off the kid in Game Six.

The old saying goes something like this, "Opportunity knocks only once but temptation leans on the doorbell." In Bob's case the opportunity was baseball, and alcohol was his temptation. For most adult fans, beer is as much a part of baseball as "Cracker Jacks" and hotdogs. At 6' 3" tall and weighing 190 pounds, he was a fine-looking kid. The joke was, he had the looks of Dean Martin and smelled like Foster Brooks. Bob Welch had a wild side and loved to party. "The fact is, I'm crazy when I'm drunk," said Welch. "There's every chance I would have been dead by now if I was still drinking." The game of baseball had been his only real friend. Baseball is a teacher; it reveals your heart and soul, and the game tries to reveal it to you. We can use the game to help people discover themselves. They can use those discoveries to confront anything in their life, including alcoholism. What Welch failed to realize at a young age is that if you try to chase two rabbits you end up losing them both. The Los Angeles Dodgers intervened and helped Bob Welch with his fight against alcohol. The Dodgers required him to attend the 12-step program for alcoholism. In January of 1980, Bob attended rehab in Arizona for 36 days. "I had been drinking since I was 16," said Welch. Bob was the kind of guy who stayed out all night and would show up at the ballpark the next day wearing the same thing he left in yesterday. Yes, he drank; this guy had been on more floors than Johnson Wax. General George Patton once said, "Success is how high you bounce when you hit bottom." Welch hit bottom, recovered and became a successful pitcher in the Major Leagues. Life is like riding a bicycle. To keep your balance you must keep moving forward. This is a story of success and redemption worth knowing.

Robert Lynn "Bob" Welch was born on November 3, 1956, in Detroit, Michigan. He played baseball at Hazel Park High School. In 1973, Bob was drafted right out of high school by the Chicago Cubs, but his parents talked him into going to college first. He attended Eastern Michigan University located in Ypsilanti, Michigan. Welch would help lead the Eastern Michigan Hurons to a 43-14 win-loss record and the 1976 College World Series. The Hurons beat Maine, Clemson, and Arizona State in that order, to get to the finals. There, they would end up losing to the University of Arizona twice in the championship round. Bob Welch was the 20th pick in the first round of the 1977 amateur draft, by the Los Angeles Dodgers. He was handed #35. Welch, after spending a little more than a year in the Minors, entered his first Major League game on June 20, 1978.

By 1980, Welsh had cracked the starting rotation for the Dodgers. Bob went 14-9 that season and pitched three innings in his first All-Star Game. On May 29, 1980, Bob Welch pitched a one-hitter against the Atlanta Braves. The Dodgers won 3-0 and Welch faced the minimum 27 batters. Only Larvell Blanks reached base on a single, but was later retired on a double play. Welch was not afraid to live in the strike zone. This guy's pitches were sharper than a video game. Welch always had front-line "stuff." Hitters swore they could see a vapor trail behind his fastball. Heck, even his change-up measured 88 mph. He understood that most home runs were thrown, not hit. This was also the year that

Bob Welch revealed his troubles with alcohol addiction to the public. As a young man, Welch believed you would never have a hangover if you stay loaded. The Dodgers' intervention more than likely saved his career or, better still, his life. In 1981, Welch would collaborate with writer George Vessey of the *New York Times* and reveal his troubles in a book entitled <u>Five O'clock Comes Early: A Young Man's Battle with Alcoholism</u>.

Welch would continue to pitch well, winning at least 13 games a season, six times with the Dodgers, yet he was eventually traded in 1987, to the Oakland A's of the American League. Welch continued to shine and had his finest years with the A's, going 17-9 and 17-8 in his first two seasons. The 1989 World Series would come down to the battle of the two Bay Area teams, the San Francisco Giants of the National League and the Oakland Athletics of the American League. A's skipper Tony LaRussa, would trot out to the pitching mound, Dave Stewart, Mike Moore, Bob Welch and Storm Davis, in that order. Both Stewart and Moore held serve and won their two games, placing the A's up two games to none, as Welch got ready to take his turn. Welch had just pitched and beaten the Toronto Blue Jays in the American League Championship Series.

On October 17, 1989, Game Three of the World Series would turn out to be more than anyone could have imagined. At 5:04 pm local time, just minutes before Welch was to take the mound at Candlestick Park in San Francisco, this entire area was struck by the Loma Prieta earthquake. The intensity of this quake measured 6.9 on the Richter scale; it caused extensive damage in the nearby region and forced the postponement of Game Three. Broadcasters Tim McCarver and Al Michaels of ABC Television were set to call the game, when the stadium began to move and the light poles in the outfield began to sway. Michaels said on air, "We're having an earthquake," as power was lost and the television feed was interrupted. Luckily, the stadium itself did not incur any damage, and everyone attending the game was safe and unharmed. This became the first major earthquake to be broadcast live on television. Interestingly, it turns out that loss of life and injuries were held at a minimum for two reasons. First, because of the game being played at that time, the freeways were relatively empty and most rush-hour traffic was light due to the 62,000 fans in attendance. Secondly, most of the fans had not yet reached their seats, which lowered the amount of weight being carried by the upper deck structures. Still, in other locations, 63 people were killed and 3,757 were injured, as several bridges and other transportation structures within the area collapsed. The game may have saved lives.

So, Game Three was postponed for 11 days. This additional time gave Athletics Manager, Tony LaRussa, time to rethink his pitching rotation. LaRussa decided to use his Game One starter, Dave Stewart, in place of Game Three starter, Bob Welch, and use his Game Two starter, Mike Moore, in Game Four instead of Storm Davis. As a result, neither Welch nor Davis would throw a single pitch in the 1989 World Series, while both Stewart and Moore would win two games each, to sweep the San Francisco Giants, four games to none. Today this World Series is referred to as the "Earthquake Series."

The following season, Bob Welch would get his due against the Cincinnati Reds. He would be selected to start Game Two of the 1990 World Series for the Athletics. Another interesting note is that this game, played on October 17, 1990, fell exactly one year after what would have been his first World Series start, had it not been for the 1989 earthquake. Welsh would pitch 7.1 innings at Riverfront Stadium and be lifted for reliever, Rick Honeycutt, with a 4-3 lead. Jose Canseco had given Welch the lead with a monster home run. Welch gave up a total of four runs on nine hits, and recorded two walks and two strikeouts. A's closer Dennis Eckersley would end up the loser, as the Reds scored late, to win 5-4.

Bob Welch was selected to the 1990 All-Star team. He finished with a career-high 27 wins with only 6 losses, for a .818 winning percentage. No one since Welsh has won as many games in a season. Bob Welch beat out Roger Clemens and Dave Stewart and won the 1990 Cy Young Award, on an A's team that won 103 games. Bob Welch's teammate, pitcher Dave Stewart, also won 22 games in 1990 making these two the last pitchers on the same team with the most wins in their league. Welch, a power pitcher extraordinaire, finished with a .295 ERA. This strong-armed right-hander pitched his last game on September 11, 1994.

Bob continued to stay close to the game. He coached at Arizona State University and then joined the Arizona Diamondbacks as their pitching coach. It was there that he won his third World Series ring, as the Diamondbacks defeated the New York Yankees in the 2001 World Series. During the 2006 World Baseball Classic, Welch served as the pitching coach for The Netherlands baseball team. After leaving the Diamondbacks, Welch would join the Athletics as a special instructor during their Spring Training camp.

Bob Welch, a great competitor, beat the odds. He won 211 games while losing 146, in a 17-year career. He spent ten years with the Dodgers and seven years with the Athletics, winning at least 14 games in eight different seasons. Welch pitched in 3,092 innings, recorded 1,969 strikeouts, and compiled a 3.47 ERA. Bob threw 61 complete games and recorded 28 shutouts. Bob played on five World Series teams 1978, 1981, 1988, 1989, and 1990. He won two World Series rings as a player (1981-L.A. and 1989-A's) and a third ring as a coach (2001-Arizona). I never got a chance to meet Bob Welch in person, but I did get to see him pitch against the Houston Astros. I loved the pop of the catcher's mitt when Welch let one go. Welch would be listed third among all pitchers in the 1980's, with 137 wins. Only Jack Morris and Dave Stieb finished with more victories during that decade.

Oscar Wilde once said, "I can resist anything but temptation." Bob Welch tried his best to strike out death, and it seemed his "stuff" was good enough to win. So, there he stood on top of the mound, as death dug in at the plate. It was not to be. On June 9, 2014, local police responded to a medical help (911) call and found Bob Welch, age 57, dead in his bathroom. It is believed that Welch died of a heart attack. Welch is survived by his ex-wife, Mary Ellen, a daughter, Kelly, who was 18, two sons, Riley age 23, who was drafted by the Oakland Athletics' in the 10th round in 2008, and Dylan who is 25 years old.

"This is a sad day for the A's organization," said general manager, Billy Bean. "He was one of the greatest competitors to wear the Dodger uniform," said Dodger President and CEO, Stan Kasten.

THE LOOK OF A WINNER

I've always heard that every ending is also a new beginning; we just don't know it at the time. I would like to think that it's true. He didn't look like a football player. This fellow knew that the brutality of this game would turn your knees into egg salad. He was a strong man; some said he ate barbells for breakfast. He wasn't a guy you looked at and thought, we will play him at this position. Nevertheless, he became a linebacker and offensive lineman for the Cleveland Browns; his job was to take in plays from the sidelines as a messenger and keep his quarterback clean. He didn't look for attention, he was an NFL lineman. Zone blocking, reach blocking, engage and sustain, and stretch plays, dominated his vocabulary.

The one thing we can never do is get inside a person's head completely. No one knows exactly what you're thinking. He understood that anything that hurts you can teach you; and if it keeps hurting, it's because you haven't yet learned the lesson. Nobody cares about your team injuries; did you win? His motto was play as hard as you can and respect your opponent. He was a bright man, a teacher, a father figure for some and, later on, an extremely successful coach. He left nothing to chance and would spend an hour teaching a newly-drafted college All-American lineman how to get down correctly in a three-point stance. For years, the Pittsburgh Steelers were like a bad musical that closes before the curtain goes all the way up. Someone once asked, "How do you eat an elephant?"

"One bite at a time," was his answer. He understood that concept; he may have been born with a whistle around his neck. No matter how big the problem, he had a plan and believed the most important thing coaches can teach their players is how to get along without them. Leadership is the ability to get men to do what they don't want to do and like it. Chuck Noll used the game and "tough love" to teach his players something about life. He didn't beat you with the screen pass; he beat you with perfection.

Noll's Steelers wanted you to be afraid; they wanted your city to shake with fear when they landed at the airport. It was always going to be a double chin strap game with Pittsburgh. Blocking and tackling were his weapons of choice. You knew you were going to spend some time in the training room after this game. Noll would bring his take-your-head-off defense, along with a formidable offense, and dominate your hometown team. Hiring Chuck Noll as your head coach was like giving U.S. Grant a division of his own. Victory was right around the corner. Noll was once asked by a reporter about a Steelers' dynasty. Noll said, "Dynasty! Is that a place to eat?"

General George Patten once said, "Success is how high you bounce when you hit bottom." Chuck Noll was like a magician saying "Abracadabra." The turn-around by the Pittsburgh Steelers was astounding. Although Noll never took the field for the Steelers, he was the "steel" in the steel curtain defense. Only the truly special teams get their own nickname, "Steel Curtain." You have to respect excellence. When you think of Chuck Noll, you think of the Steelers. Chuck knew that the more you win, the harder it would be to lose. He always had the look of a winner.

January in Cleveland is typically cold and grey. Charles Henry "Chuck" Noll was born the son of a butcher in Cleveland, Ohio, on January 5, 1932. Chuck's father, who only had an eighth-grade education, later developed Parkinson's disease. His mom attended grade school for just five years before dropping out. Chuck grew up on 7215 Montgomery Avenue in Cleveland, not far from a Catholic high school known as Benedictine. Chuck started working during his seventh-grade year at Fisher Brothers Meat Market for .55 cents an hour, in an effort to save enough money to attend Benedictine. Noll played fullback at first, but was later switched to nose tackle on defense and right guard on offense, as he grew bigger and stronger. Noll was selected All-State at both positions. He was also smart and applied himself, never complaining about having to work to pay for his education. He graduated from Benedictine High School in 1949, and won a scholarship to play football at the University of Dayton, as a lineman. Noll finished high school ranked number 28 out of 252 students in grade average.

In 1949, Chuck Noll was recruited by head coach Joe Gavin to play football for the University of Dayton Flyers. Noll was 17 years old. Noll was called "The Pope" by his teammates, because of his endless knowledge of the game. Noll was the co-caption of the only Flyers team to play in the post season. In 1952, the Flyers went 7-3 and played in the Salad Bowl, located in Phoenix, Arizona. The Salad bowl was the forerunner of the Fiesta Bowl. In 1962, Noll was inducted into the Dayton Flyers Sports Hall of Fame.

In 1953, Chuck was drafted in the 20th round by Head Coach Paul Brown and his hometown Cleveland Browns. He was given #65 to wear. Noll would get to play in four NFL title games and with some of the greatest teams in Cleveland Browns' history. The Detroit Lions beat Cleveland 17-16 in 1953, for the title. The Browns returned the favor and beat the Detroit Lions 56-10 for the 1954 NFL Championship, at Cleveland's Municipal Stadium. There is a great picture from this game with Noll on the sideline, kneeling between quarterback #14 Otto Graham, defensive end #83 Doug Adkins, and end #86 Dante "Gluefingers" Lavelli, all future Hall-of-Fame players. The Browns also had future Hall-of-

Famers, Lou "The Toe" Groza and fullback Marion Motley. In 1955, the Browns beat the Los Angeles Rams 38-14, for the title. One of Noll's best seasons occurred in 1955, when he intercepted five passes during the season. Jim Brown was the Browns' first pick of the 1956 NFL draft. Jim could tell right away how smart Chuck was. "Noll was the only Cleveland Brown who could score a 100% on Paul Brown's playbook exam," said Jim. In 1957, the Lions ran up the score on the Browns 59-14, for the NFL title. In 1959 at the age of 27, Chuck retired a two-time NFL champion.

Chuck Noll proceeded to become an assistant coach for the next nine seasons, and he learned from Sid Gillman with the Chargers and Don Shula of the Colts. Noll joined the L.A. Chargers, soon to become the San Diego Chargers, in 1960. From 1966 to 1968, Noll coached the defensive unit for Shula's Baltimore Colts. Under Noll's guidance, the 1963 AFL Champion San Diego Chargers allowed the fewest points in the league. Noll's 1968 Colts defensive unit gave up only 144 points in a 14-game season and tied the NFL record for fewest points allowed in a single season. These results warranted a promotion.

In 1969, the Steelers fired Bill Austin and offered Penn State Head Coach Joe Paterno a five-year $350,000 salary and the head coach's job. Paterno turned it down. At that point, Colts' Don Shula intervened on Noll's behalf and vouched for Noll's ability to coach the Steelers. The Pittsburgh Steelers made Chuck Noll their 14th head coach on January 27, 1969. At that time, Noll was the youngest NFL coach in the league. Pittsburgh had never won an NFL Championship Division Title or playoff game before he became head coach. When Noll took over, the Steelers were 105 games below .500. The first thing Noll did was take all the numbers off the practice jerseys. It made no difference what was their name or number; no one was safe and they would have to earn the right to play. Noll introduced himself to the team in July of 1969 with this statement: "I've been your head coach for the past five months, and I've watched every film of every practice of every game that you've played in over the past three years, and I can tell you why you've been losing. You're just not any good. You have no talent, you have no authority, you can't cover, and you have no discipline. By the time this training camp is over, most of you will not be here." "Chuck loved teaching moments," said Steelers' running back, Rocky Bleier. He also wrote on the bulletin board in the Steelers' locker room, "When geese fly in formation, they travel 70% faster than when they fly alone." It would be a sign of things to come. Six years after Noll took over; the Steelers would win their first Super Bowl.

The dreaded Steelers had accomplished only seven winning seasons during their 37 year history. In fact, they had once cut a young quarterback named Johnny Unitas, in 1955. Joe Gordon, the Steelers' public-relations director, once said, "Every Monday, team founder Art Rooney would take the back streets to work so he didn't run into any fans." Pittsburgh had been labeled by local reporters as "The City of Losers." "We'll change history," said Noll. "Losing has nothing to do with geography." Chuck Noll brought his reputation as a defensive coach to Pittsburgh and, in 1969; he drafted future Pro-Football Hall-of-Fame defensive lineman, "Mean Joe" Greene with the Steelers' first pick and then grabbed quarterback, Terry Hanratty, and little known defensive end, L.C. Greenwood. Greene, who stood 6' 4" tall and weighed 275 pounds was from Temple, Texas, and had wanted to play for the Dallas Cowboys. The following year, 1970, Noll drafted his quarterback of the future, Terry Bradshaw, along with defensive back Mel Blount; both would become Pro-Football Hall-of-Fame players. In 1971, Noll drafted linebacker, Jack Ham, along with defensive linemen, Dwight White and Ernie Holmes. Then Noll selected power running-back Franco Harris in the 1972 draft, also a future Hall-of-Fame selection. Noll then outdid himself. The success of the Steelers' 1974 draft may never be duplicated, as four of his picks would also become NFL Hall-of-Fame players. They are as follows: wide receivers Lynn Swann and John Stallworth, middle linebacker Jack Lambert, and center extraordinaire Mike Webster. If you're counting, that's nine Hall-of-Fame players drafted in five years.

"Friendship doesn't have a play clock," said Chuck. Noll got rid of the petty rules players hated. No more dress code and no strict curfew. His thought was simple: dress codes didn't improve performance. Noll was always calm and very fundamentally oriented, but when it came to the on-field conduct, he was a monster. They would run the same play until their tongues fell out, if not done with precision. He would spend twenty minutes explaining why the defensive back's right foot must be lined up two inches outside of the wide receiver. After 23 seasons, Noll retired after the 1991 season with a combined win-loss record of 209-156-1. In 1993, Chuck Noll was elected to the Pro-Football Hall of Fame just two years after he retired. That class also included Walter Payton, Larry Little, Bill Walsh and Dan Fouts.

Besides recording an 88-27-1 win-loss record and winning four Super Bowls (IX, X, XIII, XIV), the Steelers made the playoffs every year from 1972-1979. Pittsburgh also ran off 13 consecutive winning seasons and posted a 16-8 post season record. Noll was elected Coach of the Year in 1989. Chuck Noll was quoted, "The thrill isn't in the winning; it's in the doing." His legacy also includes his desire to put the best people in place to get the job done. This process of affirmative action on his part would place Joe Gilliam at the starting quarterback position, the first African-American to hold that position in the NFL. Franco Harris would become the first African-American to win the Super Bowl's Most Valuable Player Award and Tony Dungy would become the first African-American coordinator in the NFL.

I wanted to talk about two players who I believe embodied the spirit of a Chuck Noll team. "Mean Joe" Greene may have been the most important single draft pick in Pittsburgh's history. There was the time Mean Joe went after Dick Butkus of the Bears, after Butkus blindsided L.C. Greenwood, and the time Joe was taunted by Carl Eller and Alan Page of the Vikings. Greene didn't respond verbally, he just went to the sideline and got a pair of scissors and chased them down the field. In Philadelphia, Greene was so upset at the referees for not calling "holding," that he threw the ball into the stands. Noll never said a word.

John Harold "Jack" Lambert, better known as "Smilin' Jack" was really mean. I wanted to ask Lambert, "What he did with the fangs, was his coffin comfortable." Mean Joe Greene once said, "Lambert was so mean, he didn't even like himself." At the age of 24, this All-Pro middle linebacker had earned two Super Bowl rings in his first two seasons in the NFL.

Former NFL offensive lineman, Chuck Noll, was no slouch either. In 1960, Chuck once got into a scrap with Hall-of-Fame linebacker, Chuck Bednarik of the Philadelphia Eagles. Chuck Bednarik was known as one of the meanest players in all of football. His nickname was "Concrete Charlie." Noll smashed Bednarik in the mouth with his elbow during a fourth-down punt play in Philly; and Bednarik, spitting out some of his teeth, took his revenge on the next kickoff, by blindsiding Noll. Noll swore revenge after the game. Bednarik screamed, "I'll be right here waiting for you." Sure enough, at the end of the game both men squared off. Bednarik hit Noll so hard it knocked his helmet clean off. Bednarik then took Noll's helmet and started to hit him with it as some of the Browns rushed to Noll's defense. Bednarik pointed at them and said. "No one crosses that line," and they didn't.

Steelers' Hall of Fame wide receiver, John Stallworth, summed up Noll's impression on the team. "One of the lessons we learned from him was that you've never arrived. You never get to the point where you are the best that you can be, and you should admit you are always striving to be better and to get better in whatever it is, as a football player, as a father, as a business person, as someone who is active in the community."

On August 2, 2007, the Steelers' practice field located at St. Vincent College in Latrobe, Pennsylvania, was dedicated and renamed Chuck Noll Field. Noll was also honored on October 27, 2007 at Heinz Field during the pre-game ceremonies. On September 30, 2011, Noll had a street named after him. Chuck Noll Way runs along the North Shore of Pittsburgh.

Chuck and his wife Marianne maintained a residence in Pittsburgh, Pennsylvania and Florida. "When you marry a coach, you marry the game too," said Marianne. Their one son, Chris, teaches private school in Connecticut and has two children. Noll suffered from chronic back and heart problems and eventually Alzheimer's disease. Chuck died at home in his Pittsburgh condo on Friday, June 13, 2014, of natural causes. Chuck Noll was 82 years old.

Chuck Noll made everyone in the Steelers organization, all the way down to the ball boys, look like a winner. For his players, Chuck Noll will be remembered more as a teacher than their head coach.

GENIUS WITH THE BAT

The news hit me hard. Nothing makes you feel older than the death of a ballplayer you remember from your childhood. Yes, I had known he had cancer, but I didn't realize how far along it had traveled. He was very much a private person. He used phrases like "Oh man" and "Are you kidding me?" when he was happy, and he was happy most of the time. His voice sounded funny like a car radio when it is on scan. I'll miss that high-pitched country cackle. Baseball writer Tim Kurkjian said, "He loved to smile as much as he loved to hit." How true, and no one ever accused him of taking steroids. At 5' 11" and weighing 200 pounds, he looked like a baked potato. The standing joke was he had a "Body by Betty Crocker." His hands were tiny, his hips wide, and he couldn't touch his toes. Some said all he could do was hit, but then all Frank Sinatra could do was sing, Secretariat~run, and "Fats" Domino~play the piano. This guy put up Play Station kinds of numbers; he was a master at squaring up a baseball. Watching him play, you would swear he went 5 for 4 every night. He owned 20-10 vision and could hit a BB with a fly swatter. He was a surgeon, a doctor with a bat, and a genius in spikes. I was 80% sure he was not of this world. His favorite player growing up was Los Angeles Dodgers' outfielder, Willie Davis, but he admitted to following Rod Carew, Pete Rose and George Brett in the newspapers. "I would have paid good money to see Babe Ruth play," he once said. His favorite place to eat was Tony Roma's. He loved pork chops, ate pizza, drank root beer, and owned terrific hand-to-eye coordination. His closest friends called him "T." If you rated him from zero to ten as a hitter, he would be a twelve. He was such a good player that even the pigeons were afraid to sit on his statue out in left centerfield. Ralph Waldo Emerson once wrote, "An individual has a healthy personality to the exact degree to which they have the propensity to look for good in every situation." That was Tony Gwynn. As Casey Kasem would say, "The hits just keep on coming."

Meeting Tony Gwynn reminded me of a scene in the movie *The Natural* where the manager, Pop Fisher, played by Wilford Brimley, says to the star, Roy Hobbs, played by Robert Redford, "All I know is that you're the best damn hitter I ever saw." I was lucky enough or old enough if you will, to see Brett, Boggs, Carew and Rose, all great hitters, but Tony Gwynn hit like he owned a magic wand. There was no book on how to pitch to Tony Gwynn. He wasn't afraid of any pitcher and he couldn't spell lucky. I met Tony in Cooperstown, New York. He was there signing autographs at a little memorabilia shop on the main drag. I purchased his jersey and had him sign. He was kind and funny and having a ball. It was a great day.

Anthony Keith "Tony" Gwynn was born in Los Angeles, California, on May 9, 1960, to Charles and Vandella Gwynn. Tony grew up in Long Beach with an older (Charles) and younger brother (Chris). After work, their father coached Pop Warner Football and Little League Baseball. His mother once said, "We focused on making hoops and hits rather than making bail." Tony loved the game of basketball and attended Long Beach Polytechnic High School. Tony was highly recruited by the San Diego State University Aztecs (SDSU) and offered a basketball scholarship as a point guard. Gwynn became a college two-sport star, playing three years of baseball and four years of basketball. His mother encouraged him to play baseball. He was chosen a two-time All-American outfielder in baseball. His senior year, he batted .423 with six home runs and 29 RBI's. Tony also still holds the Aztecs' basketball records for assists in a game, season, and career. He was twice named to the Western Athletic Conference team. Interestingly, he could dunk a basketball but could not palm a basketball because of his tiny hands. Tony Gwynn was selected by the San Diego Padres in the third round of the 1981 draft. Tony was also drafted by the NBA San Diego Clippers that same year. Gwynn chose baseball and reported to the Padres Class-A team in Walla Walla, Washington. By 1982, you could find him with the Hawaii Islanders, the Triple-A team for the Padres.

His first Major League hit was a double, on the day he debuted in the Big Leagues. It came against the Philadelphia Phillies on July 19, 1982, during his fourth at-bat. The magic of baseball history would find Pete Rose playing first base that day. Pete said, "Congratulations. Don't catch me in one night." Pete Rose had no idea he was talking to a future first-ballot Hall-of-Fame hitter. Gwynn always said, "I learned the most from Pete Rose." Tony later discovered the magic of video and lugged his own video equipment from city to city. "It turned my career around,' said Tony.

Gwynn and his Padres played in two World Series, in 1984 against the Detroit Tigers and 1998 against the New York Yankees. Tony did not hit very well against the Tigers, but recorded 8 hits in 16 at-bats against the Yanks, and also hit a home run in Game One off pitcher, David Wells.

Tony Gwynn met Ted Williams for the first time at the 1992 All-Star game. They became instant friends. They constantly argued about power hitting versus singles. At the 1999 All-Star Game, Ted Williams was the star attraction. He was surrounded by all the All-Stars as he arrived on the field. Ted chose Tony to help throw out the first pitch. "That's my favorite moment in this game. It was unbelievable to be the last guy standing out there with Ted Williams as he threw out the first pitch. It was...

it was the best. It was the best. I hope twenty years from now someone will be talking about me in the same vein as I'm talking about Ted Williams," said Tony Gwynn. Ted Williams believed there were only two players who could ever hit .400, Tony Gwynn and Nomar Garciaparra.

"Tony was the greatest hitter I ever played against" said Steve Sax. "He was a class act and this is a huge loss for Major League Baseball and his family." "He taught me how to watch video tape," said John Kruk. Tony Gwynn was a left-handed right fielder. Try saying that five times in a row.

He called it the 5.5 hole, a sacred space between third base and shortstop, where Gwynn made his living. The system of scoring in a baseball game gives every player on the field a number. The third baseman was number 5 and the shortstop, number 6. Therefore, the space between these two players was labeled the 5.5 hole by Gwynn. Tony as a left-handed batter hit thousands of ground balls into and through the 5.5 hole for base hits. If you turned the flaps of his shoes over, on top of the laces you would find 5.5 written there.

Gwynn accomplished some incredible feats. Gwynn had an interesting way of mistreating a baseball and could get hotter than Georgia asphalt. He always hit the ball hard and could wait until the last split second to go to left field with ball. They say the most important pitch in baseball is strike one, which is true unless you're Tony Gwynn.

Okay, here we go and hang on. Yes, these numbers are correct. He played 20 seasons for the San Diego Padres and retired October 7, 2001. He won eight batting titles, seven Silver Slugger Awards and five Gold Gloves. He participated in fifteen All-Star Games and won the Branch Rickey Award in 1995, the Lou Gehrig award in 1998, and the Roberto Clemente Award in 1999. Gwynn still owns 17 Padres' team records and underwent 13 operations during his career, eight of those operations on his knees. Gwynn was inducted into the Baseball Hall of Fame in 2007, along with Cal Ripken, Jr. Tony received 97.6 % of the writers' votes. It was the first year of eligibility for both players. Only 46 players have been inducted who have played their entire career with one team. Over 75,000 fans turned out to see Cal Ripken, Jr., and "Mr. Padre," Tony Gwynn, receive their induction plaques. Gwynn's last line of his Hall-of-Fame speech went like this: "When you can laugh, laugh at yourself and others; it makes the game a whole lot easier to play."

Tony batted .338 for his career and never batted below .309 after his first season. He collected 3,141 hits, 135 home runs, 1,138 RBI's, and stole 319 bases. He struck out only 434 times, or once every 21 at-bats. Only once during his career did he strike out three times in a single game; and it has been reported that he could have gone 0-for-1,109 at-bats at the end of his career and would have still hit .300. He faced Hall-of-Fame pitcher, Greg Maddux, 107 times and never struck out. He recorded his 1,000th hit off of Texas legend, Nolan Ryan, and batted .444 during his career with the bases loaded. On Opening Day of the 1987 season, Marvell Wynne, Tony Gwynn, and John Kruk hit back-to-back-to-back home runs to start the game. It was the first time ever in Major League history. His best hitting month was in June of 1987, where he batted .473 in 93 at-bats. I also thought it was very cool that his 2,000[th] hit and his 3,000[th] hit were both accomplished on August 6th, his mother, Maria, birthday.

Although not thought of as "fleet of foot," Tony stole 56 bases in 1987 and 40 in 1989. His quick first step allowed him to be deceiving on the base paths. He could do anything with a bat. It was like the wood was an extension of his arms. A pure hitter, he was the reason you showed up at the ballpark. He signed his autograph so often for his fans that he once joked, "They're probably not worth a nickel." He was what you hoped he would be, genuine. The kids around Long Beach measured the size of their feet in the depression dug by Tony Gwynn's spikes. If you were a young player, who liked to hit, and you wanted to learn the ingredients of success from Tony Gwynn, just remember his favorite slogan was, "You need a lighter bat."

Tony Gwynn stayed in baseball by becoming the Head Coach of his SDSU (San Diego State University) Aztecs. He also worked for ESPN as a part-time analyst. In 2007, a 9½ -foot statue was unveiled inside the park just beyond Petco Park's outfield wall. It reads, "Tony Gwynn, Mr. Padre." At the bottom of the statue reads, "If you work hard, good things will happen."

In 1997, Tony had three noncancerous growths removed from his parotid gland. By 2010, he had been diagnosed with cancer of the salivary gland and had both lymph nodes removed on the right side of his face. Still, he went back to dipping tobacco. He had been dipping tobacco since 1981. Streams of tobacco juice punctuated his sentences. It may have been the only bad habit he ever had; it more than likely took his life. If you will not stop dipping tobacco for yourself, then stop for Tony.

Tony had been confined to a wheelchair in his last years. When you're dying, every moment has meaning. His heart gave out early Sunday morning, June 16, 2014, due to complications from cancer. He was but 54 years old. Tony reached home sooner than most of us and he was standing as usual. Tony was rushed to Pomerade Hospital in Poway, California. It has been said that he suffered a lot at the end. The world of baseball was heartbroken. The flag at the Baseball Hall of Fame Museum was lowered the following day to half-staff in his honor. "He lived so much in the moment, it's hard to think of him in the past," said Keith Olberman.

Tony married Alicia and they had two children, Anisha Nicole and Tony Gwynn, Jr. They also have three granddaughters. Tony Gwynn, Jr., of the Philadelphia Phillies tweeted out to the world. "Today I lost my dad, my best friend, and my mentor. I'm gonna miss u so much pops. I'm gonna do everything in my power to continue to make u proud."

Albert Schweitzer once said, "Success is not the key to happiness. Happiness is the key to success. If you love what you are doing, you will be successful." One of Tony's last recorded appearances went like this. "So I will leave this game with a smile on my face, knowing that I've had a good career, I've met a lot of people, but I will miss you, miss you a lot. So, with that I will say goodbye and thank you." Tony Gwynn.

One of my favorite Tony Gwynn stories goes like this. During the 1994 All-Star Game, the National League was down by 2 runs in the ninth inning. Fred McGriff hits a home run off Lee Smith to tie the game at 7. Gwynn then hits a hot grounder up the middle for a base hit. Will Clark is playing first base for the American League. The next batter, Moises Alou settles in at the plate. Gwynn says to Clark, "If Smith tries to sneak a fastball in on Alou, this game is over." Alou hits the ball into left-center field and it goes to the wall. Gwynn takes off and when he rounds third base he sees "Pudge" Rodriquez with his hands up getting ready to catch the ball. Tony sticks his leg in between Pudge's legs and touches home plate before the tag, for the win. "It was the only time I acted like I was in high school," said Tony.

Tony Gwynn thought he was lucky to be a Padre, I thought it was the other way around. Tony's #19 was cut in the outfield grass at Petco Park before the next home game. The current Padres formed a semi-circle and stood for a 19-second moment of silence in Tony Gwynn's honor. Tony would have said, "Oh man, are you kidding me?"

HOUSE

Comedian Richard Pryor was once asked how he would like to be remembered. He said, "I want people to look at my picture, remember, and laugh. I would like to leave some joy." This guy was always a pleasure to watch and a joy to have known. He was shorter than the program stated, with 44-inch thighs that resembled twin jet-engines. At 209 pounds, power was his forte. Built close to the ground like a fire hydrant, he could churn up defenses like a high-speed lawnmower. Undersized for a pro football player, his stats didn't measure his heart. His ticker weighed a ton. Handing this guy a football was like giving Wyatt Earp a rifle, LeBron James an outlet pass, or Mike Trout an extra strike; something incredible was about to happen. This guy ran tough; it was like trying to tackle a Pepsi machine. He simply sawed defensive linebackers in half at the line of scrimmage. He was never late to anything in his life including moving the chains for a first down. His job was to cut a path to the end zone for the running back or stop all oncoming traffic in the backfield, while keeping his quarterback standing upright and his uniform clean. Dallas Cowboy offensive guard, John Niland, once said, "If we needed three yards or less for a first down, we knew we had it. Give Robert the ball, and we had it. We'd block a yard and a half, and he'd get the other yard and a half on his own. It was a given." Robert Newhouse played like he had invented the fullback position. I can hear Verne Lundquist now, "There goes Newhouse busting it up the middle." His teammates called him "House."

Robert Fulton Newhouse was born on January 9, 1950, in Longview, Texas, and played football at nearby Galilee High School in Hallsville, Texas. Although he rushed for 200 yards and sometimes over 300 yards per game in high school, he was only recruited by one Division I school, the University of Houston. With Robert Newhouse running the ball, Houston finished 9-2 in 1969 and was ranked 12th in the nation. In 1970, Houston finished 8-3 and was ranked 19th. In 1971, before his senior season started at Houston, Newhouse cracked his pelvis in a car accident. He chose to play though the pain and propelled Houston to a 9-3 record and a ranking of 17th in the nation. Newhouse was selected Second-Team All-American by the Associated Press.

Newhouse still holds the University of Houston's all-time rushing record for a single season with 1,757 yards. Newhouse broke many other school records, some of which still stand today. He had ten 100-yard games in a season (1971), sixteen 100-yard games in a career, and the most 200-yard games in a season, with three. Back when the College All-Stars played the Super Bowl Champions from the year before, Newhouse scored a touchdown against the Cowboys. I always wondered if that touchdown had anything to do with the Cowboys' drafting him. Robert Newhouse also played in the Hula Bowl and was inducted into the University of Houston's Athletics Hall of Honor in 1977. Robert Newhouse is also a member of the Texas Black Hall of Fame.

Newhouse played 12 seasons under the "Man with the Hat" legendary Hall-of-Fame Coach Tom Landry. House was selected by the Cowboys in the second round of the 1972 NFL draft. He was given #44. During the 1973 season, House recorded his longest run from scrimmage, 54 yards, against the Philadelphia Eagles. He switched from halfback to fullback to replace a retiring Walt Garrison and became a starter in 1975. He would make his presence felt that year by leading the Cowboys in rushing with 930 yards and was listed ninth in the league with 4.4-yards per carry. By 1977, Tony Dorsett had been drafted and House became more of a blocking back for Preston Pearson, Calvin Hill and Dorsett. By 1980, Newhouse began splitting time in the backfield with Ron Springs. He would continue to play sparingly until he retired after the 1983 season.

The play was called: "brown right, X-opposite shift, toss 38, halfback lead, fullback pass to Y." Dallas was leading 20-10 with seven minutes to go, in Super Bowl XII. The Denver Broncos had just fumbled and Dallas recovered the ball on the Broncos' 29-yard line. Coach Landry sensed that Denver was on the ropes and called for a trick play to seal the victory. Newhouse was nervous in the huddle. "I was worried because I had all this stickum on my hands, said Newhouse. "Preston Pearson handed me this rag, and I was in there, scrubbing it all. They'd seen us run the play right but not to the left, and so they didn't recognize it in time." At the snap, Newhouse took a pitch from quarterback Roger Staubach and began running to his left, as if he were going to run down the sideline. Instead, he stopped quickly, turned and threw back to the right, over the outstretched hands of Denver defensive back Steve Foley, hitting wide receiver Golden Richards in stride for a 29-yard touchdown. The Dallas Cowboys would go on to win their second Super Bowl title by a score of 27-10. Landry said after the game, "Newhouse's pass play won it for us." Robert Newhouse became the first running back to pass for a touchdown in Super Bowl history. "The thing I remember most about that halfback option play we ran against Denver," said former Cowboy personnel director Gil Brandt, "is that we ran it going left, and it's a lot harder to go left than right. During the week they must've practiced the play ten times, and he never completed it. And that was going right. Here it is going left, and he completed it."

Newhouse finished his Cowboy career with 4,784 yards rushing, 956 yards receiving and scored 31 touchdowns. He averaged over an astounding four yards per carry. He also participated in three Super Bowls during the 1970's (X, XII, and XIII). I believe he should be in the Dallas Cowboys Ring of Honor.

After retirement, Newhouse worked another 29 years for the Cowboys. He worked with ticket sales, the Cowboys' alumni relations programs, minority procurement, and helped with the players' development off the field. Part of Newhouse's job was providing the community opportunities to experience the Cowboys and their players in a different setting. For years the Cowboys' basketball team would travel to Corpus Christi, Texas, and play a charity basketball game at Ray High School. That's when I first met Robert Newhouse. Later on, I had a chance to do play-by-play with my radio partner, Shane Nelson, on 97.5 The Waves. I also got to meet Michael Irvin, Leon Lett, and many others. Newhouse was a class act but he couldn't shoot a lick. He left the Cowboys' employment in 2008.

Robert Newhouse suffered a stroke in 2010. Doctors had been treating him and hoping he would become healthy enough to withstand the surgery required for a heart transplant. Newhouse was confined to the Mayo Clinic in Rochester, Minnesota, at the time of his death. "My dad's last days were terrible,' said his son, Rodd Newhouse. Former Dallas Cowboy, Robert Newhouse, died from complications of heart disease on Tuesday, July 22, 2014. He was but 64 years old. He is survived by his wife Nancy, twin daughters Dawnyel and Shawntel, two sons Roderick and Reggie, a former wide receiver for the Arizona Cardinals.

"House was a great football player," said Roger Staubach. "Off the field, he was a great man, kind and caring, solid as a rock."

Motivational speaker Jim Rohn once said, "Time is more valuable than money. You can get more money, but you cannot get more time." The only thing that could keep Robert Newhouse out of the end zone of life was time. Come on, admit it. He was the kind of guy you wished you had on your team.

THAT'S FOOTBALL

This guy wasn't scouted; he was caught in a snare and then captured. I wanted to ask him if his coffin was comfortable and what time he turned into a monster. Some said he was so mean and evil his image didn't show up in the team picture. He was loud when he ran, like a freight train. You could hear him coming with the stands full of fans, and he hit people so hard you could hear the wind leave their bodies. From his defensive-end position, he could dial up pressure faster than you can call 911. He descended on quarterbacks like a dark cloud of locusts. This guy could have been the poster child for concussions. No one was safe. He should have played an extra in *The Wild Bunch*. This guy was so mean birds stopped singing when he entered the stadium. He played like he was five squares short of a Bingo and was strong enough to slam a revolving door shut. No one in life is all good or all bad, but he was scary, outrageous, "doctor death." He learned the power of intimidation and thought nothing of throwing you down a flight of stairs. His handshake was so strong it made you feel weak. He lived with the pedal to the floor and the throttle wide open. This man could overdose on confidence and he was one of those guys that would hit back.

Football is not about the war; it's about the warriors. The list of the meanest and dirtiest players includes the names of Bill Pellington, Chuck Bednarik, Dick "Night Train" Lane, Conrad Dobler, John Henry Johnson, Hardy Brown, Joe "Bucko" Kilroy and Dick Butkus. Sprinkle can be found right near the top. That's right, Ed hurt more people than the plague; and with a last name like Sprinkle you had to be mean. "The Grim Reaper" sometimes gets the last laugh, but until then it was Ed Sprinkle's turn. Thirteen players, more than half of the NFL's All-Time Team, played in the 1950's.

Edward Alexander Sprinkle was born in Bradshaw, Texas, on September 3, 1923. He grew up in Tuscola, Texas, located just south of Abilene. His folks were sharecroppers. Ed graduated from Tuscola High School and played football and basketball at Hardin-Simmons University in Abilene. He won three letters in football and two in basketball, and earned All-Border Conference honors in football. While there, Ed was coached by a part-time assistant coach named, Clyde "Bulldog" Turner. Turner became a Hall-of-Fame center and linebacker for the Chicago Bears. Ed left Hardin-Simmons after three years and enrolled at the United States Naval Academy, where he continued to play football. Hardin-Simmons' athletic program had been cancelled due to the war effort. In 1943, Ed earned All-Eastern honors, while at Navy. In 1944, at Turner's insistence, Sprinkle tried out for the Bears. Ed initially made the team as an offensive guard and end, but at 6' 1" tall and weighing only 210 pounds, Coach George Halas decided Ed was too small to play on the offensive line. After two years, Halas moved Ed to the other side of the ball where he concentrated on rushing the passer from the right defensive-end position. "They were going to put me at left end," said Sprinkle. "But I wanted to be a right end because I'm left handed and I could reach over with my left arm."

At Wrigley Field, in November of 1946, against the dreaded Green Bay Packers, Ed and a teammate by the name of Mike Jarmoluk forced a fumble that Sprinkle recovered and returned 30 yards for the winning touchdown, as the Bears defeated the Packers 10-7. That win helped the Bears capture the 1946 NFL Championship.

Ed Sprinkle, nicknamed "The Claw," played in 132 games in 12 years. As an offensive end, Ed caught 32 passes for 451 yards and scored seven touchdowns. While on defense, Ed intercepted four passes and returned them for a total of 55 yards, but did not score a touchdown. He recovered 12 fumbles for 111 yards, while scoring two touchdowns, and also recorded a safety during the 1949 season.

Part of Ed Sprinkle's success of rushing the quarterback could be attributed to the T-formation and its passing game, which replaced the single wing. All of a sudden, quarterbacks like Sammy Baugh of the Redskins or Bob Waterfield of the Rams were sitting ducks.

When Halas was asked about Sprinkle's rough house play he responded. "Every team in the league has a passer who can beat you if you give him time to throw. The only way to stop them is to knock them down before they throw. He's got to push and shove and claw his way past those blockers; and if somebody gets an unintentional whack in the nose now and then, well, that's football," said Halas. "I never really played dirty football in my life, but I'd knock the hell out of a guy if I got the chance," said Sprinkle.

One of the meanest men to ever put on a football helmet played from 1944 to 1955. Sprinkle was selected to play in four Pro Bowls and was named to the National Football League's All-Decade team for the 1940's. Ed's four Pro-Bowl appearances occurred in his last six seasons, as the Pro-Bowl concept did not start until 1950. Ed was inducted into the Chicago Sports Hall of Fame in 1984 and also the Helms Foundation Hall of Fame. He joined the Hardin-Simmons University Hall of Fame in 1990 and was inducted into the Big Country Athletic Hall of Fame in 2007. In 2008, Ed was named to the 75th Anniversary All-Sun Bowl Team and joined the Chicago Bears' Ring of Honor in 2009.

George Halas honored his prize pass rusher with the #7, the same number Halas had worn during his career. Halas referred to Ed as "The greatest pass rusher I've ever seen."

"Ed was one of the toughest defensive ends I've ever seen in football. He was fierce," said Ralph Jecha, who played beside Sprinkle in 1955. "He wasn't that big, but if you came around the end, he got you around the throat, and you suffered. You really suffered." "If you got a chance to kill a guy, you killed 'im," laughed Sprinkle.

There are many stories told about the violence of Ed Sprinkle. Here are just a few. "That guy, Ed Sprinkle of the Bears, was a tough one," said Marion Motley of the Cleveland Browns. "I fixed him one day. Coach Paul Brown warned us about him. 'He'll hit you anywhere and anytime,' said Brown. Well, early in our game, Sprinkle hit Tony Adamle a terrible blow on his Adam's apple and then ran off the field laughing. He was holding his sides, he thought it was so funny. Well, when we got back on offense, I told Otto Graham in the huddle to call a pass play which would put me into Sprinkle's area. I tried to hit him in his Adam's apple but something went wrong and I got him much farther south of there, if you catch my meaning. Down he went," said Motley smiling.

In an interview given in 1985 to the *New York Times* Hall-of-Fame running back, Hugh McElhenny said, "Sprinkle would drive you ten yards out of bounds and the official would be taking the ball away from you, but Sprinkle would still be choking you."

One of the few guys who got Sprinkle back was Charley Trippi of the Chicago Cardinals, who got so angry he pulled Sprinkle's helmet off with one hand and punched him with the other, and then walked off the field.

During the 1946 NFL Championship game against the New York Giants, Sprinkle sent two Giants' running backs to the sidelines with injuries. Sprinkle separated George Franck's shoulder and broke the nose of Frank Reagan. Sprinkle also broke Frank Filchock, the Giants' quarterback's, nose with his patented "claw" move, which involved using his forearm and hand to hammer and swipe his opponent's eyes, nose, neck and jaw. Players did not wear facemasks in the early days of football. In today's game, this move would be known as an illegal "clothesline tackle." While under pressure from Sprinkle, Filchock did manage to get a pass off, but it was intercepted and returned for a touchdown. The Bears beat the Giants that day, 24-14.

Chicago Cardinals' halfback Elmer Angsman claimed that Sprinkle deliberately stepped on his chest during a game and had five cleat marks as proof. Los Angeles Rams' fullback, Dick Hoerner, spent the night in a hospital with a concussion after being bombarded by Sprinkle during a Bears-Rams game. "Just because I was a good, tough player doesn't mean I was dirty," said Sprinkle, while smiling.

Sometimes greatness is about struggle, not victory. It's about finding out what's inside, the reason for being who we are. When asked about his chances to enter the Pro-Football Hall of Fame, he answered, "My personal opinion is that politics played into getting players into the Hall of Fame that didn't deserve it. I feel like I deserve to be in the Hall of Fame. It probably won't happen."

In the off season, Ed worked as an engineer at Inland Steel. In 1962, Ed became the head coach of the Chicago Bulls, a semi-pro team in the (UFL) United Football League. After football he opened his own tile and carpet company and owned a bowling alley. He also enjoyed playing golf in charity events.

Ed Sprinkle lived until he was 90 years of age. He died of "natural causes" on Monday, July 28, 2014, while living in Palos Heights, Illinois, with his daughter Susan Withers and her husband. His wife, Marian, died in 2003. Sprinkle is survived by two sons, Alan and Steven; five grandchildren; and nine great-grandchildren. Perhaps they should consider sprinkling his ashes at Soldier Field in Chicago.

LITTLE BIG MAN

Oscar Robertson never won five. Neither did Robert Parrish, Shaquille O'Neal, Paul Silas, James Worthy or Kevin McHale. Heck, Wilt won only two and Larry Bird only has three. What am I talking about? Rings, NBA championship rings. This guy has won five rings, just like Magic, Kobe and Tim Duncan, and I bet you've never even heard of him.

This guy was as quick as a cat, a bulldog, country tough, a bundle of energy, and a tremendous competitor. He owned a great personality, was one of the first athletes to wear contact lenses, and could sell a blind man a newspaper. This fellow played like he had a one-year contract and in fact he did. He was a catch-and-shoot guy when flying one-handed push shots dominated the league. One sports writer wrote, "He's the Eddie Stanky of basketball. He's too small to play, he can't shoot, he's not a fast runner and he doesn't do tricks with the ball; yet he's one of the greatest clutch players and defensive stars the game has ever seen." Slater Martin could play the stars of the game to a standstill. A defensive wizard, he wasn't considered a great scorer, yet he ranked 11th in post-season scoring and finished on the top 25 All-Time scoring list, when he retired. One of the last of the truly great little men, Martin once slugged it out with 7-foot Wally Dukes of the Detroit Pistons. It took several players to separate them. Slater Martin was a modern day "David" who spent eleven years in professional basketball cutting down Goliath.

Slater Nelson "Dugie" Martin Jr. was born on October 22, 1925, in Elmina, Texas. Don't bother to look it up, it isn't there anymore. You see, Slater's father operated a railroad station and general store in Elmina, until the entire family decided to pack up and move 70 miles to Houston. Dugie was two years old at the time. When the Martin family left, the town ceased to exist. Folks called him Dugie, a nickname his grandfather had given him, after Dugan's Tavern, a bar featured in the "Mutt and Jeff" comic strip.

Martin attended Jefferson Davis High School in Houston, Texas, and starred for the baseball, football, and of course basketball teams. He also enjoyed slipping on a pair of boxing gloves on occasion. At 5' 7" tall and weighing about 130 pounds, Slater ate, drank, slept, dreamed and lived basketball. He would play a big part during his junior and senior years (1942-1943) in helping Jefferson Davis High School win consecutive Texas State Championships in basketball. Martin's size made him difficult to recruit. The story goes that Slater hitchhiked to Austin for a tryout at the University of Texas and made the team. Longhorn Head Coach H. C. Gilstrap was impressed with Martin's desire and determination. Slater enrolled at Texas in the fall of 1943 and played in several varsity games as a freshman. In 1944, Martin's college career was interrupted by World War II. Slater joined the Navy and grew to 5' 10" tall while he was away. He returned to school in 1946 and helped the Longhorns, now coached by Jack Gray, to reach the 1947 NCAA Final Four. In a tournament that included eight teams, the "Mighty Mice" of Texas would beat Wyoming before losing to Oklahoma by one point, 55-54. This placed them in the consultation game where they beat City College of New York (CCNY) 54-50, to claim third place. Holy Cross, with a freshman guard by the name of Bob Cousy, would beat Oklahoma for the title. Slater would remember watching Cousy play. These two would make some history together. On February 26, 1949, Slater Martin scored 49 points in an 81-60 victory over Texas Christian University (TCU) and set the Southwest Conference single-game scoring record that stood for years. He was also selected an All-American that year, while finishing his career with 1,140 points, to become the highest scorer in Texas team history at that time.

Only three Texas Longhorn players have had their numbers retired: Slater Martin #15, T.J. Ford #11, and Kevin Durant #35. Of these three, only Slater is apart of the Naismith Memorial Basketball Hall of Fame. He was inducted on May 3, 1982.

"I saw Slater sit on a basketball during a game for ten minutes," said my pal, Dotson Lewis. "Texas was playing the University of Arkansas in Fayetteville, and the Razorbacks loved to run-and-gun under Head Coach Eugene Lambert." This game was played in the early forties during the days of no shot clock, no five-second call, and when goal tending was allowed. "Arkansas had a big kid in the middle named George Kok who was 6'10" tall, so Texas slowed the game down by stalling the ball," continued Dotson. "Slater brought the ball over the center court line uncontested, and then sat down on top of it like he was sitting on a pumpkin. It was the darnedest thing I've ever seen. No one from Arkansas came out to confront him. I think the final score ended up in Texas' favor," exclaimed Dotson. Dotson Lewis became a Hall-of-Fame Supervisor of Officials and officiated college football, basketball, baseball and volleyball in many conferences.

Martin joined the Minneapolis Lakers in 1949. He was married and had a family. "Although the pay was horrific," said Slater, "I wanted to play basketball for a living." After the Lakers paid George Miken, Vern Mikkelson and Jim Pollard, there was little money left over for Martin and the others. Martin held out for more money at contract time for four of the seven years with the Lakers. Martin and the Lakers won four NBA Championships in his first five years with the Lakers. Martin scored 32 points against the Knicks in 1952, to clench the NBA Championship for the Lakers. Eventually, the Lakers decided to trade Slater Martin. The Hawks inquired about him but the Lakers did not want to trade him to St. Louis because both teams were in the same conference. So, in 1956, Martin was traded to the New York Knicks for center, Wally Dukes. New York then traded him in December to St. Louis, for Willie Naulls. Hawks' owner, Ben Kerner exclaimed, "Martin saved my franchise. I'd have gone broke without him." Slater Martin's financial troubles were over. "Martin gave us great leadership," said Bob Petit. "He was the glue who held us together." Before the 1956-57 seasons, the St. Louis Hawks lost their head coach, "Red" Holzman. So, Kerner made Martin the coach of the Hawks, but Slater really disliked the job. Martin appointed his roommate and teammate, Alex Hannun, to succeed him, and then resigned after eight games as coach.

"Buddy" Blattner was the St. Louis Hawks' radio announcer and roomed with Slater on the road. "One year, the team got to Boston at three o'clock in the morning, and I fell asleep almost immediately," said Blattner. "I woke up three hours later and saw Martin pacing the floor. I asked him what was wrong." Slater responded, "Nothing, I'm just thinking about Cousy." "At six o'clock in the morning?" exclaimed Blattner. "I'm always thinking about Cousy," said Martin. Slater was the only guard in the league who could check Bob Cousy at the door. In the 1957 NBA Championship game, Martin held Bob Cousy to two baskets out of 20 shots and outscored Cousy 23 to 12, but the Hawks lost in double overtime to the Celtics. "He never left you alone," said Cousy. "I don't know where he gets all the energy." In 1958, Slater Martin, with Bob Pettit and Cliff Hagan, led the St. Louis Hawks to their one and only NBA title. It took six games to bring down the mighty Boston Celtics. While with the Hawks, Martin and Cousy would meet on the floor of battle a total of three times, in the NBA finals. Slater Martin once shut out Bob Davies of the Rochester Royals; it was the first time in 16 years that Davies didn't score. Martin retired in 1960 from injuries. He was 34 years old. In 1962, Slater Martin was elected to the Texas Longhorn Hall of Honor. He was also inducted into the Texas Sports Hall of Fame, in 1964.

In 1966, Martin was hired as the general manager and head coach for the Houston Mavericks of the American Basketball Association (ABA). On February 2, 1967, the Mavericks became one of the ABA charter members. They played their home games at Sam Houston Coliseum. Martin tried his best to draft Elvin Hayes and Don Chaney, but both opted instead for the NBA. In 1968, Martin coached the Mavericks to the ABA playoffs against the Dallas Chaparrals. Houston was defeated three games to none. With attendance dwindling, the Mavericks were purchased by James Gardner and the team was moved to North Carolina. There they became the Carolina Cougars from 1969-1974. It was in North Carolina that my dad took my brother and me to see our first professional basketball games. The Cougars drafted local stars like Doug Moe, Bob Verga, Larry Miller, and Ed Manning (the father of Danny Manning). We got to see, firsthand, stars like Julius Erving (Dr. J), George Gervin, Charlie Scott, and Moses Malone. By 1975, the Cougars had moved again and became the Spirits of St. Louis. After several more moves, this original franchise is now known as the Utah Jazz.

Slater Martin had been chastised all his life for being short; too short to play basketball. Some teammates joked, "Give him an inch and he would be 5' 11". There have been very few players who stood less than six feet tall that were good enough to play with the big guys. Martin was one of the best of the little big men.

Slater Martin died suddenly on Thursday, October 18, 2012, while living in a skilled care nursing home in Houston, Texas. He was 86 years old and survived by his sons, Slater

Jr. and Jim. Wearing the #22, Martin had become a five-time NBA Champion (1950, 1952-1954, 1958), a seven-time All-Star (1953-1959), and was selected to five All-NBA Second Teams (1955-1959). Martin collected 7,337 points, 2,302 rebounds, and dished out 3,160 assists, during his NBA career. Slater Martin averaged 9.8 points per game and 4.2 assists per game, in 745 regular-season games played. He averaged 10.0 points and 3.2 assists per game, in 92 post-season games. The season after Slater Martin retired, the Minneapolis Lakers moved to Los Angeles, where they reside today. In April 2002, the Los Angeles Lakers honored Martin and other surviving members from the Minneapolis years, in a celebration at the Staples Center.

John Ruskin once said, "Dream lofty dreams, and as you dream, so shall you become. Your vision is the promise of what you shall at last unveil." The giants of the game had nothing on the little big man, Slater Martin.

WINNING ISN'T EVERYTHING

So much of our sports psyche is focused on winning at all costs, but for some of us, just being a small part of our favorite sport on the big stage would have been enough. I, like most of my friends, would have given anything to be able to say, hey, I played professional (fill in the blank). I wanted to play professional football. I was big enough, strong enough and fast enough, but I didn't have that killer instinct, the ability to give up everything that is required to separate myself from other great athletes. As a result, I was a good athlete but not good enough to play at that level.

So, let me tell you about a guy who never accepted "no" for an answer, a guy who understood the meaning of sportsmanship, a fellow who competed against incredible odds and was willing to see the bigger picture besides winning. Gleason had Carney, Abbott had Costello, Martin had Lewis and the Globetrotters had "Red."

Louis Herman "Red" Klotz was born to Robert and Lena Klotz on October 21, 1920, in Philadelphia, Pennsylvania. At the age of ten, Red discovered the wonders of basketball while attending Thomas Junior High. Red later enrolled at South Philadelphia High School and led his team to the 1939 and 1940 Philadelphia City Championships, from the point guard position. Both years, Klotz was selected the Philadelphia Player of the Year. Red received an athletic scholarship to Villanova to play basketball and became part of the Wildcats undefeated freshman team. World War II would intervene and Klotz, like thousands of other boys his age, joined the U.S. Army.

After the war, Klotz played anywhere and for anybody. Being Jewish, Klotz spent most of his time playing for the South Philadelphia Hebrew Association (the Philadelphia Sphas) of the American Basketball League (ABL). During this time, Klotz led the Sphas to an exhibition victory in his first ever meeting against the Harlem Globetrotters. Trotter owner, Abe Saperstein, would not forget Red. Klotz's time with the Sphas ended in 1947. By 1948, Klotz had become a household name in basketball circles. He joined the Baltimore Bullets and helped his new team win the Basketball Association of America Championship. At 5' 7" tall, Klotz is the third shortest person to play an NBA game and the shortest to play on a championship team.

In 1952, Klotz was approached by Abe Saperstein of the Globetrotters. Abe was having trouble finding quality local opponents for his Trotters to play. These one sided games bored the audiences. So, Abe asked Red to form a team that would tour with the Globetrotters. This team would be called the Washington Generals, named after General Dwight D. Eisenhower, and would help introduce the game of basketball worldwide as the Globetrotters' nightly opponent. This team would change its name many times over the years from Shamrocks, Seagulls, Reds, All-Stars, and Nationals back to Generals, but the ownership never changed. Red Klotz and now his family still own the team. At first the games were played for real. Klotz wanted sound fundamentals and straight-up basketball from his team. Even though Klotz played point guard and recruited some of the best players at that time, the Globetrotters would continue to beat up the Generals on most nights. So, the Globetrotters began to do tricks.

Red's short stature and hair color made him a perfect target for the Globetrotters' high jinx. Legends such as Meadowlark Lemon and Goose Tatum took turns yanking down Red's pants more than once during a game. Curly

Neal would bounce the basketball off his head and mimic Red's one-handed set shots. "I got involved in that stuff mainly to take it away from my players," said Klotz. "I wanted them to play ball and not feel like they were going to be humiliated." Klotz drilled his teams constantly. Even though they were getting their brains beat out on a nightly basis, he still wanted them to play hard and play to win.

The Generals were never owned by the Globetrotters and were never told who they could have on their team. Those decisions were all left up to Red. It's true that the initial goal was to provide incredible entertainment, but Red always drove his team to be the best they could be.

Over five decades, the Generals won somewhere between four to six games of the over 16,000 games played against the Trotters as "Sweet Georgia Brown" blared from the gym sound system. Even Red was uncertain of the Generals' record against the Trotters. The last General win recorded occurred in 1971 in a college gym in Memphis, Tennessee. Klotz, who was 50 years old at the time, made a last second shot for the win. The crowd, along with the Globetrotters, was stunned. Red said, "Guys, we just won the game. We better get to the locker room before the Trotters find out." The only thing the Generals had in their locker room was orange soda. So, they poured orange soda on their heads as they celebrated. "The crowd wanted to kill me," said Klotz. "I didn't get famous apparently until I became the biggest loser that ever lived," said Klotz. "I'm the losing-est coach in the world," laughed Red. "I accepted losing as part of something much more," said Red. That record alone should qualify him for the Hall of Fame as a contributor.

Red performed in 117 different countries for Presidents, Popes, prisoners and Kings. Millions of everyday people have flocked to see the Globetrotters. The Trotters still play about 400 games a year. They have performed worldwide on aircraft carriers, on the bottom of empty swimming pools, tennis courts, and frozen lakes, inside Spanish bullfighting rings, airstrips and on a plywood floor placed on top of beer barrels, in Berlin.

Red's awards were many. Klotz was inducted into the Jewish Sports Hall of Fame in 2001. On March 10, 2007, Red was given the Legend Award of the Harlem Globetrotters. The Philadelphia Sportswriters Association presented Red with the 2009 Living Legend Award. Red joined Philadelphia icons Robin Roberts, Wilt Chamberlain, Harry Kalas and Chuck Bednarik. In 2011, the Harlem Globetrotters retired Red Klotz's #3 for all time. Red became the sixth player in their history to join a group that includes players like Meadowlark Lemon and Wilt Chamberlain. In November of 2013, The Legend of Red Klotz was published.

Current Globetrotter CEO, Kent Schneider said, "Red was truly an ambassador of the sport and as much a part of the Globetrotters legacy as anyone. He was a legend and a global treasure." Remarkably, Red played until he was 63 years old and then became the team's fulltime coach until he was in his seventies.

"I just called him Red," said my referee friend, Dotson Lewis. "I never knew his last name, but it was obvious that he was the captain, coach and choreographer of the Generals." During the late 1940's, Dotson once officiated a Globetrotter game in Japan. The event drew 103,000 people. "The Japanese people were very quiet," said Dotson. "Curly Neal said to me during a timeout, 'Why are they not clapping?'"

Off the court, Red Klotz was a quiet, talented man who loved working in his garden, taking care of his pets and talking basketball. On July 12, 2014, Red Klotz died at the age of 93 of cancer. He was living with his wife, Gloria, of 72 years, in Margate, New Jersey. Together they had six kids, 12 grandkids and nine great grandkids. He had won two city championships at South Philadelphia High School, another with the Philadelphia Sphas and a fourth with the NBA's Baltimore Bullets. Red Klotz was the oldest living

NBA Champion at the time of his death. Klotz waited for his call to the Naismith Basketball Hall of Fame until he was 93. Now his family hopes the telephone will one day ring. The life and legacy of Red Klotz is concrete proof that winning isn't everything.

In a surprise move, the Harlem Globetrotters announced on Friday, August 14, 2015, that they will no longer play the Washington Generals. Maybe the death of Red Klotz had something to do with that decision. They will be missed.

THE HUMAN INTERNET

Before there were computers in the press box, there was this guy, the human internet. Before every trip to the ballpark that night, he had already spent the entire day preparing for that game. Short, baldheaded with thick glasses, he looked more like your Sunday school teacher than a baseball broadcaster. His collection of stats and stories kept him ahead of the listeners and engaged in the game on a personal level. Most folks think his recall of baseball facts and research earned him the title, "The Professor," but that's not true. He received the nickname from his partner, Ernie Johnson, Sr., because he looked like pitcher Jim Brosnan. Legions of Atlanta Braves fans (95 million to be exact) would tune in each night to the Turner Broadcasting Systems (TBS) to listen to "Skip" Caray, Ernie Johnson, Sr., and Pete Van Wieren. Ted Turner could not have picked a better title for his fledgling endeavor, that later became known as "The Superstation." Pete was the last surviving member of this extraordinary broadcast team.

The "Three Amigos," Skip, Ernie and Pete were made for each other. Skip was the fly in the ointment, a sharp-tongued character that had deep bloodlines in broadcasting, while Ernie brought with him a taste of the game as a real Major League pitcher, who even had his own 1957 Topps baseball card with the Milwaukee Braves. Pete, well, he was just Pete; and his job was to tell you about the game. Pete had no signature line, never screamed out "Holy Cow" or some other tag line. He wasn't remembered for any particular historic call; he just told us about the game. His ego never reared its ugly head. Pete let the other two tell the jokes and dish out the sarcasm. Pete just talked baseball. His pregame "Diamond Notes" info would allow Southern folks to learn something about the grand old game every night. He made you feel smart. On a nightly basis, his baseball knowledge and intellect placed many Atlanta Braves fans on the edge of their seats. Baseball is about history, not hits, and Van Wieren understood that. Pete's voice was as smooth as maple syrup and his knowledge of the subtleties of the game was unparalleled. While the nation listened to Bob Costas, Tony Kubek, Vin Scully or Joe Garagiola once a week, the cable folks got Ernie, Skip and Pete every day. With these three together, it was as if the TBS had caught lightning in a bottle. Many farm kids grew up in South Georgia listening to baseball. Pete and his mates made it fun, even though the Braves teams of those days were terrible.

Pete Van Wieren was born in Rochester, New York, on April 7, 1944. Pete attended and graduated from Cornell University. In the late 1960's, after school, Pete worked for the *Washington Post*. Pete never said what his job was at the paper, but one of his favorite stories was about meeting sportswriter Shirley Povich, while he was there. Pete would work eight hours at a Binghamton, New York, radio station and then race across town to broadcast a game for the Yankees' Double-A affiliate. Pete was broadcasting play-by-play for the Tidewater Tides, a Triple-A team of the Atlanta Braves, located in Virginia, when he was discovered By Ernie Johnson, Sr.

Pete was also a television broadcaster in Ohio, New York and Virginia. Pete Van Wieren and Thurman Munson will always be linked together in baseball lore. In 1968, Pete jumped at the chance when asked by his television station to go to the airport and pick up a player who had just been promoted to the Yankees' farm club in Binghamton, New York. That player's name was Thurman Munson.

Interestingly, 11 years later, the great Yankee catcher, Thurman Munson, died when a small private plane he was piloting, crashed. Pete later passed away 35 years to the day after Munson passed. The Braves will continue to celebrate Pete's life as do the Yankees for Munson. Pete was eventually hired away from Tidewater by the Atlanta Braves. Pete joined the TBS staff in September of 1975, along with future broadcast partner, Skip Caray.

The radio booth at Atlanta County Stadium is named after Pete Van Wieren. I think it is fitting to share a day in his life as a baseball announcer. Pete's day went something like this. By 3:30 pm he arrived at the stadium and parked. He grabbed a cup of coffee and would sit with Atlanta Braves' skipper, Bobby Cox, for a minute or two and find out about team injuries. By 3:50 Pete would begin to visit several websites for current baseball updates. At 4:45, he would find his way into the television booth and test the microphone. At 5:10 Pete would meet with his partner, Skip, and share info if needed. They sat down to dinner around 5:20 in the media cafeteria. From 6 to 7 pm, they would set up in the broadcast booth and make a final check of any new media releases. First pitch occurred at 7:30. By 8:45 these two would switch over to the radio booth to finish out the game. On most nights, a quick snack around 11:30 would help them complete the game. Another night of Atlanta Braves baseball was in the books.

After 33 years, (1976-2008) Pete Van Wieren unexpectedly retired from broadcasting, on October 21, 2008. Pete left the Braves less than three months after the death of his longtime partner, Skip Caray (August 3, 2008). Ernie Johnson Sr. died on August 12, 2011. Van Wieren was later diagnosed with B-cell lymphoma cancer on November 4, 2009. "This is certainly not what I planned to do when I retired," said Pete. After treatment, the cancer returned before the year was out. Pete Van Wieren died on September 2, 2014, from cancer. He was living in Alpharetta, Georgia, with his wife,

Elaine, who had stood by Pete's side for fifty years as his biggest fan. Together they had two sons, Jon and Steve, and three granddaughters.

Dodgers' president and former Braves' president, Stan Kasten said, "Van Wieren was the soundtrack for every great memory of the Braves during the era the team became a power."

Future Hall-of-Fame third baseman, Chipper Jones, responded when he heard the news. "Sad day in Braves Country as Pete Van Wieran has passed away. I grew up watching him every night. We will miss you, buddy! I can't help but think that Pete, Skip and Ernie Johnson, Sr. are up there right now sharing a couple of laughs, sharing a couple of drinks, getting ready to watch the Braves do their business tonight; rest in peace, Professor."

Pete also broadcast games for the NBA Atlanta Hawks from 1991-1994 along with the Atlanta Flames professional hockey. Pete also called some Atlanta Falcons pre-season football games, as well as football for the Big Ten Conference, all for TBS and TNT. Pete also became a sports reporter for CNN. Nobody knew or loved the Braves more than Pete. "Baseball was meant to be enjoyed," said Pete. "It's not brain surgery."

Should Pete Van Wieren be in the Baseball Hall-of-Fame Museum as an announcer? I would say, "Yes." Van Wieren won the Georgia Sportscaster-of-the-Year Award, eight times during his 33-year career, and was elected to the Atlanta Braves Hall of Fame in 2004, along with broadcast partner, Skip Caray. Pete and Skip joined an impressive group including Warren Spahn, Hank Aaron, Eddie Mathews, Lew Burdette, Del Crandall, Tommy Holmes, Ernie Johnson, Dale Murphy, Johnny Sain, Ted Turner and "Kid" Nichols. Van Wieren also co-wrote a book with Jack Wilkinson entitled <u>Of Mikes and Men: A Lifetime of Braves Baseball</u>. The release date was April 2010.

"We interrupt this marriage to bring you the baseball

season," laughed Pete's wife, Elaine. "Pete loved the 1991 season best. That's the year the team went from worst to first." According to Elaine, Pete turned down many opportunities to go elsewhere. "He was a Brave to the core," said Elaine. "He, Johnson and Caray were a team and he also had tremendous respect for Ted Turner." Pete was also an avid reader and owned two rooms full of books and reading material that he never got around to reading. "If you were playing Trivial Pursuit, you would want Pete on your team," exclaimed Elaine. Pete was also a terrific poker player and loved playing the game Jeopardy.

"He took me to Cooperstown to the Baseball Hall-of-Fame Museum," said his son, Jon. "He knew so much about so many of the ballplayers that I sort of got the grand tour with the inside scoop." Pete's source of pride came from his three granddaughters. He was a frequent spectator at their events and loved being around them. If Pete Van Wieren could speak with us now, I think I know what he would say. Love unconditionally. Hold your family close because, in the end, they are all that really matters.

What is it about broadcasting that keeps them coming back? They come into our homes regularly and become part of our family. Folks like Dick Enberg, Marv Albert, Brent Musberger, Lee Corso, Al Michaels, Bill Rafferty, Vern Lundquist and Dick Vitale are all in their seventies and still going strong. And how could we forget the king of broadcasters, 86-year-old, Vin Scully? I'm sure I may have forgotten one or two. Maybe it's the magic of the games that keeps these golden voices returning year after year. All I know is that there is work and there will always be work, what's rare is when we find someone who makes us happy. Thanks Pete.

SWAMP FOX

Irene Peters once said, "Just because everything is different doesn't mean anything has changed." They still call it baseball. Ninety feet between the bases may be the most perfect invention of our time. Baseball is the smell of fresh cut grass mixed with hot roasted peanuts. He played during a time when we listened to the game on our transistor radios. It was the 1950's. He was known in baseball vernacular as a violinist, a hitter with an especially smooth swing. This guy could hit the skin off the baseball and rip your heart out with a double. No since in shifting the infield for this guy as he could drag bunt, hit behind the runner, or push the ball to the opposite field. He would become the first National League shortstop to hit 20 or more home runs more than once, and he once took the great Sandy Koufax deep. Watching this guy hit a home run was like eating a fresh cinnamon roll; wow, that's good. This guy wasn't a morning person. He had to have two cups of coffee and a nap to wake up, but he loved baseball. This fellow owned a big smile underneath sad eyes, and he was as southern as a dirt road. He was brilliantly awkward in the infield, but there was a good chance his inner circle was actually square. His throws to first base made your hand sting. He was not a religious man as much as he was a spiritual man. He grew up playing baseball in the heat of Louisiana, where the best place to park your car was determined by the amount of shade. Playing in the hot sun made the bases look like partly-melted marshmallows. Alvin Dark claimed he was

168

tall for a shortstop, but you'd have to put him on a rack to stretch him to six feet.

Alvin Ralph "Al" Dark was born in Comanche, Oklahoma, on January 7, 1922. Born poor, this guy couldn't pick up a check, much less a girl. But boy, could he pick up a ground ball. Alvin was the third of four kids born to Ralph and Cordia Dark. As a child Alvin battled malaria and diphtheria and survived, but could not attend school until he had turned seven years old. His family later moved to Lake Charles, Louisiana. He was selected to the All-State and All-Southern Football teams as a tailback. He was elected captain of the basketball team and played American Legion baseball because his high school had no baseball team. In 1940, after Dark graduated from Lake Charles High School, he enrolled at Louisiana State University where he played baseball, basketball and starred on the football team as a running back. He had also been offered a basketball scholarship from Texas A&M, but declined in order to attend LSU. In 1942, Dark carried the football 60 times for 433 yards for a 7.2-yard per carry, and also lettered in all three major sports.

In 1943, with World War II underway, Dark joined the Marine Corp's V-12 program which allowed him to stay in school one more year. He was sent to Southwestern Louisiana Institute in Lafayette. While there, Dark played on SLI's greatest team. They were undefeated at 4-0-1 and beat Arkansas A&M University 24-7 in the very first Oil Bowl played. Dark did his part by scoring a rushing touchdown, passed for another touchdown, and kicked three extra points and a field goal. Dark then completed his basic training at Parris Island and Camp Lejeune. He was commissioned at Quantico, Virginia, in January of 1945, and sent to the Pacific Theater. Although he never saw combat, in the summer of 1945, he was sent to China after the Allied victory to support the Nationalists against the Communists.

When Dark returned home in 1946, he found out he had been drafted by the NFL's Philadelphia Eagles, but his first love had always been baseball. Boston Braves' scout Ted McGrew cornered Dark and worked out a deal to sign him to play professional baseball. Dark signed on July 4, 1946, and was 24 years old when he finally joined the Boston Braves on July 14. His contract called for a $45,000 signing bonus and a yearly salary of $5,000. Alvin Dark recorded his first hit on August 8, 1946, in Philadelphia, off pitcher "Lefty" Hoerst. Dark played in only 15 games that season and was then optioned in 1947 to Milwaukee by Braves Manager, Billy Southworth. Dark had a terrific year in the Minor Leagues and was brought back up to the Braves in 1948 as the opening day starter at shortstop. Dark performed well enough to be chosen the 1948 Rookie of the Year, though he had played in 15 games in 1946. Dark had hit .322 while leading the Braves to their first pennant in 34 years. The rules at that time stated that if a player had participated in less than 25 games during a season he could still be considered on the ballot for ROY. Boston won the 1948 National League pennant but lost the World Series to the Cleveland Indians in six games. Alvin Dark and Eddie Stanky would become the premier double-play combination for years to come. These two were traded to the New York Giants in 1950.

The Giants found themselves tied with the Brooklyn Dodgers for the 1951 NL pennant. The three-game playoff was tied with one win apiece when Alvin Dark came to bat in the bottom of the ninth inning at the Polo Grounds, trailing the Dodgers, 4-1. Dark fouled off several pitches before hitting a single. Four batters later, after Dark had scored, Bobby Thomson hit the "Shot Heard Around the World," to beat the Dodgers 5-4. The Giants then lost the 1951 World Series to the dreaded New York Yankees in six games, but Dark had done his part. He hit .417, with three doubles and one home run, and drove in four RBI's, but it had not been enough. He and Stanky were then traded to the St. Louis Cardinals, in 1956. Dark signed for $40,000, the highest one-year amount he had ever played for. By 1958, you could find Dark with the Cubs in Chicago. He would also play briefly with the Phillies and Milwaukee Braves in 1960, before retiring. His final game was played on October 2, 1960. Dark was 38 years of age. The Golden Age of New York baseball had provided us with terrific shortstops like "Pee Wee" Reese, Phil Rizzuto and Alvin Dark. Dark is the only one of the three not in the Baseball Museum Hall of Fame, although he had a higher career batting average and had hit for more power.

Alvin Dark will be remembered as one of the best shortstops in Giants' history. He played 14 seasons with five different teams and became the 1948 Rookie of the Year and a three-time All-Star. Dark had played in 1,828 games, batted .289, recorded 2,089 hits, 358 doubles, 126 home runs and 757 RBI's, while batting mostly second in the lineup. Dark played shortstop on three pennant winners: 1948 Braves, 1951 Giants and the 1954 Giants.

Dark was named the San Francisco Giants' Manager in 1961. In 1962, Dark led his San Francisco Giants to a 103-62 win-loss record and their first National League Championship. He also earned the nickname, the "Swamp Fox" for initiating his plan for slowing down their hated rivals, and the Dodgers' shortstop by the name of Maury Wills. Wills was en route to 104 stolen bases that season but not on Dark's watch, if he could help it. Dark had his groundskeepers put extensive amounts of water around first base. During one three-game series with L.A., the umpires had no other choice than to have the grounds crew place sand on the wet surface to provide adequate footing. The plan worked, as the Dodgers found the trip from first to second base extremely slow. A smiling Dark suggested he knew nothing about it.

Dark could be terse. He was the kind of guy that would

say things that would stick with you the rest of your life. "The two easiest things to do in baseball are to hustle and be prepared. Everything else is hard," said Dark Especially for Dark who managed five different teams over 17 seasons. He simply hated to lose. In 1964, it had been written that Dark alluded to his displeasure in managing Hispanic and African-American athletes. According to the article written by Stan Isaacs of *Newsday*, Dark was quoted as saying "We have trouble because we have so many Negro and Spanish-speaking players on the team. They are just not able to perform up to the level of white players when it comes to mental alertness." Dark responded that he had been severely misquoted. Was Dark a racist? Some said yes, others say no. Most of his players like Willie Mays, whom Dark had selected as captain of the Giants, Felipe Alou, and others felt he had treated them fairly. Alou went as far as saying that Alvin Dark was a "very nice man." Even Jackie Robinson came to his defense by stating "I have found Dark to be a gentleman and, above all unbiased. Our relationship has not only been on the ball field, but off it." Dark, a devout Christian, eventually released a statement. "I do not believe you can judge people by groups—Negro, Spanish-speaking, white or any other way," said Dark. Others, like Orlando Cepeda and Juan Marichal, voiced a different story. Cepeda claimed he was upset when Dark asked him not to speak Spanish, because the other players feared what they might be saying. When we spoke to Bobby Valentine on the *Dennis* and *Andy's Q&A Session* sports talk radio show, Bobby included Dark in his all-time favorite managers, along with Walter Alston, Tommy Lasorda and Dick Williams. Regardless of how much truth is involved, Dark weathered the storm. We all get to the point in life where we have to live with the choices we made, the good ones and the bad ones.

As for losing, Dark was dubbed the "Mad Genius" by the Bay Area newspaper reporters. On June 7, 1964, Dark used four different pitchers in the first inning against the Philadelphia Phillies. Walk a batter and out of the game you come. His madness paid off, as the Giants won in ten innings 4-3.

In 1964, longtime Dodger, Duke Snider, who wore #4, was traded from the New York Mets to the San Francisco Giants. Duke wore #28, because the Giants had retired the #4 worn by Mel Ott. Once before a game against the Los Angeles Dodgers, S.F. Giants' Manager Alvin Dark gave Duke $100 to take tomorrow's opposing pitcher, Don Drysdale, to dinner the night before. "Take the big donkey out, on me, and get him good and drunk," said Dark. "We had dinner and lots of Crown Royal," said Snider. The next day, Duke, sitting on the bench with a hangover, was asked to pinch hit in the ninth inning against Drysdale. Don struck Duke out on three pitches. After the game, Duke sent a note to the Dodgers' clubhouse addressed to Drysdale. It said, "Dear Donnie, don't know what the last pitch was when it went by, but it sure smelled like Crown Royal. Love, Dookie." The Dodgers and Drysdale had won the game, 8-0. "I always wondered if Dark wanted his money back," said Snider.

Giants' owner, Horace Stoneham, fired Dark in the sixth inning of the last game of the 1964 season. In 1966, Dark was promoted from an assistant to Charles O. Finley, to Manager of the Kansas City Athletics. He was let go in August of 1967, by a disgruntled Finley in regards to player discipline. Dark was then hired by the Cleveland Indians, in 1968. Dark was replaced in 1971, with his team in last place. By 1972, the A's had moved from Kansas City to Oakland and their manager Dick Williams had resigned. Finley rehired Dark, who led the team to a third straight World Series Championship in 1974, but was fired again after losing the 1976 American League Championship. Yes, it's true what they say about managers. They are hired to be fired. In 1977, Dark was hired again, this time by the

San Diego Padres. While there, Dark discovered a young shortstop by the name of Ozzie Smith. Dark found himself without a job again when he was fired during Spring Training on March 21, 1978. In 1980, Dark penned an autobiography with John Underwood entitled <u>When in Doubt, Fire the Manager</u>.

Dark found success as a manager by leading the S.F. Giants to the 1962 National League pennant, won a World Series Championship with the 1974 Oakland Athletics, and won a division title with the 1975 A's. That made him the first to manage the All-Star Game for both leagues, the National League in 1973 and the American League in 1975. He finished his career with a 994-954 win-loss record as a manager.

One of the first stories I ever heard about Alvin Dark involved Gaylord Perry. My dad had grown up just down the street from Gaylord and his brother Jim Perry. The Perry's lived in Williamston, North Carolina, and my dad grew up in nearby Oak City. Gaylord pitched for Alvin Dark and the San Francisco Giants from 1962 until 1964, and he was not a very good hitter by any stretch of the imagination. Perry, a .131 career hitter, had showed some pop in his bat during batting practice one day. Dark responded to a question by reporter Harry Jupiter about Perry's new-found power by saying, "There would be a man on the moon before Gaylord Perry would hit a home run." As fate would have it, on July 20, 1969, Gaylord hit a home run in the third inning, off Dodgers pitcher, Claude Osteen. This feat occurred shortly after the Apollo 11 module had landed onto the lunar surface of the moon. Dark's prediction had indeed come true. Neil Armstrong actually stepped onto the surface of the moon six hours later, on July 21, 1969. Perry hit five more home runs before he retired.

I enjoy collecting bubblegum cards and equipment from the past. All these item speak to me. I never met Alvin Dark in person but I do own a piece of his baseball past.

I purchased a game-used glove of his that has his name printed in the pocket. It's a typical infielder's glove from the 1950's with thick padding around the wrist and fingers. It has a small web, and the glove itself is only about 15% bigger than the actual size of his hand. It folds neatly to be placed in his back pocket or it can be laid flat upon a table; a true relic of baseball past.

In 1983, Dark created the Alvin Dark Ministries, a program designed to financially support other Christian ministries. He had been married twice and had four children of his own and two adopted. Alvin Dark was 92 years old when he left us on Thursday, November 13, 2014. He had suffered from Alzheimer's disease for several years. He left behind 20 grandchildren and three great-grandchildren. Dark was living in a small community called Easley, South Carolina. He was the oldest living manager of a World Series-winning, pennant-winning, or post-season team. Dark has been inducted into the Oklahoma Sports Hall of Fame, the Louisiana Sports Hall of Fame, The Louisiana State University Sports Hall of Fame and the New York Giants Baseball Hall of Fame.

Alvin Dark may have been a visionary before his time. He once said, "Learning used to be a three-legged stool. School, Church and your parents all taught you the same things. Now schools and church teach different things, and some parents don't teach at all." Athletes can have an amazing influence on our lives. They give us their effort, their sweat and determination. We give them our hearts. But Father Time always has the last at-bat.

CARDBOARD HEROES

At the age of ten I stood on a wooden Coke Cola crate and ran a cash register at Gordon's Market, a convenience store similar to Stripes, owned and operated by my father, William Gordon Purvis. There I learned to stock shelves, check in product, sweep up, clean the premises and interact with people. I also discovered comic books, Slurpies, roasted cashews and baseball cards in a pack. For a nickel, you would receive a pack of six baseball cards with pictures of Major League players and a strip of gum. I am embarrassed to tell you how many of those packs I opened. I'm sure my father never made a penny profit from baseball cards. Those days were spent pitching or flipping baseball cards against the wall in order to win cards that I did not have. Flipping, trading or simply storing my cards in a shoe box was fun. Eventually we placed the extras in the spokes of our bicycle tires to make a cool sound. I even remember cutting a 1968 Johnny Bench rookie card in half because I didn't like the other player on the card (Ron Tompkins).

During the fifties, and sixties, baseball cards were distributed and sold by print runs. If there were 407 cards in a complete set, like there were in 1952, they were broken up into three or four print runs. An example might be: at the beginning of the baseball season, only cards numbering 1-80 were sold in the first packs printed. Later that summer, cards numbering 81-250 were sold, with the next print run of cards numbering 251-310. The last prints runs included cards 311-407, and were sold at the end of the season in

September and October. The idea was that you would have to purchase packs of baseball cards all year long to complete your set. Interestingly, the original idea behind selling these sports cards was to sell gum. Many kids quit buying the last print run of cards as football and basketball season had started. Mothers threw out cards as their sons moved on to college. As a result, these cardboard heroes of ours became valuable beyond belief.

Cards depicting professional athletes from many sports had already been used for a half a century to sell other products, notably tobacco. Baseball cards have been sold in seven different sizes since 1871. They originally came in tobacco pouches or packs of cigarettes. Some of those companies were known as Goudey, Diamond Star, Play Ball, Turkey Red, and Allen & Ginters. Cards of all sizes were later added to boxes and cans of food or soft drinks. Topps, a Brooklyn based company, was founded in 1938 as a chewing gum company. As the industry exploded, Topps created Bazooka Bubble Gum and helped stimulate the gum sales by creating and enclosing cardboard cards of comic characters like the Three Stooges, Davy Crockett, and Hopalong Cassidy.

Seymour Perry "Sy" Berger was born July 12, 1923, in the Lower East Side of Manhattan, New York. Louis and Rebecca Berger later moved their family to the Bronx. Louis was a furrier. Sy would grow up in the Mecca of professional baseball, where the Brooklyn Dodgers, New York Giants, and New York Yankees ruled America's National Pastime. Sy served in the Army Air Forces during World War II, and then graduated from Bucknell University with an accounting degree. Berger had a friend whose father was one of the four Shorin brothers who founded Topps, in 1938. In 1947, Sy Berger joined Topps. Topps released the 1952 set which became a disaster. First, it included taffy, not gum, and second it was a poor design with little information. Berger would spend hours at his kitchen table at home with cardboard and scissors creating a baseball card that would contain gum. Berger understood that in order to sell gum, the baseball trading cards had to be the best. The cards needed to be large and have the name and picture of the player, birth date, the team logo, and beautiful striking color that would jump off the card. Other innovations included adding the player's stat line from the previous year and a facsimile of the player's autograph below their image. Berger's innovations would shift the focus from the gum to the cards themselves. Sy became the father of the modern-day baseball trading card.

Berger sent paid photographers to take pictures of the players during Spring Training, and he eventually had them signed to exclusive contracts. In the beginning, some of those contracts were valued from $75.00 to $125.00 a year. With everything in place, Berger created the 1952 Topps baseball card set. Those contracts started a bidding war with rival company, Bowman, for the best players in the game. In 1953, the cards were made from pictures of paintings of the players. Even though they were eye-catching and included gum, the set did better, but not as well as expected. Many players had cards in both sets, Bowman and Topps. Mickey Mantle signed exclusively with Bowman in 1954 and 1955, but returned to Topps in 1956. Stan Musial signed with Bowman and did not appear on a Topps card until 1959. Everything changed in 1956, when Topps purchased their rival Bowman, and Sy Berger settled on the size of the modern day baseball card that would fit nicely in a little boy's hand. The magic size of the 1957 Topps card is 2 1/2 inches by 3½ inches. They have stayed the same size since then.

In 1968, the players' union negotiated a deal with Topps to receive a percentage of the trading card revenue. Each player would now receive $400.00 per year for the rights to print their baseball card. By the mid eighties, gum was removed from the card packs, as the card itself became more important than the gum. The baseball card collecting business was in full bloom, and they were printed by the thousands.

Sy Berger was inducted into the National Jewish Hall of Fame on April 29, 2012. Berger died at the age of 91 on December 14, 2014. Sy is survived by his wife Gloria, his daughter Maxine, his sons Glenn and Gary; five grandchildren and two great-grandchildren. Berger worked for Topps for 50 years, 1947-1997, and then served as a consultant for another five years. In honor of the father of the modern-day baseball cards, Topps created card #137 in their 2004 set. The photo is of Sy Berger in a jacket, white shirt and blue tie. And yes, it has a facsimile autograph.

It has been reported that many years after the 1952 Topps cards were produced, that Berger had the equivalent of three garbage trucks full of unsold 1952 Topps cards loaded onto a barge and then dumped into the Atlantic Ocean to help create space at their warehouse. "Around 1959 or so, I went around to carnivals and offered them for a penny apiece and it got so bad I offered them at ten for a penny," Sy told "Sports Collectors Digest" in 2007. "They would say, 'We don't want them.'" Those cards were from the final print run of that year and included the trading cards of Mickey Mantle, "Pee Wee" Reese, Jackie Robinson, and Eddie Mathews, among others. With so many of the cards destroyed, it created a very small sampling of those players' cards, which in turn drove up the prices to outrageous levels. The Mantle rookie card is the most valuable card in the baseball card world after the 1909-1911 Tobacco cards known as the T206 Honus Wagner card.

In 1909, a company known as American Tobacco Company (ATC) sent out letters to 524 players asking permission to use their photo on a baseball card. Wagner did not give his consent and threatened legal action if they went ahead and created his baseball card. Unfortunately, ATC did not anticipate any resistance and about 40 of the Wagner cards were printed and distributed before production was stopped. The reason Wagner resisted has been a question of speculation. Although Wagner chewed tobacco he did not want young fans to purchase tobacco just to get his card and second, players were not paid enough for their likeness to be used. A 1952 Topps Mickey Mantle "rookie" card #311 graded in mint condition sold for around $3,000 in the early eighties, but is now currently valued at $165,000. In April of 2013, a T206 Wagner card sold for 2.1 million.

Topps continues to own the card business as they have produced series devoted to Elvis, Batman, "Star Wars" and Charlie Brown. In 2010, Justin Bieber could be seen on Topps cards. Despite the many different cards, baseball players are still tops in the trading card business. "A kid can readily identify with a ballplayer," Berger once said. "They're not terribly tall or physically enormous. A kid can look at one of our cards and see himself."

Now that's what I call a real cardboard hero.

How to Bite Through a Helmet

The sight of this man breaking the huddle would quicken your heartbeat. With their adrenaline flowing, opposing linemen called him "Sir." They asked about his family, his dog, and how things were going at home. Most of these giants stood several stories higher than the rest of us, and they hated the sound of a whistle. Whistles meant you had most-likely been caught doing something illegal, and the play was being called back. Wasted effort ticked these guys off. They owned faces that looked like they had blocked a punt, and no one could out-cuss them. Even Keith Jackson called them "The Big Uglies." To be a good offensive lineman, you have to have been born with a football name. Names like "Chuck" Bednarik, Mike Munchak, Jim Otto and Art Shell come to mind. If Munchak had been named Robby Phillips, he would have run track or played in the band. As an offensive lineman, you learned to live with a high jersey number and the screaming sounds of pain and horror in a pile of human flesh. You can't imagine what grown men will do to each other in the "pit." It's not uncommon to see linemen come stumbling out of a game like drunks being thrown out of a bar.

These guys loved nothing more than getting the back of a defensive lineman's jersey dirty. They understood the power of intimidation. He led the offensive linemen down the field like Sherman marching through Georgia. They wanted to hit you and the words "trap play" and "sweep" made them smile. The key to being a good offensive lineman is that you have to make your guy look at you, fight with you and focus on you and not the ball carrier or quarterback. "Their eyes can tell you when a stunt is on. I focus on their jersey number, never their head or hips. Those areas can be used to fake you out. When I make them look at me, eye to eye, I've got a chance," said Fuzzy. "That's when they usually start yelling, 'He's holding me.'" If Fuzzy Thurston could have learned how to bite through a helmet he would have.

Frederick Charles "Fuzzy" Thurston was born in Altoona, Wisconsin, on December 29, 1933. His father, Charles, was a common laborer who passed away when Fuzzy was two years old. His mom, Marie, found it tough to raise a family of eight by her self so Fuzzy spent some time growing up with an aunt who lived in Florida. He got his nickname for his curly hair as a baby. Fuzzy graduated from Altoona High School and received a scholarship to play basketball at Valparaiso University in Indiana. Remarkably, Altoona High School did not have a football program. Fuzzy was such a fine athlete that he was finally persuaded by the football coach to try out for the football team, before his junior year of college. In 1954, Fuzzy led the Crusaders of Valparaiso to the Indiana Collegiate Conference title and was selected All-American twice. Fuzzy was also named All-Conference for the 1954 and 1955 seasons, while being named the Conference's Top Lineman, in 1955.

Thurston was drafted in 1956 by the Philadelphia Eagles, but he did not make the team. He then joined the Army for a couple of years and later tried out and made the Baltimore Colts' team as a backup, in 1958. He would wear #64 for the Colts. That was the year that Baltimore beat the New York Giants in sudden death overtime, in what many referred to as the greatest game ever played. The offensive coordinator for the Giants was none other than Vince Lombardi, who liked what he saw in the film of Thurston's play. In 1959, before the season began, Lombardi became the head coach of the Packers and worked a trade with the Colts for Thurston. Fuzzy wore #63 for the rest of his career and played for Lombardi for nine seasons in Green Bay. He was the bedrock of the 1961, 1962, 1965, 1966 and 1967 championship teams, which included the first two Super Bowls.

The NFL locker room before game time is quieter than a Church on Monday morning. Guys are sitting in front of their lockers looking like they have lost their mothers. The defensive guys try to read or remember what they had watched on film all week. Offensive linemen apply Vaseline on their jerseys; clear for white jerseys and dark for the colored jerseys. Yes, it's illegal but done anyway. The intensity fills the room.

Offensive linemen would rather run block than pass block. They are aggressive by nature. "Take the game to the enemy" was their mindset. Paul Hornung once wrote in his book, Golden Boy, that Fuzzy, an otherwise excellent pass blocker, had a tough time pass-blocking the behemoth defensive tackle, Roger Brown, of the Detroit Lions. "So Fuzzy invented the Lookout Block," said Hornung. "In one game, Bart Starr had been sacked about six times. It got to be a joke," said Hornung. "So when the next pass play was called, just as Starr was getting ready to take the snap from center Jim Ringo, Fuzzy yelled out, 'Look Out, Bart.' That cracked everybody up," said Hornung.

Thurston was also well known for an answer he gave to a sportswriter's question after the "Ice Bowl." The temperature of that game in Green Bay against the Dallas Cowboys was played at 13 degrees below zero. The referees claimed that it was so cold that their whistles stuck to their lips. The sportswriter asked Fuzzy how he prepared to play in such cold weather. Thurston responded that he drank "about ten vodkas" in order to stay warm. The fact is Fuzzy would have never had the guts to drink before a game for fear that Lombardi would find out.

Offensive linemen are the worst golfers in the world. Maybe it's because they spend so much time in a three-point stance. They have bad breath on purpose and most of them take out their false teeth before the game. Offensive linemen never want to hear their opposing guys' names mentioned on the public address system. That means they made the tackle. Offensive lineman is really a misnomer. The offensive guy is really trying to defend his quarterback. Offensive lineman hate quick defensive linemen like Deacon Jones. "The offensive lineman's best friend is most times a good running back. They can fake the defensive player right into your block," smiled Fuzzy. "Offensive guards have three different pulling plays; short pull, long pull and the deep pull," said Thurston. "Defensive players come at you in different ways, that's why we watch film. I may have to hook a linebacker in or kick a cornerback out of the play." Defensive linemen have three options to attack. They can meet you head on, dodge you or undercut you. At 6 feet 1 inch tall and weighing 245, Fuzzy was one of the brooms in Green Bay's famous sweep.

Forever the optimist, Thurston was once hit so hard by defensive tackle Buck Buchanan of the Kansas City Chiefs that his steel face mask was bent. "As he came to the sideline," said Jerry Kramer, "I asked him how things were going with Buchanan? Fuzzy answered, 'I'm kicking his butt.'"

Fuzzy Thurston was adored by people everywhere. I think it was because he was both a player and a fan. His motto to future Green Bay Packer players was simple: avoid the distractions, enjoy the game and respect the team. Teammate Dave Robinson referred to Thurston as "the heart and soul of the Packers. He was the thing that made us a team." Fuzzy played in 116 games and is one of only three in NFL history to participate on six NFL championship teams. The other two were teammates Forrest Gregg and Herb Adderley. Thurston retired in 1967 and was inducted into the Green Bay Packers' Hall of Fame in 1975.

After football, Fuzzy built and owned a chain of taverns around Wisconsin known as Fuzzy's #63 Left Guard Bar & Grill. Even the phone number to the bars ended in 6363. Fuzzy would have turned 81 years old on December 29, 2014. Cancer made it difficult for him to speak and Alzheimer's disease stole away his memories. Cancer had claimed Thurston's larynx in the early eighties and three years ago he was diagnosed with colon and liver cancer. Thurston died on Sunday December 14, 2014. He has been staying in an assisted living facility in Howard, Wisconsin. Alzheimer's is a bad way to die, but a worst way to live. His #63 will never be worn again in Green Bay, as it has been retired. Over three hundred gathered at Lambeau Field on Friday December 19 to say good-bye to one of the architects of the "Green Bay Sweep," at that time one of the most unstoppable plays in professional football. Most interior offensive linemen remain obscure, but with a name like Fuzzy, you had to be a guard. This was not the case with Jerry Kramer and Fuzzy Thurston. Their names will be linked together for all time. They were like peas and carrots; it's impossible to say one name without the other. Eleven players from the 1964 through 1967 Packer's teams have been enshrined in the Pro Football Hall of Fame. That's half the starting team. Why not Jerry Kramer or Fuzzy Thurston? These two will always remain frozen in time.

As a junior in high school, I once spent a week at the Johnny Unitas sports camp during the summer. During camp we watched game film at night. One of those films was about the "Green Bay sweep." The message: the sight of Kramer and Thurston leading either Paul Hornung or Jim Taylor around the line of scrimmage made defensive backs faint. Stopping these guys was like trying to halt a rockslide.

Fuzzy was named to the 1961 and 1962 All-Pro teams.

Thurston was elected to the Indiana Football Hall of Fame in 1982 and the Wisconsin Athletic Hall of Fame in 2003. Fuzzy lost his wife after 55 years of marriage. Sue passed away in 2012. Fuzzy also left behind a daughter Tori, two sons Mark and Griff, and three grandchildren.

Oklahoma quarterback and now in the House of Representatives, J.C. Watts once said, "It doesn't take a lot of strength to hang on. It takes a lot of strength to let go." When the end comes for our heroes we find ourselves asking how could this be true. The answer sometimes: It just is. Fuzzy realized at the end that he had influenced a lot of people along the way, guys like me. He knew he had done the best he could and lived a clean life. He was a great player but also a nice guy. "It's such an honor to be a Green Bay Packer, and I cherish that every day of my life," said Thurston.

Of the 43 men who played on Lombardi's last team in 1967, 15 are now deceased. The average age of those alive is 72.2. The Glory Years are becoming the Golden Years. We have already lost Henry Jordon, Lew Carpenter, Lionel Aldridge, Max McGee, Ron Kostelnik, Elijah Pitts, Gale Gillingham and Ray Nitschke. Teammates Paul Hornung and Jerry Kramer are both 79. Bart Starr turned 80 and Forest Gregg is now 81. Father time moves on. I can still close my eyes and see Fuzzy and Jerry in perfect step, running at a 45 degree angle, a search-and-destroy mission if there ever was one.

FACING THE ENEMY

Elvis Presley once said, "When things go wrong, don't go wrong with them." What Elvis meant was, don't do something permanently stupid just because you are temporarily upset. This fellow was fast and fearless; he got into his opponent's head like a bad sinus infection. He guarded you to death, teeth in your stomach, just not going to let you beat him. He was scary, a strong guy; if he ever decided to rush the court, he could turn the place into an empty parking lot. If you talked down to him, he would beat you up so badly you'd be the only guy in Heaven in a wheelchair. He owned length and ball skills, and he could shoot it from the concession stands. "Bad News" didn't just catch a basketball, he attacked it. He was a big fellow who could catch and finish. He may bloody your nose, poke you in the eye, anything to break your will. Some say he was hooked on a feeling. The same feeling he got when he snorted cocaine. In the end, he became "fool's gold," a great player that you could not depend on.

Marvin "Bad News" Barnes, a basketball shooting star, disappeared faster than the ABA's red, white and blue basketball. It would only take thirty minutes to film his life story. When they discover the center of the universe, a lot of people will be disappointed they are not it. Barnes would have been one of those people. The only thing this guy loved more than basketball was himself. The game of basketball came easy to him. It was real life that was much harder. In the end, Marvin Barnes was not able to outplay his own demons. Every time he looked in the mirror, he was facing the enemy.

Marvin Jerome Barnes was born July 27, 1952, in North Kingstown, Rhode Island, but grew up in Providence. His father served in the Navy while Marvin shared a bed with his mother and sister at home, until he became a teenager. Marvin grew up wanting to play football, but his mother said "No." This right-handed power forward would grow to 6'9" tall and weighed 230 pounds. Barnes attended and won a state championship at Central High School in Providence, before enrolling in 1971 at Providence College. *The Providence Journal* claimed Barnes was "the greatest basketball talent the city had ever produced." It was at Central High School that Barnes began to earn his nickname, "Bad News." Barnes joined a gang that attempted to rob a city bus. He was identified quickly since he was wearing his state championship jacket. What was he thinking? His name was embroidered on the jacket.

One of the most talented basketball players, Barnes was considered unstoppable. Marvin Barnes averaged 20.7 points per game while playing 89 games at Providence College (1971-1974). On the court, he shot over 51% from the floor, while pulling down 17.9 rebounds per game. In 1972, Barnes lost his cool and attacked a teammate, Larry Ketvirtis, with a tire iron. Barnes pled guilty to assault, paid his teammate ten grand, and was placed on probation.

Marvin set the Providence scoring record on December 15, 1973, by pouring in 52 points against Austin Peay. That record still stands today. Barnes became the first basketball player in NCAA play-off history to score ten times in his first ten field-goal attempts. He is currently tied at second place behind Kenny Walker, who connected on his first 11 shots in the NCAA play-offs in 1986. Marvin led the nation in rebounding during the 1973-74 season, while at Providence. Marvin Barnes was chosen first-team All-American that season. With Ernie DiGregorio and Kevin

Stacom, Barnes led Providence, coached by Dave Gavitt, to the 1973 NCAA tournament played in St. Louis. The Fryers lost to the Memphis State Tigers in the National Semifinals.

At 22 years of age, Marvin was drafted with the 2nd pick of the first round of the 1974 National Basketball Association (NBA) Draft by the Philadelphia 76ers. Bill Walton went to the Portland Trailblazers with the first pick. Marvin was also drafted in the first round by the Spirits of St. Louis of the American Basketball Association (ABA). Marvin chose the ABA and played for the Spirits from 1974 to 1976. The choice was easy as Philadelphia offered him a two-year 1.6 million dollar contact, compared to the St. Louis 2.2 million dollar offer. His ABA debut occurred on October 18, 1974. Barnes played well enough to be chosen Rookie of the Year. During his first two seasons with the Spirits, he averaged more than 24 points and 13 rebounds a game.

Still, he remained unhappy and once disappeared from the team for several days before being found in a pool hall in Dayton, Ohio.

There is a story told that Marvin owned a Rolls Royce and he would drive around and pick up kids and take them to McDonald's. He would arrive at the arena with the kids, French fries and quarter-pounders, fifteen minutes before the game was set to begin. The coach would come unglued and then Barnes would go out and put up 40 points in a win.

The Spirits of St. Louis met the New York Nets in the 1975 ABA Eastern Division Semi-finals playoffs. Barnes poured in 41 points in the first game and 37 points in the second game. The Spirits closed out the Nets four games to one, to meet the Kentucky Colonels in the Eastern Division Finals. Kentucky, the eventual ABA Champion, beat the Spirits four games to one behind the play of MVP, Artis Gilmore. "During that series, Julius Erving of the Nets was second best player on the court," said the 22-year-old

Spirits' announcer named Bob Costas. "During the season, I saw him go for 35 and 25 in games against Dr. J and be the best player on the court."

But Marvin's success was not enough to keep him from the downside of lots of money and no self-discipline. Marvin later admitted that he started using drugs during his second season while in St. Louis. His skills eroded as his drug use spiraled out of control. On August 5, 1976, Barnes was picked by the Detroit Pistons from the Spirits of St. Louis in the dispersal draft and played his first NBA game on November 24, 1976. Barnes violated his probation in October of 1976, when an unloaded gun was found in his carry-on bag at the Detroit Metropolitan Airport. He was sentenced and served 152 days in the Rhode Island State Prison. Barnes returned to the Pistons after his release and was later arrested for burglary, drug possession and trespassing. Barnes was on a fast train to nowhere.

Barnes would end up playing for four different NBA teams during his next four years, as his average dropped to 9.2 points per game and 5.5 rebounds. On November 23, 1977, Barnes was traded to the Buffalo Braves for Gus Gerard and John Shumate. In 1978, the Braves moved their franchise to San Diego and became the Clippers. On August 4, 1978, Marvin was on the move again, to the Boston Celtics from the San Diego Clippers. On February 7, 1979, Barnes was waived by the Celtics. He had played in just 38 games with Boston, before being released. Barnes later admitted to snorting cocaine while sitting on the bench as a member of the Celtics. On September 30, 1979, Barnes signed as a free agent with the Clippers for a second time. By this time, Barnes was carrying two guns, which he hung up in his locker during the game. Barnes was then caught stealing x-rated videotapes to sell for drug money and was sentenced to 13 months in prison. While in prison, he began to study the Bible and went to church services. There seemed to be some hope for Barnes. He was waived by San Diego on

October 10, 1979, and signed again on January 30, 1980, by these same Clippers. By 1980, his drug use had stolen away his basketball career, and he ended up homeless and destitute in San Diego, California. It was reported that, at times, he lived in abandoned buildings and junk cars. It has also been said that he had enrolled in nineteen different drug rehabs and served four separate prison terms. He was no longer considered a threat to anyone but himself.

In 1980, Barnes played basketball in Italy and then continued to play until 1986, with several other teams of the Central Basketball Association (CBA) located in Detroit, Ohio, and Evansville, Indiana.

He was finally able to get much needed help in a rehab center which allowed him put his life back together. Marvin Barnes returned to South Providence and made an attempt to reach out to kids in Rhode Island, urging them not to make the same mistake he had. He worked for the Rebound Foundation, a nonprofit organization supported by the former owners of the Spirits. It was reported that one day Barnes took twenty kids off the playground and bought them all new sneakers and ice cream.

In the end some nice things and some not-so-nice things were said about Barnes. Spirits' owner Donald Schupak was quoted in a 1976 *New York Times* article, "He's just totally unreliable. He's probably in the top five players in basketball, talent-wise. In terms of value to a team, he's probably in the bottom ten percent."

Celtics' legend Dave Cowens said, "He did things easily. Other people made it look hard. I'd say he was a combination of Alex English and Connie Hawkins."

British politician, Gilbert Parker, once wrote, "There is no refuge from memory or remorse. The spirits of our foolish deeds haunt us with or without repentance." Marvin Barnes died on a Monday afternoon, September 8, 2015. Barnes was 62. He had missed his latest court appearance scheduled that Monday morning. He is survived by his mother, Lula, and his sister, Alfreda. Barnes was married two times and divorced twice. It has been written that after several years of living clean, he relapsed into a life of more drug use. People are defined by how they act at their lowest point. Interestingly, everyone liked Marvin and he never blamed anyone else for his troubles. Marvin Barnes played in two ABA All-Star Games, in 1975 and 1976. He scored 5,034 points, snatched down 2,873 rebounds and blocked 438 shots. The only thing that could stop Marvin Barnes on a basketball court was cocaine.

In one of Barnes' last statements before he died, he said, "I got introduced to some drug dealers and I got real close with them. They became like my family. I was living my fantasy. I always wanted to be a "gangsta," a drug dealer, a pimp, a player, a hustler. I was, like, I'm gonna die young, die fast, gonna die quick, and I'm gonna have fun. That's it." Too bad, he got his wish.

TEAM PLAYER

Albert Schweitzer once wrote, "One thing I know, the only ones among you who will really be happy are those who will have sought and found how to serve." He loved and served the game of basketball for 17 years. His first words may have been Bill Russell or Oscar Robertson. This is the story of a tall man that left an extra long shadow. At 6' 11" he was so big he had his own climate. He was also thin enough to have problems with wind. This guy weighed so little he didn't even leave any footprints. His arms and legs looked like a spider spinning a web on the court. Some said he was so skinny he could sleep in the barrel of a 12-gauge shotgun. He was raised to work hard and to play hard. If the results were not satisfactory, he worked harder and played harder. His secret to success was he never gave up. This guy knew how to play "big boy basketball." He was turtle quiet and some said one-half enforcer and one-half asleep. This fellow was a great defender and always had an appointment with the rim. Coach Larry Brown was asked by *USA Today*, "What do you think of Caldwell Jones?" "When he retires," said Brown. "I think they should have a farewell tour for him." Caldwell Jones just played basketball, no chest bumping, hand signals or facial expressions. If Denzel Washington had been 6' 11" with a hook shot, he could have been Caldwell Jones.

Caldwell "Pops" Jones was born on August 4, 1950, in McGehee, Arkansas. Caldwell was one of eight very tall children born to Caldwell Sr. and Cecelia. The Jones families were cotton farmers. The shortest of the bunch was their only daughter, Clovis, who would grow to 6' 3" tall. In 1969, Caldwell graduated from Desha Central High School, located in Rohwer, Arkansas, before attending Albany State University in Georgia. Caldwell was rather skinny and would top out at 6' 11" tall, but weighed only 217 pounds. For 18 straight years (1961-1979), six of the Jones brothers, starting with Oliver, played center for Albany State University; and they loved playing in pick-up games. Oliver would eventually become the basketball coach at Albany State for 28 years. Oliver retired in 2000. I guess you could say they were "keeping up with the Joneses."

In 1973, after four years in college, he joined the San Diego Conquistadors of the ABA (American Basketball Association). His head coach was none other than Wilt Chamberlain. Pops averaged scoring 15.8 points per game, led the ABA in blocked shots his first season, and then played in the 1975 ABA All-Star Game. His ABA all-time record of 12 block shots in a single game still stands.

Caldwell played with three more ABA teams (San Diego Sails, Kentucky Colonels and Spirits of St. Louis) before joining Head Coach Gene Shue and the Philadelphia 76ers when the two leagues merged together, prior to the 1976-77 season. They handed him the #11. The 76ers were loaded with great players like Julius Erving, George McGinnis, Joe "Jellybean" Bryant, Doug Collins, Darryl Dawkins and Bobby Jones, just to name a few. In Pops' first season with the 76ers, he took a more defensive role, while blocking 200 shots and helping the team to a 50-32 win-loss record. His play helped provide Philly with a trip to the NBA Finals, against the Portland Trailblazers. Portland upset the 76ers by winning four games to two. The following year, Philly reached the Eastern Conference Finals only to lose again, this time to the Washington Bullets. There were so many great players on the team that Jones wore out his uniform sliding up and down the bench. The 76ers played in the

NBA Finals twice more in 1980 and 1982, losing both times to Kareem Abdul-Jabbar and the Los Angeles Lakers. Jones was twice named to the NBA All-Defensive team while with Philadelphia. It has been said that Jones would sit and answer questions from the media after every Sixers game, while drinking a six-pack of beer.

After six years with Philadelphia, Jones was traded to the Houston Rockets for Moses Malone. Sooner or later everyone gets replaced. Human nature is always, 'What about me?" That was not the case for Caldwell. The good news was that in Houston he got to play with his brother Major Jones. The bad news was that the 76ers won the 1983 NBA title with Malone at center. 76ers coach Billy Cunningham offered Caldwell Jones his own NBA Championship ring, but Jones turned him down. Caldwell joined the Chicago Bulls for the 1984-85 season. It would be Michael Jordan's rookie season. Pops was traded again the following year and spent four seasons in Portland. His final season (1990) was spent in San Antonio, Texas, with the Spurs, tutoring a young kid from the Naval Academy named David Robinson. The old-timers say that Caldwell Jones and Michael Cooper were the only defenders that gave Larry Bird fits.

Caldwell Jones retired at the end of that season, at the age of 39. Caldwell played for eight teams in 17 seasons and he never did anything to draw negative attention to himself. Jones played in 1,299 games, scored 10,241 points, pulled down 10,685 rebounds and managed to block 2,297 shots. It was quite a career.

Caldwell and three of his brothers (Wilbert, Charles and Major) would play professional basketball in either the NBA or ABA or both, for a total of 37 years. Two other brothers found playing time in minor league basketball.

Jones understood we only get a short amount of time to be great at what we want to be. But he managed to play for 17 years. Jones was reliable and hard working, owned a fluid hook shot, a short-range jump shot and was an awesome rebounder. He shot better than 47 percent from the floor, for his career. I never got to meet Caldwell Jones, but saw him play many times in person with the Spurs. Every time I turned the television on, he was there doing the dirty work. He would battle the big men as best he could. He once said in an interview with NBA writer, Fran Blinebury, "You know how to stop Kareem Abdul-Jabbar? You push him and you push him and you push him and you push him. And then you hope he just steps out of bounds." Jones wore two big knee pads and one high-top and one low-top shoe to provide support for a damaged ankle. I've been told he loved watching old westerns and cartoons.

Caldwell Jones died of a massive heart attack while hitting golf balls at the driving range in Stockbridge, Georgia. The date was September 21, 2014. He was but 64 years old. Caldwell and his wife Vanessa were doing what they always did on Sundays. They attended church with their three daughters Zori, Maya and Leah, and then headed out for a bite to eat. The Sunday meals at the Jones table included turning off all electric devices and talking about that day's sermon or discussing a topic of Mom's choosing. On that day, Vanessa asked everyone one question. "If you could do one thing, and only one thing every day for the rest of your life, what would you pick?" Caldwell gave a sports answer to that question. "Caldwell had never been much of a golfer," said Vanessa. "He discovered the game late in life. But you know, he wrote that he would play golf if that's the only thing he could do. That's what he would do every day for the rest of his life."

It had started out as just a normal day for the Jones family. You know, there is such a thing as a simple life. Jones believed that we do deserve everything good that happens to us. He also enjoyed every moment that he was with his loved ones. Those moments can never be taken away from you and will be with you when the dark days come. I would like to think he got his wish. It reminds me of something I read one time: "Live your life with a plan and die empty.'

TEACHING THE T-FORMATION

Sports writer Howard Bryant once wrote, "You don't have to win the last game of the season to be important." Most fans would believe that this statement is contradictory to why we play sports. Every player should want to win the Super bowl, World Series or NBA Championship, but the odds are long and sometimes unattainable, just ask General Manager Billy Bean of the Oakland Athletics or the Buffalo Bills. In Bryant's case he focuses on the word "important" and with that I agree.

This fellow, about whom I will tell you, became very important to the world of football, especially in New York, yet his teams never won an NFL Championship Game. With this guy in charge, if you didn't play hard you would find yourself standing on the sidelines with the cheerleaders. He was intense and demanded more from you than you demanded from yourself. Yet, he spoke to his players like a father talks to his son. They respected him for that. He was a good-looking guy who grew up as a left handed quarterback, small in stature and very smart. As a coach, this man's office looked like the headquarters for the invasion of Normandy. He may have watched more game film than Siskel and Ebert. He believed there are only two things we can control, energy and effort; and this guy had lots of both. He seemed to notice everything. It was like he had eyes in the back of "your" head. His teachings of the T-formation offense may have been the greatest thing since the invention of penicillin. He was also a real wheeler-dealer; with enough time, he could get the Fourth of July moved to another day. He once said "No matter what you are told there is no such thing as an even trade."

Famous high school basketball Coach Morgan Wooten once said, "A player will never forget his coach. He may forget his teachers but never his coach and what kind of person they were." Allie Sherman coached the New York Football Giants from 1961 until 1969, earning two NFL Coach of the Year Awards in 1961 and 1962, the first time in league history that a coach won that honor in back-to-back seasons. Missed yes, forgotten, never.

Alex "Allie" Sherman was born in Brooklyn, New York, on February 10, 1923, into a Jewish family that had emigrated to the U.S. from Russia in 1920. Allie attended Boys' High School in Brooklyn and, at the age of 13, tried out for the football team. He weighed only 125 pounds. The coach convinced him to play handball instead. Allie became the captain of the high school handball team that won several titles. He graduated in 1939 at the age of 16, with honors, and enrolled in Brooklyn College. A little bigger and a lot smarter, he tried out again for football. Only this time his smarts and dedication, not his size, allowed him to stick on the team. Allie Sherman became the starting quarterback in 1940. Sherman was one of the few who ran the T-formation and led his 1941-42 Brooklyn College team to an upset win over City College. One of his teammates was none other than Johnny Most, the former Hall of Fame play-by-play voice of the Boston Celtics. Sherman graduated in 1943 (cum laude, a psychology major).

By 1943, his knowledge of this new offense called the T-formation earned him a backup quarterback job with the Philadelphia Eagles, where he would help Head Coach Earl "Greasy" Neale by mentoring the Eagles' All-Pro quarterback, Roy Zimmerman. "Never have I seen a player with a greater understanding of the game. He was so dedicated, he insisted on rooming with a lineman. He wanted to absorb the way a lineman thought," said Neale about Allie. Sherman once said in jest, "During my five NFL seasons, I was the best left-handed holder on extra points in the league." Sherman would also play both quarterback and defensive back for the Eagles (1943-1947). In 1947, Sherman led the Eagles to the NFL Championship Game, where they lost 28-21 to the Chicago Cardinals. Sherman played in 51 games and completed 66 passes for 823 yards and nine touchdowns. He also threw 10 interceptions. Allie rushed 93 times for 44 yards and four touchdowns.

He retired from playing at the end of that season and in 1948, joined the coaching staff of the Patterson Panthers, a minor league football team located in New Jersey. His team won that league's championship. In 1949, he was hired as the backfield coach for the New York Football Giants, under Giants' head coach Steve Owen. Sherman's job was to convert Charlie Conerly to a T-formation quarterback. When Owen retired in 1953, Allie was passed over for the head coach's job, so he headed north to coach the Winnipeg Blue Bombers of the Canadian Football League. His team made the playoff three years in a row. One of Sherman's players was future head coach of the Minnesota Vikings, Bud Grant.

In 1957, Sherman returned to the Giants as a scout. He became the offensive coordinator in 1959, replacing Vince Lombardi, who had been hired by the Green Bay Packers as their head coach. Lombardi tried to persuade Sherman to go with him to Green Bay, but Allie decided to stay with the Giants. Allie Sherman became the New York Football Giants' head coach in 1961, replacing Jim Lee Howell. He went out and got several young players to help his roster. Y.A. Tittle, Joe Walton, Del Shofner and defensive back Allan Webb, to name a few. The Giants' record would improve from 6-4-2 in 1960 to 10-3-1 in 1961, and then win the NFL Eastern Division. As luck would have it, Sherman's Giants would meet Lombardi's Packers for the NFL Championship. Green bay won 37-0, but Sherman was named the NFL Coach of the Year because of the dramatic improvement of wins and losses. In 1962, Frank Gifford returned from injury and helped the Giants claim another NFL Eastern Division title, with a 12-2 win-loss record. Again, Sherman would be voted Coach of the Year even though the Giants lost the NFL Championship to Green Bay again, 16-7. Don Shula and Joe Gibbs are the only other coaches to duplicate back-to-back Coach of the Year Awards. The Giants would win their division again in 1963 and faceoff with the Chicago Bears. The Bears knocked Tittle out of the game with a leg injury and won 14-10.

The Giants' record fell to 2-10-2 in 1964 and fans were calling for his release. Sherman had traded the popular linebacker Sam Huff, Rosey Grier, Don Chandler and tackle Dick Modzelewski all before the season, and the fans were beside themselves.

It was Allie Sherman who broke the news to Rosey Grier that he had been traded to the L.A. Rams. Rosey was stunned. He later said about Allie Sherman, "I had nothing in common with him. He was a good football coach and I respected him."

Pete Gogolak, the NFL's first soccer-style kicker joined the N.Y. Giants in 1966. He played nine seasons and is still the franchise's career scoring leader with 646 points. "Allie always treated me well," said Gogolak. "He didn't try to change my form. He was really a good guy to play for."

In 1965 and 1966, Sherman hired Emlen Tunnell and Rosey Brown, the first two African-American assistant coaches in the NFL. Sherman would never have another winning team with the Giants and, after losing all five preseason games, was fired before the start of the 1969 season, with five years remaining on his ten-year contract. He was replaced by Alex Webster.

Sherman and his staff would coach three consecutive

NFL Pro Bowl Games. Sherman's eight-year record with the Giants stands at 57-51-4. Steve Owens, Bill Parcells and Tom Coughlin are the only other men to coach the Giants for at least eight seasons. The Giants would not appear in an NFL Championship Game again until Super Bowl XXI, in 1986.

Allie Sherman was also the first professional head coach to cross over into the media, serving as an on-air analyst after his coaching days were done. Allie was very media-friendly and conducted never-before-done daily press conferences, during team training camp. Every Monday, after a game, he provided film clips and evaluations, while answering questions. He even held a huge Christmas party every year, for all the New York media. He produced and owned the first pro football coach's weekly television show that included guests. Sherman also co-produced a Monday Night radio program called "Ask Allie." He hosted the first nationally syndicated TV show called "Pro Football Special." He even appeared on ESPN as a pre-game pro football analyst. Sherman was also involved with Ed Sabol in creating NFL Films.

Eventually Sherman was asked to join Steve Ross, the CEO of Warner Communications Inc. Together they purchased cable television companies around the country. They not only worked with universities, but also professional baseball teams like the Pittsburgh Pirates. This company was eventually purchased and is known today as Fox Sports Networks. Sherman even dabbled in World Cup Soccer and became the president of the New York City Off-Track Betting Corporation.

Allie Sherman died at his home in Manhattan, New York, on Saturday January 3, 2015. He was surrounded by family. It was a good death. Sherman is survived by his wife of 63 years, Joan, one son and two daughters. He also had two grandchildren. He is a member of the National Jewish Hall of Fame in Long Island and the Brooklyn College Sports

Hall of Fame. This guy was a good man, he didn't even jaywalk. Sherman was one of the great citizens of the game. Groucho Marx once said, "Getting older is no problem. You just have to live long enough." Allie Sherman lived 91 years.

STU

George Bernard Shaw once said, "The single biggest problem with communication is the illusion its taken place." There was never any doubt with this guy. He took us to the barbershop, spoke to the hip-hop culture, and added a healthy dose of church. He touched a whole segment of sports fans out there in the real world with his words. He was "Cool & The Gang," "Earth, Wind and Fire," and "Sly & the Family Stone" all rolled into one. With his catchphrases and street cred, he became a master at the language of sports for the inner-city kids. He needed the spotlight and attention, like the rest of us need sunlight and oxygen. His nickname could have been "Sideshow." Giving this guy a script to read was like giving Ricky Henderson the steal sign, feeding Dr. J. an outlet pass, or throwing Jerry Rice a post pattern; the results were going to be fantastic. He spoke with a voice that was unafraid, and he was as friendly as a newborn puppy. He may have been born wearing a three-piece suit, and some say he owned a heart two sizes too big. He also had North Carolina Blue pumping through his veins.

His motto was "Don't sweat the small stuff, and everything is small stuff." His grin would give you a headache, and he had a way of getting beyond the media reports. In his business he was known as a catch-and-shoot guy. He was better than a bowl full of "Lucky Charms." I've even heard his mother's fried chicken could bring peace to the Middle East. This man helped create the word "celebrity" for sportscasters. He's completed more commercials than passes and couldn't buy a bucket on EBay. He was a charmer, a warrior and a father but, in the end, for all of us he was just "Stu." Why? Boo-Yah! Because he was a sportscaster; Stuart Scott was as cool as the other side of the pillow.

Stuart Orlando "Stu" Scott was born in Chicago, Illinois, to Orlando Ray and Jacqueline Scott. The date was July 19, 1965. The Scott family, consisting of four children, moved to Winston-Salem, North Carolina, when Stuart was seven years old. His father became a postal inspector. Stu graduated from Richard J. Reynolds High School in 1983. He had been the captain of the football team, ran track and as a senior, was elected Vice President of the Student Government. Scott enrolled at the University of North Carolina (UNC) and graduated in 1987 with a degree in Speech Communications. While at UNC he worked at the student-run radio station, known as WXYC. Scott claimed that he and his roommate did not have cable while in college. Therefore, he never watched ESPN. Interestingly, ESPN became his first fulltime job in television.

In 1987, Stuart's first job landed him in Florence, South Carolina, as a news reporter and weekend sports anchor for WPDE-TV. Stu had originally sent out 27 resumes and had heard back from none of them. He would leave a year later (1988) for WRAL-TV5 in Raleigh, North Carolina. By 1990, you could find Stuart in Orlando, Florida, working as a sports reporter and sports anchor for WESH, an NBC affiliate.

In 1993, Al Jaffe hired Stuart Scott to work for ESPN2. Jaffe was the Vice-President for talent and he was looking for personalities who would appeal to a younger audience. Scott's first gig was called *SportsSmash*. This assignment consists of two short sports casts per hour during ESPN2's *SportsNight* program. Scott represented new-school. He owned the two most important qualities for television; he was entertaining and right. After Keith Olbermann left

SportsNight for *SportsCenter*, Scott took his place. He would soon become a regular on *SportCenter* and, over time, he was teamed up with Rich Eisen, Steve Levy, Kenny Mayne and Dan Patrick.

In 1996, the team of Stuart Scott and Rich Eisen aired at 1:00 a.m. on *SportsCenter*, nightly. These two loved nothing better than singing a good duet every night, coming and going, in and out of commercial breaks. My radio partner, Dennis Quinn, and I continue this strategy on our own radio show, *The Q & A Session*, which airs on ESPN 1440 KEYS, located in Corpus Christi, Texas. We don't sing well, but more importantly, we have fun. By 2002, Scott was a studio host and eventually became the lead host in 2008. When *Monday Night Football* moved to ESPN in 2006, Scott hosted the on-site show.

On a Sunday morning, in 2007, before he was to cover the *Monday Night Football* in Pittsburgh, Scott experienced a stomach ache which got progressively worse. He decided to go to the hospital instead of the game. There he had his appendix removed and then learned he had cancer. Two days later, Scott underwent colon surgery and started chemotherapy. Stuart Scott continued to cover major events for ESPN while being treated for cancer. These events included the Super Bowl, NBA Finals, World Series and NCAA basketball tournament. His cancer went into remission until it returned in 2011. More treatment put him back in remission, but not for long. He was diagnosed with cancer again on January 14, 2013. By 2014, Scott had received 58 infusions of chemotherapy. Radiation and more minor surgery was required, all while Scott continued his life as a father and host on ESPN. On July 16, 2014, Scott was honored with the Jimmy V. Award for his ongoing fight against the dreaded disease. He was suffering from kidney and liver complications, and the prognosis did not look good. Scott told the audience, "When you die, it does not mean that you lose to cancer. You beat cancer by how you live, why you live, and in the manner in which you live." He ended his speech with, "Have a great rest of your night, have a great rest of your life." That in essence was Stuart Scott, a better man when he knew he was dying. His talent, work ethic and faith were never called into question. The V Foundation for Cancer Research has now established the Stuart Scott Memorial Cancer Research Fund.

I briefly met Stuart Scott at the 2002 ESPY Awards. The show occurred on July 10th and this was the first year that the awards show was being held in Los Angeles, at the brand new Kodak Theater. I was with a group of about fifty sports radio broadcasters who worked for ESPN affiliates around the country. The night before the event, there was a party held at the Kodak Theater that we all attended. It was there that I met Linda Cohn, Rich Eisen, Bob Ley and an injured Stuart Scott. On April 3, 2002, three months before the ESPY Awards show, Stu got hit in the face with a football while attending the New York Jets training camp. He had been there filming a special for ESPN. The blow damaged his cornea. He did receive surgery afterwards but soon began to suffer a drooping eyelid. Scott began to wear glasses shortly thereafter.

The next night before the ESPY Awards, we were all introduced individually and walked down the Red Carpet into the event. I followed Green Bay Packer Hall-of-Fame football player, Paul Hornung, and preceded tennis star, Serena Williams. Samuel Jackson hosted the show, and I sat in the upper deck between the late Ralph Wiley, a writer for *Sports Illustrated,* and *Kansas City Star* writer, Jason Whitlock. This place was pure energy.

Stu died early Sunday morning, January 4, 2015. He was but 49. Stuart Scott married Kimberly in 1993. They had two daughters Taelor and Sydni and they lived in Avon, Connecticut. They divorced in 2007. Scott was in another relationship with Kristen Spodobalski at the time of his death.

He was paid tribute by many athletes and his former partners of the ESPN. "Stuart Scott changed the way we talked about sports," said Michael Wilbon. At one point, Stu became as famous as the athletes he covered. For twenty-one years, Stu blended sports talk and African-American culture in a way that had never been used before. He became the sound of change. He talked the way kids talked at home. He appealed to a younger demographic, and no one had ever seen or heard anyone like him on television. ESPN understood that 80 percent of the players in the NBA were African-American and 70 percent, in the NFL. What they didn't know was how important it was to have someone these players could relate to. Stuart Scott's voice filled that roll with style and passion.

Scott became known as "the king" for his many catchphrases like "Boo-Yah," "Game recognizes game," "Just call him butter 'cause he's on a roll," and my favorite, "You ain't gotta go home, but you gotta get the heck up outta here." Stu received a lot of hate mail because people resented his hip-hop style and although ESPN had issues in the beginning with his delivery, they stuck with him.

Tim Meadows of *Saturday Night Live* portrayed Scott in 1999. Stu appeared in music videos and also displayed his writing talents by contributing monthly to *ESPN the Magazine* in his column referred to as *Holla*. Some of his more impressive interviews included Michael Jordan, President Bill Clinton, Sammy Sosa, "Tiger" Woods and President Barack Obama.

Stuart Scott would have told you, it's okay to fail and it does not mean you're a failure. Scott continued to work because it made him feel normal. He never claimed to be Superman, but youth doesn't bother to wave goodbye. In the end, Stuart Scott's courage was staggering. He wore a tee-shirt with "EVERYDAY I FIGHT" printed on it, when he worked out, and never asked the doctors what stage of cancer he was in. "I haven't wanted to know...I'm trying to fight it the best I can," said Scott. There's an old Chinese proverb that goes like this, "As long as there's one person on this earth that remembers you, it isn't over." I've got a feeling the name Stuart Scott will be remembered for a while.

UNSUNG HERO

Ralph Waldo Emerson once said, "Do not go where the path may lead, go instead where there is no path, and leave a trail." This guy was so big he was worth three electoral votes. He had no choice but to leave a trail. If you saw his footprints in the sand you'd run. He owned the toughness of a sidewalk, and his shoulders were as wide as a door. The man was about the size of your average four-lane bridge. The word "fear" was not in his vocabulary. In his day, defensive linemen were taught to come in high when they tackled a quarterback. That way you could either destroy their vision in the passing lanes or break their arms. He wasn't complicated, just consistent, and he could muster the speed of a racquetball. This guy looked so calm on the outside that he made Tom Landry look kinky, but the fact is he was so intense at game time that he could change the temperature on the field. He didn't just ride in on a bale of hay from North Carolina; he made the kind of plays that made you lean forward in your seat, and you knew no one on the field was safe. As a great athlete he had the willingness to pay the price, to give it his all for a moment in time. I wondered how many times a running back came to the sidelines and told his coach, we need to change the game plan. We can't run against this guy. He was so young when he was drafted, he didn't know how to shave; but he sure knew how to rush the passer. He loved hitting quarterbacks and, no matter what he did to them, he never felt bad. The guy was so good you would get a lump in your throat watching him hit ball carriers. As a kid he was hungry and poor, and he never had two twenty-dollar bills to rub together. He would eat anything that wouldn't eat him. Jethro Pugh became the unsung hero of the "Doomsday Defense," a group that hurt more people than the plague.

Jethro Pugh Jr. was born in Windsor, North Carolina, on July 3, 1944. Very intelligent, Pugh graduated from Bertie High School and then enrolled at Elizabeth City State University, at the age of 16. He played on both sides of the ball and became a two-time All-CIAA (Central Intercollegiate Athletic Association) defensive end, in 1963 and 1964. Pugh is only one of five players to have his jersey retired at ECSU.

In 1965, Pugh became an 11th round draft pick out of Elizabeth City State University, for the Dallas Cowboys. He was just 20 years old. Pugh was also offered a contract by the Oakland Raiders of the AFL that same season. All man, Pugh stood 6' 6" tall and weighed 260 pounds. He was given $1,000 as a signing bonus and a one-year contract worth $10,000. There is no telling what he would receive in today's market. "He was big, long arms, very athletic, very fast; just a great competitor and smart. He was beyond his years," said Cowboy personnel director, Gil Brandt.

Pugh was given the nickname "The Buzzard," by his teammates because he always kind of hunched over when standing. He was tall and lean and it looked like his shoulders were higher than his head, so he looked like a buzzard sitting on a tree limb waiting for his prey. It was later shortened to "Buzzy" and then just "Buzz."

No. 75, Jethro Pugh, played during a time when your team's knuckles-in-the-dirt ground game was designed to annihilate the other team. There were no VCR's, no nets in the end zone, and no NFL properties (logos, cheese heads, jerseys or gear) for sale. There were no network sponsors, just local sponsors. There were no names on the backs of jerseys and the joke was that the PA announcers didn't introduce the players by name. They went up into the stands and shook hands with the fans. Pugh played in 183 games over his 14 years, all with the Cowboys. Pugh recorded 95.5 sacks and led the Cowboys in sacks for five straight years (1968-1972). He recovered 14 fumbles, two safeties and had one interception, while playing in Tom Landry's "Flex Defense." He was selected Second-Team All-Pro in 1968. Pugh retired on January 29, 1979, with five NFC Championships and two Super Bowl rings. Dallas beat Miami in SB VI and Denver in SB XII.

Pugh has been inducted into four different Halls of Fame. In 1979, he was inducted into the CIAA Hall of Fame. In 1980, he was added to the North Carolina Sports Hall of Fame and, in 1981, he was inducted into the ECSU Sports Hall of Fame. In 2010, Pugh was inducted into the National Black College Alumni Hall of Fame. I hope that Jerry Jones sees fit to eventually place Pugh in the Cowboys' Ring of Honor.

Pugh roomed with Hall-of-Fame offensive tackle, Rayfield Wright. Jethro would become one of the unsung heroes of the "Doomsday Defense." That group included Larry Cole, Bob Lilly and George Andrie. In 1979, after Jethro Pugh finally decided to retire, his teammates on the defensive line had been Hall-of-Famer Randy White, Ed "Too Tall" Jones and Harvey Martin.

I can close my eyes and see it even now, December 31, 1967, 47 years ago. The temperature was listed at minus 13 degrees at kickoff, with a wind-chill factor of minus 48. "I remember the officials yelling to stop play during the game rather than blowing their whistles," said Cowboys' Lee Roy Jordan. Head referee, Norm Schachter, tore off a piece of his lip at the start of the game while trying to remove his whistle from his mouth. "He bled for almost all the game," exclaimed Jordan. "That guy looked pitiful. His shirt was bloodied all the way to his belt. After that game, the NFL went to plastic whistles." It was so cold, CBS announcer

Frank Gifford was heard saying on air, "I'm going to take a bite out of my coffee." Steve Sabol of NFL Films claimed it was so cold that some of the cameras quit working.

Packers against Cowboys, Lombardi against Landry, Starr against Meredith; there were 16 seconds left on the clock at Lambeau Field. The winner of this game would represent the National Football Conference in Super Bowl II. Green Bay had the ball first-and-goal on the Cowboys' one-yard line. Packers' halfback Donny Anderson ran the ball twice, but was stopped both times at the two-foot line. I remember "Mr. Cowboy" Bob Lilly digging furiously with his cleats, trying to carve out a place to get his footing. Starr called timeout to confer with Lombardi. On third and goal, they decided to run a play called "Brown Right 31 Wedge." As the play unfolded, center Ken Bowman and right guard Jerry Kramer double-teamed Pugh, as Starr took the snap and shouldered his way for a touchdown on a quarterback sneak. The scoreboard would now read "Packers 20, Cowboys 17," with the extra point to be kicked. "It wasn't Jethro's fault, they could have gone over anybody; we were standing on pure ice," said Bob Lilly. NFL lore would remember this game as the "Ice Bowl."

Pugh later commented on that play. "You are responsible for your situation, good or bad," said Pugh. "That is how it is. I had a tough time with it for about a year, but I had a good season in 1968 and decided to look to the future."

I had the privilege to meet Jethro Pugh in Dallas on the sidelines of a football game against the Seattle Seahawks. Pugh, Randy White and Calvin Hill were there as guests of Jerry Jones. Jethro was quiet and reminded me of a nice Deacon Jones. They both had worn the #75; they were about the same height and weighed about the same; yet their demeanor was totally opposite. (I was in football heaven.)

Pugh retired to a fine career where he was successful running airport concessions and western-themed gift shops at the Dallas-Fort Worth International Airport. He also hosted the Jethro Pugh Celebrity Golf Tournament each year, to raise funds for the United Negro College Fund.

The old saying is, every athlete dies twice, once when he retires. According to his family, Jethro Pugh died in his sleep of natural causes on January 7, 2015. He was 70 years old. His pal Bob Lilly said, "I think the world of him and am so sad to hear this news. He was tough. He played through a case of appendicitis one year and kept taking shots of penicillin to take the field." The truth is always far stranger than fiction, and I find it interesting that Pugh would leave us four days before the Cowboys travel to Green Bay for a post-season game. I hope they took his memory with them.

Do You Know Andy?

While waiting on a pitch, his fingers moved like a piano player against the handle of the bat. Hands back, right elbow up, hunched in the batter's box, he was doing exactly what he wanted to do, play baseball. He was the best player on a bad club for 19 years. He had started out as a shortstop and, like many who played for awhile; he ended up a first baseman. In the early 1950's, before reaching the Major Leagues, this fellow played for $7 dollars a game with Kansas City Monarchs of the old Negro Leagues. "Cool Papa" Bell and Satchel Paige were two of his teammates. As a young man, he was not all about baseball; it was the other way around. Baseball is supposed to be all about guys like him. He was a winner in life, which is far bigger than a game of baseball. He became more important to baseball than hotdogs and nachos. Heck, they named streets after this guy. It became obvious that the "C" on his cap stood for class. His joy was not defined by something that happened on the field. He was able to filter out the down times that occurred in the game. With his wonderful attitude about others and his abundance of enthusiasm about life, he could have been a Hall-of-Famer at anything he chose to do. This guy may have invented sunshine. In ten minutes he could own the room.

"Do you know Andy?" Those were the first words I ever heard him say in person. We were standing on the field at Minute Maid Park in Houston, Texas, before the 2004 All-Star Game. He was tall and walked with the bend in his back of an old ballplayer. His knees had been surgically replaced from the many slides into second base by his opponents with their spikes showing. His eyes twinkled and were still sharp. His face was thin with time. I listened carefully as he said to Joe, "I've had 19 years of doing and 32 years of remembering." When Ernie asked, "Do you know Andy?" he was talking to Joe Booker. The great Ernie Banks was actually introducing me to Joe. Ernie had only seen me once before years ago but here he was introducing me to someone else as if we were old friends. It's the first and so far the last time that has ever happened to me. I was astounded. Yes, I knew Joe Booker quite well. Joe and I had spent lots of time over the years in the media section, discussing the game of baseball and covering the hometown Houston Astros. Banks had been a friend of Booker's for years. Ernie Banks saw me standing there quietly; waiting to interview him, and he read my name on my media credentials. How cool is that? Banks was one of the warmest and most sincere guys I have ever met. I enjoyed being around him. Baseball lost one of its best friends today, another part of my childhood taken away too soon for me.

Born at home on January 31, 1931, in Dallas, Texas, Ernest "Ernie" Banks would have turned 84 in eight days. Ernie's parents were named Eddie and Essie Banks and Ernie was the second of 12 children. His father worked in a warehouse for a grocery chain, and his mom encouraged him to follow his grandfather's career and become a minister. Ernie loved swimming and playing football and basketball. He never showed much interest in baseball until his dad bribed him with a store-bought glove for three dollars and gave him loose change to play catch. Eddie had played baseball for several black semi-pro teams in Texas. In 1950, Ernie graduated from Booker T. Washington High School. Interestingly, Washington High School did not have a baseball team, so Ernie played softball at church and baseball during the summers, for a team known as the Amarillo Colts. A natural athlete, Banks received athletic letters in football, basketball and track.

There seem to be two stories about how Banks joined the K.C. Monarchs. A Monarch scout by the name of Bill Blair claimed to have discovered Banks, while a Kansas City player named James "Cool Papa" Bell says he influenced Banks to play for Kansas City. Bell operated a team known as the Junior Monarchs and they were touring Texas, when he saw Banks play. The story goes: Bell telephoned "Buck" O'Neil, manager of the Monarchs, and told him about Ernie. Buck signed Banks to a contract without ever seeing him play. Either way, 19-year-old Ernie Banks joined the Monarchs in 1950, after high school. It's hard to believe that according to Buck, Ernie was shy and somewhat introverted at the beginning, when he arrived in Kansas City. Banks always looked up to Buck O'Neil as a father figure. "I patterned my life after him," said Banks. I guess you could say Buck's pleasant demeanor rubbed off on Banks.

In 1951, Banks was drafted into the U.S. Army and served in Germany during the Korean War, where he injured his knee in basic training. Banks later served as the flag bearer in the 45th Anti-Aircraft Artillery Battalion at Fort Bliss, located in El Paso, Texas. While there, he occasionally played basketball with the Harlem Globetrotters. Banks was discharged in 1953 and returned to Kansas City to play with the Monarchs. Ernie's roommate was a fellow you might remember, Elston Howard. At the end of the 1953 season, the K.C. Monarchs sold Banks' contract to the Chicago Cubs for $10,000 in cash. Banks signed on September 14, 1953, and became the first African-American player for the Cubs. The Chicago Cubs became the ninth of 16 Major League teams to integrate. His first Major League at-bat occurred on September 17th. Ernie was 22 years old. Banks' first home run was hit out of Sportsman's Park three days later. Cardinals' pitcher Gerry Staley provided the fastball. It was the first of 512 home runs to be hit during Banks' 19-year career. Banks would hit 40 or more home runs five times during his career. He contributed his power to switching to a lighter bat (34-31 ounces), and developing strong wrists by playing handball. Ernie Banks would become the ninth player in Major League history to reach 500 home runs. Clyde McCullough said, "He swings the bat like Joe Louis used to throw a punch, short and sweet."

Shortly thereafter, in 1954, second basemen Gene Baker would join the team. These two would not only be roommates on the road, but turn into one of the best double-play combinations in the National League. The first baseman at this time for the Cubs was Steve Bilko. Cubs' announcer, Bert Wilson, could be heard describing a double play as "Bingo to Bango to Bilko." After hitting 19 home runs, Banks finished second to Wally Moon in the Rookie-of-the-Year race. In 1955, 44 home runs left Ernie's bat and he played in his first All-Star Game. Banks also set a record by hitting five grand slams in a single season. It was quite a year for "Mr. Sunshine."

Banks became the first player to win the National League MVP Award in back-to-back seasons, 1958 and 1959. Wrigley Field may not have had lights, but they had Ernie Banks. In 1960, Banks won his first and only Gold Glove at the shortstop position. Banks was moved to left field at the beginning of the 1961 season, but soon found a new home at first base. On a Friday during the 1962 season, Banks was hit in the head by a ball thrown from pitcher Moe Drabowsky, a former Cub. Banks left the field on a stretcher, unconscious. He spent two days in the hospital and then sat out Monday's game. On Tuesday, incredibly, Banks returned to the lineup and hit three home runs and a double. Ernie Banks played with many stars, but his favorite was Lou Brock. Banks roomed with Lou while playing with the Cubs. After Lou moved on to the Cardinals, Ernie roomed on the road with Billy Williams.

Banks finished playing the game of baseball on September 26, 1971, at the age of 40. He had been a 14-time All-Star, and a two-time National League home run (1958-1960) and RBI (1958-1959) champ. This North Side hero taught everyone how to lose gracefully, as he never got the chance to win it all. The incredible amount of joy he received back from the fans easily replaced any World Series ring he may have won. Banks did convey onetime that he felt an empty feeling inside, because he never got a chance to play in a World Series. He continued to serve the Cubs as a coach, instructor and administrator.

There is an amazing story that has been told by the late umpire, Tom Gorman. Tom recalled, "In 1957, Banks was knocked down four times by four different pitchers: Don Drysdale, Bob Purkey, Bob Friend and Jack Sanford. Each time he was knocked down, Banks hit their next pitch out of the park." Hall-of-Fame umpire, Doug Harvey, mentioned that Banks was equally respectful of the umpires. "Banks was never ejected from a game," said Harvey.

My first time meeting Ernie Banks was actually on the telephone. My wife and I watched QVC on television and occasionally they would sell sports memorabilia. On this particular show, their guest was "Mr. Cub," Ernie Banks. I saw an item that I wanted and called in to order. When I completed my order the fellow on the phone said, "Would you like to speak with Ernie Banks." Stunned, I said, "Sure." When I came on they asked me my name and where I was from. "Corpus Christi, Texas, I answered." Ernie said, "Hello Texas! How are you doing?" He asked me what I ordered and then told me he was from Dallas, Texas. It was short and sweet, but I'll never forget it. Who knew that I would meet him in person several years later in Houston, and then interview him for a radio show at the 2004 All-Star Game?

There they sat, three of the best Chicago had to offer. Billy Williams, Ernie Banks and Ron Santo were in Houston,

Texas, at the Astro Hall, signing autographs for fans during a weekend series between the Astros and the Cubs. This was the first time I had met any of them in person. I had each one of them sign a jersey for me. I asked Williams and Banks to add their Hall-of-Fame year. When I got to Santo I said, "Promise me, Ron, when you get in the Hall of Fame you will add your year to my jersey." When Banks and Williams heard my request they began to clap, and then folks standing close by also began to applaud. Ron smiled and nodded his approval.

When asked about his 500th home run, Banks said, "People said, 'How does he do it, twenty-one years old and 150 pounds, hitting home runs.' It was May 12, 1970, at 2:03 PM in the afternoon, on a Monday, when I hit number 500 against Pat Jarvis of the Atlanta Braves. He threw me an inside fastball and I hit my 500th home run. I didn't know if it was going to go out at first," said Banks. "When I hit that home run, I was in my forties; after I touched home plate, I felt like I was 20 years old."

"I had guys tell me 'You kept me out of jail,'" said Banks. 'I used to run home from school in the seventh, eighth and ninth inning to watch you play instead of running off with that gang.'"

After retirement, Banks became a Ford car dealer and a motivational speaker. Cubs' owner P.K. Wrigley bought the first Ford from Ernie. Banks was living in Los Angeles and had tried finance. He also worked for several different charities. Banks was married a fourth time in 1997. Hank Aaron was his best man, and Ernie and his new wife Liz adopted a baby girl in 2008.

Banks won the 1968 Lou Gehrig Award. Ernie had a lifetime batting average of .274. He recorded 2,583 hits and 512 home runs, and batted in 1,636 runs. With a vote of 83.8%, Banks was inducted into the Baseball-Hall-of-Fame Museum in 1977, on the first ballot. Ernie became the third of the players who also played in the Negro leagues to land a place in Cooperstown. Banks was selected after Jackie Robinson in (1962) and Monte Irvin in (1973). In 1982, Ernie's #14 was the first to be retired by the Cubs. In 1999, Banks was named to the Major League Baseball All-Century Team. In 2008, The Cubs unveiled a statue of Banks just off the third-base side of Clark and Addison streets. The Library of Congress named Ernie a "Living Legend" in 2009. On August 8, 2013, Ernie Banks was awarded the Presidential Medal of Freedom by President Obama. "I handed him a bat that belonged to Jackie Robinson," said Banks. "He was trilled to hold that bat."

Other thoughts by Ernie Banks are as follows: Some of the Negro League players were illiterate but wise beyond their years. They knew how to play the game. Banks was 16 when Jackie Robinson started. Ernie met Jackie in 1954 at Wrigley Field. "He told me, 'Congratulations! Now just keep your mouth shut when you play; just be quiet.' That's what I did," said Ernie. "Mr. Cub" was on hand the day Warren Spahn gave up a home run to 75-year-old Luke Appling in the Old Timers' Game in Washington D.C. Manager Leo Durocher gave him a hard time, but he did that to everyone. "He was tough and a smart guy. He knew all the writers, but I just killed him with kindness," said Banks.

"Ernie was playing first base when we played them at Wrigley," said my pal, Bart Shirley. Bart was playing with the Dodgers when he ended up at first. "I don't remember if I got a hit or a walk, but I do remember Ernie," said Bart. "He was just like everyone remembers. He looked at me, smiled, and said, 'Great day for two.'"

Ernie Banks claims that a sportswriter named Jim Enright was the first to use "Let's Play Two" when writing about Ernie. "It was something he heard me say in the clubhouse one hot July afternoon. My teammates were upset with me for wanting to continue playing in the heat," said Ernie.

Mr. Sunshine took his place in the heavenly lineup on

Friday, January 23, 2015. He died of a heart attack at Northwestern Memorial Hospital in Chicago. I'm positive he died laughing, or eating, or both. Baseball's brightest light flickered and went out. Expect the Cubs to honor Ernie during the season, especially during the Major League home opener set for Sunday night on April 5, 2015, against the St. Louis Cardinals. His #14 with a circle around it will be placed on the turf behind home plate. The flags attached to the foul poles will have #14 on them and the stands, which are under construction, will have pictures of Ernie during his career with the Cubs.

In the end, Ernie Banks honored his mother and father by becoming a great baseball player and an ordained minister. There's a good chance there will be a double header in Heaven this weekend. I wondered if my dad and Ernie are playing catch. At a time where drugs, steroids, cheating and spousal abuse fill the sports pages, Ernie Banks was a breath of fresh air. He was a reminder of all that is good in the world of sports. Perhaps Major League baseball should have every team play a double-header next year in his honor. I will remember the rhythm of his voice and that smile. Ernie Banks just might have been what baseball's all about. For Ernie, one game was great, but two was better. Thanks, Ernie.

I will end with a quotation by Ernie that will stand the test of time. "There's sunshine, fresh air, and the teams behind us. Let's play two."

Reid Ryan   Reid, President of Business operation for the Houston Astros, has always been kind enough to give me some of his time. This photo was taken during the Astros Caravan, 2014.

Tony Gwynn   I met Tony in Cooperstown, 1999, where he signed a jersey for me. One of the finest hitters in the game.

Kenny Stabler   One of the best left-handed quarterbacks in the
NFL. Met and took this picture of Kenny in Houston in 1993.

Larry Dierker   Pitcher, manager, and broadcaster, Dierker has done
it all in Major League baseball. Photo taken in 2015.

Milo Hamilton   Milo and I spent lots of time together on the air
and in person. I will never forget our friendship.

Ernie Banks   Ernie and I actually visited on three different
occasions. The last time we were together was at the
2004 MLB All-Star Game.

Yogi Berra   One of the greatest catchers in MLB history.
Everyone should have someone like Yogi in their life.

Willis Wilson   I met Willis for the first time at the 2011 NCAA
Final Four. A fine coach, we have become great friends.

J.R. Richards   The big man has so many funny stories. We could
laugh for days when we are together.

Frank Gifford   Met Frank on the field before a game in the
Astrodome. The Oilers were playing on Monday Night Football.

Meadowlark Lemon   Met Meadowlark in 1995. He had one of the most well- known faces and names in the world of basketball.

Dotson Lewis and Bart Shirley   I was honored to have these two sit with me during one of my book-signing events. Dotson has been enshrined in the College Football Officiating HOF and Bart played for the L.A. Dodgers in the 1960's.

Joey Crawford   Joe honored me with this photo and many kind
words about my first book.

Pat Dwyer   Pat and I have become close friends. He spent 20
seasons as a Scout for the Houston Astros.

Craig Morton   In 1998, Craig joined Shane Nelson and me on
the air at 97.5 "The Waves."

Chuck Bednarik   No one hit harder than "Concrete Charlie."

Bobby Smith   Bobby and I met at lunch in 2015. The two-time
AFL champion running back of the Buffalo Bills is
a fine man and friend

Billy Casper   As a young man growing up in N.C., I followed
Doug Sanders, Lee Trevino and Billy Casper. Casper was a
fine golfer and tremendous family man.

Calvin Peete   Calvin's ability to overcome obstacles to become a
terrific golfer is an amazing story.

Andrew Helton   Andrew, head basketball coach at Eastern New
Mexico, and I have become great friends. His ability to spot
talent is uncanny

Don Zimmer   I took this photo at a Cubs-Astros
game in the Astrodome. "Zim" only had one job in
his life, baseball.

Carlos Espinoza   No one has been a better friend to me than
Carlos. Carlos played as a professional all over the world and has
been paired with many of golf's greatest players.

"Hot Rod" Hundley   I met Hot Rod in Salt Lake City during the 1993 NBA All-Star Game. The man was a magician with the basketball.

Scott Malone   Scott is a fine head coach for the Texas A&M Islanders baseball club. We have become fast friends.

Matt Hicks   Matt, the voice of the Texas Rangers, has been my friend for many years. His passion for baseball and broadcasting continues to make him one of the best.

Dean Smith   I only met Dean once in Houston, Texas, but I did have the pleasure of watching his teams play for many years. One of the best.

Jack Ramsey Spent some time with Jack in Orlando, Florida, at the 1992 NBA All-Star Game. He was a very smart coach with a real feel for people.

George Springer I interviewed George during the 2015 Astros Caravan. A superstar in the making, he was kind, humble and very talented with a bat.

Andy Pettitte   Met Andy at a memorabilia event where he
signed some things for me.

Minnie Minoso   The first Black Latin baseball star to play in the
Major Leagues.

Chuck Noll   Noll became a four-time Super Bowl Championship
Coach for the Pittsburgh Steelers. One of the very best in the NFL.

Steve Castillo   Steve is the coach of a two-time Texas State
Championship Baseball team and a member of the Texas High
School HOF.

Jake Marisnick   A fine center fielder with the 2015 Astros. I look
for bigger and better things from Jake in the near future.

Marques Haynes   Haynes, the first Harlem Globetrotter to be
inducted into the Naismith Basketball HOF, is joined in this photo
by legend, Bill Russell.

Jerry Tarkanian   One of the most interesting college basketball
coaches who drew national attention at UNLV.
I met Jerry in San Antonio.

Jason Castro   Castro continues to hold down the Astros'
catching position. I met Jason at a Corpus Christi Hooks event.

240

Ralph Kiner   One of the greatest HOF power hitters of his era.

Hector Salinas   Coach Salinas constructed not one, not two,
but three college baseball programs from scratch. He is a fine
man and friend.

Bill "Fireball" Beverly   Bill and I became instant friends.
We met in Houston in 1997. He loved talking about the
Negro Leagues, especially the Birmingham Black Barons.

Ronnie Arrow   A fine coach and a better friend,
Ronnie and I have spent hours talking about the game
we love, basketball.

ONE GIANT STEP

Joseph Ferrell once said, "The man who most vividly realizes a difficulty is the man most likely to overcome it." He didn't have an intimidating name like Tiger, Shark or The Golden Bear, but this guy could toast it off the tee. He would cut the fairway right down the middle like a ripe watermelon. Humble and often shy, he spurned the spotlight. He hit golf balls, smoked big cigars, and dodged haters for a living. His drives had "deep threat" written on them, and he played with a chip on his shoulder. He was a funny guy. He once said, "My 3-wood lost six new balls the other day. When I put the club back in my bag, I swear I heard it laughing." He also said, "Golf will make you take up another sport." He understood that he who controls others may be powerful, but he who has mastered himself is mightier still. Oh, he was good. He even once hit an alligator swimming in a pond about 140 yards away. This fellow won despite the hardships he faced. An exceptional talent with a golf club, he remained emotionally tough against adversity at every turn. Unlike Jackie Robinson, he had no team around him, protecting him and cheering him on. It was him against the culture, against the times, and against the golf course. He was the very definition of "speak softly and carry a big stick." He could chip with the best and he would swear at times that his putter wriggled like a garter snake. "My putter has a built in tremor and I think it eats mice at night," said Sifford. Famous sportswriter, Grantland Rice, once said, "Eighteen holes of match play will teach you more about your foe than 18 years of dealing with him across a desk." Charlie Sifford opened the door for African Americans and took the game of golf one giant step further than anybody else.

Charles Luther Sifford was brought into this world on June 2, 1922. He was born in Charlotte, North Carolina. His dad was a factory worker and taught Charles the meaning of hard work and the value of a dollar. Sifford became a caddie at a local whites-only golf course at the age of 13. The story goes that he was paid 60 cents a day for his efforts. He gave his mother 50 cents and spent the rest on himself and cigars. He would play the course with other caddies on Mondays when allowed, and often broke par. At the age of 17, his family moved to Philadelphia, Pennsylvania, and Charlie turned pro. He would grow to 5' 8" inches tall and weigh a sturdy 185 pounds. Charlie served his country in the segregated Army of the Pacific Theater, during World War II. He endured the hardships of the Battle of Okinawa and returned home wanting to play golf for a living. Sifford began playing golf professionally in 1948. He started playing on the United Golf Association Tour, where African-American golfers played for relatively small purses on mostly public courses, because most private clubs would not allow minorities to play. Charlie won six Negro National Open Titles before making his PGA Tour debut, at the ripe old age of 38. Charlie first attempted unsuccessfully to qualify for a PGA Tour event at the 1952 Phoenix Open. He was allowed to play in an all-black foursome that included the great boxer, Joe Louis. In 1957, Sifford won the Long Beach Open, which was not an official PGA Tour event but was co-sponsored by the PGA and had many well-known white golfers in the field. He also played in the 1959 U.S. Open and finished in a tie for 32nd place. In October of 1960, Charlie finished second to Billy Casper at the Orange County Open.

Sifford became the first black golfer to participate on the

PGA Tour in 1960. Players whose last names were Hogan, Casper, Nicklaus, Palmer, Player, and Snead dominated the links in the world of golf. Even after the PGA Tour had dropped its "Caucasian only" membership rules in 1961, Sifford and other black golfers endured all kinds of racial threats and hazards. Wonderful black players like Pete Brown, Lee Elder, Calvin Peete, Jim Dent, and Jim Thorpe would follow in his footsteps. In fact, it was Brown who became the first black golfer to win an official PGA Tour event in 1964, at the Waco Turner Tournament, played in Oklahoma. They were often barred from clubhouses and the club restaurants, so they had to leave the course to change their shoes, to shower, change clothes and get something to eat. Sifford claims he was once given $20 by a tournament sponsor and asked to eat somewhere else, but not in the clubhouse. They found black cats in their beds at the hotel. They also heard the ruffled curses from the gallery and often found their balls kicked into the rough. Charlie struggled to overcome his anger and used counseling to help him along the way. Still, Sifford was able to win the 1963 Puerto Rico Open.

Charlie Sifford won $341,000 on the PGA Tour and almost $1 million on the Senior Tour (now called the Champions Tour) with seven wins. Sifford was an original member of the Senior Tour created in 1980. At the age of 64, Charlie was the oldest Senior Tour player and finished 28th on the money list in 1986. Sifford won the 1967 Greater Hartford Open and the Los Angeles Open in 1969. He also won at Sea Pines in 1971. One of his greatest wins came after a 22-foot birdie putt on the first hole of "sudden death" in the 1975 PGA Senior Championship. Sifford said smiling, "Up to that point, I had played so bad my clubs started to drink and stay out late at night." He collected $7,500 for the victory. It was of small consequence after not being invited to the 1974 Masters, even though he had qualified. His last tournament appearance came in 2011, at the Liberty

Mutual Legends-of-Golf Tournament. This event was part of the 70 and older players of the Champions Tour. His partner was none other than Lee Elder.

In 1975, Lee Elder became the first black player to participate in the Masters Tournament. Charlie Sifford never played in the Masters Tournament or The Open Championship. Clarence Rogers of the National Negro Golfers Association (NNGA) said, "There would have been no 'Tiger' Woods without Charlie Sifford, at least in our lifetime. He was a beacon of life." Woods concurred. Earl Woods, Tiger's dad, and Charlie became friends when Tiger was a junior golfer. Tiger wrote, "My pop likely wouldn't have picked up the sport, and maybe I wouldn't have either." Tiger paid tribute to Charlie many times calling him the grandfather he never had, and Sifford referred to Tiger as his adopted grandson.

"Charlie won tournaments, but more important, he broke a barrier," said Nicklaus. "I think what Charlie Sifford has brought to this game has been monumental."

Charlie Sifford wrote in his autobiography, Just Let Me Play, about the trials and tribulations he fought to play the game he loved. The following is a funny story about a fellow golfer who would become one of his best friends. "How the hell did he shoot 63?" asked Arnold Palmer, after the first round of the 1955 Canadian Open. Of course, he was talking about Charlie Sifford. Sifford led Palmer by one stroke and was standing right behind Arnold when he said that. Sifford responded to Palmer's surprise, "The same way you shot 64. That's how we met," laughed Sifford.

Charles Sifford died on a Tuesday at the age of 92. The date was February 3, 2015. It seemed almost appropriate for Charlie to leave us during Black History Month. Charlie's wife Rose had died in 1998 and they had two sons, Charles Jr. and Craig, three grandkids and one great grandchild. More than two hundred mourners attended his funeral, yet it is sad to say that no current PGA Tour golfers were present. Sifford had experienced a stroke one month before entering a hospital in Cleveland, not far from his home in Brecksville, Ohio. Charlie had lived in Northeast Ohio, for many years and was the former club pro at Sleepy Hollow in Brecksville. At his funeral, twenty-seven of the local members of (NNGA) each placed a golf ball in a container that was to be given to the family. In 2004, Charlie Sifford won his most important match by becoming the first black player inducted into the World Golf Hall of Fame. Interestingly, Charlie chose his dear friend, Gary Player, a South African player, to present him for induction. Sifford was also presented with the Old Tom Morris Award in 2007.

Fortunately, in November of 2014, three months before Charlie passed away, he received the Presidential Medal of Freedom from President Barack Obama at the White House. Jack Nicklaus and Arnold Palmer are the only other golfers who have received this honor. The medal was promptly displayed next to his casket along with a photo of Charlie with a big cigar in his mouth. Former Chief Justice of the Unites States, Charles Evans Hughes, once said, "When we lose the right to be different, we lose the privilege to be free." Charlie Sifford was both different and free and one heck of a golfer. Save me a tee time, Charlie.

PLAY IT WHERE IT LIES

Groucho Marx once said, "I've had a perfectly wonderful evening, but this wasn't it." We all go though the process of finding out what we're good at. This guy became an amazing golfer. He was harder to beat than Floyd Mayweather. He could play as calm as a morning in May, and his middle name should have been money. It was like he could reach down inside and find an extra gear. When all was said and done, all he did was win. He never seemed to have a bad round, a quiet round, but he never beat himself. This guy had magic in his hands, and his personality matched the size of his physique. It was like he had a pocket full of "gimme's." On the golf course, he was all business, like a hit man with a 7-iron. His high arching approach shots rained down like death from above on his opponents. This guy could land an iron shot on the side of the Empire State Building and stop it. His putter was a born outlaw. If it were human it would rob banks. He just exploded off the tee and would use his short game to drive a stake through your heart. He could get up and down out of a trash can with his 9-iron. Someone once said if he missed a putt it's because the hole moved. There are stories that he practiced putting in the dark. "On a pitch-black night, when you walk up to the hole just to see where it is, it stamps a very strong image in your mind," Casper told *Golf Digest* in 2005. "You develop a feel for everything: the moisture on the grass, the small change in elevation, the exact distance to the hole, and all kinds of things your eyes alone can't tell you." "Billy" Casper always played it where it lay. At times, he seemed to be bullet proof.

William Earl Casper, Jr., was born on June 24, 1931, in San Diego, California. His family soon moved to Chula Vista. His father was an avid golfer who built a three-hole golf course on their farm. It was here, at the age of four, that Billy received his first golf lessons from his dad. As a kid, Billy was called "fatso" and other unflattering things at school. He caddied at a golf course close by during the day and practiced putting at night. At 16, Billy got a chance to see the great Ben Hogan play in an exhibition match and marveled at his shot-making abilities. After graduating from high school, Billy attended the University of Notre Dame for a while before joining the U.S. Navy.

Casper turned professional in 1954 and won his first PGA Tour event within two years. Billy would soon stand among the game's finest golfers. The great Jack Nicklaus said, "When I played in a tournament and I came to the turn, I always looked at the leader board for three names: Arnold Palmer, Gary Player and Billy Casper."

Casper's hand to eye coordination was something to behold. He was a genius with his short game. He once claimed, "I could look at a telephone pole 40 yards away, take out a 7-iron and hit it ten times in a row." It took Billy Casper 25 years on the PGA Tour before he recorded his first hole-in-one. He eventually made 23 before he retired. Casper won at least once every year for 16 straight years. Only Jack Nicklaus and Arnold Palmer surpassed Casper with a win, in 17 straight years. "I had to play well to feed my family," said Billy. "I never got caught up in the history of the game."

Billy Casper's first major win occurred in 1959, at Winged Foot, in Mamaroneck, New York. There Billy set a tournament record with only 114 putts over 72 holes. The crowd was so quiet you could hear ice melt.

His most thrilling win was played at the Olympic Club

in San Francisco, California, during the 1966 U.S. Open. Casper trailed Palmer by seven strokes with only nine holes to play. Billy caught him with a four-under 32 on the back nine and beat Arnold by four shots in an 18-hole playoff. Incredibly, Casper never three-putted over the 90 holes played. Palmer was quoted afterwards, "He's the greatest putter on the pro tour."

It has been said, "It's never spring until The Masters." The 1970 Masters was the scene of another thrilling victory by Casper. It took another 18-hole playoff to beat Gene Littler. It was in this match that Casper claims he hit the best shot of his career. Casper's ball was tucked down inside tall grass, with a small log two or three inches behind his ball on the par-5 second hole. Casper took his 9-iron and lofted a shot up over the tall pine trees onto the fairway. That shot allowed him to save par.

Casper also won nine events on the senior Tour including two more majors, the 1983 U.S. Senior Open and the 1988 Senior Tournament Players Championship. His last win on the Senior Tour occurred in 1989.

I do not know how Billy Casper had time to play golf, as he fathered five children and adopted six with his wife Shirley Franklin Casper. He was held as a wonderful husband and family man. Billy and Shirley had 71 grandchildren and there is no telling how many great-grandchildren. He was known for his charitable side and oozed kindness towards others. He enjoyed the outdoors, especially fishing. "Fishing not only rests and relaxes me; it also provides me with a muscle exercise that makes me stronger on the golf course," said Casper. In July of 1966, Billy also gave his time to our troops in Vietnam.

Casper suffered from all kind of allergies from most meats and fruit and vegetables where certain pesticides were used. He turned to eating venison, buffalo, elk, caribou, moose and organic vegetables. He also converted to Mormonism in 1966.

"Billy Casper Golf" was a company Billy created which designed, built and operated 140 courses across the United States. At present, it is the second largest company of its kind.

Billy's oldest son David is in prison in Nevada, serving a life sentence for committing many felonies and armed robberies. "He will never get out," said Casper. Billy and his wife struggled with David's fate and reached deep down inside trying to make sense of it all. They never came to terms on how they could have done better as parents. Sometimes, life gets in the way.

Billy Casper played in 584 events and recorded 69 total professional wins, including 51 PGA Pro-Tour events and 31 second-place finishes. He was listed at #7 in all-time career wins behind Sam Snead, "Tiger" Woods, Jack Nicklaus, Ben Hogan, Arnold Palmer and Byron Nelson. Some of his wins came at famous golf courses and events such as Doral Country Club, the Greater Greensboro Open, the Bob Hope Dessert Classic, the Bing Crosby National Pro Am, and the Colonial National Invitational. From 1962 to 1970, Casper and Nicklaus won 33 times on the PGA Tour. Palmer won 30 times. Casper's advice to other golfers: "Play more and practice less off the tee." Nicknamed "The Gorilla," Casper was elected Player of the Year twice in 1966 and 1970. He was the leading money winner twice and holds the American record in the Ryder Cup for most points. He participated on eight Ryder Cup Teams and captained the team in 1979. Casper has also won the Vardon Trophy five times, a trophy given for best stroke average. Over the years, Casper wrote 37 articles for *Golf Digest*. Casper was inducted into the World Golf Hall of Fame in 1978. In 2000, Casper was ranked the 15th greatest golfer of all time in *Golf Digest* magazine.

"I think people recognize what I did more readily now than when it happened," said Casper before he died. "In my best years, everybody was talking about Palmer, Nicklaus and Gary Player." In 2014, Billy Casper passed out in the clubhouse at The Masters in Augusta, Georgia. He had been going to cardio rehab for the last four months and seemed to be doing fine, when suddenly he began to feel bad. He died quickly and quietly from a heart attack, at home in Springville, Utah, on Saturday February 7, 2015. His wife of 62 years, Shirley, was by his side. It has been said that Father Time always eagles No. 18.

The Dean's List

He was a master of the last two minutes of a game and constantly preached that five minutes early meant you were late. He saw teaching as the most important thing he was doing. The game of basketball was so much more to him than wins and losses. He could have been John the Baptist with a whistle. His voice sounded like a distant avalanche, and he had enough nose to mind everybody's business. Early on, he was perceived as arrogant because everybody in the room wanted to beat his team. He thought in much broader terms and taught a sense of responsibility to his guys. "Coach" held his players accountable and treated them all alike and like men. He also protected his players at every turn. This fellow made you want to be a better player, a better person, a better man. He was one of those guys against whom other coaches measured themselves. This man may have been the real MVP of his teams. He practiced and believed in social justice and was considered a champion of all people. He enjoyed a good book, a round of golf and church. In fact he has recorded two holes-in-one. He made his players go to church every Sunday, and he worshiped in the only integrated church in Chapel Hill, during the 1960's. He remained positive, always in control, and prepared his players for the future. His goals were about helping people find their balance, not just in basketball, but in life. He once took his team to Central Prison in Raleigh, N.C., to play the prison team. He explained to his kids, "If you know what's right, you try to do what's right." He would enter the quarters of death row inmates to speak with the prisoners. Watching him made me wonder if Moses ever coached basketball. He also enjoyed letting his players be different. His memory was legendary, as he knew every one of his players' names as well as their wives' and kids' names. One of his greatest contributions to society may have been about the 300 or so players who did not play in the NBA. "It never takes courage to do what's right," said the University of North Carolina (UNC) Head Coach, Dean Smith. Everybody in basketball wanted to be part of "The Dean's List."

The name Dean Smith will always stand for excellence in college basketball. He was brilliant and knew how to treat people. Dean was more powerful than the Governor of North Carolina, and a lot of opposing coaches thought Smith had advantages they did not have. Maybe he did, but Smith understood that you either evolved as a team or you died. Smith demanded discipline. It has been said that the only guy who could hold Michael Jordan to 20 points or less was Dean Smith. He respected the game and expected everyone around him to do the same. Many of his players' life decisions after basketball were not made without his counsel. "Off the court, we try to be a servant and help them reach their goals," said Coach Smith.

Dean Edward Smith was born in Emporia, Kansas, on February 28, 1931. His mother and father were both teachers and his dad, Alfred, was the basketball coach for the Spartans of Emporia High School. Alfred Smith had a black player by the name of Paul Terry on his 1934 team, who won the Kansas State Championship in basketball. Terry was not allowed to play in the state tournament by Kansas State officials, because of his color. The Smith family later moved to Topeka, Kansas, when Dean turned 15. Dean played catcher on the baseball squad, quarterback on the football team, and guard on the basketball team at Topeka High School. Dean made good enough grades to be offered an academic scholarship to the University of Kansas. At 5'10" tall, Smith tried out for the Jayhawks' varsity basketball team and made the team as a substitute guard. Smith also made the varsity baseball team and played on the freshman football team. Dean was part of Coach "Phog" Allen's 1952-53 NCAA National Championship team at the University of Kansas. It is also interesting to note that Kentucky Coach Adolph Rupp also played for Phog and Kansas in 1923. Phog Allen played at Kansas for James Naismith, the guy who invented the game of basketball. Smith majored in math. Dean once told a story of how Coach Phog Allen wanted his players to shoot free throws underhanded. After graduation, Dean coached at Kansas and the Air Force Academy, until he was hired in 1958 by then UNC Coach, Frank McGuire. UNC was coming off a 1957 undefeated season and a triple-overtime victory over the University of Kansas, led by Wilt Chamberlain, for the National Championship. McGuire's basketball program at UNC was under pressure and eventually placed on probation for recruiting issues. In 1961, Frank McGuire left UNC to become the head coach for the Philadelphia Warriors. Frank McGuire said, "The two best moves I ever made were marrying my wife and hiring Dean Smith." Thirty-year-old Dean Smith replaced him. In his first season, Smith's record stood at 8-9 for the year. After a 22-point loss to Wake Forest on the road, UNC returned home to find a dummy hung in effigy from the door to the gym. Billy Cunningham quickly tore down Dean's likeness. Dean Smith's success followed shortly, as UNC would make the Final Four, three years in a row (1967-1969). His 1968 team lost in the finals to John Wooden's UCLA Bruins. Smith described his keys to success as simple: recruit, develop and then coach. "There were no situations we didn't practice," said Roy Williams.

One of Dean's favorite lines was used by the coach at the start of every new season: "You're in Chapel Hill now."

His players came to understand that the expectations of them as players and students were going to be great. Smith expected sustained excellence. Every year his former players gathered in Chapel Hill for an old-timers game. One Friday in February of 2010, some 70 players from their 20's into their 80's gathered to say thank you to Dean Smith. It was the 100th anniversary of Carolina basketball.

Dean Smith's innovations as a coach were numerous and far-reaching. Coach invented the run-and-jump defense. He created a rotate-and-trap defense. His teams were taught to stand and applaud when a substitute came off the bench. Players were instructed to give the "tired" sign by holding up a clinched fist when they needed to come out of a game for rest. Smith created the "thank you" point where the player who had just received an assist and scored gave recognition by pointing to the guy who had passed them the ball. "We brag about the guy who makes the unselfish play," said Dean Smith. He divided his team into first and second teams, and referred to them as the Blue team and White team. Many times when things were not going well for the Tar Heels, Smith would take out all five of his starters and send in the White team so he could address the starters as one unit. Smith's use of the "four corners" offense forced the use of a shot clock in college basketball. Although fellow Kansas alum, John McLendon, actually invented the four corners offense, Smith was better known for utilizing it in games. Dean was one of the first to use the team huddle at the free-throw line to set his defense before a free-throw shot. "As a coach you're in charge, and I take that seriously," said Smith.

Dean also practiced what he called "Senior Day," at Carolina. He always started his team's seniors on the last home game of the season. This was his way to honor their contributions. In one particular season, Dean had six seniors on his team and started all six rather than having to choose which one to leave out. His team was given a technical foul at the start of the game. Smith also made it a point to schedule a game on the road in the hometown of his seniors. In 1994, Carolina had a 7'0" tall senior out of Houston, Texas, named Kevin Salvadori. Smith scheduled UNC to play Houston. One of my favorite radio sports announcers was a guy by the name of Art Casper. Art always sent me the Houston Cougars' schedule each year and allowed me to come to Houston four or fives times a season and sit next to him at the scorers' table, while he and his partner broadcast the games. He had me chart turnovers, rebounds, or whatever he needed. I was in Heaven. It was here that I got to meet some of the all-time great coaches and players like Dean Smith. Art would introduce me to the opposing coaches before the game. Dean and I spent about 30 minutes together talking basketball. Unless you were close to Dean you probably would not know that he was an avid smoker. He had tried to quit for years but was unsuccessful. I remember following him and his team to the dressing room at halftime, where he stopped and lit up a cigarette as soon as he was out of sight of the fans. I also met Guy Lewis, Digger Phelps, Ray Meyer, and many others. It was also great to meet national television announcers like Gary Bender and Don Criqui.

Eighty-three of his Tar Heel players reached the professional level. Their names ring from high: Michael Jordan, James Worthy, Sam Perkins, Billy Cunningham, Vince Carter, Walter Davis, Bob McAdoo, Eric Montross, George Lynch, J.R. Reid, Brad Daugherty, Kenny Smith, Mitch Kupchek, Rick Fox, Doug Moe, Harrison Barnes, Hubert Davis, Bobby Jones, Danny Green, Phil Ford, Charlie Scott, Dick Grubar, Joe Wolf and many more.

Some of Dean Smith's most well-known coaching tree includes, Eddie Fogler, Jeff Lebo, Buzz Peterson, Matt Doherty, Bill Guthridge, John Kuester, George Karl, Roy Williams, and Larry Brown.

There were many players and coaches who spoke about

their relationship with Dean Smith. I have included some of their comments where they helped tell his story.

Brad Daugherty told how he was recruited by Dean Smith to come to UNC. "When Coach and I visited, he said, 'You may or may not become a good basketball player, but I promise you that if you come to North Carolina, you will get a first class education.'"

"Six or seven years ago, while I was at the Final Four, I don't even remember what city, I was out at a restaurant and Dean Smith was there. He said 'Hello' and he called me by name and even asked about some of my players. He acted as if he had known me all my life," said former South Alabama Coach, Ronnie Arrow. "I didn't know what to say."

Former Georgetown Coach, John Thompson, said, "I loved him, I lost a friend."

Duke Coach, Mike Krzyzewski, stated about Smith, "His greatest gift was his unique ability to teach what it takes to become a good man." Dean Smith and Coach K had one thing in common, winning. They became friends.

"He was like my second father," said Michael Jordan. "Dean Smith taught me how to play basketball. I was just an athlete." To fulfill a promise Smith made to Jordan's parents, he had the Chicago Bulls contract include additional money if Michael returned to UNC and graduated.

UCLA Coach, John Wooden once said Dean Smith was the best teacher of basketball he had ever seen.

Former Notre Dame Coach, Digger Phelps, tells how he wrote Dean Smith a letter back in 1964 or 1965. "I asked if he would hire me as an assistant," said Digger. "Dean wrote me back and said 'Sorry, I'm going to hire a guy named Larry Brown.' I kept the letter," said Digger.

"When I was being recruited for college, both Steve Fisher from Michigan and Dean Smith from UNC was scheduled to come visit me and my family at my house on the same day. My mother fixed a few items to eat while Coach Fisher was there, but had BBQ ribs and "the works" laid out for Coach Smith. It was obvious where she wanted me to go to college. Coach Smith could undress you like anyone else with his words, yet no one ever heard him curse," said Jerry Stackhouse.

"Ninety percent of the things I do today, I got from Coach Smith," said currant UNC Coach, Roy Williams. "He may have been one of the best coaches in any sport, not just basketball."

"Everyone talks about all the All-Americans that Coach Smith had. They forget that we weren't All-Americans when we went there," said Phil Ford. If you screwed up or embarrassed the school, you received one of Smith's handwritten notes. "We called it 'The Wrath of Dean,'" said Ford.

The fine baseball sportswriter, Peter Gammons, is a UNC graduate. Once when Peter was starting out, Dean was being interviewed by Frank DeFord of *Sports Illustrated*. Dean asked Peter to come join him during the interview so Gammons would have firsthand knowledge on how to conduct a proper interview.

"Every minute of practice had a purpose. Coach Smith always tried to get his players to open up their minds. To see more than what was right in front of them," said Charlie Scott.

Former Coach, Gary Williams of Maryland said, "I think Dean Smith will be remembered most for graduating 96.6% of his players."

Dean Smith was a shy man. He didn't like for you to say Dean Smith and the Tar Heels. It was always about his players, not himself. He made it a habit to attend every one of his players' weddings and hated the 9:00 P.M. start times for television games, as it did not allow his players time for enough sleep to make their early classes. He also had a rule: miss a class and you miss a game. He once had a player (name withheld) who missed 28 classes before the season started. Therefore, he sat out 28 games and had to be red-shirted in order to play the following season. He also said that as his program became more and more successful, he had to hire additional personnel to handle the players' mail for autographs. By the 1990's, Smith had gone from one to five in the mail room.

The death of Coach Dean Smith hit pretty close to home for me as I grew up in Raleigh, 29 miles from Chapel Hill, during his tenure. I will end the list of quotations from others with two of my own favorite Dean Smith stories. The 1980's of Atlantic Coast Conference (ACC) Basketball could be summed up in two words: Dean Smith. Coach Jim Valvano told a story about going to get a haircut after he was hired at N.C. State. Jim found a barbershop on Hillsborough Street in downtown Raleigh, across from the N.C. State Campus. When he entered the barbershop, the barber said, "Hey you must be Jimmy V., that new basketball coach they just hired at State. I hope you do better than the last guy they had." Valvano said, "You know, that last guy (Norm Sloan) won a National Championship in 1974." The barber then smiled and said, "Yeah, but just think of what Dean Smith could have done with that team."

The second story was told to me by former Coach Bobby Cremins of Georgia Tech. Cremins said jokingly, "The first several years I coached in the ACC, I thought Dean Smith's name was 'That Damn Dean,' because every time Lefty Driesell called me from Maryland he began every conversation with, 'Hey Bobby, do you know what that damn Dean is doing now?'"

In 1966, Dean Smith recruited and signed the first African-American player in UNC history. He gave that scholarship to #33, Charlie Scott, an outstanding high-school forward from New York City. Charlie Scott became a two-time All-American and a three-time All-ACC selection. He was also named the MVP of the ACC Tournament. Scott joined the ABA's Virginia Squires and later became an NBA All-Star with the Phoenix Suns.

Earlier in his freshman year, Dean Smith had said to Michael Jordan during a practice, "If you can't pass, you can't play." With 32 seconds left in the 1982 National Championship Game against Georgetown and behind by one point, Dean Smith called a time out. (I get chills just typing this.) Assistant Coach, Roy Williams reveals what was said: "Coach Smith said, 'We're in great shape. We're exactly where we want to be. We are going to determine who wins this game.'" As the UNC team broke the huddle, Smith said to Michael Jordan, "If it comes to you, knock it down." The rest is history. Fifteen seconds later, #23 Michael Jordan, then a 19-year old kid, knocked it in. UNC and Dean Smith won their first NCAA Title 63-62. It's the stuff that legends are made of.

Smith's second title came in 1993 against the "Fab Five" of the University of Michigan Wolverines. In a close game, the Tar Heels eventually won 77-71 with the help of a misguided timeout called late in the game by Chris Weber, when Michigan was out of timeouts. This mistake led to a technical foul on Michigan, and two free throws and a win for North Carolina.

Dean Smith's first game as head coach at UNC occurred on December 2, 1961. It was his only losing season. Dean Smith was one of the winningest coaches in college basketball history. Smith won 77.6% of the games his UNC teams played and recorded 27 straight 20-win seasons. Smith was chosen the ACC Coach of the Year nine times, and his teams won 13 ACC Conference Titles. Smith's Tar Heels won the 1971 National Invitational Tournament. In October of 1997, Smith passed Kentucky Coach, Adolph Rupp, with an 879-254 win-loss record. Smith's Division I record for wins has since been passed by Indiana's Bob Knight, Jim Boehein of Syracuse, and Duke's Mike Krzyzewski. UNC qualified for 23 consecutive tournament appearances under Smith. His teams played in 11 Final Four tournaments. Smith won two National Championships, eleven years apart, in 1982 and 1993. Only Smith and Knight have played for and coached a Division I National Champion. Smith also coached the U.S. Olympic team to a Gold Medal in 1976. Dean Smith was selected the NCAA National Coach of the Year four times (1977, '79, '82 and '93). Coach Smith received the Presidential Medal of Freedom from President Barack Obama in November of 2013. Due to health reasons, Smith was unable to attend the ceremony. Smith was also given the Arthur Ashe Award. The best attribute I can give Dean Smith is that his players always checked with Coach, before making life changing decisions.

If there is a Hall of Fame by any name, Dean Smith is in it. Smith's last game coached occurred on March 29, 1997. Smith ran a clean program for 36 years (1961-1997). The essence of Dean Smith can be summed up in this quotation, "Wins, losses and championships do not determine a good coach," said Smith.

UNC plays their home games in the new Dean E. Smith Center, referred to by basketball fans as the "Dean Dome." A humble Smith never wanted the credit; he did not want the new area named after him. Smith announced his retirement on October 9, 1997. It was unexpected. His assistant for 30 years, Bill Guthridge, took his spot on the UNC bench.

In December of 2007, Smith suffered neurological complications after he underwent knee replacement surgery. His forgetfulness increased dramatically. It was but a matter of time before the outside world would know. On July 17, 2010, Coach Smith's family released a statement that he had been diagnosed with a "progressive neurocognitive disorder" and had developed some memory problems. Although he continued to go to his office each day, he suffered his last seven years with signs of dementia.

Dean Smith died on Saturday night, February 8, 2015. He was 83 years old. Smith was surrounded by his wife, Linnea, and his five kids, from two different marriages. Dean's first marriage to Ann ended in divorce. Every coach in a gym tonight is borrowing or has already borrowed something from Dean Smith. Smith was buried on Thursday, February 12, 2015. They came from near and far to honor a man they all called coach. Duke's Mike Krzyzewski wore a Carolina Blue tie. Dean would have loved seeing that.

The first home game for UNC after the death of Dean Smith was against Georgia Tech. To honor his mentor, Head Coach Roy Williams chose to open the game with Dean Smith's Four Corner offense. They scored on a backdoor layup and never looked back.

A little over one month after his death, approximately 180 players who lettered at UNC under Coach Dean Smith, each received a surprise in the mail. Coach Smith had set aside a trust fund in his will, that each of those players would receive a check for $200 dollars and a note. The note said "Enjoy a dinner out, compliments of Coach Dean Smith." He was still ahead of his time," said former player, Kenny Smith. I wonder how many will actually cash their check.

Sometimes we say "thank you" too late; but as long as there is a kid dribbling a basketball on some playground somewhere, the legend of Dean Smith will live on. Smith is defined by basketball and how he used the game to tear down social barriers, and for that he will always be remembered. Dean Smith would want to leave you with this: "Whatever you do in life, you are there to serve." In the end, every great leader is a teacher.

Since I wrote this story, UNC has been accused of academic fraud among their athletes from 1993-2011. Nearly 1500 athletes out of 3100 students who took the courses were given credit for non-existent classes in Afro-American studies to keep them eligible. UNC performed an internal investigation and exposed the athletic department of also inflating grades. The Wainstein report found that Dean Smith was not aware of any wrong doing. The NCAA placed the UNC Athletic Department on a one-year probation.

HE MADE US DREAM

He was naturally creative and tormented by routine. He never acted his age, his whole life. He was born old and remained young. As a young man, he swam so fast, swordfish were jealous. With color film, he helped you feel a part of the conversation. He always said, the media spins the truth but film never lies. He could really see people as they were, and he was tighter with his money than Elvis Presley's pants. This man reinvented normal for all the sports fans of the game of professional football. With the help of his son, Steve, he placed football, music and "the voice" in a video format that captured the American imagination then and even now. "Dad was a storyteller at heart," said Steve. His father had always said, "Tell me a fact and I will learn. Tell me the truth and I will believe you, but tell me a story and it will live in my heart forever." The ultimate compliment occurred when people approached him in super slow-motion. "Big Ed" Sabol once said, "Vince Lombardi was my hero." Ed convinced Lombardi to be miked-up for a game in November of 1967. Green Bay got beat that day and Lombardi refused to allow the sound to be used. Ed knew he was onto something big.

Most of us never grow up to be who we really want to be. Most red-blooded American boys would love to hit a baseball like Ted Williams, tackle a ball carrier like Dick Butkus, or dunk a basketball like Dr J. But the fact is only one percent of us ever get the chance to play at the professional level. Ed Sabol made us dream when he created NFL Films.

The only event in history to be documented more than the National Football League is World War II.

Edwin "Ed" Milton Sabol was born in Philadelphia, Pennsylvania, on September 11, 1916. He became a championship swimmer at Blair Academy, located in Blairstown, New Jersey. In 1935, Ed set a World Interscholastic Swimming record in the 100-yard freestyle race. He attended Ohio State University (OSU) on an athletic scholarship for swimming and was named an alternate on the 1936 United States Olympic team. Ed refused to attend the Olympics in Berlin, Germany, because of the connection with Adolph Hitler. In 1937, he participated on the OSU BIG TEN Championship team that set the 400-yard freestyle relay record. He also swam on the 1937 National AAU Championship team in the 400-yard freestyle relay.

Ed dropped out of Ohio State after two years and worked as a comic in a vaudeville act and even appeared in a Broadway play. Ed Sabol eventually joined the U.S. Army to fight in Europe against the Germans during World War II. Ed married in 1940, Audrey Siegel, a sculptor and art enthusiast. After the war, he joined his wife's father's business as a clothing salesman. It would not last.

In 1956, Ed Sabol had just turned 40 years old and was not happy with where he was in life. He grew tired of selling overcoats for his father-in-law's company. So, he retired with the intentions of reinventing his life. He built a new house and learned to fly. With his new-found hobby, he traveled around the world. He rediscovered a 16-millimeter camera that he and his wife, Audrey, had received as a wedding gift and took it with him to document his travels. He also loved filming his son, Steve's high school football practices and games, for fun.

Ed Sabol's son, Steve, was born October 2, 1942, and he played and loved the game of football. By 1945, Ed had hatched the idea of forming a film production company.

Steve had a sister named Blair and their dad decided to name his new company "Blair Motion Pictures" after her. This company was founded in 1962 and its first major project was to film the 1962 NFL Championship Game between the New York Giants and the Green Bay Packers at Yankee Stadium in New York City. Sabol had won the filming rights with a $3,000 bid. It has been said that it took all of Ed Sabol's wit and charm to convince NFL Commissioner, Pete Rozelle, that his experience in filming high school games was enough to prepare him for the job. As Mother Nature would have it, the game was played in 15-degree weather with 30 mile-per-hour winds. Sabol built bonfires in the baseball dugouts to keep his cameras thawed out. After the game, Rozelle claimed it was the best football film he had ever seen.

In 1964, Blair Motion Pictures became NFL Films. Steve joined his dad and the company that same year as a full-time cinematographer. Fifty years later, NFL Films produces about 800 miles of game footage into 2,000 hours of programming each year. Their headquarters in Mount Laurel, New Jersey, holds the only visual record of games played in the 1960's and 1970's, when network videotape was not preserved. Ed retired in 1995. During his tenure, NFL Films had won 52 Emmy Awards.

The great George Halas once said to Ed Sabol, "You guys are the keepers of the flame."

In 1987, Ed received the Order of the Leather Helmet from the NFL Alumni Association and the Bert Bell Memorial Award. In 1991, he accepted the Pete Rozelle Award. Ed was inducted into the International Jewish Sports Hall of Fame in 1996. In 2003, both father and son received Lifetime Achievement Emmys from the National Academy of Television Arts and Science. On February 5, 2011, Ed Sabol was elected to the Pro Football Hall of Fame as a contributor. His son Steve was his presenter. In November of 2011, Steve Sabol and his dad were inducted into the

Philadelphia Sports Hall of Fame, and in December 2011, Steve was placed in the Sports Broadcasting Hall of Fame. Even though Ed Sabol turned over the business to his son in 1985, Steve Sabol continued to look at the Pro Football Hall of Fame from the outside. As a company, NFL Films has won 107 Emmy Awards.

There is no doubt that Big Ed Sabol and his son played a large role in accelerating professional football to America's #1 watched sport. His idea of using multiple cameras from all different angles brought the game up close for the fans. The use of stop-action, super slow-motion film, and sound effects made the game's violence very real. And not unlike Hollywood, the company thrived with an annual income surpassing the $50 million mark. It was even reported that supreme filmmaker, Sam Peckinpah, had used slow motion in his gunfight scenes in his movie *The Wild Bunch*, after watching a Super Bowl highlight film that had been created by NFL Films. Former television anchor man, John Facenda, became famous in football households as the voice of the NFL.

They say one of the worst experiences a parent can have is the loss of their child no matter what their age. In this case, Steve Sabol was diagnosed on March 11, 2011, with an inoperable tumor on the left side of his brain. He passed away eighteen months later on September 18, 2012. Steve was 69 years old. His father Ed was 95 years old at that time. Even though Steve lived a relatively long life, his death made it extremely tough on his father.

Have you ever noticed that when a person leaves this life in their seventies we tend to mourn their loss, but if they are able to stay with us into their nineties we celebrate their life. Ed Sabol died on a Monday at the age of 98 at his home in Scottsdale, Arizona. The date was February 9, 2015. Ed is survived by his wife, their daughter Blair, and grandson Casey by their son Steve.

Ed Sabol once said, "When you're in the moment behind

the camera and everything is quiet, you can't hear the fans. That's when I knew we had something special."

JERRY'S WORLD

He was cool, colorful, funny and a great storyteller. He loved the fans that showed up to watch his team practice, and a good cigar. Baldheaded and unafraid, he moved through life with a raspy voice, while being brutally honest. Some said he looked a little like Uncle Fester on *The Munsters* and spoke like Yoda on *Star Wars*. He could fool you with his lovable puppy-dog eyes, but the fact was, you were either with him or against him. If he wasn't chewing on a towel for good luck, he was placing it on top of his head to help him cool off and think. This fellow was a basketball junkie whose teams practiced hard and played like they were always in a fist fight. This man hung his coaching hat on guarding the ball and disrupting the opposing offense. He created the "Amoeba" defense--a gambling zone defense that led to steals and fast break opportunities. His games were like a prize fight, run, gun and press. He seem to feud with everyone, everyone but his players. Hanging a hundred points on the opposing team was just another day at the office. He liked recruiting kids with "baggage," guys who were academically challenged and economically depressed. He thought everyone deserved a second or maybe a third chance. You could say he was colorblind. Maybe he saw some of himself in his players. He had grown up on the poor side of town and had needed junior college to keep his dreams alive. He told a story of how he recruited a kid on a stairwell in one of the Oakland project.

Coach Jerry Tarkanian was always in on the gag. He once

said, "I like transfers from the Pac-Ten; their cars are already paid for." When UNC was running the "Four Corners" and UCLA was playing fundamentally sound basketball, there was a time when Syracuse, Georgetown and Vegas were known for fun basketball. "Tark the Shark" put the run in "Runnin' Rebels" and I'm sure he never paid for a meal in Vegas in his life. What happened in Jerry's world was never intended to stay in Vegas.

Jerry Esther "Tark" Tarkanian was born in Euclid, Ohio, on August 8, 1930. The town of Euclid is located right outside of Cleveland. Jerry was the only child of Rosie, a refugee of the Armenian genocide, which occurred in World War I. Rosie and the rest of her family escaped the Ottoman Empire and settled in Lebanon, where she met George Tarkanian. The couple married and later moved to the United States. Jerry's father died when he was 13. Rosie remarried and Jerry's new stepfather disliked sports and did not approve of Jerry's involvement. "He told me I should become a barber," said Jerry. His mother, on the other hand, gave her blessings. Jerry enrolled and attended Pasadena City Junior College, in California. While there, Jerry made the basketball team and played during the 1951-52 season. Then he transferred to Fresno State College and played for the Bulldogs during the 1954-55 season, as a back-up guard. Jerry graduated in 1955 and earned his master's degree in Educational Management from the University of Redlands.

Tark spent the next five years (1956-1960) coaching basketball at three different high schools located in California: San Joaquin Memorial, Antelope Valley, and Redlands High School. He then moved on to Riverside City Junior College where he coached for six years (1961-1966), and then he coached at Pasadena City Junior College from 1966-1968. Four of his junior college teams won California Junior College Championships, three at Riverside, and one at Pasadena. With Tark, it did not matter where you were from, only where you were going. He signed black kids from the playgrounds of Watts and Inglewood. No one was written off. During his seven years in coaching junior college, his teams went 196-13 (.938).

In 1968, Tarkanian took the big step to Division I basketball and accepted the Head Basketball Coach's position at Long Beach State. While there, he recruited several black players and proceeded to break one of the unwritten rules of college basketball, where at least three of the starting five players had to be white. He also became one of the first coaches to recruit junior college players. A rebel was born. Tark's team scored 100 or more points in 23 games that season. And this was before the shot clock or three-point shot. His program was looked down upon, and he was labeled a renegade. By 1970, his Long Beach State program had made the NCAA Tournament, and Tark boasted his team was made up of mostly junior-college transfers. Long Beach qualified for four straight NCAA Tournaments and established itself as a regional power. Even John Wooden of UCLA refused to schedule a regular season game with Long Beach. These two schools did eventually meet in the 1971 NCAA West Regional Finals. Long Beach led by 12 points at halftime, but lost 57-55 to UCLA. Tarkanian left Long Beach at the end of the 1973 season, for the University of Nevada, Las Vegas (UNLV). Tark's win-loss record at Long Beach State was an astounding 122-20 over five years.

In 1973, Tarkanian proceeded to take a small desert program and turn it into a national powerhouse. There was little if any fan support and the program has been down for quite a while. The locals referred to UNLV as "Tumbleweed Tech." His teams began play in the Las Vegas Convention Center, which sat 6,400 fans. The success of his program allowed them to build the Thomas & Mack Arena which seats 18,500. UNLV became a Division I program when Tark arrived. After his second year at UNLV, his team made "Sweet 16." Two years later (1977), they arrived at his first

Final Four. UNLV lost in the semifinals to Dean Smith's UNC Tar Heels. Tarkanian was offered the Los Angeles Lakers' job after the 1977 season, but turned it down. Jerry West became the Lakers' head coach.

Tark's Rebels returned to their second Final Four in 1987, where they lost again, but this time to Bobby Knight's Indiana Hoosiers in the semifinals. In 1990, Tark arrived in Denver with a team that resembled a basketball machine. In the finals of the West Regional of the NCAA tournament, the favorite, Loyola Marymount, had suffered the terrible death of their star, Hank Gathers. Tark's Rebels ran the Lions out of the gym. Several days later, in Denver, Colorado, UNLV played in Tark's third Final Four and scorched Duke 103-73, a record for margin of victory in a championship game. This win provided Tark with his first NCAA National Championship. His team went undefeated (34-0) the following year (1990-91), before losing a rematch to Coach Mike Krzyzewski and the Duke Blue Devils, 79-77, in the semi-finals of his fourth Final Four appearance, held in Indianapolis, Indiana. Tark's 1991-92 team went 26-2. Tark won his final game at UNLV 65-53 over Utah State. He resigned at the end of that season.

"Red" McCombs signed Jerry Tarkanian to coach the San Antonio Spurs during the 1992 season. His pro experience lasted but twenty games before he was fired. I happened to attend one of Tark's games while he was still there. He looked completely out of place. I even took a picture of him pacing the sideline. Tark and Red never got off on the right foot and argued constantly about the point-guard position. The Spurs had just lost Rod Strickland to Portland, and Red signed "Vinny" Del Negro and Avery Johnson. Tark felt he could not compete without an experienced point guard and said so in the press. It was but a matter of time before he was told to leave. Tark said publicly after his release, "I always liked college more than the pros." After twenty games his professional win-loss record was 9-11. Tark accepted a $1.3

million settlement.

In 1995, Jerry Tarkanian returned to the college ranks to coach his alma mater, Fresno State University. The Bulldogs won 20 or more games, six times from (1995-2002). They participated in five NIT and two NCAA Tournaments. Tark retired in 2002, at the age of 72; with a final win-loss record of 778-198.

Coach Jerry Tarkanian was a very superstitious man. Over the years he became known as the coach who chewed on a towel. There were many other superstitions, some known and some not so well-known. Here's the story of how it all began. In 1956, Tark's high school team was playing an important league game in a sweltering gym that had no air conditioning. There was but one water fountain in the gym, and Tark kept going back and forth during the game to get a drink of water. He often suffered from a dry throat as was made known by the sound of his voice. Eventually, he got tired of going back and forth, so he took a white towel with him and soaked it in water and returned to his seat. After getting the victory, Tark continued to take a wet towel into each game with him. Over the years he had his trainer provide two towels each game, one wet and one dry. The chewing of a towel evolved into his good-luck charm and then became his trademark. There were other superstitions. The seat on the right of Tark was to always remain empty as he did not like anyone sitting next to him. It became known as the "ghost chair." He threw away sport coats he had worn to a game that his team had lost. If his team lost a road game, he refused to have his team stay in the same hotel the next time they played.

Part of the Jerry Tarkanian's story is his career-long battle with the NCAA. Like Daniel in the lion's den, nothing bothered him. He had no problem with poking the bear (NCAA) or sticking his fingers in the parrot cage. His catch-me-if-you-can attitude resulted in each of the three universities where he coached eventually being placed on probation for rules violations. The NCAA visited UNLV eleven times while Tark was the head coach. Their visits resulted in ten players being suspended at different times over different rule violations. Even Tark was suspended, but he appealed his suspension and continued to coach. In short, Tark believed that the small schools were being picked on, while the major universities were allowed to do whatever it took to field a great team. He felt that the NCAA leadership was only concerned about power and money. Tark said that he had witnessed large schools paying athletes and parents, while fixing their grades. Yet only the small schools got investigated and then punished, while the NCAA beat their chests and claimed they were cleaning up the system. A couple of my favorite quotations from Tark were: "The NCAA is so mad at Kentucky, it's going to give Cleveland State two more years probation." And second, "Nine out of ten schools are cheating. The other one is in last place."

In the end, Tarkanian sued the NCAA for violating his due process. In 1998, the NCAA settled out of court to the tune of 2.5 million. I'd call that a win. He called it, "My greatest victory."

Another part of Jerry's history are the stories of his recruiting exploits. There is a wonderful story told by Dan Wetzel of Yahoo Sports. It goes something like this: In 1985, the President of UNLV (Robert Maxon) decided they needed more intelligent kids enrolled at the university. So, he came up with the idea that any student in the country who was named valedictorian of their high school class would receive a full academic scholarship if they enrolled at UNLV. There was a 6'10' kid, a fine basketball player, serving time in the El Paso de Robles Youth Correctional Facility, for robbery. Tark went to the prison and spoke with the kid on the phone through the glass. The kid had earned his GED while behind bars and was their valedictorian. Tark got the idea that this guy would qualify for the free academic scholarship, which would get him a good player and another athletic scholarship to use for his program. The fellow's name was Clifford Allen. So Tark had Allen sign a Letter of Intent to play for UNLV upon his release. It didn't work out. After being released and before Allen could play, he was caught stealing cars in LA and returned to prison. Although very few of his kids actually graduated from UNLV, Tark always claimed he had successfully recruited a valedictorian for his program. Other tales had Tark sending Frank Sinatra to the house of a recruit who lived in New Jersey, because his mother was Italian.

Ronnie Arrow, a fine basketball coach and friend, knew Tarkanian very well. In fact, Tark recruited two of Arrow's players (David Butler and Moses Scurry) from San Jacinto Junior College to play for the UNLV Runnin' Rebels, who won the 1990 NCAA National Championship over Duke. "Tark understood he couldn't get UNC-type players," said Arrow. "He was left with economically-challenged kids. Lots of my coaching ideas came from Tark. He was all about basketball and family, and nothing else. His kids loved him and played hard." Arrow continued, "He wouldn't hire an assistant if they played golf, because he thought golf was a waste of time. So they didn't tell him."

"He was not an early person," said Arrow. "There was a time in the eighties and nineties when coaches respected one another. Those were the days. There was no internet or social media. They competed like crazy against each other, and then spent time together after the games at dinner. I loved hearing the stories late into the night," said Ronnie. "Now coaches will do almost anything to win."

At UNLV alone, Tark had 39 of his players selected in the NBA draft. You will remember some of the names: Larry Johnson, Greg Anthony, Stacey Augmon, Reggie Theus, Sidney Green, Armen Gilliam, Anderson Hunt, and of course his son, Danny Tarkanian. Then there's the name Lloyd Daniels from New York City. In 1987, Daniels was caught buying crack cocaine from an undercover policeman. Daniels would never play a game at UNLV. Interestingly, Daniels was good enough to play professional basketball and signed with the San Antonio Spurs while Tark was coaching there.

Jerry Tarkanian coached college basketball for 31 years. His teams failed to win 20 games a season only twice. In his 19 seasons (1973-1992) at UNLV his teams went to four Final Fours and won 30 tournament games. Since he left, they have won only three. His time at UNLV will show that his win-loss record was 509-105. Yet, very few of his kids would graduate. The Thomas & Mack Center became the place to be. In 2005, the basketball floor was named "Jerry Tarkanian Court." He lived in the moment with no playbook. His pregame ceremonies included indoor fireworks and light shows. He created "Gucci Row" where Vegas headliners would pay top dollar to sit courtside. Bill Cosby, Don Rickles and Frank Sinatra were considered regulars. In 2013, Tark was finally inducted into the Naismith Memorial Basketball Hall of Fame. UNLV also placed a life-size statue of Tark outside of the arena. Yes, he's chewing on a towel.

Family and basketball drove Jerry to get up every morning. He married Lois in 1966. They had four children together and eleven grandchildren. Lois was a Las Vegas City councilwoman. Jerry Tarkanian died on February 11, 2015, just three days after Dean Smith, the head coach at the University of North Carolina. Tark was 84 years of age. Together, these two legendary coaches amassed 1,657 wins between the two of them. They were each very successful in very different ways. Jerry had his second heart attack in April of 2014 and suffered from pneumonia that November. He was taken to Valley Hospital Medical Center with difficulty in breathing. The flags at City Hall were flown at half-staff.

Tarkanian must have known how hard it would be to run a clean program in a city known worldwide for gambling.

It reminded me of an old saying: "Never rob a bank that's across the street from a diner that serves the best donuts in three counties. The place is full of cops." Vegas honored Tarkanian the only way they knew how. On Wednesday, February 18, 2015, the casinos agreed to dim their lights on the Vegas Strip for three minutes at 10:30 PM local time. This coincided with the end of UNLV-Boise State basketball game, the first game UNLV had played since Tark's death. Jerry Tarkanian's name now joins the list of JFK, Frank Sinatra, Sammy Davis Jr., Dean Martin, George Burns and Ronald Reagan.

LAST OF THE FIRST

Charles Dickens once said, "It was the best of times, it was the worst of times." True greatness is most often hard to understand. He fell in love with the game with the first basket he made. He had all the physical riches: speed, power, vision, energy and size, but was never one to toot his own horn. This guy could motor, one of the most exciting guys on a basketball court. He was so big he had his own climate. This fellow had no respect for Sir Isaac Newton's law of gravity; he could jump over your car. He could also fill it up. When the lights went on, he could do it all. When he had paint under his feet, he was almost impossible to stop. The fans berated him, his opponents tried to hurt him, but his teammates accepted him when they learned he could play. It was 1950, he was African American, his skin looked like melted butterscotch, and his name was Earl Lloyd. Before there was Earl "The Pearl" Monroe, there was Earl "Big Cat" Lloyd. Both would end up in the Naismith Memorial Basketball Hall of Fame.

"Chuck" Cooper, Nat Clifton and Earl Lloyd were the first three African Americans to play in the NBA during the 1950-51 season. Chuck Cooper was the first black man to be drafted by an NBA team, the Boston Celtics. Nat "Sweetwater" Clifton of the Harlem Globetrotters became the first black to sign an NBA contract with the New York Knicks, but it was Earl Lloyd, drafted in 1950 in the ninth round by the Washington Capitols, who became the first black man to actually play in an NBA game against the

Rochester Royals. The date was Halloween night, October 31, 1950. The defensive-minded Lloyd scored six points and pulled down ten rebounds. There were 2,184 fans in the stands in Rochester that night. "That first game was really uneventful, and there was no publicity on it," said Lloyd. With some luck in the scheduling, Lloyd played one day before Cooper and four days before Clifton. The Royals beat the Capitols that night, 78-70. A fourth black player, Hank DeZonie, of the New York Rens, entered the NBA later in the season on December 3, 1950, but only played in five games with the Tri-City Blackhawks before quitting out of frustration. Cooper passed away in 1984, Clifton died in 1990, and DeZonie left us in 2009. Earl Lloyd was the last of the first to pass away.

Many incredible black basketball superstars would follow shortly after these first three. In 1950, when Lloyd started playing in the NBA, Bill Russell was 16, Wilt Chamberlain was 14, and Earl Monroe was but 6 years old. Michael Jordan had not even been born yet.

Earl Francis "Big Cat" Lloyd was born in Alexandria, Virginia, on April 3, 1928. Theodore and Daisy Lloyd taught Earl to never dignify ignorance. If people were saying nasty things, it meant he was playing well. "It just made me want to play harder," said Lloyd. Earl played basketball and graduated (1946) from Parker-Gray (all black) High School in Alexandria, Virginia. T.C. Williams High School, the subject of the motion picture *Remember The Titans,* was built as a combined, desegregated high school twenty years later. In 2007, the newly-built basketball court at T.C. Williams High School in Alexandria was named in Earl Lloyd's honor.

At 6'6" inches tall and weighing over 230 pounds, Lloyd was the biggest player at West Virginia State College when he enrolled in 1947, on scholarship. This defensive specialist led the Yellow Jackets of West Virginia State to two (CIAA) Central Intercollegiate Athletic Association conferences and tournament championships in 1948 and 1949. It was at West Virginia State, that Earl Lloyd received the nickname "Moonfixer," which would later become the title of his 2009 autobiography he wrote with Sean Kirst. Lloyd was named All-Conference, three years in a row (1948 to 1950), and was also named All-American by the *Pittsburg Courier* in 1949 and 1950. He averaged 14 points and 8 rebounds a game. In the 1947-48 season, West Virginia State was the only undefeated college basketball team in the nation.

Earl played in only seven games in 1950, after being drafted. The Washington Capitols went out of business on January 9, 1951, while Earl was serving in the Army. One of Earl's teammates was Hall-of-Fame player, Bill Sharman, and the player-coach for the team was "Bones" McKinney, who played at the University of North Carolina. Bones would later coach at Wake Forrest University. There is a wonderful story concerning Bones McKinney that occurred during the Capitols' second game on the road. Washington was playing in Fort Wayne, Indiana, and Earl was prohibited from eating in the hotel restaurant with the team because he was black. "My coach, Bones McKinney, a southerner came up to my room and said he wanted to eat with me," said Lloyd. "I said, 'Bones, you've got nine other players downstairs; you gotta take care of your team. The important thing is I know how you feel.' I told Bones how much I appreciated the gesture." This act of kindness from a white man stayed with him the rest of his life.

Earl Lloyd joined the U.S. Army at Fort Sill, Oklahoma, and served two years. The Syracuse Nationals picked him up on waivers in 1952, where he played for the next six years. Lloyd joined a fine team that included Johnny "Red" Kerr and Dolph Schayes. They were coached by Al Cervi. Lloyd, wearing #11, posted his best year in Syracuse during the 1955 season when he averaged 10.2 points per game and 7.7 rebounds. The Nationals beat the Fort Wayne

Pistons for the 1955 NBA Championship, four games to three. Lloyd, as a starter, and teammate Jim Tucker would become the first African Americans to play on an NBA Championship team.

In 1958, Lloyd and Dick Farley were traded to the Detroit Pistons where he would finish his career in two years, retiring in 1960 at the age of 32. "I didn't think I was ready to stop playing until we played in Philadelphia in an exhibition game and I saw Wilt Chamberlain for the first time," exclaimed Lloyd. "I quit right there and said, 'Coach, this guy isn't real. You've got your assistant coach.'" The Pistons also had two other black players at that time, Nat Clifton and 7-foot center, Walter Dukes. In 1968, Lloyd became the NBA's first black assistant coach in the NBA.

Lloyd fell in love with Detroit, Michigan. "I had a real love affair with the town," said Earl. Lloyd would spend the next 42 years in the "Motor City." He served as a scout for five years and a television commentator throughout the sixties. He became frustrated because the Pistons did not follow up on several of his prospects from small black colleges. Earl Lloyd was credited with discovering Wally Jones, Ray Scott, Willis Reed and Earl Monroe. In November of 1971, the Pistons' head coach, Butch van Breda Kolff, resigned without notice. Lloyd left his position with Chrysler Corporation and joined Detroit as the NBA's second black head coach, after Bill Russell. Even with future Hall-of-Famers, Bob Lanier and Dave Bing, the Pistons went 20-52 in Lloyd's first year. Earl was fired after seven games into his second season (1972) and replaced by Ray Scott.

Lloyd worked for the Detroit Board of Education for more than ten years and later for Dave Bing in his steel and auto parts company. In 1999, Earl moved his family to Tennessee.

Of course Lloyd was compared by many writers to the great Jackie Robinson who, in 1947, broke the color barrier in Major League Baseball, with the Brooklyn Dodgers.

Lloyd would have none of it. Lloyd stated, "I'm no Jackie Robinson." Lloyd experienced a fairly easy transition from college to the pros, because he was accepted by his white teammates. Lloyd told the *Detroit Free Press* in 2004, "Throughout my career, I never experienced one covert racist incident with a teammate or opponent, perhaps because the basketball players were college-educated and many had played with blacks before." He continued, "So you get to training camp with these guys from Southern Cal and Ohio State and UCLA and Georgetown and N.C. State, you kind of ask yourself: 'Do I belong?' For a young black man from Virginia to compete at that level and learn that he belongs there, it was a true defining moment."

As for the opposing cities and their fans, that was an entirely different story. He was not allowed to eat or stay with the team in St. Louis, Fort Wayne, or Baltimore. He heard fans screaming racial comments on a nightly basis. He was called the N-word and, in some cities, fans asked him if he had a tail. Fans yelled stuff like, "go back to Africa." "I learned to manage my anger," said Lloyd.

Lloyd was relatively unknown by today's players until he joined the Naismith Memorial Basketball Hall of Fame as a contributor in 2003. After that he made it a point to attend every induction and become a part of the NBA Rookie Transition Program. This program allowed players from the early days to tell their story and remind today's players it was not as easy to play in the recently-formed NBA as it is now. Former Commissioner David Stern once said, "A reminder in the flesh is a better way to communicate than in a book or by someone else communicating the story." In today's world, a decade is a long time ago.

Earl Lloyd left us on Thursday, February 26, 2015. He was 86 years old. Lloyd is survived by his wife, Carlita, three sons, and four grandchildren. They were living in Fairfield Glade, Tennessee. Lloyd was selected to the CIAA's Player-of-the-Decade Team for the 1940's. In 1993, the Big Cat was inducted into the Virginia Sports Hall of Fame. He was named to the NAIA Silver and Golden Anniversary Teams. Lloyd was tough and never backed down. He led the NBA in personal fouls and disqualifications during the 1953-54 season. Earl played during nine seasons in the pros. He scored 4,682 points while pulling down 3,609 rebounds. He also dished out 810 assists. Earl was ranked 43rd in scoring at the time of his retirement in 1960.

Like most athletes who played during the "Golden Era" of sports, Earl Lloyd's sacrifice-for-the-good-of-the-team playing style was expected and appreciated. Never one to blow his own horn, I wondered why Lloyd tried so hard to fit in when he was born to stand out.

HITTING HIS WAY OFF
THE ISLAND

"It's love that makes the world go 'round," said W.S. Gilbert. If that's true, then the world spun a little faster with this guy in it. He was special. He was superstitious, loved to cook and watch old black-and-white westerns on television. But baseball, yes baseball, that's what made him tick. Baseball is all about memories, and he left us with a stack of them. His voice was thick, as if he were speaking with a mouth full of eggnog. A Cuban rock star in spikes, his skin was as black as an umbrella. This man knew baseball like the back of his glove. He was fast, as elusive as smoke from a pipe, and he played like he was trying to get away from something. At times, because of the color of his skin, he felt like a sparrow facing a cobra, yet he was a symbol of all that was good about the game of baseball. His wrists were as thick as the bat he held in his hands. There was no two-strike approach for this guy; he was up there to hit. The sound his bat made was never quiet. Each time he connected, it sounded like a cannon from Robert E Lee's artillery. This fellow could "crack" out line drives. His bat should have had TNT written on the label instead of Louisville Slugger. He made a living destroying sliders and cutters, and he loved showing off that arm. He may not have broken the land speed record, but he could steal second base in a heartbeat. He was quicker in the outfield than the Red Cross after a hurricane and routinely beat the first baseman to the dugout from leftfield, at the end of an inning. He was an on-base machine and had juice in his legs. A quiet mind and a quiet body were his secret to hitting. The old saying was, the only way to escape from Cuba was to hit your way off the island. When I saw "Minnie" Minoso, I didn't see an old man. I saw a fresh-faced kid throwing a baseball with stars in his eyes. The "Cuban Comet," Minnie Minoso, was an ageless slugger.

Saturnine Orestas Armas "Minnie Minoso" Arrieta was born about 100 miles from Havana, Cuba, in the small town of Perico. No one really knows exactly when he was born, and there is no birth certificate available. In his autobiography, Just Call Me Minnie, written with Herb Fagen, Minoso listed his birth date on his visa as November 29, 1922, but folks close to him swear he was born on the same date in 1925. Minnie grew up working in the sugar cane fields and playing sandlot ball. He eventually joined a semipro team in Cuba before coming to the United States in 1945.

In 1946, Minoso joined the New York Cubans of the Negro Leagues and played with them for three years. In 1947, the New York Cubans won their only Negro League World Series title defeating the Cleveland Buckeyes. Luis Tiant Sr., Martin Dihigo and Minnie Minoso were apart of that championship team.

In 1949, Minoso was signed by the Cleveland Indians as a third baseman. His signing came just two years after Jackie Robinson. Minnie struggled with English and the hatred of the times for black players. He debuted on April 19, 1949, but only played in nine games that season before being sent down to the Indians' Class-A Minor League team located in Dayton, Ohio, for the rest of that year and the 1950 season. We must remember that Cleveland had just won the World Series in 1948 and the team was still filled with stars, therefore limiting Minoso's playing time. Minnie's first full season occurred in 1951, where he hit .326 while driving in 112 runs. Minoso also led the American League with 14 triples and 31 stolen bases. Unfortunately, Minoso lost the Rookie-of-the-Year Award to New York Yankees' Gil McDougald on the baseball writers' ballot, but was chosen by *The Sporting News* as their choice for the 1951 Rookie of the Year. On April 30, 1951, Cleveland sent Minoso to the Chicago White Sox, in a three-team trade with the Philadelphia Athletics. On May 1, 1951, in his first at-bat as a White Sox, #9 Minnie Minoso hit a home run off Yankees' pitcher, Vic Raschi. That made Minoso the first black player to hit a home run at Comiskey Park. A white Venezuelan shortstop named Chico Carrasuel also joined the White Sox in 1951, making it easier for Minnie to fit in. There were times when Minnie was turned away from a restaurant, so Chico would go in and get them both something to eat.

From 1951 to 1957, Minoso would hit over .300 five times and receive five All-Star selections. His best year by far came in 1954, as Minnie batted .320 with a .410 on-base percentage. He drove in 119 runs by hitting 19 home runs and 18 triples. Minoso missed out on playing with the White Sox pennant winners of 1959 (the Go-Go Sox), because he was again traded back to Cleveland, before the 1958 season. After two years in Cleveland he was sent packing back to the White Sox for the 1960 and 1961 seasons. You could find him in St. Louis with the Cardinals in 1962 and in Washington with the Senators in 1963. And yes, you guessed it; Minoso was then traded back to the White Sox in 1964. He would make two more appearances with Chicago where he played in three games in 1976. After not playing for twelve years, he hit a single to leftfield against California Angels' pitcher Sid Monge, with two outs in the second inning and Chet Lemon on first base. It was his only hit in eight at-bats as a designated hitter that year. In 1980, he recorded two at-bats with no hits in three games. Minoso's last official Major League at-bat occurred on October 5, 1980. White Sox owner, Jerry Reinsdorf, did petition the Baseball Commissioner, Fay Vincent, to allow Minnie to play in a game in 1990, but Vincent would not allow it. Fay felt it would make a mockery of the game. The story is not over. Mike Veeck, Bill Veeck's son (former Cleveland Indians' owner) was running the St. Paul Saints of the Independent Northern League. Mike signed Minoso for one game in 1993, and he bounced back to the pitcher in his only at-bat. Minoso signed a one-game contract again in 2003, his seventh decade of appearing in a professional game, and he drew a walk.

Several of my favorite Minnie Minoso stories are as follows: Minnie Minoso was once hit by a pitch and then homered in the same at-bat. How, you ask? It has always been customary to be awarded first base when hit by a pitched ball. In a Minor League game, Minnie, who was notorious for standing very close to home plate, turned his shoulder into a pitched ball and was hit. The umpire claimed Minnie made no attempt to get out of the way and called the pitch a strike. Minoso hit a home run several pitches later in that same at-bat. As he rounded the bases and crossed home plate, the umpire asked him if he was happy with the way things turned out. "Give me my first base the first time," Minoso told the ump. Interestingly, Minnie led the American League ten out of his seventeen seasons in number of times being hit by a pitch. He was "plunked" a total of 192 times.

The second story goes like this: Minnie Minoso was the first black man to play in old Comiskey Park. In April of 1991, when the White Sox moved into the new Comiskey Park (now known as U.S. Cellular Field), Minnie showed up at the park. He told a sportswriter of the Chicago Tribune, "Before anybody played there, I went up there and ran against the wall in left field and ran around the bases and slid into home plate. The players said, 'Minnie what are you doing?' I said, 'I was the first black guy to play in the old stadium, and I want to be the first black guy to run against the wall and run around the bases in the new stadium. And that's what I did.'" Tony Perez once said, "Every young player in Cuba wanted to be like Minnie Minoso, and I was one of them."

Last but not least: White Sox centerfielder and teammate, Jim Landis, tells a story of how Minoso once showered after a game with his entire uniform on. Being very superstitious, Minnie believed he could wash away all the bad sprits that had caused him to be in a hitting slump. The next day," said Landis, "Minoso had four hits, including a home run." His other superstitions included taking the same route to the ballpark every day, eating the same food, at the same time, wearing the same clothes when they won, and talking to the same folks at the park, in the exact same order.

At 5' 10" tall and weighing 175 pounds, handing Minnie Minoso a bat was like giving Roberto Duran a pair of boxing gloves; something remarkable was going to happen. Minnie Minoso's complete stats will read: He played in 1,835 games over 17 Major League seasons. He hit .298 with 1,963 hits, 336 doubles, 82 triples, 186 home runs, 1,023 RBI, and scored 1,136 runs while stealing 205 bases. He still ranks among the White Sox leaders in many categories. Minoso played in nine All-Star games during his career. In 1983, Minoso's #9 was retired by the Chicago White Sox, and they also erected a statue of him outside U.S. Cellular Field, in 2004.

My favorite quotation from Minnie goes like this: "The most important thing in my life is the fans, to receive a smile and pay them back with a smile." Minoso was an interesting man. He understood that you really do learn some neat things if you have enough luck to hang around this life for a while. His looks could be intimidating to some until he let loose that marvelous smile and said, "Hello my friend." Minnie was the ninth black player in the Major Leagues and recognized as the first Cuban player. Minnie won three Gold Glove Awards, though he was 35 years old before the award even existed. He was elected into the Chicago Sports Hall of Fame in 1984 and the World Baseball Hall of Fame in 1990. Minoso was one of two players to play baseball in five different decades. Nick Altrock, a pitcher, who began his career in 1898, was the only other five-decade player.

Minoso's first manager, Paul Richards, once said, "He hit a home run in his first at-bat for the Sox and a home run in his last at-bat for the Sox. He was even better in between." The highest support Minnie received from the baseball writers regarding the Hall of Fame was 21.1 % in 1988. How do we let Gil Hodges, Buck O'Neil, and Minnie Minoso die without a plaque in Cooperstown? They shared their talents and we will miss them like an old friend. Their play will stand, and there will never be anyone like them again.

The Chicago White Sox statement said "Mr. White Sox has died." Baseball's Cuban ambassador, Minnie Minoso, was found slumped over, dead, in his parked car at 1:09 AM Sunday morning March 1, 2015, near a gas station in North Chicago. Minnie had a pacemaker installed awhile back, and his son said his dad had been experiencing breathing problems recently. Minnie had gone to a friend's house on Saturday night to celebrate a birthday. It appears his heart just gave out, and he pulled his car over and parked. It doesn't really make any difference how old he was. The Good Lord got himself a Hall-of-Famer that day. Beloved by everyone but his opponents on the baseball diamond, Minoso will be missed. As he got older, Minnie had often said, "When I die, I want to be playing baseball. They don't bury me without my uniform. If I die, I die happy because I was wearing my #9 with the White Sox." Left behind is his wife of 30 years, Sharon, and four kids: Orestes Jr., Charlie, Marilyn and Cecila. In less than six weeks, The Windy City of Chicago has lost two of its most iconic athletes in the passing of Minnie Minoso of the White Sox and Ernie Banks of the Chicago Cubs. I never had the chance to meet

Minnie, but I wish I had. As our country moves towards reconciliation with Cuba, Minoso could very well be the future of Major League baseball.

My pal, Bill "Spaceman" Lee, once said, "You don't work baseball, you play it." I'm sure Minoso felt the same way. And yes, as the funeral ended, they played and sang "Take Me Out to the Ballgame," in unison. Ernie Banks would have been proud.

CONCRETE CHARLIE

"The greatest teams in college football came after WWII when all the players returned at 22-23 years old," said "Beano" Cook. "Football was easy after fighting Japan and Germany." This game called football was the most important thing in his life then, now, and always. He may go down as the toughest son-of-a-gun to have ever played. He was mean and absolutely unforgiving. He didn't have any friends; he only had family. This guy was like some sort of creation that stepped out of a steel blast furnace located in Bethlehem, Pennsylvania; chiseled out of iron ore. He developed a fondness for train wrecks. His idea of a good time was a mass murder. Genghis Khan may have been a middle linebacker. There is no doubt that he gave his era a backbone. He owned the dirtiest uniform and hated to go off the field. "Forty-three players trotted on and off the field and there I would be, alone, waiting," he said. He was so emotionally spent at the end of a game; it took him an hour to get his shoes off. "It's hard to describe staying out there with only the officials." "He would have been as great as Spartacus," said Tommy McDonald. He was "blue collar," with a wide nose, talked tough, and hit hard. "He once tore his right bicep during a game. He went to the sideline with the muscle hanging down. He massaged the muscle up his arm and then, pointing with his index finger, told the doctor to put the tape right here. Then he flexed his arm a couple of times, nodded, turned and went back into the game," said Tom Brookshire. "If he had been with

Custer, he would have been standing right beside him." He was a professional at gritting his teeth when he spoke. "Other players were afraid of him. He was loud, and talked a lot," said "Sonny" Jurgensen. Someone once said if you had a magic wand and you owned a football team, you would want to make eleven Chuck Bednariks. Chuck was considered the "Spirit of Philadelphia" and the last of the 60-Minute Men.

Charles Philip "Chuck" Bednarik was tough, grew up angry, and the last of the two-way players; they called him "Concrete Charlie." He was born on May 1, 1925, in Bethlehem, Pennsylvania, among the steel mills. He had six brothers and sisters. One brother was named "Jeep." His father had emigrated from Czechoslovakia, in 1920. Chuck made his first football from his mom's stocking stuffed with cloth and leaves. Chuck attended Bethlehem Liberty High School and was drafted into the service in 1942. Called up to serve at 18 years old after his senior year in 1944, Chuck became an Army Air Corps waste gunner on a B-24 Bomber. He once counted 175 holes in his plane after a mission, and he flew 30 missions. "I had a number of buddies who never came back; thank God I was able to survive," said Bednarik. When he returned stateside in 1945, he enrolled at the University of Pennsylvania. The post-war years were the days of the "Golden Boys" like Glenn Davis, Johnny Lujack, Doak Walker, and "Doc" Blanchard. Bednarik was the best of the college linemen. Chuck once intercepted two passes against the 1946 unbeaten Army team. He was selected All-American twice in 1947 and 1948, and also won the Maxwell Award, an award given to the best college football player in the nation that year. Chuck finished third in the Heisman voting in 1948, while punting, playing center and linebacker.

Chuck was the first player drafted in 1949, by the Philadelphia Eagles. He was given the #60 and started at center and linebacker. Still, he had to have a job during the off-season to pay the bills. So, he worked as a concrete salesman for the Warner Company. It was here and on the football field that he earned his nickname, Concrete Charlie. Chuck Bednarik is as hard as the concrete he sells. "We played during a time of no holds barred," said Baltimore Colts' defensive tackle, Art Donovan.

On December 18, 1949, Bednarik and the Philadelphia Eagles took the muddy field, in a driving rain storm, against the Los Angeles Rams, at the L.A. Memorial Coliseum. Harry Wismer and Red Grange broadcast the game for ABC. The Eagles shut out the Rams 14-0 that day in front of 27,980 spectators and won the NFL Championship. It was a great way to start the career of Chuck Bednarik.

The NFL really came on strong in the 1950's as television became the newest form of media. "Suddenly, the camera loved the game of football," said writer, David Halberstam. "It allowed us to see the violence of the collisions." During the 1950's, Chuck always felt overshadowed by the Giants' linebacker Sam Huff and the Lions' linebacker Joe Schmidt. Why? Because Schmidt won several championships with the Detroit Lions: in 1952, 1953 and 1957. Sam Huff won a championship in 1956 with New York and played in the media capitol of the world.

"He was a monster. Chuck would lead the team in exercising drills and one day we were doing jumping jacks, and he just stopped and weaved his way in between players until he came to big Jessie Richardson who weighed over 300 pounds. Chuck just unloaded on him and I thought to myself, how can you screw up jumping jacks? I was scared to death," said quarterback, Sonny Jurgensen.

Bednarik once got into it with Cleveland's Chuck Noll, who had hit him in the mouth with a forearm during a game. So Concrete Charlie runs Noll down after a kickoff and knocks him to the ground and kicks him. Noll says, "I'll get you after the game." Chuck says, "I'll be right here waiting for you at the end of this game." Bednarik approached Noll after the game and hit him so hard in the face his helmet flew up in the air. A bunch of the Browns' players ran towards Chuck, and Bednarik turned and pointed at them and said, "Don't cross that line," and none of them did. New York Giants' middle linebacker, Sam Huff once said, "Linebackers are born like that."

Chuck tried to retire at the end of the 1959 season but was convinced to come back in 1960 at 35 years of age. The story goes, he needed the money to build a bigger house and his wife was pregnant again. The New York Giants played the Philadelphia Eagles for the Eastern Conference Championship in late November of 1960. Norm Van Brocklin was the quarterback for the Eagles. The two teams met at Yankee stadium. Frank Gifford was from California, smooth, with movie-star looks, and Chuck was from Pennsylvania, old-school and ugly. It was a collision of two different cultures. Near the end of the game, Frank Gifford caught a pass and was tackled hard at the Eagles' 30-yard line by Bednarik. "He was flat on his back, shaking, and he turned white. I thought he was dead," said Sam Huff. "We were leading 17-10 with one-thirty-five left and the Giants were driving," said Chuck. "Charlie Conerly threw Gifford a pass as he headed toward me. I'm ugly. He's handsome. I'm 240. He's 190. He never made a bigger mistake." Bednarik is now smiling when he says, "He took his eye off of me and I ran right through him. 'Giff' went five feet in the air and landed hard. He didn't move. Gifford fumbled and Chuck Weber recovered, and I knew we had the game won. Their team doctor ran out to work on Giff and as the Dr. passed by me, he made a snide comment. I told him he was next," Bednarik snickered. Frank Gifford was unconscious for the next 36 hours, and the doctors forced him to sit out for 18 months. Gifford returned in 1962 and played until 1964. Some fan had a heart attack in the stands during the game and was brought into the locker room. When the players saw someone covered with a sheet, they thought Frank Gifford was dead. Interestingly, opposing Giants' linebacker, Sam Huff, said afterwards, "Linebackers dream of making tackles like that." The Eagles would now face the Packers for "all the marbles."

The Eagles had won ten games during the regular season. In the NFL Championship Game, played on December 26, 1960, Vince Lombardi's Green Bay Packers had the ball on the Giants' 16-yard-line with 14 seconds to go in the game. Bart Starr threw a little swing pass to Jimmy Taylor, coming out of the backfield. Bednarik tackled him on the 10-yard line and stayed on top of him while the clock ran down, 4, 3, 2, 1, zero. "You can get up now, this &>8@4g* game is over," screams Bednarik. The final score was 17-13 in favor of the Eagles. Bednarik was on the field that day for every play except two kickoffs.

Chuck Bednarik was indeed an "Iron Man." He played for the Eagles from 1949-1962 and only missed three games in his fourteen seasons. He retired in 1962 and was inducted into the Hall of Fame in 1967, his first year of eligibility. "He had such a sense for the game," said teammate, Tom Brookshire. "You could do all that shifting and put all those men in motion, and Chuck still went right where the ball was. He just snapped them down like ragdolls." Chuck was named the All-NFL center in 1950. In 1953, Chuck intercepted six passes and returned one for a touchdown. During his NFL career, Bednarik intercepted a total of 20 passes and returned them for 268 yards and the one touchdown mentioned above. He was named All-NFL linebacker from 1951-1957, and then again in 1960.

In 1969, Chuck was elected to the College Football Hall of Fame. He was also selected to the NFL's 50th Anniversary All-Time Team and later to the NFL's 75th Anniversary All-Time Team. You can also find him as a member of the NFL's 1950's All-Decade team. In 1987, the Eagles retired his #60 and placed him in their Hall of Fame. The Chuck Bednarik Award is presented yearly to college football's best defensive player. Chuck, with his hands broken and mangled, was an eight-time Pro Bowl choice and the Pro Bowl MVP in 1954.

Bednarik served as the chairman of the Pennsylvania State Athletic Commission, which oversaw boxing and wrestling in the state, for many years. He also served as an analyst on the HBO program *Inside the NFL* during its inaugural season in 1977-78.

Chuck was taken to St. Luke's Hospital in Bethlehem on March 26, 2011. He was suffering, and passed out from shortness of breath and low blood pressure. He was released shortly thereafter.

Chuck Bednarik died a slow, agonizing death from complications with dementia. His time of death was recorded at 4:23 a.m. on Saturday, March 21, 2015. He was 89 years old and staying in an assisted-living facility located in Richland, Pennsylvania. His long battle took its toll on his family. Chuck's wife, Emma, their five daughters, ten grandchildren and one great grandchild survived their father's ordeal.

Bednarik once said, "A linebacker is an animal; he's like a tiger or a lion that goes after prey. He wants to eat them. He wants to kick the s#7&k% out of them; that's a linebacker." Over the years, good becomes great, great becomes super human. The facts about Chuck are greater than the myth. We will never see anyone do what he did, again. The highest amount he had ever been paid was $27,000 a year. "I don't go to football games anymore. It's not like it used to be. I don't respect the game anymore, the hell with it. All I do now is play golf and practice with my accordion," said Chuck. He remained a bitter critic of the modern-day players, who only played on one side of the ball. Chuck said, "They suck air after five plays, and Deion Sanders couldn't tackle my wife, Emma."

How Sweet It Is

Comedian Jerry Lewis once said, "In order for comedy to work, you must have pace, a tempo; without tempo you have no joke, no visual, and you lose the spirit of comedy." The same can be said about basketball. Some folks say he was the early version of "Pistol Pete" Maravich. He drank, he smoked, he hung out in pool halls and he played basketball, not necessarily in that order. He was a gifted athlete, with an infectious personality, whose parents gave up on him when he was very young; so he was raised by distant relatives and lived at times in some of his teammates' homes. He was every bit a showman; he drew people to him like horseflies on beef ribs. This guy could jump-shoot you out of the building, and he was better at reading zone defenses than books. A self-made basketball player, he could go thru' you, past you, over you, under you, around you, eat your lunch, steal your girl and talk bad about your mama, all at the same time. The only thing that could stop him from scoring was food poisoning. Make no mistake; he wanted to win and to be great. While playing college basketball, he would sit on the other team's bench on purpose; shoot behind his back, dribble behind his back and with his knees. He would spin the ball on his finger tips and roll it down his arms. He even attempted free throws with a hook shot from the foul line. Before it became illegal, he would hang on the rim waiting for a lob pass from a teammate, and you could run holes in your sneakers trying to guard him. He had more tricks than a clown's pocket. Still, he averaged a double-double by scoring 24.6 points and grabbing 10.6 rebounds per game, during his three varsity years in college, and was picked first overall in 1957 NBA draft. He also became the first white basketball player to be recruited by Abe Saperstein of the Harlem Globetrotters. Nothing fazed "Hot Rod" Hundley; they didn't teach "scared" at the University of West Virginia.

Rodney Clark "Hot Rod" Hundley was born in Charleston, West Virginia, on October 26, 1934. He was an only child. His mother abandoned him while looking for work during the depression era, and his father only came into his life on occasion. Hot Rod loved the attention and hated quiet. Silence reminded him of when he was young. It seemed that no one wanted him in the beginning, but in the end, he became a household name, loved by millions. He would grow to be 6' 4" tall and spend a lot of time at the local Y.M.C.A. gym. Everybody called his dad "Butch" Hundley. "I even called him Butch," said Hot Rod. "He was, without a doubt, the best pool player in West Virginia."

Hundley's talent with a basketball was evident at an early age. He was also a pretty fair baseball player. While at Thomas Jefferson Junior High School, he set the state basketball scoring record by pouring in 441 points in a single season. When he wasn't out drinking, smoking and carousing, Hundley attended Charleston High School and averaged 30 points per game, while breaking the state's four-year scoring record in just three years. Hundley scored 45 points for the West Virginia All-Stars against the Kentucky High School All-Stars. He was named a high school All-American and received tons of offers to play ball on the college level. He may not have been able to read the letters, but he surely enjoyed getting them in the mail.

He decided to stay close to home and play for the University of West Virginia Mountaineers. I do remember that N.C. State went after Hot Rod pretty hard to come play basketball for the Wolfpack in Raleigh. From 1954 to 1957, West Virginia made their first of three appearances in the NCAA tournament with Hot Rod leading the way, and they also won three Southern Conference titles in a row. When Rod played on the freshman team, they outdrew the varsity and outpointed just about everyone they played. Hot Rod averaged 35 points per game as a freshman. Once on a breakaway against a team who was way behind on the scoreboard, an overweight opponent tried to keep him from getting to the basket. Rod did a little "juke" step and the guy fell down flat on his back. Instead of driving around him and making a layup, Hundley stopped, put the ball under his right arm and bent over laughing. Then he reached down and helped the guy up. "The place went wild," said Hundley. "That's when they started calling me Hot Rod." He holds the freshman record with 62 points in a game against Ohio University. Fans would come from near and far to pack the Old Field House to see him play.

During his junior year, Hundley scored over 40 points per game, six times. He led the Mountaineers to scoring 100 points as a team, in nine different games, and a No. 4 ranking in the nation. Hundley set the varsity record by scoring 54 points against Furman.

Hundley became only the fourth player in NCAA history to score over 2,000 points (2,180) in his college career and he did it in three years, not four. At that time, freshmen were not allowed to play on the varsity basketball team. Hot Rod was chosen first team All-American twice and still holds eight West Virginia basketball records. He was named to five different All-American Teams in 1957. For West Virginia Head Coach, Fred Schaus, Hot Rod led the Mountaineers to a stunning 72-16 record during his three years of varsity basketball and was chosen the Southern Conference Player of the Year in 1957. Hundley, not Jerry West, is still the only Mountaineer to be drafted first overall in an NBA draft.

Hot Rod was drafted in 1957 by the Cincinnati Royals with the first pick, but was traded immediately to the

Minneapolis Lakers. He would play in Minnesota for three years (1957-1959), before moving to Los Angeles. He would call it quits at the end of the 1963 season because of bad knees. He was only 28 years old and had played in two NBA All-Star Games (1960-61). His NBA career totals in six seasons were 3,625 points scored, 1,420 rebounds and 1,455 assists. It is fair to say that Hot Rod's professional career never rivaled his college career. "I partied all night, slept all day, and fit basketball games in between," laughed Hot Rod. Hundley was the deciding factor on why Jerry West attended West Virginia, and they became tremendous friends and even teammates with the Los Angeles Lakers, from 1960 to 1963. "I first met Rod when I was 18, and he encouraged me to attend West Virginia," said Jerry West. Ten years after Hundley left West Virginia, the university was raising money to build a new basketball coliseum. Both Hundley and West were invited back to play in a charity pickup basketball game. After the game Hot Rod turned to Jerry and said, "I built this building." West replied, "Yeah, but I paid it off."

After basketball, Hot Rod moved to the broadcast booth. He worked four seasons with the Phoenix Suns and then four more seasons with the Los Angeles Lakers. Along the way he teamed up with Dick Enberg to call games aired on TBS and CBS. He worked four NBA All-Star Games on television and two All-Star Games on radio for ABC. In 1974, Hot Rod became the lead voice of the New Orleans Jazz. He would follow the team to Salt Lake City in 1979. As he got older and made announcing basketball his living, he began using clichés when speaking. "How sweet it is," "Home away from home," and "It's been a little slice of heaven," were all woven into his courtside conversation. "Stockton to Malone, hammer-dunk," and "From the parking lot, good!" became some of his signature calls. His broadcast would be simulcast on radio and television for many years before the NBA forced the Jazz to use different broadcasters for each venue.

On the 19th of February, 1993, my friend, Mike Patranella, and I flew to Salt Lake City, Utah, for the NBA All-Star Game weekend. It was a three-day event. It was also snowing when we landed and, being from central and south Texas, neither of us was used to driving on ice and snow. The event at that time was called the NBA JAM and included a sports memorabilia show, with many NBA players from the past and present signing autographs. In addition to the NBA All-Star game, there was also an NBA Legends Game followed by the Slam Dunk contest and the Three-point Shoot-Out. All the events were held at the Delta Center in downtown Salt Lake City. It was here that Mike and I met Hot Rod Hundley and many other players. At the age of 59, former NBA player, Hot Rod Hundley, decided he was going to play in the Legends Game for the West team. I have pictures that I took of Hot Rod along with teammates Zelmo Beaty, Bobby Jones, Maurice Lucas, Calvin Murphy and Clifford Ray. The East team included such stars as Dave Cowens, George Gervin, Artis Gilmore, Connie Hawkins and Lou Hudson, to name a few. The 1993 NBA All-Star Game itself was thrilling as the West team, coached by Paul Westhead, outlasted the East team, coached by Pat Riley, 135-132 in overtime. Unfortunately, 1993 was the last year for the NBA Legends Game to be played.

Once while announcing a Jazz game, Hot Rod had arranged a post-game interview with Jazz player, "Truck" Robinson. The only problem was that after the game, Truck was nowhere to be found. So Hot Rod did the interview without him by playing both parts and answering his own questions. At the end of the interview Hot Rod presented himself with a gift certificate for doing the post-game interview and ended the segment by saying, "Thanks for joining us, Truck." That was pure Hot Rod Hundley.

In 2005, Craig Bolerjack took over the television duties, and Hot Rod continued the Jazz radio broadcast for another four years before retiring for good. The real reason he retired is because most NBA teams moved their radio broadcast teams from courtside to high above the playing floor. The walk up the stairs on Hundley's surgically repaired hips and knees became too much for him to bear. After broadcasting 3,051 games for the Utah Jazz, he announced his retirement on April 24, 2009.

Hundley once said, "My biggest thrill as a pro player came in 1960, when I teamed up with Elgin Baylor to score 73 points in a single basketball game. Yeah, he scored 71 and I scored two."

In 1992, he was inducted into West Virginia Sports Hall of Fame. In 1994, he received the NBA's Distinguished Broadcaster Award. In 2000, forty-three years after he left college, Hot Rod graduated from WVU and received a bachelor's degree in physical education. In 2003, Hundley received the Curt Gowdy Media Award from the Naismith Memorial Basketball Hall of Fame. In 2004, Hot Rod was voted into the Utah Broadcast Hall of Fame. His rapid-fire voice was so distinctive that directory assistance operators always asked "Are you Hot Rod." Hot Rod's #33 was retired by West Virginia on January 23, 2010, at halftime of the Ohio State game, making his number only the second number retired after Jerry West. When the ceremony was over, the fans were standing and chanting, "One More Shot, One More Shot," 76-year-old Hot Rod Hundley grabbed the basketball and threw up a hook shot from the foul line. It hit nothing but net.

In 1998, he co-authored a book with Tom McEachin entitled Hot Rod Hundley: You Gotta Love It, Baby. As a player and announcer, Hot Rod saw every player play, from George Mikan to LeBron James. The Utah Jazz honored him with the naming of the "Hot Rod Hundley Media Center." He conducted basketball clinics in off-season and hosted the Hot Rod Hundley Celebrity Golf Tournament to benefit the Salt Lake Shriner's Hospital. Rod also supported the Boys' and Girls' Clubs in the area.

This is hard for me, as this is not the way I wanted to remember him. Even now I don't think I have all the right words to define all that he was. He must have watched the Kentucky game against West Virginia the other night and died from a broken heart. The Wildcats won, 78 to 39. Hot Rod died from Alzheimer's disease on Friday, March 27, 2015. He was 80 years old and living at his home in Phoenix, Arizona. He was everybody's friend and survived by three daughters. "Hot Rod was the first real basketball hero in West Virginia," said Jerry West. Perhaps a movie about his life would be in order, but who would play him? I think I know what he would have said: "Nobody did the things I did on the court, and nobody has done them since."

STANDING TALL AT QUARTERBACK

In the average fan's mind during the 1950's, football was a college game, played on Saturdays by amateurs. Texas Head Football Coach, Darrell Royal, once said, "There are 22 million people in Texas and all of them majored in coaching football." He may have been correct. This guy wasn't a great player because everything went right. It's because when things went wrong, no one could tell. He understood that great players make simple basic, easy plays. For guys like him, the circus never came to town. He was as wholesome as a Boy Scout, motorcycle-fast and, so little he didn't leave footprints. With this guy at quarterback, the play was never over. He was the kind of guy who would give you everything he had left. It was like being in a gun battle and running out of ammunition. His ability to hide the ball with his little hands, after the snap, was magnificent. He would turn his back to the defense while pretending to hand the ball off to a running back, only to tuck it to his hip. The next thing you know, he's standing tall in the end zone with the ball, for a touchdown. With quick feet and a rifle arm, his ability to run the play action pass was a sight to behold.

You see, he stood 5'7 inches tall and weighed only 165 pounds. In fact, he was one of the shortest quarterbacks to ever play in professional football. No matter what nickname was used to identify him, the word "little" always preceded as in the "Little General," the "Little Magician," or simply the "Little Man." He was so short, he lent a whole new meaning to the words "shoestring tackle." The standing joke with his teammates was that he had to ask his wife to kneel down on one knee, so he could propose marriage to her. As good as he was at quarterback, he also managed to throw lots of interceptions. Part of that was due to his size and part due to the fact he played with the Washington Redskins and Dallas Cowboys, two mediocre teams at that time. While with the Cowboys, he threw so many interceptions that he led the league in tackles for three years. Once while blowing out the candles on his birthday cake, his wish was intercepted and returned for a touchdown. Let me tell you about Eddie LeBaron, one of my father's favorite players.

Edward Wayne "Eddie" LeBaron, Jr., was born in San Rafael, California, on January 7, 1930. He was an only child. His dad was in the farming business. "An uncle gave me a football when I was four or five years old," said Eddie. "I played with it every day." Eddie started high school at the age of 12 and graduated from Oakdale High School at the age of 16. Not only did he play football and began running the single wing formation, but he even drop-kicked extra points. He also played basketball and ran the hurdles for the track team. Eddie was accepted at the University of Stanford, but chose the College of the Pacific (now called the University of the Pacific), because several of his high school teammates were going to play football there. Not only was Eddie pretty smart, but the community was so small in San Rafael that sometimes there were not enough kids to have a class, so students were just moved to the next grade level. As a result Eddie attended first grade and then third grade and moved along rather quickly.

Eddie LeBaron played quarterback at Pacific from 1946 to 1949 and ran the T-formation. He also lettered all four years, while leading the 1949 team to an undefeated season, and they were ranked tenth in the nation. His first college coach was the legendary Amos Alonzo Stagg. Stagg had played end for Yale University and was elected in 1889 to the very first College Football All-American Team. Stagg, then 70 years old, had become a legend while coaching at the University of Chicago for the past 40 years. Stagg coached the Tigers from 1933-1946 and left Pacific in 1947. The coaching reins were given to his assistant, Larry Siemering, who had played professional football for the Boston Redskins in 1935 and 1936. Before he died, Amos Alonzo Stagg said, "Eddie is one of the greatest T-formation quarterbacks in America and one of the finest passers I've coached in 60 years." Stagg would live to be 102. LeBaron achieved Little All-American honors for three straight years and, in 1949, was awarded the Pop Warner Trophy as the Pacific Coast Most-Outstanding-Player. LeBaron quarterbacked an offense that averaged 503 yards per game and scored 575 points in eleven games and broke the NCAA scoring record. The Tigers also played in three consecutive bowl games: the Optimist, Grape and Raisin Bowls. Eddie did his part while playing both quarterback and safety on defense, at the East-West Shrine Bowl and the Senior Bowl. He also punted on special teams, a true 60-minute man. Eddie was showered with gifts his senior year, including a brand new Studebaker, two suits of clothes, luggage, a television set, and a new 12-gauge shotgun. Stagg (1951) and LeBaron (1980) are the only two from the University of Pacific to be inducted into the College Football Hall of Fame.

In February, LeBaron was chosen and signed in the tenth round of the 1950 NFL draft by the Washington Redskins. He played in two exhibition games before being called into active duty by the U.S. Marines. LeBaron served as a lieutenant for nine months in the Korean War. He was wounded twice and received the Purple Heart. He was also awarded the Bronze Star for heroic action taken, while serving on the front lines. He returned to the Redskins in

1952 and played very well for most of the season, finishing as the sixth leading passer in the league. Remarkably, Eddie was starting his NFL career as one of the great professional quarterbacks of all time was ending his. "Slingin' Sammy" Baugh from TCU was in his 16th and final season of professional football. Eddie claimed he never learned much from Baugh, as their styles were so different. "He didn't go into long dissertations, but he knew the game," said Eddie. LeBaron was named the 1952 NFL Rookie of the Year. Eddie banged up his knee in 1953 and did not play much.

In 1954, Eddie left the Redskins and joined the Calgary Stampeders of the Canadian Football league. He joined Calgary for two reasons. His old college coach, Larry Siemering, was coaching there and Eddie did not get along with Redskin Head Coach, "Curly" Lambeau. While with the Stampeders, Eddie passed for 1,815 yards, eight touchdowns and threw 24 interceptions. He also continued to play defensive back and punted.

In 1955, Eddie returned to Washington after Lambeau was fired and Joe Kuharich was named head coach. The Redskins would finish 8-4 that season, and Eddie LeBaron earned his first Pro Bowl appearance. Although LeBaron liked Redskins' owner, George Preston Marshall, Eddie felt Marshall never fully invested enough money to build a better team. On September 25, 1955, Eddie led Washington against the Cleveland Browns, a team that the Redskins had never beaten. In fact, the Browns had won last year's contest, 62-3. LeBaron called this game his greatest. LeBaron threw for two touchdowns and had the Redskins leading 20-17, late in the fourth quarter. Eddie, an unlikely star, guided the Redskins to the Browns' 13-yard line. With time running out, he dropped back to pass, but found no receivers open. So, he scrambled toward his right sideline and then cut back through the entire Browns' defense to score a rushing touchdown in the left corner of the end zone.

In 1958, Eddie LeBaron led the NFL in passing. In January of 1959, LeBaron threw a late-game touchdown pass to help his East team beat the West team in the NFL Pro Bowl. At that time, the winner's share was $300 each, a lot of money in those days. Gene "Big Daddy Lipscomb of the West team was not happy. Eddie was standing with his new bride outside the locker room after the game when Big Daddy, all 6' 6" inches and 282 pounds of him, emerged from the opposing locker room. He approached Eddie, pointed toward him and said, "You little s.o.b., I'll get you next year." "My wife was scared to death and wanted me to retire right there on the spot," laughed LeBaron.

Tom Landry once said, "The worst thing I ever did for Eddie was talk him out of being a lawyer in Midland." By 1959, LeBaron had received his law degree from George Washington University by going to class during the off-season. That same year, Landry and "Tex" Schramm talked LeBaron out of retirement from football at the age of 29. Dallas was not able to participate in the 1960 NFL draft so, with Eddie's blessing; Dallas traded their first round and a sixth-round draft pick in the upcoming 1961 draft to the Redskins for Eddie LeBaron. His contract paid him $20,000 dollars a year and provided him a law partnership in Dallas. Eddie would be the Cowboys' first starting quarterback for their first three seasons, 1960-1962. LeBaron scored the Cowboys' first-ever touchdown in their first exhibition game, against the San Francisco 49ers, on August 6, 1960, in a game played in Seattle.

Being the Cowboys' starting quarterback wasn't as wonderful as you might expect. On September 24, 1960, the Dallas Cowboys made their franchise debut. Eddie LeBaron started at quarterback and passed for 345 yards and three touchdowns, in a 35-28 loss to the Pittsburgh Steelers; yet he was never mentioned in the cover story. During that game, Steelers' quarterback, Bobby Layne, had broken Sammy Baugh's Cotton Bowl passing record. Over the next four years, Eddie helped paved the road for the Don Meredith era. Those early times were tough. The Cowboys did not win any games in 1960, finishing with a 0-11-1 win-loss record. They only won four games in 1961. The Cowboys won a total of five games with Eddie LeBaron at quarterback.

Eddie LeBaron still holds the NFL record for the shortest touchdown pass ever thrown in a league game. On October 9, 1960, Eddie LeBaron, quarterback of the Dallas Cowboys, threw a touchdown pass to Cowboys' receiver, Dick Bielski, against his former team, the Washington Redskins, from the 2-inch line.

From 1952-1963, Eddie LeBaron played twelve years of professional football, seven with the Redskins, one year in Canada and four with the Dallas Cowboys. Eddie's NFL career totals are as follows: He played in 134 games and completed 898 passes for 13,399 yards, while attempting 1,796 passes for a 50% completion rate. He threw 104 touchdowns and 141 interceptions. Eddie also rushed for 650 yards and scored nine rushing touchdowns, while losing 28 fumbles. LeBaron punted 171 times in five NFL seasons for 6,995 yards. He was selected to play in four Pro Bowls (1955-1957-1958-1962). Eddie was the shortest quarterback to ever be selected to the Pro Bowl.

From 1966 to 1971, LeBaron worked as an NFL announcer. He became the Atlanta Falcons' general manager from 1977 to 1982 and their executive vice president from 1983 to 1985. Eddie also served on the NFL's Competition Committee with Tex Schramm, Don Shula and Paul Brown. In 1980, he was voted the NFL's Executive of the Year.

LeBaron joined the Washington Redskins' Ring of Fame and as mentioned earlier, was elected to the College Football Hall of Fame in 1980. In 2004, Eddie joined the Bay Area Sports Hall of Fame. In 2008, LeBaron was elected to the United States Marine Corps Sports Hall of Fame. During his career, LeBaron played on only two winning teams. You could say his career was mediocre at best.

Eddie LeBaron and I sat together for almost an hour that day and talked football. It was 1992 and we were at the Astro Hall behind a huge white curtain in the players' area, where they sat when they were not signing autographs. A friend of mine in the memorabilia business named Doug Coleman ran a shop called Boxseat Sportscards, located in Dennison, Texas, and he was a huge Cowboys fan. Doug had invited me to come meet Eddie LeBaron in person, after he had finished signing. I was thrilled. With me, I had a Washington Redskins helmet that had been signed by Sonny Jurgensen, Billy Kilmer, Sammy Baugh and Joe Theismann. I grew up in Raleigh, North Carolina, a Redskins fan because of my dad. He had been born poor and raised on a farm in Eastern N.C. and had never seen a television or a football game until he was well over twenty-one years of age. One of the first things he watched on television was a Redskins game. He immediately fell in love with football and the Redskins. Eddie would become one of my dad's favorite football players. Unfortunately, my dad passed away on July 10, 1984, so I was not able to share this story with him. So, I will share a portion with you. My dad was also small in size and he hated it. He always pulled for the underdog and Eddie LeBaron was indeed the underdog in a game where size does matter.

Eddie LeBaron swore to me his size never interfered with his ability to throw the football downfield. He claimed it was an advantage that the defensive backs could not see him behind his linemen. "I knew where the receivers were supposed to be; the defensive backs did not," said LeBaron. He claimed that he could confuse the defense. It is important to realize that, as a group, the players of the fifties were not as big as today, yet there were several who were noticeably large. Gene "Big Daddy" Lipscomb stood 6' 6" tall and weighed 282 pounds; "Rosey" Grier was 6' 5" inches tall and weighed 285 pounds; and "Gino" Marchetti topped out at 6' 4" inches tall and weighed in at 245 pounds. "I never had a problem. I didn't have balls knocked down. I released it high and quick," said Lebaron. Still, Eddie LeBaron was a wizard with the football. He could hide the ball after the snap as good as any quarterback that played the game. His ability to run misdirection plays and scramble when needed made him a true threat to score on every play.

So, now he is gone, the littlest of QB's; the heavens must have needed a quarterback. Old #14, Eddie LeBaron left us on April 1, 2015. Eddie would have laughed at the thought of April Fools, because he had accomplished everything he had ever wanted. It seemed the joke was on us. He died of natural causes and is survived by his wife, Doralee, three sons and five grandchildren. Eddie was being taken care of in an assisted living facility in Stockton, California. LeBaron was 85 years young.

In the beginning, everybody is just a kid from somewhere, but Eddie LeBaron passed the football like little boys do in their wildest dreams. Eddie once said, "Never lose your sense of humor. It's a tough league if you do." Rest well, Eddie, and tell my dad I said, "Hello."

RAW, NOT RARE

Standing 6' 9" tall and weighing over 270 pounds, he could not be overlooked. He had what I called a "caveman aura" around him. He reminded me of a Roman Gladiator. His shoulders were as wide as Goliath and his legs resembled tree stumps. Not only was he big, but he was loud and overwhelming. He cursed and laughed with his head back, like he was possessed. Some said he was one of the most powerful men in the game. He could move mountains and was so mean his motto was, "Finish them off; you don't leave any wounded." Newspaper guys wrote that he was terrifying and would cut your heart out and eat it in front of you. He once leveled Sam Huff, who was standing beside a pile of bodies at the goal line. He hit Huff so hard that the dust flew off the back of my television. He credited eating raw meat as the source of his strength. As a kid, he became addicted to the high protein energy-producing properties of uncooked meat. At the age of five, his grandmother fed him chunks of raw meat from the cutting block, while preparing dinner. He also loved raw eggs. As he got older, he chewed tobacco, ate raw honey, drank beer in quantity and enjoyed vodka screwdrivers. His teammates nicknamed him "The Geek." Ordering a steak in a restaurant went something like this. "I want my steak served raw," he said. "You mean rare?" responded the waitress." "No, raw, take it out of the icebox and put it on a plate," he exclaimed.

Robert Bruce "Bob" St. Clair was born on February 18, 1931, in San Francisco, California. As a kid, Bob ran with gangs on the mean streets of the Mission District in San Francisco. He was scrawny and weak and, according to his high school football coach, too small to play. From his sophomore year to his junior year, Bob grew six inches and gained 60 pounds. He now stood 6'4" and weighed 210 pounds. He also had surprising speed and ran the 440-yard hurdles in high school with the best. Bob graduated from Polytechnic High School, which was located across the street from Kezar Stadium. He would continue to grow, while he was in college.

Bob enrolled and played football with the 1951 Dons of the University of San Francisco's (USF) undefeated (9-0) team. He played offensive tackle and tight end on occasion. Six Dons from this team were good enough to play in the NFL, including future Hall-of-Fame players, Ollie Matson and Gino Marchetti and St. Clair. In fact, USF is the only college in the nation to have three Hall-of-Fame members from the same team. The Dons were invited to play in the Orange Bowl at the end of their season, but were told that their two black players, Ollie Matson and Burl Toler, were not welcome and could not attend. The team voted to take a courageous stand against racism. Bob said "We told them, 'Hell no.'"

USF, a Catholic Jesuit school, dropped their football program after the 1951 season. They were losing about $70,000 a year trying to maintain the program. Bob transferred to the University of Tulsa for his senior season. There, he received a bachelor's degree in Public Administration. Tulsa finished with an 8-1-1 record and received an invitation to play in the Gator Bowl. St. Clair was the only player to vote against playing in the Gator Bowl, as he was invited to play in the East-West Shrine Game to be played in his hometown at Kezar Stadium.

Bob St. Clair was chosen in the third round of the 1953 NFL draft by the San Francisco 49ers. "I grew to love raw liver and dove and quail hearts," said Bob. "I would sit down with the rookies at their training camp table and cut a piece of raw liver and put it in my mouth, and I'd crunch it, and let a little of the blood trickle down my chin. They would always get up and leave with great haste. That night when they called home, I bet they said to their family, 'I don't know if I can make this team. There's one guy here that's crazy.'" Bob played with a leather helmet early in his career, and the results yielded a broken nose on at least six different occasions.

He would spend the next eleven years protecting and opening holes for what would become known as the "Million Dollar Backfield." The backfield of Quarterback Y.A. Tittle and running backs, John Henry Johnson, Hugh McElhenny, and Joe Perry are the only group to be inducted into the Pro-Football Hall of Fame.

Because of his height, St. Clair also played defense in goal-line situations and on extra-point and field-goal attempts. He blocked ten field-goal and extra-point attempts in 1956 alone. Bob also lost five teeth while blocking a punt by Los Angeles quarterback, Norm Van Brocklin. St. Clair blocked the punt but in return got kicked in the mouth. They filled his mouth with tissue to stop the bleeding and gave him a Novocain shot and sent him back in. Ah, the good old days, when men were men. His height also created another problem, finding a bed big enough for him to sleep in, on the road. Bob would throw the mattress on the floor and add some pillows at the top to create length and then sleep on his homemade bed.

Now don't be mistaken, there have been other NFL players who were as tall as Bob St. Clair. Morris Stroud, tight end of the Kansas City Chiefs, stood 6'10" tall and defensive tackle, Ed "Too Tall" Jones of the Cowboys was measured the same height as St. Clair, at 6' 9". Philadelphia Eagles' tight end, Harold Carmichael, was 6' 8." Ravens' offensive tackles, Jonathan Ogden and Jared Gaither both stood 6'9," and the tallest NFL player was Richard Sligh, of North Carolina Central, who topped out at 7' 2," for the Raiders. Sligh only played in ten games before his career ended.

St. Clair was one of the 49ers' team captains and one of twelve players to date to have his jersey (#79) retired by San Francisco. Bob was a five-time Pro Bowl selection and was chosen nine times as an All-Pro. He is also listed on the 1950's NFL All-Decade Team. Bob St. Clair was inducted into the Pro-Football Hall of Fame in 1990.

Bob became a City Council member and the Mayor of Daly City, California from 1958-1964. He also became a paid lobbyist in Orange County, from 1979-1980. Bob worked in several different businesses including air freight, insurance, a meat distribution plant, and he bought and sold several liquor stores. In 2001, the City of San Francisco honored Bob St. Clair by naming the Kezar Stadium field the St. Clair Field. Bob had played 189 games during his 17-year career on this field.

Bob St. Clair loved hitting, and he broke fingers and toes on several occasions. Bob also played an entire quarter of football with a broken shoulder, in 1957. He twice had Achilles tendon surgery and wrote that he had taken 23 Novocain shots during his career, in order to continue playing. St. Clair never made more than $20,000 a season playing professional football.

One of the few faceless offensive linemen that became well-known in the 1950's, Bob St. Clair, died on Monday, April 20, 2015 in a Santa Rosa Hospital, in California. He was 84. Bob had fallen in February and died from complications of a broken hip. He is survived by his third wife Marsha, four daughters and two sons. He also had 19 grandchildren and three great grandchildren. All six of his kids were with his first wife, Ann.

We all realize that the athletes today, on average, are bigger, stronger and faster than the athletes of fifty years ago, but are they as tough? They asked Bob St. Clair and you know what the answer was; he said it while smiling.

GOOD WHISKERS

On December 26, 1992, a legendary broadcaster said in his final broadcast, "Just keep swinging; I'm Marty Glickman." I was immediately reminded of a great two-time middleweight boxing champion who made his reputation because he just kept swinging. As a young man he seemed to fail at everything but making trouble. He grew up in a rough family, even his father's nickname was "Tuff." His mom, Mary, could execute a perfect sleeper hold if needed. Having a simple conversation with this guy might require a referee, a bell in the corner, and a mouthpiece. On fight day, he looked like something put together by an eight-year-old, about thirty minutes before the first bell. He was extremely awkward, with an oversized head and a graceless gait. He certainly didn't look like a boxer. The man was so ugly he looked like he had been washed on scalding hot, several times in a row. He had been blessed with two bazookas hanging from his shoulders where his arms used to be; and he held his ground like Andrew Jackson against the British in the Battle of New Orleans. Built like Charles Atlas, he was one strong son-of-a-gun. Some say he could crush a cue ball in his bare hand. The word "grit" may have fit him better than his boxing trunks. It was said that when he fought in the squared ring, he was so mean he could make onions cry.

Gene Fullmer entered the sport of boxing with the strength of Sampson and the aggressiveness of Ivan the Terrible. This guy could turn your lights out with a straight right hand and became great at cutting the ring in half against his opponents. He just kept moving forward and could get in your way faster than a New York cab. With necessary roughness, Fullmer hit guys so hard they crumbled up like a napkin being thrown to the ground. He rang more guys' bells than Quasimodo (Hunchback of Notre Dame). Fullmer may have hurt more guys than polio and had what others referred to as "good whiskers" (he could take a punch).

In a sport where you wouldn't take a shower with most of the people involved in professional boxing, Fullmer's reputation was born. Actually, he was a good guy, and many referred to him as "Gentleman Gene;" but you never mistake kindness outside the ring as a weakness.

Lawrence Gene Fullmer was born in the town of West Jordan, Utah, on July 21, 1931. He was named Lawrence after his dad and Gene after the 1926 World Heavyweight Champ, Gene Tunney. Fullmer's father had done some amateur boxing and gave Gene a pair of boxing gloves when he turned six. Trainer Marv Jensen would become Gene's manager. Gene started fighting in youth exhibitions by the age of eight. His two brothers, Don, a middleweight, and Jay, a lightweight, also boxed. Fullmer had tried other sports. Gene hurt his knee while running track and hit his head face first on the floor, while playing basketball. He knocked out his two front teeth. So he turned to, of all things, boxing. Gene and his family were devout Mormons, prompting his opponents to label him the "Mormon Mauler." Jensen saw at once what nobody else did. "He had it," said Marv. "I knew the minute I tried him out. He had three things I could work on: strength, a good mind, and fast reflexes. I took advantage of those three things." Gene worked with his father in a Utah copper mine while growing up. He later opened his own mink farm with his brothers, and eventually created the Fullmer Brothers' Boxing Gym in South Jordan, Utah.

In June of 1951, Gene Fullmer made the world of boxing take notice as he started his string of 29 middleweight wins in a row, 19 by way of knockout. Fullmer's orthodox stances hid the tremendous power he carried in both his fists. He won his first eleven fights all by knockout, and KO'd 18 fighters in his first 21 bouts. Sixteen of those KO's occurred in the first four rounds. Fullmer's first loss did not occur until April 4, 1955, against Gil Turner at the Eastern Parkway Arena located in Brooklyn, New York. Fullmer would avenge that loss by outpointing Turner two months later on June 20, 1955.

On January 2, 1957, Fullmer brought his 38-3 win-loss record into the ring at Madison Square Garden against the champ, "Sugar Ray" Robinson. Fullmer built an early lead and opened a cut over Robinson's left eye, while scoring a knockdown in the seventh round. After 15 brutal rounds of boxing, Fullmer defeated the great Sugar Ray in a unanimous decision and won the World Middleweight Title. Robinson looked like an unmade bed after their fight. These two would meet again five months later on May 1, at Chicago Stadium. Everything went according to plan for Fullmer, now 40-3, as he forced the action by bullying Robinson around the ring for the first four rounds. At 1:27 of the fifth round, the 36-year-old Robinson got off what boxing tacticians have called the perfect left hook. This hook caught Fullmer flush on the chin and knocked him out for the first time in his career. Fullmer stumbled backward a few steps before falling down. Referee Frank Sikora counted to ten. Fullmer later said about the count out, "It must be on me, because I never heard any of it." It would be the first and only knockout Fullmer would experience in his entire career.

Fullmer became champion again when he stopped Carmen Basilio in the 14th round on August 28, 1959. This was the first time the tough chinned Basilio had ever failed to go the distance in 75 career fights. Fullmer won the National Boxing Association crown that had been vacated by Sugar

Ray Robinson for failing to defend the title. Gene stopped Basilio again, this time in 12 rounds, to defend his title on June 29, 1960. Carmen Basilio once said about Fullmer, "He did everything wrong, but he did it right." Only a boxer would understand. Fullmer fought Robinson to a draw in their third fight on December 3, 1960. Gene received the Edward J. Neil Award for "Fighter of the Year," in 1960.

There was another fight that would define Fullmer's toughness. On April 20, 1960, Gene Fullmer and Joey Giardello would fight to a draw in what became a vicious foul-filled bout. Giardello thought he was the greatest thing since popcorn. They may as well have thrown the rulebook away as both fighters engaged in a swarming, bruising, head-butting affair. They locked up one another's arms, rabbit-punched from behind, and hit each other with their fists, their elbows, and then their shoulders. Fullmer suffered a deep cut to his head. Even after the fight had been called a draw, the Giardello brothers threatened to continue the fight with Fullmer outside the ring. The old-timers still talk about this fight.

In their fourth and last fight, Fullmer pounded out a 15-round unanimous decision over Ray Robinson on March 4, 1961, at the Las Vegas Convention Center. Paul Pender and Gene Fullmer were the only two fighters to defeat Sugar Ray Robinson twice each during a championship fight.

Six months later on September 5, 1961, Fullmer fought Cuban fighter, Florentino Fernandez. Late in the fight, Fullmer took a vicious blow from Fernandez that fractured a bone in his right elbow. Fullmer had built a solid lead and was able to hold on, despite not being able to throw a punch with his right hand. The Boxing Writer's Association of America voted Gene the 1961 "Fighter of the Year."

Ah, Saturday nights with my dad were made just for us. I have pictures of him and me lying on the couch in our den watching the "Saturday Night Fight of the Week" on the Cavalcade of Sports, brought to you by Gillette Safety

Razors Company. It was here at the age of ten (1962) that I would learn about Gene Fullmer from my dad. Fullmer would eventually lose the title to Dick Tiger on October 23, 1962, by unanimous decision and later retired after losing to Tiger a second time, when he was TKO'd in seven rounds by Tiger on August 10, 1963. These were two of the fights I watched with my father on television.

In 1962, Gene Fullmer appeared on "What's My Line?" and in 1968; he had a role in the movie, *The Devil's Brigade*. Gene Fullmer continued to coach young boxers after retirement. He also refereed a few fights between 1967 and 1990. He helped establish a Golden Glove franchise in the Rocky Mountain Region.

Gentleman Gene Fullmer suffered from the effects of Alzheimer's disease and died from a bacterial infection on Monday, April 27, 2015. He was 83 and living in Taylorsville, Utah. His brother Don died in 2012 and sadly, his brother Jay died five days before Gene. Gene actually passed away the day his brother Jay was being laid to rest. Gene was laid to rest on May 4, 2015. The bell in an old makeshift gym where he learned the sweet science of boxing was struck ten times by his nephew. A U.S. Flag was draped over his casket to honor his service to his country during the Korean War. Karen, his wife of 31 years said, "His fists were as hard as iron, but his heart was soft and kind." Gene left behind his wife Karen, four children, and a number of grandchildren and great-grandchildren. Gene Fullmer entered the ring 64 times in 12 years and came away a winner in 55 bouts (24 by knockout). He lost six times and fought three draws. His straight-ahead style and lack of grace made him tough to watch, but you could not argue with the results. He reminded others of the great Rocky Marciano. Gene Fullmer was inducted into the International Boxing Hall of Fame in 1991. In the end, it's not our friends; it's our opponents that define who we are.

NEVER TOOK A LESSON

I once heard someone say that God made the world round so we could not see too far down the road. I think what they meant is that we need not know about everything that is going to happen to us in the future. Don't try to figure out your whole life. It's not important to see A to Z, just get started. It is important to keep moving forward, discovering and learning. That's why hard work and faith are so important. This man understood this; he may have been a decade ahead of his time. Make no mistake; he wanted to win and to be great, but this wasn't about him winning a round of golf. It was much bigger than that. For him it was about hope. Men like him showed us the way. All that was required of us was to follow.

Comedian Groucho Marx once said, "I refuse to join any club that would have me as a member." He may have been talking about the PGA, Professional Golf Association. Calvin Peete wore a white cap and loved the color purple. He wore cowboy boots with spikes, drove a pink Cadillac and had diamond chips in his front teeth. He grew a Fu Manchu mustache and swung a golf club, while clinching a cigarette between his teeth. He could consistently hit the ball in the fairway and made a living keeping his golf ball dry. A classy guy, Calvin Peete never talked down to others. He was short, 5'10" with a slim build. He only weighed 165 pounds but, boy, could he drive a golf ball. Peete once said, "I loved seeing my ball fly straight and long." Great players always find a way to slow the game down. Calvin Peete hit a golf ball as if he had a personal grudge, and his idea of a great evening was shining his putter.

The amazing thing is that Peete didn't pick up a golf club until he was 23 years of age. "I grew up thinking golf was a game for 'sissies,'" he said. "If I happened to turn the channel and see golf on television, I'd be like most people I knew; I'd turn to a basketball game or a war movie." Without ever taking a lesson, Calvin Peete was breaking 80 after six months and reached par in 18 months. In a game where it has been said that a right-handed golfer must keep his left arm straight to hit a golf ball correctly, Peete defied logic. Even with a permanently-bent left arm, he was a natural. He started out hitting golf balls on a baseball diamond, at night. His bony hands became raw from practicing. Eventually, Calvin cut out Dr. Scholl's foot pads and placed them in his golf gloves to help ease the pain.

Calvin Peete was born in July 18, 1943, in Detroit, Michigan. He was the eighth of nine children. When he was the age of 11, his parents divorced and he moved south with his father Dennis to Pahokee, Florida, a small town located in central Florida. His father married again, so Calvin would then become one of a total of 19 children. Shortly after the move, Calvin at age 12, fell from a tree and broke his left arm and elbow into several pieces. It would remain permanently bent for the rest of his life. In fact, the doctor claimed the break was so bad that amputation would be in order if he ever injured it again. By the age of 14 Calvin dropped out of school after the eighth grade to help the family financially. He could not do heavy lifting because of his arm, and he and other boys in the neighborhood took jobs picking green beans and corn in the hot sun. They got paid according to how much they picked. "On a good day, I could make $10,' said Peete. Moving away from Detroit had not been easy for Calvin. "I was poor; which I realized after the fact, but as a kid growing up in Detroit, I really didn't want for much," said Peete. "I had clothes, food, and shelter. I had friends. A couple of my greatest memories as a child was playing hopscotch, kick the can, hide and go seek, and marbles."

By 1960, at 18 years of age, with the help of his grandmother, Calvin had financed the purchase of a 1956 Plymouth station wagon. He filled the car with goods, clothes and jewelry to sell to the migrant workers. During the day, Peete would play on public courses and read all kinds of instructional books written by Ben Hogan, Sam Snead, Jack Nicklaus and Doug Ford, on how to play golf. His goal was to teach himself the game, while peddling goods to migrant workers at night, up and down the east coast. It took nine years and three trips to the PGA-qualifying school, before he was able to earn the right to join the PGA Tour in 1975. He was 32 years old at the time.

In 1962, the PGA lifted what had been called the Caucasian-only rule. African-American golfers like Charlie Sifford, Lee Elder, Jim Thorpe and Jim Dent, gave Peete the confidence to play golf on the PGA Tour. There was one other black golfer, who appeared in tournaments occasionally and had actually become the first African-American golfer to win a PGA Tour event. His name was Pete Brown.

Some said Calvin was so calm that he could go to sleep with a fly on his nose. "I get my accuracy from my tempo and rhythm," said Peete, in a 1982 N.Y. Times interview. "Some of the players still drive farther than I do, but I'm always in the fairway, and they're sometimes in the trees." In 1980, Calvin became the second black golfer to play in Augusta at the Masters' Tournament. The first was Lee Elder in 1975.

It took him four hours to take the hardest test of his life, his GED. "My hands were sweating and I felt more nervous than I did looking at a big putt on the 16th hole in the Milwaukee Open," said Peete. It would be several days before he learned the results. His wife Christina was a high school English and drama teacher. She had prepared Calvin by tutoring him in English, math, history and geography. Calvin had always wanted to get his diploma, and it was also required for any golfer who wanted to play on the Ryder Cup Team. In 1982, 24 years after he had dropped out of school, Peete got the word that he had passed. Peete played on two U.S. Ryder Cup teams and compiled a 4-2-1 individual record. The 1983 team was made up of all-stars. It included Jack Nicklaus, Tom Watson, Curtis Strange, Ben Crenshaw, Calvin Peete and several others. The 1985 team was equally impressive.

In 1984 Peete averaged a score of 70.56 shots per round. It was good enough to win him the Vardon Trophy, given annually to the PGA Tour's overall scoring leader. He had edged out the great Jack Nicklaus.

Between the years of 1976-1986, Peete won 12 times on the PGA Tour, including the prestigious 1985 Player's Championship, and in 1982, captured a career-best four victories and $318,470 in earnings. Those earnings placed him fourth on the money list just ahead of Tom Watson. Players that finished second to Peete during his career include Lee Trevino, Jerry Pate, Hal Sutton, Bruce Lietzke and Mark O'Meara. He also led the PGA Tour in driving accuracy for ten consecutive years from 1981-1990.

Peete qualified for 98 percent of the tournaments he attended. He played in 344 PGA tournaments and won 12. He also won two tournaments on the Japanese Golf Tour. He finished in the top ten in 73 events and earned over $3 million on the PGA and Champions Tour, not bad for a vegetable picker. Peete tied for 3rd in the 1982 PGA Championship and his best U.S. Open finish was a tie for 4th in 1983. His best finish in the Masters' was a tie for 11th, in 1986. Even with the odds stacked against him, Calvin Peete became the most successful black golfer on tour, before Tiger.

PGA Tour Commissioner Tim Finchem exclaimed that Calvin gave back so much to the game he loved so dearly. His work with "The First Tee" program for junior golfers in the Ponta Vedra Beach area in Florida made such a huge difference. Peete also became an instructor at the World Golf Village. There are many stories of Peete taking four golf balls out of his pocket on the last day of school and, without any warm-up; he would hit each one true and straight for about 275 yards down the fairway. It was said that they were always easy to retrieve, as they all landed in an area about ten feet apart.

Peete had an elephant's memory. He never forgot the injustice he had to endure as a poor black child from a broken home who picked vegetables to survive instead of going to school. Peete understood that he was just a piece of the puzzle. He was not the puzzle. Calvin Peete is gone but his memory will live on, as long as African American golfers like "Tiger" Woods continues to play professionally.

In the spring of 2001, Calvin retired from competitive golf. Two years earlier, Peete had been diagnosed with Tourette's syndrome and suffered from a neurological disorder that caused involuntary movement of muscles. Calvin Peete left us at 71 years of age. He died on a Wednesday, April 29, 2015. He and his family were residing in Atlanta, Georgia. Calvin Peete, a true champion and even better man, is survived by his wife, Pepper, and his seven children: Calvin, Dennis, Rickie, Nicole, Kalvanetta, Aisha and Aleya. He and his first wife, Christina Sears Peete, had divorced in 1987. Calvin joined the African-American Ethnic-Sports Hall of Fame in 2002, and was inducted into the Michigan Sports Hall of Fame in 2005.

There is no expiration date on greatness. Peete understood that pressure is what makes a golfer great. With the absence of pressure, it's hard to do great things. When he swung a golf club, sweet music played.

FALL ON THE BALL NEXT TIME

That's what Head Coach Don Shula said to him, as he hid down at the end of the bench, with his face in his hands. With his team leading 14-0, he had been sent in to attempt a 42-yard field goal with 2 minutes and 7 seconds left in the game. This time the field goal was blocked by Washington's Bill Brundige. But this was no ordinary block, as he picked up the ball and tried to pass downfield. The ball slipped out of his hand and went straight up in the air. He then tried to knock the ball out of bounds but instead batted it back up in the air again. Millions had watched as the Miami Dolphins attempted to do the impossible, go through an entire NFL season undefeated (17-0). The Washington Redskins had other plans and sent everyone to try and block the kick. Cornerback Mike Bass of the Redskins (a former Lions' teammate) intercepted the wobbly pass and ran 49 yards the other way for a touchdown. Not only had his pass been intercepted, but he had also missed tackling Bass. The final score of Super Bowl VII (1973), played at the Los Angeles Coliseum, would stand at 14-7, and Miami did become the first team in the 53-year history of the NFL to go through a season undefeated and untied. "Garo" Yepremian told reporters after the game, "This is the first time the goat of the game is in the winner's locker room." Interestingly, Shula admitted years later that while standing on the sideline, he liked the idea of winning the Super Bowl by the score of 17-0 in a season where they won all 17 games. That's why he had sent Yepremium in to attempt the field goal. "What a great way that would be to remember that game," said Shula. After that play, Shula's reaction on the sideline was to tell Garo, "Fall on the ball next time." The following training camp, one of the first drills implemented by Shula was a missed snap field-goal-attempt drill. Shula instructed Garo to fall on the ball. Garo did and strained his ankle. They never ran that drill again.

In 1985, Mike Ditka's Chicago Bears came the closest to an undefeated season, as they went 18-1 through the regular season and postseason.

Nobody called him Yepremian, it was Garo. The word "blooper" may have been invented by his poor decision. He was a short 5'8" and had more hair on his upper lip than his head. He was left-legged and from the country of Cyprus. Try finding it on the map. Garo was a happy-go-lucky guy with a bubbly personality and mutton-chop sideburns. He came to the U.S. at the age of 22 and kicked in the first NFL game he had ever seen in person. He had never been to college and had only watched the game of football on television. "I can do that," he said to the Detroit Lions.

Garabed Sarkis "Garo" Yepremian was born on June 2, 1944, in the small town of Larnaca, located in the country of Cyprus. Garo was Armenian and fled with his family to London in the 1960's when the Greeks took up arms against the Turks. We may have never heard of him if his brother Krikor had not come to America to play college soccer. Garo visited Krikor in Indianapolis, Indiana, during the summer of 1966. Garo played soccer well enough to get college offers from Butler and Indiana, but he had no high school diploma.

Garo tried out for the Atlanta Falcons, and they were impressed. "He's not a very big guy," said Falcons' coach Norb Hecker, "but he was knocking them through consistently from 55 yards out." Atlanta made him an offer, but he had promised the Lions he would work out for them before signing with anyone. In Detroit, Yepremian made 19 of 20 from 45 to 55 yards. Those were the days where NFL kickers converted about 55% of all field goals attempted. Even Lions' current linebacker and placekicker, Wayne Walker said, "He's the best I've ever seen." Krikor and Garo convinced the Lions to hire him as their placekicker, and he was signed midseason on October 13, 1966. Detroit also had an Armenian Church and Atlanta did not. That season, Garo set the NFL record by kicking six field goals in a single game against the Minnesota Vikings. Jim Bakken of the St. Louis Cardinals broke that record with seven, the following year.

Garo would be the team leader in points scored during the 1966 season. In a shortened season, he had scored 50 points by kicking 11 extra points and 13 field goals in 22 attempts. The Lions' placeholder for Garo in 1966 was Wayne Rasmussen. Garo played in Detroit through the 1967 season and then left to join the U.S. Army in 1968. When he returned a year later, the Lions refused to sign him, so he signed a one-year contract to placekick and punt for the Michigan Arrows of the Continental Football League. The Arrows were terrible and only won one game all season. They folded at the end of the 1969 season. Garo joined the Miami Dolphins in 1970, and stayed for nine seasons. In 1971, he led the Dolphins in scoring with 117 points.

Garo's 37-yard field goal in the second overtime of a 1971 playoff game ended the longest game in NFL history (82 minutes and 40 seconds), as Miami would beat Kansas City 27-24, on Christmas Day in Kansas City. Every event seems to have a back story. The morning of this game, the NFL coaches voted Kansas City placekicker Jan Stenerud to the Pro Bowl, even though Garo was the AFC's most accurate kicker that year. Garo was hurt by the snub but did congratulate Stenerud. Then with the game on the line, Stenerud missed a field goal to win it. Garo did not. Miami won back-to-back NFL titles in 1972-73.

Garo's start in pro football was somewhat a comedy of errors. He spoke four languages, but none of them was football. It has been written that Garo Yepremian was the last NFL player to wear a helmet without a facemask. In fact, he had never worn a helmet of any kind and didn't like wearing one now. He didn't even know how to put on his uniform, and shoulder pads were a mystery. All that quickly changed in Week 4 of his first season (1966) when Green Bay Packers' linebacker, Ray Nitschke, badly injured Garo by knocking him to the ground. Opposing players considered pro football an American game and foreign players were not well received, especially placekickers. Garo may have helped coin the term, "roughing-the-kicker." Opponents tried their best to take his head off. Lions' coach, Harry Gilmer, instructed Garo to head to the bench immediately after kicking off. This resulted in Yepremian running to the wrong sideline and sitting on the opposing team's bench.

There is also an interesting story that has Garo down on his knees at midfield before the start of a game. It seems that Lions' Coach, Harry Gilmer, told Garo, "We have lost the coin toss." Garo, concerned, promptly ran to the middle of the field and got down on his knees, in search of the coin.

In 1966 there were only three soccer-style kickers in the league, Pete Gogolak (New York Giants) and his brother Charlie (Washington Redskins) and Yepremian. Pete Gogolak joined the Bills in 1964 and became the first soccer-style kicker in professional football. My pal, running back Bobby Smith, joined Buffalo the same season. Bobby thought Pete was very gifted and helped the Bills win the 1964 and 1965 AFL Championship titles. The Cowboys' Tom Landry tried his hand at signing soccer-style kickers, Efren Herrera and, eventually, Raphael Septien.

They were known as straight-on kickers before the soccer-style kickers came along. Most placekickers were usually position players. Halfback Paul Hornung kicked for Green Bay. Quarterback George Blanda kicked for the Oakland Raiders and Houston Oilers. Guys like Lou Groza of the Cleveland Browns and Lou Michaels of the Baltimore Colts played tackle. The last fulltime straight-on placekicker was Mark Mosley who retired in 1986 from the Cleveland Browns.

I remember place-kicking some in junior high school. After watching other kickers we took an extra shoe lace and ran it underneath the first cleat on our kicking foot and pulled back the toe of the shoe. Then we tied the shoelace behind our ankle to hold it in place. This created a wider kicking space which would help control the direction of the kick.

Straight-on placekicker Tom Dempsey was born with a deformed foot. His right foot was missing the lower half of the foot and toes. He was also missing the fingers on his right hand. Dempsey had a specially designed kicking shoe made. On November 8, 1970, he set the NFL record against the Detroit Lions with a 63-yarder at Tulane Stadium for a 19-17 win for the Saints. This newly-designed shoe did have more of a sweet spot to insure a clean square kick, like some of these new drivers that are used in the game of golf. Some also thought he had the shoe loaded with extra weight to give him more distance. The NFL checked his shoes several times but found nothing unusual. In 1977, the NFL outlawed any shoe that provided more kicking space than a normal shoe used by straight on kickers. It was only a matter of time before every team had a soccer-style kicker. On December 8, 2013, Denver soccer-style placekicker Matt Prater broke Tom Dempsey's record with a 64-yard field goal.

Lions' tackle, Alex Karras, told a story on the Johnny Carson show that has become famous. In his first season, Garo had kicked a game-winning extra point with seconds left in a game. He came running off the field, jumping up and down and celebrating. Karras asked him, "What the hell are you hollering about?" "I keek a touchdown," yelled Garo. Yepremian spent 1979 with the New Orleans Saints before joining the Tampa Bay Buccaneers for his final two years (1980-1981). He kicked 14 years in the NFL.

The success rate for made field goals in 2014 was 84% inside the 50-yard-line and 61% over 50 yards. These days, any field goal inside the 40-yard-line is now considered a chip shot, and extra point attempts are automatic. So much so that the NFL just voted to move the points after touchdown try to the 15-yard-line, making this attempt 33 yards.

Yepremian converted 210 of 313 field goals (67%) and made 444 of 464 extra-point attempts for a total of 1,074 points. Although not considered very good results by today's standards, he did lead the league in field goal accuracy for three different years. Garo made two Pro-Bowl appearances and was named to the NFL All-Decade Team of the 70's as a kicker, by *Sports Illustrated* and the Pro-Football Hall-of-Fame Committee. Garo played in three Super Bowls: VI, VII, and VIII. He was also chosen the 1973 Pro-Bowl MVP. He has been nominated to the HOF but as of this writing has not been elected. Garo was elected to the Florida Sports Hall of Fame in 1981 and named one of the Miami Dolphins' all-time greatest football players during the Dolphins' 40th Anniversary.

On the funny side, Garo was in an episode of "The Odd Couple" and kicked a football-shaped meatloaf out of Felix and Oscar's apartment window. In the off-season Garo created a company that made and sold neck ties and clip-on ties. Yepremian was a motivational speaker and the Founder and CEO of the Garo Yepremian Foundation for Brain Cancer Research. Interestingly, more than a decade earlier, Garo had created the foundation devoted to fighting brain cancer after his daughter-in-law was diagnosed with a brain tumor.

There is an interesting side story to Garo's failed pass attempt in the Super Bowl. As you would imagine, he was devastated by the screw-up. During the off-season, he received a letter at home. The letter told him how important he was to the team and to not get too down on himself. The letter was signed by Don Shula. Garo kept the letter for years. Years later, Garo and Shula were at an event together and Garo told Shula how much he appreciated the letter he had received after Super Bowl VII and wished he had taken the time to thank him. Shula's response was, "What letter?" They finally figured out that Shula's first wife, Dorothy, who had since passed away, had written the letter and signed Don's name.

Garo Yepremin died at a hospital in Media, Pennsylvania, during the morning of May 15, 2015, from brain cancer. The cancer had been diagnosed in May of 2014. He was 70. His wife, Maritza, was with him. John Maxwell once wrote, "Greatness is by what we give, not by what we receive." Garo was great in his own place and time. Garo Yepremian, a fellow who technically never stood a chance, beat the odds and will always be #1 in the Miami Dolphins fans' minds. He remains a part of the only team to record a perfect season.

ONE MAN PARADE

John Maxwell once said, "Greatness is by what we give, not by what we receive." When writing about these wonderful athletes from all walks of life, my desire is to tell you who these people really are, not who you think they were. Hall-of-Fame Basketball Coach, Bobby Knight, once said, "He's the greatest basketball player of all time." Have you ever heard of Bob Cousy, "Hot Rod" Hundley, "Pistol Pete" Maravich, Fred "Curly" Neal or Oscar Robertson? All five of these guys and many more were influenced by this man. At the end, half the planet knew this fellow; it was said that he could draw a crowd at the North Pole, and he did. Giving him a basketball was like handing Zorro a sword; he could cut through the best defenses ever played. He was unimpressed with himself, but the only thing that could stop this guy was maybe food poisoning.

You see, sometimes it has to get dark enough to see the stars. He was a star, a brilliant player, an extraordinary shooter, a tenacious defender and an expert in passing. But as a ball handler, he had no peers. It was his skill with a basketball and two hands that made him different, made him a magician. Whether the ball was two inches from the floor or three feet, he was able to weave in and out between defenders. He dribbled on one knee and both knees, lying down on his side and while sitting on his backside. He was the greatest dribbler of his era or any other era. It was estimated that he could dribble a basketball six times a second with either hand. Although I saw him do this in person, I still have some doubts about the six times a second, but isn't wonderful to wonder whether are not he really could do it? Isn't it so much better than having a replay from 16 different angles and having a hundred-plus reporters asking him about the feat, after the game. There is no doubt that Marques Haynes traveled through life as a one-man parade.

Marques Haynes, an American original, played hard since the moment he was born. Haynes lived, ate and breathed basketball every day, and no building could hold him. This guy was the energy source of the team. Marques was smooth, like a warm glass of milk. To make your team better you just signed this guy, added water and stirred. They should have called him Jell-O because teams congealed around him. Haynes didn't want to hear anything but the basketball bounce and the crowd roar their approval. Marques Haynes of the Harlem Globetrotters helped sell the game of basketball to the American public, and then to the world.

Everybody is just a kid from somewhere, but Marques Oreole Haynes was the fourth and youngest, born in Sand Springs, Oklahoma, on March 10, 1926. His father worked with the railroad and left when Marques was around 3 or 4 years old. His mother, Hattie, was a laundress and took care of her family by herself in a three-room house with no electricity or running water. It has been said that his sister, Cecile, taught him how to shoot a basketball. His brother, Joe, taught him how to pass and his older brother, Wendell, how to dribble on the solid dirt courts of his hometown. "As a kid, I practiced dribbling with a tennis ball or rubber ball," said Haynes.

Kevin Sherrington of the Dallas Morning News tells a wonderful story about Haynes. He would wait until all his friends got off work and then he would put on an exhibition on the railroad tracks that divided his town. Marques would dribble a tennis ball up one side of the tracks and then down the other side, never missing a rail. All the white people in town would line up on the north side of the track to watch, and the black folks would stand on the south side.

Marques played basketball at Booker T. Washington High School. He would top out as a 6-foot point guard. As captain, his team traveled to Tuskegee, Alabama, in 1941 and won the Negro Basketball National Championship. He attended Langston College, located about 45 minutes north of Oklahoma City, and played basketball for the Lions and local legend, Coach "Zip" Gayles. There he became the leading scorer on a team that won 112 games and only lost three, and at one point won 59 games in a row. In 1946, Langston College was so good that they were able to secure a game with the world famous Harlem Globetrotters. All Haynes did was score 26 points and lead Langston to 74-70 win over the Trotters. At the end of the 1946 season, the Globetrotters' owner, Abe Saperstein, offered him a spot on the team; but Haynes put them off until he graduated and then played briefly for the Kansas City Stars of the Black Professional Basketball League, before joining the Trotters.

The name Harlem Globetrotters is a bit of a misnomer as they were formed and have played since 1926 in Chicago, Illinois, and not the city of Harlem, New York. Their first game was played on January 7, 1927. In fact, the team did not play a game in Harlem until 1968. Haynes joined the Trotters in late 1946 just as the team was beginning to take on their mystique as not only a great basketball team, but also as entertainers. Reece "Goose" Tatum joined the team in 1941 and was the star of the team when Marques Haynes arrived. Tatum not only helped create the trick routines but is credited with inventing the hook shot. Haynes and Tatum became the Ying and the Yang for the Globetrotters, as together their razzle-dazzle style of basketball made millions take notice. Haynes and Tatum led the Globetrotters to two wins over the NBA Champion Minneapolis Lakers, led by Hall-of-Fame center, George Mikan, in 1948 (61-59) and 1949 (49-45).

Marques Haynes spent two different stints with the Trotters, 1946-1953 and again from 1972-1979. In 1950, the Globetrotters refused to sell Haynes's contract depriving him of being the first African American in the NBA. With the Globetrotters he traveled over four million miles and played in well over 12,000 games in 106 different countries, to the tune of the song, "Sweet Georgia Brown." Haynes left the Globetrotters in 1953 after a contract dispute. He took Goose Tatum with him. Marques turned down an offer of $35,000 a year from the Philadelphia Warriors and the 1955 Minneapolis Lakers. Instead, he formed his own team called the Harlem Magicians. The Philly offer would have made him the second highest-paid player in the NBA. Boxing legend, "Sugar Ray" Robinson, played in some exhibition games with the Magicians. Haynes would later rejoin the Trotters as a player/coach in 1972 and stayed until 1979. Haynes also played with two other teams after the Trotters. The first team was known as Meadowlark Lemon's Bucketeers, from 1979 to 1981 and then he played for the Harlem Wizards from 1981 through 1983. His last nine years of professional basketball were with his recreated Harlem Magicians from 1983 until 1992.

The Harlem Globetrotters are known as the ambassadors of basketball and showmanship. They have spread American good will throughout the world. From bullrings to dirt courts, the Trotters have displayed their unique brand of basketball. They have played in empty swimming pools, on the decks of aircraft carriers, in soccer stadiums and dim school gyms. They have also played in Madison Square Garden, the Rose Bowl, the Olympic Stadium in Berlin, Germany, and all the major sports venues in the world.

In 1973, Haynes started a clothing company that specialized in Italian wear. The company eventually failed, but it was there that he met his wife, Joan, who was a model and auditioned for the fashion show. They had two daughters. In the 1980's, you could still find Marques traveling the country in a bus, performing for the masses. He was a gypsy with a basketball. "You really do learn some neat things if you have enough luck to hang around this life for awhile," said Haynes. Marques Haynes finally retired in 1992, at the age of 66. He had played professionally for 46 years. He had spent his life playing the game he loved for paupers, regular folks, Presidents, Popes and Kings. He also played for you and me.

He was once asked if he thought he would be inducted into the Naismith Memorial Basketball Hall of Fame. "The world is my Hall of Fame," said Haynes. Marques Haynes died peacefully of natural causes with his family in attendance in Plano, Texas, on Friday, May 22, 2015. So Marques Haynes has left us. He was 89. As B.B. King would say, the thrill is gone, but for every behind-the-back pass or cross-over dribble, his spirit will live on. Although he never played in the NBA, Marques Haynes dribbled his way to the Naismith Memorial Basketball Hall of Fame on October 2, 1998. He was the first of all the Harlem Globetrotters to be inducted. Haynes has also been inducted into several other Halls Of Fame: NAIA Hall of Fame in 1985, Jim Thorpe Hall of Fame in 1993, the Oklahoma Sports Hall of Fame, and Langston University Sports Hall of Fame in 1995. Langston University also dedicated their basketball court as "Marques Haynes Court," in 2007. The Trotters will dedicate their 90th season to Marques in 2016, by wearing a commemorative patch on their uniforms. Haynes, Meadowlark Lemon, and Wilt Chamberlain are the only Globetrotters to have their jersey numbers retired.

When I write about athletes like Marques Haynes, I often think to myself, why think of the future when you can think of the past? The problem with the future is that it's the future, it's unknown. You don't know what will happen. You will always know that he won in the past. Just close your eyes and you can go back to better basketball, to where life is so much better. There you will find him; "I'm Marques

Haynes, and I'll show you how." Kurt Schneider, CEO of the Harlem Globetrotters has said, "He was the greatest Globetrotter that ever lived." If you could stop trembling when he spoke to you, you could learn something.

LUNCH BUFFET

Virgil Runnels was loud, proud and a bit over the top. He was billed as a working man and the son of a plumber. His body resembled something other than an athlete, but his charisma drew people to him like ants on watermelon. His magic with a microphone would endear him to millions of professional wrestling fans across the nation. What most liked about him was that he was real: a blue-collar, common man, who rose from nothing to become a part of American Pop culture and, therefore, the "American Dream." The only thing fake about him was his wrestling name, "Dusty Rhodes." Our paths would cross in the summer of 1977.

I would guess that most of America has eaten from the lunch buffet offered by Pizza Hut since the late 1950's. During the summer of 1977, this guy and a few other well-known wrestlers walked into the Pizza Hut restaurant located in Sumter, South Carolina. I was the assistant manager that day. The customers already seated began to stir, as they turned in their seats to see. There he was, bigger than life, The American Dream, Dusty Rhodes. Dusty also had with him two other wrestlers, "Brute" Bernard and "Skull" Murphy. You've gotta' love those stage names. A buffet (all you can eat) lunch was the perfect way for these large fellows to chow down. They were in town for a wrestling match to be held that weekend. These were big boys. Dusty was large, blond, and occasionally spoke in rhymes. Dusty reminded me of the comedian, "Buddy" Hackett. He also had the body of a cafeteria lady, as he stood a little over

6-feet tall and weighed close to 300 pounds. Everything about him was big, even his dandruff was as large as rice. The other two were equally big enough to have their own zip codes, and both were baldheaded. They joked when asked by the waitress what choice of pizza toppings they desired. "Whatever you got will be fine, and don't worry about cutting them in slices," they said, while laughing. "We'll just eat them whole." You could say they got their money's worth that day, and so did the customers. Dusty Rhodes was well-known and had been chosen the 1977 Wrestler of the Year. They ate and signed autographs, ate some more, and basically held court.

Sumter was a small town of about 30,000 people and was part of the professional wrestling tour that occurred nearly every weekend, during the summer. Every year, professional wrestlers made their way south to Georgia and Florida from the Carolinas.

Virgil Riley Runnels, Jr., better known as Dusty Rhodes, was born in Austin, Texas, on October 12, 1945. Runnels trained under Joe Blanchard and debuted in 1968. He started out in the American Wrestling Association as a rule-breaking villain and tag-team partner of fellow Texan, Dick Murdoch. They called themselves the "Texas Outlaws." He had a terrific fire, that drive that helped him dominate inside the ring. He was beer in a cup and chips, the opposite of fine wine and he was so slow, he would finish third in a race with a pregnant woman.

Runnels became famous during the height of wrestling's popularity in the 1970's and 1980's. Steroids and bleached-blond hair were all the rage, yet Runnels was quite the opposite of his opponents, who entered the ring with hulking body-builder physiques. His yellow polka-dot tights, round belly, and a conspicuous red birthmark located on his right side endured him to the common man as a chubby yet loveable outlaw. Armed with charisma, a slight lisp and the gift of gab with a microphone, Runnels would win three

National Wrestling Alliance (NWA) Championships and be inducted into the 2007 World Wrestling Entertainment (WWE) Hall of Fame. He also joined the Professional Wrestling Hall of Fame and Museum in 2010.

He was crowned the United States Champion. He won several Television, World Tag Team, and Six-Man Tag Team championships. Runnels also won many regional championships along the way.

When he heard the news, Ric Flair called Runnels his mentor. Paul Levesque who wrestled under the name "Triple H," called Runnels "A legend, teacher, mentor and friend." Wrestling broadcaster Gene Okerlund referred to The Dream as "One of the best ever." Hulk Hogan said, "This was the man who hooked me on wrestling. Without him, I would never have been interested."

During his rise, Runnels wrestled under many other names in different states. He wrestled in Florida while using a mask, and called himself "The Midnight Rider." He also used the names, "Stardust," "The White Soul King," and eventually, "American Dream." Like most wrestlers, Runnels was known for many devastating moves in the ring. Some of his signature moves were known as the bulldog, figure-four leg lock, and the sleeper hold. His finishing move was called the bionic elbow. Yes, I considered them to be athletic. You try flipping backwards off the top rope. No doubt, figure-four leg locks and getting hit with a folding chair hurt. The matches were more scripted for show than as a sporting event, but there was nothing fake about how they felt when they woke up in the morning.

Virgil Runnels had several moves he was known for. One of them became known as the "pile driver." This move required facing your opponent and pushing his head down between your legs and then grabbing him around the waist, picking him up and then sitting down. It's a wonder more wrestlers did not suffer a broken neck from the move.

Runnels became a longtime wrestling legend. "I have

wined and dined with kings and queens, and I've slept in alleys and dined on pork and beans," said Runnels. He retired from the ring in 2007.

Runnel's is the father of two other famous WWE wrestlers: Dustin and Cody Runnels. They wrestled under the names "Goldust" and "Stardust." Runnels also managed wrestlers, Ron Simmons, Larry Zbyszko, and "The Outsiders." Runnels booked promotions for Jim Crockett Promotions, made several promos and DVD's, wrote and directed several weekly television shows, and spent some time behind a microphone.

The man everyone called Dusty Rhodes died on June 10, 2015, in his home located in Orlando, Florida. He was 69 years old. It was reported that he had taken a fall, and paramedics responded to a 911 call. He is survived by his four children, three grandchildren and his wife, Michelle.

At the time of his death, Runnels was one of six men inducted into each of the World Wide Entertainment, World Championship Wrestling, Professional Wrestling, and Wrestling Observer Newsletter Halls of Fame. He was selected the Wrestler of the Year twice (1977, 1978), and the most Popular Wrestler of the Year three times (1978, 1979, 1987).

Author Graham Brown once said, "Life is about choices. Some we regret, some we're proud of, some will haunt us forever. The message—we are what we chose to be." The man we all knew as Dusty Rhodes was destined to be the American Dream.

THE REAL JOHNNY FOOTBALL

The legendary Sam Houston once said, "Do right and risk the consequences." He could have easily been talking about this guy. Unpolished to say the least; this guy was quiet. He drove a truck, wore jeans and ate hamburgers from the local drive-in. Vanilla was his favorite color and all he knew how to do was win. Standing 6' 2" tall and weighing 220 pounds, he was a big boy for his time. He was a bare-knuckles kind of a guy. His bruising running style was propelled by powerful thighs and a no-nonsense approach. He had all the physical riches: speed, power, vision, energy and size. It was like trying to tackle a Volkswagen. It was a muscle game that they played in the fifties, the "heyday" of the big running backs. Some said he was so strong he could slam a revolving door. He played during a time when you were not allowed to have a bad game. Handing this guy a football was like giving the Texas Rangers an assignment; he gave you a feeling of hope and he was as tough as an advanced course in algebra. Even while injured, he ran for 1,465 yards and scored 14 rushing touchdowns, while catching four more touchdowns, in his three-year career at Texas A&M University. He also intercepted five passes, while playing on defense. As the old saying goes, "The pain stops when the applause begins." Some players are born with championship blood, the kind you can't get at the blood bank. This just in: John David Crow was the "real" Johnny Football.

John David Crow was born in Marion, Louisiana, on July 8,

1935. His mom, Velma, experienced some difficulty during birth that left John David with some nerve damage on the left side of his face. Then he suffered from pneumonia at the age of two and almost died. His father, Harry Crow, worked at a paper mill, while John David just tried to survive. Survive he did, as John David would grow to 6' 2" tall and weigh 220 pounds. He was raised in Springhill, Louisiana, and graduated from Springhill High School in 1954. His older brother, Raymond Crow, played football at Southern State, for Head Coach, Elmer Smith. Southern State was an Arkansas College located 26 miles north of Springhill, Louisiana. In 1954, when legendary football coach, Paul "Bear" Bryant, took the job at Texas A&M, he hired Elmer Smith as an assistant. John David later said he had never heard of Bear Bryant. John David chose Texas A&M over Oklahoma, Arkansas and LSU. Seems that Coach Smith convinced the Crows that he would take care of John David and make sure he got his degree. In 1954, freshmen were not eligible to play on the varsity club, so John David missed out on the intolerable training camp that gave its name to "The Junction Boys." Coach Bear Bryant liked to say "Coach 'em hard and hug 'em later."

In 1956, John David played an integral part for the first Texas Aggie team to beat the University of Texas at the Darrell K. Royal Texas Memorial Stadium. John David Crow became only the third football player from a school in Texas to win the prestigious Heisman Trophy. First was Davey O'Brian, a quarterback from TCU, in 1938. Second was Doak Walker, a running back from SMU, in 1948. When John David was told he was a candidate for the Heisman in 1957, he confessed he had never heard of the award. The good news was that the Bear had. Bryant started his own campaign for Crow. In 1957, Crow played in only seven games. He carried the ball 129 times for 562 yards, while injured, and scored six touchdowns during his senior season. He passed for five more touchdowns and intercepted five passes while on defense. His Aggie team won their first eight games of the season and was ranked No. 1 in the Associated Press poll. Unfortunately, they lost their last three games and finished 8-3 in the Southwest Conference. Crow was named a scholastic All-American and was named to Who's Who in American Colleges and Universities.

"Don't count the yards," exclaimed Bryant, "Count the people he's run over." Bryant continued, "If he doesn't win the Heisman, they ought to stop giving it." John David Crow almost doubled his closest competitor, Alex Karras, a defensive tackle from the University of Iowa. Crow won the Heisman Trophy on December 3, 1957. Interestingly, Crow would be the only player to ever win the Heisman Trophy, while playing for the Bear. The other Heisman winners from a school located in Texas include Earl Campbell, Andre Ware, Ricky Williams, Robert Griffin and Johnny Manziel. Ty Detmer, Tim Brown and Billy Simms are Texas natives who won the Heisman trophy at universities outside of Texas.

John David Crow was chosen with the second pick of the 1958 NFL draft by the Chicago Cardinals. There he would play with the likes of Dick "Night Train" Lane, Charlie Johnson, Bobby Joe Conrad and Larry Wilson. This team later moved to St. Louis as the Cardinals. Crow played with the Cardinals from 1958 to 1964, and then ended his 11-year career with the San Francisco 49ers (1965-1968). He played in 125 games, carried the ball 1,157 times, and piled up 4,963 rushing yards, while scoring 38 touchdowns. He also recorded 3,699 yards in receptions by catching 258 passes for an additional 35 touchdowns. If that wasn't enough, he threw for 759 yards and five more touchdowns from the halfback position.

John David Crow led the NFL in 1960 with 5.9 yards per carry. With his eyes like the headlights of an oncoming train, Crow rushed for 1,071 yards and caught passes for an additional 462 yards. It was easily his finest year in professional football. He was elected to the NFL 1960's All-Decade team and played in four Pro Bowls: 1959, 1960, 1962 and 1965. John David Crow completed more passes than any other non-quarterback in NFL history with 33 completions for five touchdowns.

In 1969, John David left the NFL for the University of Alabama to be their offensive backfield coach. He remained there until 1971. You could find John David in Cleveland as their offensive backfield coach during the 1972 and 1973 seasons. And he served as the San Diego Chargers' offensive coordinator in 1974. From 1976 to 1980, Crow served as the sixth head football coach at Northeast Louisiana College, now known as the University of Louisiana-Monroe. His win-loss record stands at 20-34-1. Crow remained there until 1981 as their athletic director.

In 1983, Crow became the assistant athletic director at Texas A&M University under Jackie Sherrill, and he was promoted to Athletic Director at the end of the 1988 football season, after Sherrill resigned under suspicion of scandal. R.C. Slocum would become the new football head coach.

In 1990, Crow fired long-time Aggies' basketball coach, Shelby Metcalf. Metcalf had been there for 32 years and had won five Southwest Conference Championships, but they could not get along. Crow appointed Kermit Davis to replace Metcalf. Crow resigned from his position in April of 1993. John David invested into a limited partnership in a greyhound race track. He was succeeded by Wally Groff. Crow later returned to Texas A&M as a fundraiser.

There is a wonderful story about John David Crow being appointed associate athletic director by Jackie Sherrill. A friend of Sherrill's asked Jackie, "You realize what you're doing? John David Crow is a lot more important than you." Sherrill understood that Crow could get some things done that he couldn't, and it was true. John David had a quality about him that just invited you in. Crow would make significant changes, especially in women's athletics. Texas A&M had been an all-male military academy until 1972. "We're not supporting women's athletics because of Title XI, but because it's the right thing to do," said Crow. In 1984, John David hired Lynn Hickey as the women's basketball head coach. He made sure the women's programs had adequate funding and support to compete at the highest level.

John David Crow, a fine gentleman, was surrounded by his family when he left us. The date will read, Wednesday June 17, 2015. He was three weeks shy of his 80th birthday and living with his family in College Station, Texas, where he had finally retired in 2001. He and his wife Carolyn (his high school sweetheart) had three children (one now deceased), seven grandchildren, and five great granddaughters. Crow has been elected to the Texas Sports Hall of Fame, the Louisiana Sports Hall of Fame, the National Football Foundation and the College Football Hall of Fame in 1976. Crow also has a street named after him on the Texas A&M campus. In 2004, he was awarded the Price-Waterhouse-Cooper "Doak Walker Legends" Award for excellence in athletics and administration. Crow was preceded in death by his son, John David Jr., who died in a car crash in 1994. Jr. had been born while John David was playing at A&M and later played his college football for Bear Bryant at Alabama.

Fifty-five years after John David, another Johnny rose to prominence at Texas A&M University and won the 2012 Heisman Trophy. His name was Johnny Manziel. Although Manziel was exciting to watch on the field of play, he has yet to be able to take the next step at the professional level. In keeping with the times, Manziel has been referred to as "Johnny Football." But we all know that the "real" Johnny Football's last name was Crow.

EL KICKADOR

There he stood at about the 25-yard line. It was hard to really know exactly where he was because of the condition of the field. He used his toe to mark the spot where he wanted the football placed on the ground. Lambeau Field, with the frigid temperature of 13 degrees below zero at game time, was glazed over by a sheet of ice. It was impossible to see the yard line markers. The date was December 31, 1967, and the warm-weather Dallas Cowboys had come to Green Bay, Wisconsin, to take on the Packers for the NFL Championship. With time running out during the first half, making this field goal would close the gap, as Green Bay led 14-7 at the time. The "Ice Bowl" was underway, and the world of professional football stills talks about it.

It has been recorded as a 21-yard field goal attempted and made. The Cowboys would head to the warmth of their locker room, down by four, 14-10. No. 11, Danny Villanueva, was one of the first Mexican-American placekickers and punters to play in the NFL and one of the last straight-away style placekickers. Only he knew that this would be his last game played in the National Football League.

Daniel Dario Villanueva was born in a two-room dirt hut in Tucumcari, New Mexico, to migrant missionary workers. The date was November 5, 1937, and Danny was the ninth of 12 children born into his family. A chubby kid at 5' 11" tall and weighing over 200 pounds, Danny played football and graduated from Calexico High School. He then attended Reedley College, before receiving an offer to play football at

New Mexico State University. Villanueva not only edited the college newspaper but he also became an integral part of the Aggie football teams of 1959 and 1960. New Mexico State won back-to-back Sun Bowl titles those years, as well as going undefeated his senior year (1960). Interestingly, the Aggies have not appeared in a post-season football game since then.

Little did Danny know that a scout from the Los Angeles Rams had attended one of the Sun Bowl games to watch another player and wrote down in his notes that a kid named Villanueva had kicked a 49-yard field goal. Many months later, the Rams were discussing possible kickers to be drafted and the scout said, "I know this fat, little Mexican kicker I saw in El Paso. The Rams sent a future Hall of Fame player and current front office employee by the name of Elroy "Crazylegs" Hirsch to see if Danny had any desire to kick in the NFL. In 1960, Villanueva had just began his career as a high school teacher but chose to pay his own way to Los Angeles to try out. The story goes that when he checked into the team's hotel, there were no rooms available so they placed him in the ballroom on a rollaway bed.

The long story short is that at the age of 23, he made the team. Danny signed as an undrafted free agent and his salary was $5,500 a year with a $200 signing bonus. He later said, "And the $200 signing bonus was taken out of my last check." As a placekicker and punter, Danny kept two different pairs of shoes on game day. Entrance music is popular now in professional sports, especially baseball. That was not the case in the sixties, but the Rams made an exception for Villanueva. They would play bullfighting music when he walked onto the field, and the local media called him El Kickador. In the 1960's, segregation was also prevalent in sports, especially on the team buses. A Rams' teammate once proclaimed, "All black guys get on that bus, white guys get on that bus, and Danny, you need to take a cab."

In 1962, with the Rams, Villanueva led the NFL in punting, with a 45.5 yards per kick average. He also set the Rams team record with a 51-yard field goal. He led the Rams in scoring from 1960 to 1963, but eventually lost his job to Bruce Gossett in 1964. Villanueva was traded to the Dallas Cowboys for wide receiver and future Hall-of-Famer, Tommy McDonald. The Cowboys tripled Villanueva's salary to $15,000 a year. From 1965 to 1967, he set the Cowboys' record with 100 consecutive extra-point conversions. In 1966, Danny completed an entire season without a missed extra point, with 56, and set the Cowboys' record for most points scored in a season, with a total of 107.

After eight years in the NFL, he retired at the end of the 1967 season with 491 points scored in 110 games and a punting average of 42.8 yards per kick. His last game had been "The Ice Bowl." As for the game, it was hard fought and suddenly with 4:50 left, the Packers found themselves down 17-14 to the Cowboys. Villanueva had been perfect on that day with two extra points and a field goal. Green Bay quarterback Bart Starr marched the Packers to within two feet of the goal line, with 16 seconds remaining. With no timeouts left and the two previous running plays yielding no yardage, another running play seemed out of the question. Starr took the snap and drove into a hole created by center Ken Bowman and guard Jerry Kramer, who had combined to move Cowboy tackle, Jethro Pugh, enough for the winning touchdown.

Villanueva led the NFL in punting yards with 3,960 in 1962 and 3,678 yards in 1963 and only had two punts blocked. His longest punt from scrimmage was 68 yards. He made 236 of the 241 extra points he attempted, for 97.9%. He connected on 85 of the 160 field goals attempted, for 53.1%.

While with the Rams, to support his football salary, he took a job at a L.A. Spanish-language UHF station known appropriately as KMEX. He would work as a broadcaster, and by the early 1970's, he had become part-owner of the Spanish International network (SIN). He worked tirelessly to raise money for toys and food for needy Hispanic families in Southern California. In 1986, this company was sold and renamed Univision. Villanueva went on to become a self-made multimillionaire.

In 1970, Danny Villanueva became a member of the New Mexico State Athletics Hall of Fame. Danny was inducted into the National Hispanic Hall of Fame in 1986. In 1991, he established the Danny Villanueva Scholarship Endowment Fund to recognize New Mexico State students. This fund has paid more than 40 scholarships. In 1999, he received an honorary doctorate from New Mexico State. In 2003, he joined the Management Hispanic Hall of Fame of the National Academy of Television Arts and Sciences. By 2007, you could find his name listed in the Hispanic Sports Hall of Fame. Over the years, he had donated millions of dollars to the university over the years.

Danny Villanueva met Myrna Schmidt while working at a fruit packing plant. They married and had two sons, Daniel and Jim. Daniel went to Stanford and became President of the Los Angeles Galaxy, and Jim took after his dad and became an All-American kicker at Harvard University. Danny Villanueva died from a stroke on June 18, 2015. He was 77 years of age. His story is a tale of hard work, never quitting and of reaping the benefits of a life well-lived.

SECRET WEAPON

Henry Ford once said, "Coming together is the beginning, keeping together is progress and working together is success." That pretty much sums up the story of the 1970 Detroit Lions, the first Lions team to make the playoffs since 1957.

In 1957, Lions' coach George Wilson molded players like Tobin Rote, Bobby Layne, Yale Lary, Joe Schmidt, John Henry Johnson, and Howard "Hopalong" Cassady into a fine team, one that would lead the Lions to the championship game against Jim Brown and the Cleveland Browns. My pal Lew Carpenter scored a touchdown against the Lions in this game. The Lions won the NFL Championship, 59-14. Since that time the Lions played so bad, you wanted to call 911. They sustained so many injuries they should have moved their locker room next to a hospital. Then the 1968 NFL draft rolled around, and the Lions hit the jackpot.

He had hands as big as shovels, springs in his legs, and even his cleats smelled fast. His teammates called him "Sticky Fingers" and "Little Mackey." This man was fast all right, a real Jessie Owens and smooth as corn silk. Some said the ground would tilt in his team's favor when he ran onto the field. He was so good at catching a football and finding the end zone where the first downs end. Everything #88 did just looked right. If you liked football, this guy was must-see TV, every seven days. He was the kind of player you put on speed dial when you are building your fantasy football team. Oh, this guy was hot all right; he rubbed his hands together while talking like he was trying to start a fire. They called him their secret weapon, a tight end with the hands and speed of an elite receiver. When throwing Charlie Sanders a football, he was gone, like tear away jerseys or the wishbone offense.

Charles Alvin Sanders was born on August 25, 1946. He grew up in Richlands, North Carolina, where it was so flat that once you started running there was nothing around to stop you. His mother, Parteacher, passed away when Charlie was two and his father, Nathaniel, spent most of Charlie's early life in the Army. Charlie and his two brothers, Nathaniel and Adrian, were sent to Greensboro, North Carolina, to live with his Aunt Flora. By the age of eight, Nathaniel returned from the Army, attended college and became a teaching professor at North Carolina A&T University. His dad also married again, providing Charlie and his brothers a home. Charlie would play basketball and baseball. Charlie did not play football until the tenth grade, while attending James B. Dudley High School.

Charlie Sanders was recruited by many local colleges, especially Wake Forrest University, but chose to go north, where the weather was cooler and African American athletes were accepted more readily. Many other great football players would head west or north during this time to continue their careers, players like Bubba Smith and Mel Farr, to name two. By 1972, every college football program in America was integrated.

Charlie accepted a full athletic scholarship to the University of Minnesota, coached by Murray Warmath. He played both football and basketball. Charlie started out on defense but was switched in 1967 to tight end, as a senior. He caught 21 balls that season, for 276 yards, and scored two touchdowns in an offense where his first priority was to block. His Minnesota team was a precision team. The kind of team that you beat up and down the field only to get on the bus heading to the airport after the game when you realized you had lost. Even though he had played but one season in college on the offensive side of the ball, Charlie was selected to the All-Big-Ten Conference Team as a tight end. The Golden Gophers finished 8-2 that season, and Charlie Sanders was drafted in the third round of the 1968 NFL draft, by the Detroit Lions. At 6' 4" tall and weighing 225 pounds, The Lions had just gotten the steal of the draft.

Sanders was also contacted by the Toronto Argonauts of the Canadian Football League. They offered him $16,000 a year, one thousand higher than the Lions. Detroit stepped up and made him another offer of $17,000 a year, with a $20,000 signing bonus. That closed the deal and made Charlie Sanders a Lion for life.

Before he reported to camp, Sanders played in the College All-Star Game with the Lions' first pick that year, quarterback Greg Landry. At that time, the Lions played their home games at Briggs Field, later to be named Tiger Stadium. These two would make magic for years to come. "My sights were never getting to the Hall of Fame," said Charlie Sanders. "It was about being the best I could be." There are only eight tight ends currently in the Pro-Football Hall of Fame and there were only three chosen before Charlie Sanders: Mike Ditka, John Mackey and Jackie Smith. Charlie would have to wait 29 years before becoming a senior committee's choice for the Pro-Football Hall of Fame.

Charlie hurt his knee in 1976, but continued to play through the pain the following season. Charlie announced his retirement before the 1977 season began. He was only 31 years old. The injuries had taken their toll. Hall-of-Fame tight-end Charlie Sanders played in 128 games from 1968-1977 and made 108 starts. He played when there were only 12 games per season. Charlie caught 40 passes his first year for 533 yards, one touchdown, and averaged 13.3 yards per catch. He was the only rookie in the NFL to be named to the 1969 Pro Bowl. He caught 336 passes for 4,817 yards and found the end zone 31 times during his career. Those team records stood for 20 years until they were broken by Herman Moore, a player Sanders had coached.

As good as he was, Charlie Sanders may have outdone himself during his 2007 induction speech at the Pro Football Hall of Fame. He spoke to the crowd about his mother, Parteacher. "Of all the things I've done in football, and I've done a lot, there is only one thing I really, really regret," said Sanders. "Many times I've seen an athlete, college or pro, often look in the television camera and say, 'Hi, Mom.' I always thought that was special, and always something I wanted to do. So I take this time, right here, right now, in Canton, Ohio, at the Pro-Football Hall of Fame, to say 'Hi, Mom. Thank you for your ultimate sacrifice. This day belongs to you, for it was written.'"

Charlie walked like a man whose body had paid a toll. He had so many surgeries some said he invented scar tissue. Charlie Sanders developed a malignant tumor behind his right knee. It was not discovered until he had a knee replacement. He underwent chemotherapy but, unfortunately, he died on July 2, 2015. Charlie Sanders was 68 years old and living in Royal Oaks, Michigan. He left his wife Georgiana and ten children behind. He is one of two tight ends selected by the Hall of Fame to join the 1970's All-Decade team. The other was Dave Casper of the Oakland Raiders. Charlie Sanders was inducted into the North Carolina Sports Hall of Fame in 1997. In 2005, he co-authored a book entitled <u>Charlie Sanders, Tales from the Detroit Lions.</u> Sanders was chosen as a member of the Lions' 75th Anniversary All-Time team, in 2008. He was also inducted into the Minnesota M-Club Hall of Fame in 2013.

Charlie, a Detroit Lion for life, became one of the Lions broadcasters from 1983-1988. He coached the Lion receivers from 1989-1996. He scouted and eventually evaluated all personnel for the team. The Charlie Sanders Foundation was created in 2007, in an effort to provide college scholarships to local students in the Detroit area. He worked with and for the United Way and March of Dimes.

Someone once said, "It's not our friends, it's our enemies that define us." I don't think he had any enemies. So, in the end, it became clear that Charlie Sanders was also a Hall-of-Fame human being. "I'd like to think I played the game the way it should be played," said Sanders before he passed. A well-kept secret until the end.

SNAKEBIT

Hall of Fame football coach, John Madden, once said, "I can't wait until some of my players retire so I can go drinking with them. This was one of those guys. He loved fast boats and expensive whiskey. He was one cool country boy. Born poor, he had big ears and looked like Willie Nelson with blonde hair. He loved fishing, hunting, playing baseball and basketball. In fact, he averaged 29 points per game in high school, playing basketball. He shot pool, drank beer from a paper cup, and dated every girl in Alabama. Tall and thin, his dad called him "Bud." He had grown up straight as a string. In the ninth grade, he was not interested in playing football. His dad took him to see the Houston Oilers play an exhibition game against the New York Titans. There he would get his first autograph from quarterback, George Blanda. His father wanted him to play football, so he bought him a 1954 black Ford when he was in the tenth grade. "Hey Bud, it's yours if you play football," said his dad. He was excited to have a car and told his father, "I'm going to be a great football player." Eleven years later, he would be holding for Blanda, while George kicked field goals and extra points for the Oakland Raiders.

"Coach Madden would stand behind me when I dropped back during passing drills," said Ken Stabler. "It was his way of seeing what the quarterback sees and determining which receivers were open and when." "Ken, I don't know how you spot the open receiver and get the ball to them so fast," said Madden. "You're hitting people I can't even find looking over your shoulder. You're getting the receiver the ball between two defenders on the dead run. You've got the touch."

Kenneth Michael "Ken" Stabler was born on Christmas Day, 1945, in a farm town of about 4,000 named Foley, Alabama. His father was named Leroy, but everyone called him "Slim." Slim served his country in WWII during the invasion of Anzio. He was wounded in the leg and returned home depressed. Slim earned his living as a mechanic. He would eventually become an alcoholic and died early, at the age of 47, from a massive heart attack. Kenny's mom, Sally, worked in a doctor's office. He also had a sister, Carolyn, born in 1950. Ken Stabler had also been a fine pitcher in high school and was offered a contract with a $20,000 signing bonus his senior year, by the New York Yankees. Stabler had faced future Hall-of-Fame pitcher, Don Sutton, in high school and won. It was Sutton's only loss in high school.

Ken Stabler was a fine defensive back and kick returner in high school, before he became the quarterback. He once returned a kickoff that required him to zigzag back and forth across the field four times before he made it to the end zone. "I must have run over 200 yards," said Ken. One of his high school coaches, Denzil Hollis said, "That boy runs like a Snake," and the legend was born. "He called me 'Snake' and I loved it," said Stabler. Kenny's dad had been correct. Kenny would become a star quarterback at Foley High School and a hell-raiser like his dad. Snake and a buddy once tossed five smart alecks out of a local bar. His senior year, Ken was elected All-State, All-Southern and made two different All-American teams. He was also voted MVP of the All-Star Game. He was recruited by Auburn and Alabama. Foley High School would finish with a 29-1 win-loss record during Stabler's three varsity years. There were only 47 students in his graduating class.

In 1964, Stabler signed with Alabama, after a visit from

"Bear" Bryant. Freshmen were ineligible, so Stabler watched as senior, Joe Namath, led the Crimson Tide to a National Championship. In 1965, Kenny was given the #12, the same number Joe Namath had worn. That year, Stabler backed up Steve Sloan, as the Tide went 9-1-1 and defeated Nebraska in the Orange Bowl, 39-28. In 1965, Alabama won their second consecutive National Championship. As a junior, Kenny took over the Crimson Tide in 1966, and led the team to an 11-0 record and a 34-7 victory over Nebraska in the Sugar Bowl, but finished third in the nation behind Notre Dame and Michigan State. He was elected MVP of the Sugar Bowl and was on his way. Kenny's senior season (1967) was a little bumpy as Bryant kicked Stabler off the team for cutting classes and partying too much. Stabler was eventually given a second chance and led Alabama to an 8-2-1 record, with a 53-yard run for the winning score against rival Auburn in the Iron Bowl. This incredible run for a 7-3 victory over Auburn is most often referred to as the "Run in the Mud." Stabler finished his career at Alabama with a 28-3-2 record as the starter. He threw for 18 touchdowns and rushed for nine more. Bear would later say, "Stabler was the best quarterback I ever had at Alabama."

The Houston Astros drafted Kenny Stabler in 1968. He was the 24th player picked, even though he had not thrown a pitch in two years. He was also the last pick of the 2nd round of the 1968 NFL Draft by the Oakland Raiders. Stabler was given #12 to wear and signed a four-year escalating contract that would play him $16,000, $18,000, $20,000 and $22,000 during the next four years. He also received a $50,000 signing bonus.

With three quarterbacks on the team, Stabler was sent to the Spokane Shockers of the Continental Football League, during the 1968 and 1969 seasons, to get some playing time.

Kenny had four roommates while with Oakland: Pete Banaszak, Tony Cline, Dan Connors and Fred Bilenikoff. According to Stabler, Fred Bilenikoff perfected the ability to sleep with his eyes open at meetings.

In his autobiography entitled <u>Snake</u>, written by Berry Stainback, Ken tells many wonderful training camp stories that happened while he was with the Raiders. One of my favorites included two of his roommates, Pete Banaszak and Ken Herock, devising a way to beat curfew. Herock takes two pillows and places them long ways in the bed, and then takes a small lamp off the night stand and places it above the pillows with the shade at the top where his head would be. He pulls the covers up over the top of the lamp shade. He then turns to Pete and says, "Cover for me," and leaves for a night of fun and entertainment. A few minutes after 11:00 PM, an assistant coach comes by and knocks on the door as he sticks his head inside. He looks at Pete and then over at the other bed and says, "Is that Herock?" Pete responds. "I think he's asleep." The coach then hits the light switch on the wall beside the door and the lamp shade lights up. When Herock returns he finds a note on his pillow stating he had been fined $200 for missing curfew. Banaszak says, "You should have unplugged your head."

In 1970, Kenny played sparingly behind "The Mad Bomber," Daryle Lamonica, and George Blanda. Interestingly, Blanda had also played for Bear Bryant in college, at Kentucky. Lamonica, who came from Buffalo in 1967, would lead the AFL in passing that year.

When Stabler didn't start in 1971, he wanted to be traded. Blanda told him, "Stay put. You're on a team that will be good for a long time. I waited ten years in Chicago to get my chance." Sure enough, Kenny would get onto every game played in 1971, as George Blanda's holder.

Kenny made his presence felt in a 1972 NFL playoff game against the Pittsburgh Steelers. Stabler replaced Lamonica and scored a go-ahead touchdown late in the game with a 30-yard scramble. Oakland now led 7-6 with 1:13 left to play. The Steelers roared back with a controversial play that included a pass from Terry Bradshaw to "Frenchy" Fuqua.

Fuque was dislodged from the ball with a stinging hit by Raiders' Jack Tatum, and Franco Harris caught the football before it hit the ground and then raced 60 yards for the winning score. It has become known in NFL lore as, "The Immaculate Reception."

In 1974, the (WFL) World Football League came after Stabler. The Birmingham Americans played at Legion Field. Stabler signed a contract with them, but the team folded in mid-season of 1975. Stabler remained with the Raiders without ever playing in the WFL.

The Raiders led by quarterback Kenny Stabler won 37 of his first 45 starts. In 1976, Ken completed 66.7% of his passes, the second highest rate for completions in NFL history. Stabler was named the AFC Player-of-the-Year in 1974 and 1976. In January of 1977, Stabler and the Raiders won the Super Bowl. He also won the *Sporting News* Player-of-the-Year Award. Kenny won the Hickok Award as the best athlete and the Pro Player-of-the-Year Award. Ken also completed 66.7% of his passes; only Sammy Baugh had been better in, 1945, with 70.3%. After Oakland beat Minnesota 33-14 in Super Bowl XI in front of 100,421 people, Los Angeles sportswriter Jim Murray wrote, "The Vikings play football like a guy laying carpet. The Raiders play like a guy jumping through a skylight with a machine gun." The Raiders were always serious on Sundays. Oakland appeared in eight AFL Championship games in ten years.

In the 1977 AFC playoffs against the Baltimore Colts, Stabler completed a fourth-quarter pass to his tight end, Dave Casper to set up a game-tying field goal by Earl Mann. This play has been called the "Ghost to the Post." The game went into overtime and Oakland eventually won, 37-31.

The next two seasons were depressing as the Raiders struggled to replace several members from their Super Bowl team. In 1978, Kenny tore a tendon in his left ring finger. The results were 16 touchdown passes and 30 interceptions. Head Coach John Madden, Fred Bilenikoff, George

Atkinson and Clarence Davis had all left the team. In 1979, Snake was also saddled with a new roommate named John Matuszak. Stabler nicknamed him "Tooz." Six feet eight and 290 pounds of crazy, they made quite a pair. "Tooz looked like an ice machine with a head," said Kenny. Eventually, Kenny Stabler was traded to the Houston Oilers in 1980 for quarterback Dan Pastorini. Bear Bryant and Oilers Coach "Bum" Phillips were good friends and, when Bear heard the news of the trade, he came to Houston. Stabler had let his hair grow long and, when Bear saw Kenny he said, "Well look, here comes Davy Crockett." Armed with a beard and silver hair, Stabler looked more like country western singer. The Oilers also traded for Dave Casper and Jack Tatum. Stabler loved playing for Phillips. "At training camp, we'd be practicing in the hot sun at Angelo State, and Bum would blow the whistle and say, "Let's go drink some beer. It's no wonder everybody liked him," said Snake. Kenny led the Oilers to the playoffs, but lost to Oakland in the Wild Card game. "We only had one play in Houston," said Kenny. "Turn and hand the ball to Earl Campbell." The Raiders would go on to win the Super Bowl that season. Stabler came to the Oilers with a label as a hell raiser. "I studied my playbook by the light of the juke box," said Stabler. "How much sleep do you need to play three hours a day?" Additional protection for this renegade quarterback was devised by Bum Phillips. His name was Carl Mauck. Phillips roomed Stabler with offensive center Mauck, who stood 6'5" tall and weighed over 280 pounds. His job was not only to snap the ball to Ken, and block for Ken, but to keep Stabler out of trouble away from the field. In essence he became "The Snake Keeper." Bum Phillips was fired after the season. Snake would follow Phillips to the New Orleans Saints, in 1982. Stabler, now wearing #16, had a fine season for the Saints in 1983, but at 37 years of age, Kenny was close to being done. He retired in 1984.

Stabler was not a small guy. He was the kind of guy who

gets up out of the dirt, brushes himself off and inspires others to do the same. Kenny stood 6'3 inches tall and weighed 225 pounds. After suffering several knee injuries, Stabler was forced to become more of a drop-back passer versus a scrambler. Ken was also blessed with big, strong, quick, and agile offensive linemen. They averaged over 270 pounds and were easily the largest in the NFL at that time. Bob Brown, Art Shell, Gene Upshaw, George Buehler and Jim Otto plowed holes in the defensive lines of their opponents. It has been said that they often brought dumb bells to lunch to do curls with one hand, while they ate with the other. It also didn't hurt to have a receiving corps that included wide receivers Fred Biletnikoff and Cliff Branch, and tight end, Dave Casper.

"When Ted Hendricks joined the Oakland Raiders, he was known as 'The Mad Stork,' but we all called him 'Kick'em in the head Ted.' He was the best player I ever played with," stated Kenny. The team was labeled with a lot of different adjectives. "Misfits" seemed to be the best.

Ken Stabler was the fastest quarterback to win 100 games in the NFL, having done so in 150 games. Johnny Unitas held the record at 153 games, before Stabler. That record has now been broken by Terry Bradshaw (147), Joe Montana (139), and Tom Brady at 131 games.

Ken Stabler played in 184 games and he had guts. He threw for 27,938 yards and 194 touchdowns in his 15 NFL seasons. He also had 222 passes intercepted. He was a four-time Pro Bowl selection and the 1974 MVP of the league.

Ken and a couple of friends owned two bars in Alabama for about three years, while playing for Oakland. After football, Stabler worked as a color commentator on CBS NFL telecasts and then on radio with Eli Gold during Alabama football games. He hosted a golf tournament to help raise funds for the Ronald McDonald House of Mobile, Alabama. He was featured on *SNL* and appeared on Miller Lite commercials. He was arrested three times for

DUI: 1995, 2001 and 2008.

I met the Snake in person in 1992. Kenny could disarm most people with his humor. He was in Houston at a sports card and memorabilia show. I got his autograph, shook his hand, and took a photo. He was nice, but looked older than I would have thought. Maybe too many nights out finally catches up with a man.

The Snake left us on July 8, 2015. Father Time does not spare icons, either. He was but 69. Ken had been diagnosed with colon cancer in February. He was never meant to sit in the shade of life. Even people who didn't care about sports knew who he was. He transcended sports, and he belongs in the Pro Football Hall of Fame.

Ken had been married and divorced three times and is survived by daughters Kendra, Alexa and Marissa; his sister, Carolyn Bishop; and two grandchildren.

Sure, he drank too much, stayed out too late and raised Cain, but he also knew how to win football games. He was Bret Favre before Bret Favre. "He would cut you up on a football field," said Archie Manning. Kenny Stabler's philosophy in life was play hard, live fast and throw deep. There was lightning in his left arm. My pal, Gene Upshaw, used to say, "When we were behind in the fourth quarter, with our backs to our end zone, no matter how he had played up to that point, we could look in his eyes and you knew, *you knew*, he was going to win it for us. That was an amazing feeling."

MR. ZERO

Greek philosopher Plato once said, "Never discourage anyone who continuously makes progress no matter how slow." Baseball is an adventure, a rollercoaster. He became a great pitcher, the kind that makes your bat feel heavy. Handing this guy a baseball was like giving him the keys to an F-15; there was going to be a lot of speed involved. Standing in against this guy pitching was like facing a firing squad. He threw so easy; his windup said 85 mph, but his arm said 95. Some said he worked over-the-top like Sandy Koufax and he owned a see-you-later fastball. He mixed his stuff up and really got those batters rocking in the box. This guy was a joy to watch and nasty; he didn't throw much of anything straight. He had four pitches that could embarrass you, and he could bury all four pitches at the bottom of the box. His change-up had three speeds: slow, slower, and to-heck-with-it. This fellow understood that curveballs lead to groundballs and groundballs lead to outs. In 1944, he once pitched six shutouts as a junior in high school and earned the nickname, "Mr. Zero." Albert Einstein once wrote, "Force equals mass times acceleration." He may have been talking about pitchers like Billy Pierce.

Walter William "Billy" Pierce was born on April 2, 1927, in Detroit, Michigan. Billy was the son of pharmacist, Walter Pierce, and his mom's name was Julia. Billy grew up in Highland Park and fell in love with the grand old game of baseball at the age of ten. One of his teammates at Highland Park Community High School was future Major

League pitcher, Ted Gray. Billy's favorite player was Detroit pitcher, Tommy Bridges, who also had a slight build. Pierce used to tell the story of how his father had to offer him a real Major League baseball and good glove to have his tonsils removed. "I refused to have the operation until I got my way," laughed Billy. Pierce started out playing at first base but later switched to pitcher, as he realized that he owned a pretty good fastball. Weighing all of 140 pounds, his tall and slender build made one think that he had to run around in the shower to get wet. He was so skinny they used him to get the baseballs out of the sewer. On August 7, 1944, Mr. Zero started and became the winning pitcher in an East-West All-American Boys' Game sponsored by Esquire magazine. The game was played at the Polo Grounds in New York, home of the New York Giants. The East team, on which Billy played, was managed by none other than future Hall-of-Fame Manager, Connie Mack, of the Philadelphia Athletes. The West team included future Hall-of-Fame centerfielder, Richie Ashburn, who played catcher in high school. Ashburn went without a hit in two at-bats against Pierce. Billy Pierce was voted the game's most outstanding player and won a four-year scholarship to the college of his choice. Billy became a hot commodity and worked out for the Red Sox, Phillies, and his hometown Tigers at Briggs Field, later to be named Tiger Stadium. Billy and his parents decided to wait until after high school to decide his fate. He strongly considered studying medicine at The University of Michigan, but instead signed with the Detroit Tigers when they offered him a $15,000 signing bonus.

The beauty of baseball is that it's inexplicable. Billy actually made the Tigers' team in 1945, before he graduated from high school. He made his Major League debut a few weeks after turning 18, in June of 1945. He logged three relief appearances in June, and then spent a month in the Minor Leagues with the Buffalo Bisons of the International League, before returning in September for two more relief appearances. His manager in Buffalo was another future Hall-of-Fame Manager known as "Bucky" Harris. Billy was listed on the Detroit Tigers' World Series roster in 1945, but did not appear in a game for the champions.

Billy found himself back in Buffalo in 1946 and his manager this time was "Gabby" Hartnett. He would miss most of the season with a back injury. After the 1947 season in Buffalo, Pierce returned to Detroit in 1948 and spent most of that season in the bullpen and trying to put on weight. He was 21 now and still only weighed 148 pounds. He did start five games and posted a 3-0 win-loss record. His first start and Major League victory came on August 8, 1948, against the Washington Senators. He pitched 7 2/3 innings and struck out six, while winning 6-5. He was also handy with his bat as he drove in one run with a triple and scored. Pierce also had control problems and walked 51 batters in 55 1/3 innings that season. Concerned, the Tigers traded him to the Chicago White Sox on November 10, 1948, for Aaron Robinson and $10,000. Most historians agree that this trade would become one of the most lopsided trades in baseball history. The Tigers tried to call off the deal one day after it was completed, after they realized what they were about to give up. They even offered $50,000 to the White Sox to get Pierce back. The White Sox were not about to give up what they thought was the deal of the century.

During the first couple of seasons with the White Sox, Pierce's control problems continued, but there were also signs of brilliance. On May 29, 1949, 22-year-old Billy Pierce was matched against 42-year-old Cleveland Indians' former legendary Negro League pitcher, Satchel Paige. These two locked up in an eleven-inning game in Cleveland. Pierce was replaced after walking leadoff hitter, Ken Keltner, in the eleventh. After two bunt singles, Indians' Lou Boudreau also singled, to give Cleveland a 2-1 victory. Pierce had scored his team's only run in the eighth inning, after reaching base on a single. It got better on June 15, 1950, as Pierce threw his first shutout, a 5-0 one hitter, against the reigning World Series Champion, New York Yankees. Yankees' star, Joe DiMaggio commented on Pierce's speed to a reporter. "That little so-and-so is a marvel. So little and all that speed; and I mean speed! He got me out of there on a fastball in the ninth inning that I'd have needed a telescope to see."

Paul Richards became the White Sox Manager in 1951 and worked tirelessly with Pierce on honing his four pitches. In 1952, Billy would rank sixth with an ERA of 2.57 and would also set the White Sox record ("Doc" White-1907) for strikeouts by a left-hander, ending the season with 144. Pierce would open the 1953 season at home with a 1-0 win and his second career one-hitter against the St. Louis Browns. He would be the first White Sox pitcher to be chosen to start the 1953 All-Star Game for the American League. He gave up one hit to Stan Musial in three innings of work. Ted Williams said, "Billy probably threw harder than anybody for a guy his size. He held us in the palm of his hand that day. He threw the ball right by everybody."

Richards also arranged his rotation in a different way and was known to occasionally hold Pierce out of the rotation, so he could face the powerful New York Yankees and Cleveland Indians. It has been said that Pierce could have picked up many more wins if he had faced each opponent equally. Pierce would post a 21-21 win-loss record against the Yankees, from August of 1952 through the 1960 season. Pierce faced Whitey Ford 14 times in his career, more than any other pitcher. Pierce won seven of those contests and bested Ford and the mighty Yankees on July 28, 1959, to put the White Sox in first place. Chicago would win the American League pennant for the first time since the 1919 Black Sox scandal. Chicago White Sox Manager, Al Lopez, chose not to start Pierce in the 1959 World Series against the Los Angeles Dodgers. He did pitch in relief the last three games of the Series, allowing only two hits and no runs. By then it was too late. That decision still remains controversial today. The White Sox never finished lower than third place, from 1952-1960. The "Go-Go White Sox" were built on speed, defense and pitching. Billy's roommate, "Nellie" Fox, would kid Pierce after scoring a run. "Here's your run, now go out there and hold it."

It really was not a fair matchup. Billy's career record against the Yankees was 25-37. Whitey Ford was supported by Mickey Mantle, "Moose" Skowron, Hank Bauer, "Yogi" Berra and many others, while Billy Pierce had Nellie Fox, "Minnie" Minoso and Luis Aparicio in his corner. Interestingly, the Yankees tried to acquire Pierce when Ford was serving time in the military. Yankees' outfielder Hank Bauer said, "The guy who gave me the most problems, and I think he gave'em to most of us, was Billy Pierce." On June 20, 1961, Pierce broke Ed Walsh's White Sox record of 1,732 career strikeouts.

Billy Pierce would become the ace of the Chicago White Sox pitching staff. During his 13 seasons in Chicago, Billy led his team in wins nine times and in strikeouts eight times. Billy would be the team's Opening Day starter seven times. He received the American League Sporting News' Pitcher-of-the-Year Award for 1956 and 1957. Pierce holds the White Sox franchise record for career strikeouts (1,796) and his club marks of 186 wins, 2,931 innings, and 390 starts, are all team records for a left-hander. With an outstanding fastball, a fall-off-the-table curveball, a slider that changes lanes, and a change-up previously described above, Pierce became, in my opinion, a candidate for the Baseball-Hall-of-Fame Museum. His #19 was retired by the White Sox in 1987.

In November of 1961, Pierce was sent to the San Francisco Giants with Don Larsen for four players. Pierce was now surrounded by a team of hitters. Willie Mays, Willie McCovey and Orlando Cepeda supplied the power, as Billy

Pierce won his first eight starts of that season. In 1962, Pierce helped the Giants win the National League pennant, going 12-0 at home. The Giants matched the Dodgers with a win-loss record of 101-61 and entered a three-game playoff. Billy started in Game One against Sandy Koufax and won 8-0. He then pitched in relief during Game Three and struck out the side, to capture the National League pennant for the Giants. Against the New York Yankees, he started Game Three and took a 3-2 loss. Pierce returned in Game Six at Candlestick Park, against his long-time nemeses, Whitey Ford, and hung on, to win 5-3 and tie the 1962 Series at three games each. The Yankees would win Game Seven and the Series. Billy was chosen to open the season for the Giants in 1963. Billy threw his last shutout of his career against the Houston Colt 45's. He would gradually be moved to the bullpen and was used exclusively in relief during the 1964 season. Pierce would retire at the end of the 1964 season. His last start occurred on October 3, 1964.

Billy pitched for 18 years in 585 games. He completed 193 games including 38 shutouts, unheard of in today's game, and gave up only 284 home runs. He was selected for the All-Star team seven times. His career win-loss record stands at 211-169. His ERA is listed as 3.27 and he came up one strikeout short of 2,000. Billy Pierce was selected to the Chicago White Sox All-Century Team in the year 2000. Billy was inducted into the Michigan Sports Hall of fame in 2003. On October 4, 2005, Billy threw out the first pitch before Game One of the American League Division Series against the Boston Red Sox. The White Sox would defeat the Houston Astros and claim their first World Series title in 88 years. In 2006, Billy was inducted into the Chicagoland Sports Hall of Fame and on July 23, 2007, a statue of Pierce was unveiled in his honor at U.S. Cellular Field in Chicago.

Pierce worked as a White Sox television color analyst in 1970 and even did some scouting. He was credited for discovering 1983 White Sox Rookie of the Year, Ron Kittle. He worked at a couple of car dealerships and then joined Continental Envelope as a sales rep from 1974 until he retired in 1997.

Billy Pierce died on July 31, 2015, from gallbladder cancer. He was 88 years old and survived by his wife, Gloria, and three kids. He was living with his family in Palos Heights, Illinois. He was entombed in Chapel Hill Garden-South Cemetery in Alsip.

My question is, how can the baseball writers place Whitey Ford (236-106), Jim Bunning (224-184), and Don Drysdale (206-166) into the Hall of Fame and not give recognition to Pierce? Pierce is also listed fifth in career strikeouts (1,999) as a left-handed pitcher, behind only Warren Spahn, "Rube" Waddell, "Lefty" Grove and Eddie Plank. Pierce was 24-24 in 54 career starts against Hall of Famers from his era and achieved 12 strikeouts per game, four times.

Billy Pierce's name appeared on the Golden Era Committee election ballot in 2014. He and his teammate, Minnie Minoso, failed to receive enough votes for induction. The Committee meets every three years and votes on ten candidates who played from 1947 to 1972. I'm in hopes that Mr. Zero, Billy Pierce will be inducted into the Baseball Hall of Fame in 2017.

THE CENTERPIECE

William Faulkner once said, "Wake up the past! History is not what was but what is." He was either one of the greatest football players I've ever seen or one of the luckiest. This fellow was a gifted athlete, fluid but not flashy. He was not very big and not very fast, but a complete player, nevertheless. He played offense and defense, threw passes and caught passes, kicked and returned kicks, and he looked like James Bond in shoulder pads. He was the kind of man that would make you smile when you thought about him. This guy was like sunlight passing through raindrops; he created rainbows. And that smile; a smile is the lighting system of the face, the cooling system of the head, and the heating system of the heart. He may have breathed different air than the rest of us, and some said he was so wealthy that China owed him money. "He was the guy other guys wanted to be," said Pat Summerall. He owned a soft-spoken voice, a quick mind, and a perfect body. His face looked like it could have been carved into Mount Rushmore. This fellow looked more like a movie star than a football player. With actor's looks, he was an undisputed star of the game of professional football in the fifties. This man played like he was 18 years old for 12 years, and he never rested on his gifts. We are all competition junkies. He and his teammates were a class act. They played hard on Sundays, hung out at Toots Shore's afterwards, and they won.

Frank Gifford was so good-looking he might as well have been dipped in gold. He owned Sundays in the media capitol of the world, New York City. He built the bridge from the football locker-room to Madison Avenue. In the fifties and early sixties, it was Mickey Mantle and Frank Gifford. They were the coolest guys in the room. Attending a Giants' game and not watching Frank Gifford was like going to the Grand Canyon and not looking down. More people knew about Gifford than the President. "I sign more autographs now than when I was a player," said Frank. One time, Howard Cosell and Frank Gifford ended up at the same event. "No one asked for Cosell's autograph," said Frank. Most people make you earn their respect, but with Frank Gifford that's where you started. We should always hang onto the good people, but now we are deprived of his thoughts and words. Frank A. Clark once wrote, "Real generosity is doing something nice for someone who will never find out." That may have been the secret of the real Frank Gifford.

Frank Newton Gifford was born on August 16, 1930, in Santa Monica, California. His dad, Weldon, was a roughneck and worked in the oil fields. He went where there was work. Frank had two older siblings, Winona and Wayne. His mom, Lola, took care of the three kids at home. The Giffords lived in 37 different towns while Frank was growing up. Wayne would eventually drop out of school and work in the oil fields with his dad. Frank attended Bakersfield High School, where he played quarterback in the T-formation. Coach Homer Bailey changed the offense to the single-wing and moved Gifford to halfback. It was a stroke of genius, as Gifford's talent really began to shine.

Frank first attended Bakersfield Junior College to get his grades up. He played well enough to be chosen a Junior-College All American. He later enrolled at USC on a full athletic scholarship. Gifford accumulated 841 yards rushing on 195 carries, in his senior season. He graduated from USC in 1952. USC coach, Jeff Cravath, regarded Frank Gifford as the finest college player he had ever known. He pledged a fraternity but had to drop out, because he could not afford the dues. In 1951, Hollywood called; Frank did a bit part in a Dean Martin-Jerry Lewis football film entitled "That's My Boy." He was a double in all of the football scenes for comedian, Jerry Lewis. It was Gifford who kicked the game-winning field goal in the movie. Times were good for Frank, as he eventually ended up as a senior, marrying the USC Homecoming Queen, Maxine Ewart, in June of 1952. That same year, Frank Gifford found out he had been drafted by the New York Giants, by listening to the radio in his car.

Tim J. Mara purchased the New York Football Giants' franchise in 1925, for $500. The first ten years the NFL was in existence, 35 franchises went "belly-up." Tim would give ownership of the team to his son, Wellington Mara, in 1930. It was Wellington who had scouted Gifford when he attended the USC-Army game played at Yankee Stadium in 1951.

When Gifford left USC, he was still somewhat a shy, withdrawn kid from Bakersfield, California. While at USC, Gifford stood 6'1" tall and weighed 197 pounds. He was chosen an All-American single-wing tailback and placekicker. He also played and starred in the defensive backfield for the Trojans. He was drafted in the first round of the 1952 NFL draft, by the New York Football Giants. The Los Angeles Rams had the first pick and took quarterback Billy Wade out of Vanderbilt. Frank was taken with the eleventh pick, out of the first twelve by the Giants. During the summers, Gifford finished his college studies by attending classes from 1952 to 1955. He would earn a degree in industrial management. The Edmonton Eskimos of the Canadian League made Frank an offer, but Gifford ignored their plea.

Frank and his family moved into apartment 909 of the Concourse Plaza, an apartment building within walking distance of Yankees' Stadium. In 1953, during the first week of practice in the New York Giants' camp, Gifford was homesick and discouraged. He had lost almost 20 pounds and was down to 178 pounds. The New York Giants were not a passing team when Frank arrived. They were ninth out of twelve in passing, but third in the league in rushing. Frank tried to sneak out of camp one day and was stopped by assistant backfield coach, Allie Sherman. "My nose wasn't broken and I had all my teeth, but I didn't think I would make the team," said Gifford. Sherman told him he was the best rookie running back they had in the Giants' camp in years. Frank decided to stay. Head Coach, Steve Owens, often played Frank in the defensive backfield. Frank did fill in for halfback, Kyle Rote, when Rote injured his knee. He would begin to make the #16 famous for the "Big Blue." By 1954, Owens was out as head coach and Jim Lee Howell was in. Howell would proceed to hire two of the very best coaches in all of football.

Head Coach, Jim Lee Howell, once said, "My job is to bring the bag of footballs." With a coaching staff that included Tom Landry on the defensive side of the ball and Vince Lombardi on the offensive side, Howell's job was easy. Landry was the stoic type, mechanical and unassuming. You did it his way or you took the highway. Lombardi was smart, volatile and always grinning. You could hear Lombardi laugh from five miles away, but you couldn't hear Landry if he were sitting in the chair next to you. You need to remember that in the 1950's, each team only had 35 players and two-thirds of those played on the offensive side of the ball. Lombardi started Gifford at the left halfback position, where he thrived on the power sweep and halfback-option plays. Frank had a good burst of speed but would get run down from behind on several occasions, after running for about 30 or 40 yards. Gifford was also an interesting receiver as he caught the football backwards. Being right-handed, most receivers reached for the ball with their left on top and secured the ball with their right hand underneath. Gifford did it backwards by extending his right hand above his left.

In 1956, the New York Giants had no major injuries to the team. There were no MRI's or scopes in those days, only tape. "Professional football was much noisier than college football," said Frank. "Grunts and moans when players hit each other were easily heard." The Giants won the 1956 NFL Championship by smashing the Chicago Bears, 47-7. The winner's share came to $3,799.19. It was the Giants' first championship in 18 seasons. Frank Gifford was voted NFL MVP and received the Jim Thorpe Trophy. In a traditional "run first, pass second" offense, Frank led the entire league with 51 pass receptions, 1,422 yards receiving and 819 yards rushing.

Frank Gifford made the Pro Bowl eight times, at three different positions: flanker, defensive back and running back. He became the centerpiece of the New York Football Giants' offense that played five times in next seven years, in the NFL championship games. The game of professional football grew up during the decade of the fifties. From 1950 to 1960, the attendance of an NFL game grew from 25,353 per game to 40,106.

Bob Sheppard was the voice of New York Yankees and the New York Football Giants. In 1958, Sheppard was in his third year with the Giants. He had four rose bushes in his backyard named Andy, Rosey, Mo, and Kat. They stood for Andy Robustelli, Rosey Grier, Dick Modzelewski and Jim Katcavage; the four down linemen of the Giants defense.

Frank Gifford made $25,000 in 1958. His roommate on the road was Charlie Conerly. In his latter years, Gifford mostly remembered fumbling the ball twice in the 1958 NFL Championship game against the Baltimore Colts. He did run the ball for 60 yards on 12 carries and caught the go-ahead touchdown pass in the fourth quarter, but it was not enough. The Colts scored touchdowns on both of his turnovers and won 23-17 in sudden-death overtime. This game was crowned "The Game of the Century," because it was the first NFL Championship Game to be televised nationwide and the first to use "sudden death" to be decided. It did not carry the same meaning for Frank. In 1959, the Colts beat the Giants again, for the NFL Championship. It was a bitter defeat.

On November 20, 1960, Gifford received a devastating hit from future Hall-of-Fame linebacker, Chuck Bednarik. Frank was carted off the field unconscious. This hit ended his season. On February 10, 1961, Frank Gifford announced his retirement after sustaining a concussion from the hit by linebacker, Chuck Bednarik, of the Philadelphia Eagles. He found work instantly in radio, writing a column for the newspaper and speaking engagements. Frank rejoined the Giants team for the 1962 season. When he returned to the Giants after taking the year off, his two best friends on the team, Kyle Rote and Charlie Conerly, had both retired. Frank started the 1962 season on the bench. "All good quarterbacks like to be blitzed. Linebackers leaving their positions left huge gaps in the pass coverage," said Tittle. In the Giants' second game of the season, Frank caught two big passes, one for a touchdown, from quarterback Y. A. Tittle. It was the first time they had played together. Y.A. Tittle's motto, "Throw the ball," helped Gifford tremendously. Gifford claimed that he and Tittle clicked from the very start. In the next three seasons, the Giants reached the NFL championship game twice, losing to the Green Bay Packers in 1962 and the Chicago Bears in 1963. Gifford returned to the Pro Bowl in 1963. He retired for good on March 19, 1965.

Frank Gifford worked for CBS as an analyst during the 1967 "Ice Bowl." The NFL Championship game was played in Green Bay between the Dallas Cowboys and the Green Bay Packers. Gifford was in the booth with Ray Scott and Jack Buck. At minus 15 degrees below zero, Gifford was heard saying on air, "I'm going to take a bite of my coffee."

In 1971, Roone Arledge of ABC hired Gifford to take Keith Jackson's place as play-by-play announcer for the second season of *Monday Night Football*. Gifford would join Howard Cosell and Don Meredith. Frank hosted *Wide World of Sports* and also covered several Olympics. In 1972, Gifford sat with Celtics' legend, Bill Russell, during broadcast of the Olympic Gold basketball game. He called 588 consecutive NFL games for ABC Television. Frank also worked with some of the best, like Dan Dierdorf, Al Michaels, Joe Namath and O.J. Simpson. Frank left *MNF* in 1997. Gifford was an icon of the game. He came off honest, genuine and sincere. When he started making a lot of money and becoming famous, Frank Gifford became somewhat of a loner, kind of like Joe DiMaggio.

In 136 regular season games with the Giants, Gifford ran for 3,609 yards and scored 34 touchdowns. He caught 367 passes for 5,434 yards and 43 touchdowns. Frank completed 29 of 63 passes for 823 yards and 14 touchdown passes, while running the halfback option. The 14 touchdown passes is the most by any non-quarterback in NFL history. Frank Gifford was inducted into the Pro Football Hall of Fame on July 30, 1977. Gifford was presented by Wellington Mara, the Giants' owner at the time. "He was the ultimate Giant," said Giants' team president, John Mara. "He was the face of our franchise for so many years." The New York Giants retired Frank Gifford's white, home Giants' jersey #16, in 2000.

Frank Gifford joined the College Football Hall of Fame in 1975. Gifford won an Emmy Award for Outstanding Sports Personality in 1977. He was inducted into the inaugural Hall-of-Fame class of the University of Southern California in 1994. Frank was given the Pete Rozelle Radio-Television Award by the Pro Football Hall of Fame in 1995, for his NFL television work. In 1997, Gifford won his second Emmy for the Lifetime Achievement Award for television.

Gifford has an extensive resume of television shows in

which he appeared and was good-looking enough to sell almost anything on television, including sweaters, Vitalis hair tonic and Lucky Strike cigarettes.

On Sunday, August 9, 2015, Kathie Lee found Frank Gifford dead on the floor of their bedroom home in Greenwich, Connecticut. He was 84. His doctor declared the pro football Hall of Famer died of natural causes so there was no autopsy. We now know that the family had Frank tested for CTE and he was found to be suffering from head trauma.

I never got to meet Gifford and felt that another part of my childhood had left. Gifford married three times with the first two ending in divorce. He is survived by his current wife, Kathie Lee Gifford, including their son Cody and daughter Cassidy. Gifford also leaves behind two sons, Jeff and Kyle, a daughter, Victoria, and five grandchildren from his first marriage. Interestingly, Frank and Kathie Lee shared the same birthday.

Muhammad Ali once said, "Impossible is just a big word thrown around by small men who find it easier to live in the world they've been given than to explore the power they have to change it. Impossible is not a fact. It is an opinion. Impossible is not a declaration. It's a dare. Impossible is potential. Impossible is temporary." Like Ali, for Frank Gifford nothing seemed impossible. At the end, Frank may have been tackled by life but he was never down.

I'LL TELL YOU ONE THING

He was hard on the equipment and would wear his cars out driving so hard for so long. He never learned to pace himself and save his car. On short tracks he had a tendency to drive his car too deep into the corners and use up his brakes. By the end of the race, he had no brakes. But when it came to the big tracks, you had to deal with this guy. He was the master of the super speedways. His hammer-down approach to racing was exciting but costly, as he broke parts and blew engines with regularity. He once claimed he was the all-time winner of the Daytona 475 because his cars fell apart before he got to 500. He only knew one way: Go as fast as you can and hope the car holds up. This man would drive the wheels off his car. He could be found, in his uniform, pacing and smoking one cigarette after another before race time. Darrell Waltrip once asked him why he was so nervous. "If you had as much stuff happen to you at the end of a race as I have, you'd be nervous too," he answered.

For an entire generation, he wasn't remembered as a race car driver. He was known as the fellow who talked and told stories about race car drivers. This fellow's life was one continuous racing story. He was an extremely large man in a sport where most of his competitors were small. His father let him start racing cars when he turned 18.

My dad always said, there is a difference between story telling and telling stories, this guy could have been the only one to do both at the same time. His audiences couldn't wait to hear these five words, "I'll tell you one thing." Story time with Buddy Baker was about to begin. Here's an example. One night at a dirt track located in the mountains of eastern Tennessee, this man was running away with the race when he suddenly blew a tire, ran into a fence and broke several ribs. The Smoky Mountain Raceway only had a two-man medical team that drove a hearse which had been converted into an ambulance. It has been said that the ambulance had an American Indian head as a hood ornament, which lit up when the vehicle's lights were turned on. This sounds like something right out of the Andy Griffin show. Our driver was unable to get out of his car, so these two guys helped him out and placed his massive body on a stretcher and loaded him in the back of the ambulance. As the ambulance started to leave the track, the driver got spooked by the other cars coming off of pit row and heading toward them. So, he gunned it. Sure enough, the wheels on the stretcher were not locked and our injured race car driver hit the back door of the ambulance, which was also not closed properly. So, there he was rolling backward on the stretcher at about 35 mph, desperately trying to get his arms free to signal to the other drivers. The good news was the other cars missed him but the stretcher rolled until it hit the mud embankment on the apron of the track and flipped him over, facedown in the wet red clay. The ambulance driver and his sidekick screamed, "Are you OK?" as they tried to flip him back over. "Yes," screamed the driver. "But as soon as you get me turned over, I am going to kill you."

This colorful character, who spoke with a slight lisp, hated being called Elzie. They had to call him Buddy, not because he was so nice, but because no one could pronounce his real name. Elzie Wylie "Buddy" Baker, Jr., was built on January 25, 1941, in the town of Florence, South Carolina. All it took was a garage, some racing fuel, a few lug nuts, a side of sheet metal, and a heart the size of an 8 cylinder motor. His father was two-time NASCAR Series Champion and Hall-of-Fame member, "Buck" Baker. Buddy had a brother, Randy Baker, who would also race cars. His dad taught him everything he knew about building and racing cars. Buddy started his career in 1959 on a small track in Columbia, South Carolina. His first win did not come until eight years later, at the 1967 National 500, run at Charlotte Motor Speedway.

There is a funny story told by Dale Inman, Richard Petty's Hall-of-Fame crew chief, when the "King" was running for his seven titles. "It was 1970 and Buddy Baker was driving for us, and Richard was running for the championship. While I was preparing for an inspection and qualifying at the 2.54-mile track at Watkins Glen International Racetrack, Buddy and one of the guys had purchased two dirt bikes. They would go riding in the woods. They eventually talked Richard into riding one, and he kept falling off the bike. Eventually there was a wreck with Petty falling off his bike and the other guy landing about ten feet up in a tree. When Petty came back to the shop, he was showing me all his cuts and bruises, and I got mad. I was really giving it to him," said Inman. "Here we were in the middle of a championship and he was doing something foolish like that. Well, Buddy must have heard me and I guess he got scared and loaded up the bikes and hightailed it out of there," laughed Inman. "It was the last time we ever saw those bikes."

Buddy Baker crawled in and out of his left side car window 700 times during his racing career. The 6-foot-6 Baker found the space a little cramped, but felt right at home. Baker ranks 14th in NASCAR history with 38 pole positions to start a race. He finished 202 times in the top five, 311 times in the top 10, and won 19 races. Baker won several big races during his career but the one everybody talks about was his win at the 1980 Daytona 500. Buddy also won the 1970 Southern 500. He won the World 600 race three times, in 1968, 1972 and 1973. Baker won the Winston 500 three times, in 1975, 1976 and 1980. In 1979, you could find

Baker in the winner's circle at the Busch Clash. Baker also drove for many legendary employers such as Cotton Davis, Ray Fox, Richard Petty and Bud Moore. In 1998, Buddy's dad, Buck, was interviewed for NASCAR's 50th anniversary celebration. "People joke about how he's scared of stuff. Hell, they never saw him on those big racetracks, Daytona and Talladega," said Buck. "He could pick up speed like you've never seen. Buddy could draft off a damn hot dog wrapper." On March 24, 1970, at Talladega Superspeedway, Baker became the first driver to exceed 200 mph (200.447) on a closed-course track. This record was broken a year later by Bobby Isaac, but it has recently come to light that the Isaac car had two four-barrel carburetors in it, therefore that run was not done in a legal car.

One day the three biggest men in all of NASCAR at that time decided to go fishing in a boat on the Santee Cooper Lake in South Carolina. There was only one problem; the lake was full of alligators. "Tiny" Lund, who was not tiny in the least bit, was joined by NASCAR Hall-of-Fame writer, Tom Higgins, who was also a fairly large guy, and Buddy Baker, who was bigger than both of them. Somehow they found a way to fit into a relatively small boat. Now if you have ever been to South Carolina in the summer you know there is one word that gets a lot of use, "hot." Yes, it was extremely hot. Baker announced out of the blue that he was going to take a dip to cool off, regardless of the alligators. As he lowered himself over the side of the boat, he did not see Tiny ease into the water on the other side. Just as Baker's head broke the surface of the water he felt something grab at his crotch. Baker screamed and thrashed and tried his best to get back in the boat. He was sure an alligator was about to bite off his privates. It was only then that Lund rose up out of the water beside Baker, laughing.

I always turn to my friend, Bob Doty, when we lose a NASCAR legend. Bob knows more about the automobile racing world than any other person I know. According to Bob, Baker is one of eight drivers to have won a career Grand Slam, by winning the sport's four major races: the Daytona 500, Aaron's 499, Coca-Cola 600, and the Southern 500. Richard Petty, David Pearson, Bobby Allison, Darrell Waltrip, Dale Earnhardt, Jeff Gordon and Jimmie Johnson are the other seven. Interestingly, Baker was the only one of this group to not win the championship. Baker raced mostly part-time and only participated in every race during three seasons. Mr. Doty also reminded me of the relationship that Buddy and Cale Yarborough had with one another. Let's just say it was informal at best. I was an Area Supervisor for a Pizza Hut Franchise in South Carolina during the late seventies and early eighties. One of the huts I oversaw was located in Darlington, South Carolina, about five miles from the racetrack. The fisticuffs between Baker and Yarborough became legendary and always made front-page news.

Buddy was inducted into the International Motorsports Hall of Fame in 1995 and became a part of the Charlotte Motor Speedway Court of Legends that same year. In 1997, Baker was inducted into the National Motorsports Press Association Hall of Fame. "Leadfoot," a nickname he acquired, was named one of NASCAR's 50 Greatest Drivers in 1998. "Buddy was a person you always wanted to be around, because he made you feel better," said Richard Petty.

Buddy Baker twice did the unthinkable. He won a Grandfather Clock at Martinsville by outrunning Richard Petty, and he became one of the first NASCAR drivers to sit down behind a microphone after he retired from racing. After a wonderful television career (1994-2000) with The Nashville Network, CBS, TBS, and then TNT, he moved to SiriusXM Radio. There is no doubt that Buddy Baker was a great race analyst.

Buddy left us early Monday morning on August 10, 2015. He was 74. Buddy and his family were living in Lake

Norman of Catawba, North Carolina. He was diagnosed with a large tumor in his lung that was ruled inoperable and had resigned from the radio show on July 7. He left behind a wife, Patricia, and two sons, Brandon and Bryan.

"I'm right with the man upstairs," Baker told The Charlotte Observer in a July 27 story. "If I feared death, I never would have driven a race car." Baker once said in jest, "I'll tell you one thing; when everything seems to be coming your way; you're in the wrong lane."

Buddy Baker's life will live on in his stories and his accomplishments.

DOUBLE-D

Sportswriter Jim Murray once wrote, "He was so big he wasn't born, he was built." At 6'11 inches tall and weighing 260 pounds, he was massive, the kind of guy who would have lived at the top of the beanstalk. Crowds would part when he walked through. Kids would put away their autograph books and stare. His arms were so long he had to be careful not to step on them. His fingers measured 12 to 14 inches long, not counting the nails. He resembled a marble statue and his presence could fill up the room. He was as big as Christmas and held the record for the most "Yo-mama" during an interview. This dude was a one-man band, a hotdog with extra mustard and a happy, fun-loving kid, in a grown man's body. He also had a smile that belonged in a museum. The shoes he wore cost $500. The price alone would have killed most people. He may have been one of the first guys to have his shoe size, his IQ, and his jersey all the same number.

While watching him play basketball, you had to keep your eyes on him. If you weren't watching him it was like going to the Empire State Building and not looking up. He had always been a little bit on tilt. He would sit on the bench and eat Three Musketeers bars during the game and once wore one shoe from Pony and one from Nike because he had signed two shoe deals. The look on his face after a thunder dunk was like he had just seen the Ark of the Covenant. This guy threw down dunks that had never before been seen. His dunks were so powerful the ball hit the floor before he did. He had enough power to light up a small city and he never forgot to speak to a kid. The great Stevie Wonder gave him his nickname, "Chocolate Thunder." Stevie didn't have to see Darryl to know he was something special. Darryl Dawkins was Moby Dick in a gold fish bowl. The only thing that could have stopped Dawkins from dunking the basketball was being kidnapped. He was rough and tough and wasn't happy unless he had some flesh and blood underneath his fingernails after a game. Dawkins led the league three times in personal fouls. During the 1983-84 season, Dawkins set the NBA record for personal fouls committed, at 386. If you could stop trembling long enough when Darryl spoke to you, you could learn something.

Darryl Dawkins was born on January 11, 1957, in Orlando, Florida. He was close to his father, Frank, but reared primarily by his mother, Harriet. Darryl powered Maynard Evans High School to the 1975 Florida State Championship. Eighteen-year-old Darryl applied for the 1975 NBA draft as a hardship candidate. The Philadelphia 76ers made him the fifth overall pick. David Thompson from N.C. State was the top pick, followed by David Meyers, Marvin Webster and Alvan Adams. Dawkins became the first player to go from high school to the NBA, National Basketball Association, but he was not the first high school player to turn professional. In 1974, Moses Malone jumped from high school in Virginia to the Utah Stars, a member of the ABA, American Basketball Association. These two leagues merged together in 1976. Many others would follow in Malone's and Dawkins' footsteps: Kobe Bryant, LeBron James and Kevin Garnett entered the NBA straight out of high school.

Every legend has a beginning and this one is his. Dawkins brought with him, size, huge hands, attitude, and a fine jump shot for a big man. He would also to practice with a 70 pound boom box resting on his shoulder. The Wilt

Chamberlain comparisons began. Darryl was still a kid and, without spending time in college, he needed time to develop. Darryl was immature and, to cope with his new found fame, he developed a make-believe world he called Planet Lovetron. He wore lime green suits and pink coats that made him look like a huge bottle of Pepto-Bismol.

Darryl spent time on the bench his first two seasons, only playing in 37 games his rookie year. Dawkins would be called on more often during the 1976-77 season, as the 76ers made it to the NBA Finals against the Portland Trailblazers and Bill Walton. Philadelphia would lose to Portland in six games. Dawkins' time would be expanded during the 1977-78 season as he played nearly 25 minutes a game. With a team that consisted of Julius Erving, George McGinnis, Lloyd Free and Doug Collins, playing time was hard to come by. They advanced to the Eastern Finals before losing to Wes Unseld and the Washington Bullets, in six games.

Darryl Dawkins' hands were incredible large. They helped him not only palm and control a basketball, but allowed him to literally grab a blocked shot or rebound out of the air. This kind of thing had never been seen before and some referees called him for traveling when he returned to the floor. Of course most fans remember Dawkins as the guy who tore down backboards and rims. On November 13, 1979, Darryl shattered the backboard when he threw down a massive dunk over top of the Kansas City Kings' center, Dave Robinzine at the Municipal Auditorium. Glass went everywhere, delaying the game for 90 minutes. No one could dunk like Dawkins, not even Chamberlain. Three weeks later, Dawkins did it again, but this time at home against the San Antonio Spurs, at the Spectrum. The NBA declared that any further tearing down of the backboard and or rim by hanging on would result in a fine and a suspension. It became known as the Dawkins rule. Dawkins always claimed that the first time he broke the backboard, it had been an accident and he did not plan to tear down another rim but "All the fans were hollering, 'You've got to do one for the home crowd,' so I went ahead and brought it down. Everybody was in awe. Fans were running out and grabbing the glass. People's hands were bleeding. I felt like I was doing something no other human could do." Shortly afterwards, the NBA began to work on the so-called breakaway rims.

Darryl Dawkins would eat anything that wouldn't eat him. We may never see his likes again. I'm a huge fan of the old Negro Leagues in baseball, especially Satchel Paige, who used to name all his pitches. Dawkins did the same thing by naming his dunks. He had the Rim Wrecker, the Go-Rilla, the Lookout Below, the In Your Face Disgrace, the Cover Your Head, the Spine-Chiller Supreme, and his favorite, the Yo-Mama.

Dawkins spent 14 years in the NBA. The first seven were with the 76ers, with whom he went to three league championships and lost each time. He also played with the New Jersey Nets (now the Brooklyn Nets), the Utah Jazz and the Detroit Pistons. Along the way, injuries began to pile up as Darryl hurt his back. It would bother him the rest of his life. Dawkins averaged 12 points and 6.1 rebounds per game. His career shooting-percentage was .572, the seventh highest in league history. Darryl scored 8,733 points, pulled down 4,432 rebounds, all while blocking 1,023 shots. He would continue to play overseas with three different teams in Italy, and enjoyed a season with the Harlem Globetrotters before playing in the CBA and IBA. Dawkins would wear #53, #45 and #50 during his professional basketball career.

Darryl turned his attention to coaching. He coached professional teams in Winnipeg, Canada, and Allentown, Pennsylvania. In 2009, he also coached for Lehigh Carbon Community College in Schnecksville, Pennsylvania, not far from Allentown where he and his fourth wife, Janice lived. Dawkins managed to write a book with the help of author, Charley Rosen. It was entitled <u>Chocolate Thunder: The</u>

Uncensored Life and Times of Darryl Dawkins. He talked about the racism he had incurred and his experiences with drugs and partying.

It's been a lot of years since they chanted his name. Darryl Dawkins, one of the game's fiercest dunkers and lovable characters, passed away on Thursday, August 27, 2015. He died of an apparent heart attack in Allentown, Pennsylvania. He was but 58. He leaves behind his wife Janice, their son Nicholas, and daughter Alexis; a stepdaughter, Tabitha; and a daughter from a previous marriage, Dara. "You didn't have to know him to like him," said "Sleepy" Floyd. "He was a tremendous person."

My radio partner, Dennis Quinn, and I were on the air that night and Dennis took a minute to tell about his friendship with "Double-D," that's what he called Dawkins. Quinn had met Darryl in Florida and covered him for a local sports television station. They hit it off, played some one-on-one and had a photograph taken of the two of them. It's tough when you lose your pals.

1 TO 8

George F. Will once said, "Baseball is a habit." Never has there been uttered a truer statement. Most of you folks will not remember hearing this man, but you would have been lucky if you did. He was one of the best baseball announcers of his generation. He was a master of the language of sports. There was magic in his words. Giving him a microphone was like putting Dan Rather in front of a television camera; his information would be crisp and on target. He loved to call baseball games; he felt like he was always holding the winning lottery ticket. This guy was more likeable than Opie on the Andy Griffith Show. He owned a pirate smile and a voice that could qualify as medicinal. This man was as comfortable as an old baseball cap. The beauty of baseball is that it is inexplicable. He still believed that singing "Take me out to the Ballgame" was a privilege. On the hallowed ground of baseball, you can't run away from the history. He understood the game and accepted that some days you're the pigeon, and some days you're the statue. He could spend two weeks telling stories and you'd realize that he hadn't even gotten started. Although his broadcast style was somewhat restrained, his game notes were emblazoned with different colored markers and he always helped you feel a part of the conversation.

He was so nostalgic; he sat around picking his teeth with a 1954 Hank Aaron rookie card. He understood the value of silence at the right moment. His voice sounded like melted butter. He was a smart guy; he could have counted cards if he had wanted to. He always reminded us that a ballpark is where memories gather. Gene Elston, the original voice of the Houston Astros, made a lasting impression on all who listened, and now he has left us.

Gene Elston was born on March 26, 1922, in Fort Dodge, Iowa. By 1941, at the age of 19, he had started announcing high school basketball games. He later joined the fight for his country during World War II. When he returned to the States after the war, he received his first minor league assignment in 1946. He started broadcasting minor league games for Waterloo of the Three-I League. He also received an NFL job with a team then called the Cleveland Rams. In 1954, after eight years of broadcasting minor league baseball, he was signed by the Chicago Cubs as their number two announcer, alongside Bert Wilson. From 1955-1957, Gene made his debut in Major League baseball with the Chicago Cubs, on WIND radio of Chicago. Gene Elston spent the next three years calling baseball games on the Mutual Radio Network's *Game of the Day* with Hall of Fame pitcher Bob Feller. At that time, the Mutual Radio Network aired on 350 stations across the country. At the end of the 1960 season, Elston left them for greener pastures. The Houston Colt 45's club offered Gene a job and promptly hired him for the 1961 season, as their lead announcer for their minor league club known as the Houston Buffs. They also hired Loel Passe as the color commentator. In 1962, Major League baseball expanded and the Houston Colt 45's and the New York Mets became Major League teams. In 1965, three years later, the Colt 45's would change their name to the Houston Astros and moved into the "Eight Wonder of the World," the Astrodome. Elston stuck with the team, even though they lost 96 games in each of their first three seasons. Elston would remain the Astros' lead announcer for 25 years, until 1986, when he was fired by Astros' general manager, Dick Wagner. In 1987, Elston rejoined the national radio broadcasts. He would call the CBS Radio *Game of the Week* until 1995. Gene also called the postseason games for the National League Division Series, in 1995, 1996 and 1997. He then retired from broadcasting and joined Tal Smith Enterprises, as a consultant and researcher.

Elston told many wonderful stories about the Colt 45's and Astros in his later years. One I remember was about a 1960's pitcher named George Brunet, who pitched well into his fifties, down in Mexico. George had pitched for many minor and Major League teams during his long career. Once, when he was traded by the Braves to the Cardinals, the St Louis publicity man ended up catching hell from his wife after she intercepted a phone call at the house telling her husband what time to pick up Brunet, a name she mistook for a "brunette," from Milwaukee at the airport.

Another story included Astros' pitcher, Turk Ferrell, and centerfielder, Jimmy Wynn. Most real baseball fans know how to score a baseball game. The broadcasters always score the game so they can provide needed information to the listener as the game moves forward. For those of you who do not know what I'm talking about, here is a quick recipe: Each player on the defense is given a number. The pitcher is one, the catcher is two, the first baseman is three, and so on. The second baseman, third baseman and shortstop are numbered four, five and six. The outfield is numbered left to right, seven, eight and nine. Now when an out occurs in the field, the defensive player's numbers are used to record the play. Example, if the batter hits a ground ball to the shortstop who fields the ball and throws it to first base, beating the runner to the bag, it is recorded 6-3 for an out. If the ball is hit to left field and caught in the air by the leftfielder, it is recorded F-7, which stands for fly ball-leftfield for the out. So, in this particular game, a very unusual out is recorded that rarely happens. In fact, I have scored hundreds of games and have never heard anything else like this. Hank Aaron of the Braves was facing Turk Ferrell when Aaron lined a ball back to the mound that hit

Turk right on the top of his forehead. The ball was hit so hard, it bounced off his head and was caught in the air for an out, by Jimmy Wynn, the Astros' centerfielder, some 100 plus feet away. Elston scored the out, 1 to 8. I don't think it has ever happened that way before or since.

In 2006, Gene Elston was honored for his contributions as a baseball announcer to the great game of baseball. He was awarded the Ford C. Frick Award from the Baseball Hall of Fame Museum. At the age of 84, Elston was well enough to accept the award in person in Cooperstown.

Elston called a total of 13 no-hitters, including Nolan Ryan's fifth no-hitter and Mike Scott's 1986 masterpiece, to clinch the National League West Division. Gene also described Eddie Mathews' 500th home run as an Astros' for the fans and called Nolan Ryan's 3,509 career strike-out on April 27, 1983 to become the all-time leader.

"I feel blessed to have been a part of such a great game for so long," said Elston at his Hall-of-Fame induction. For 47 years behind the microphone, he always treated the listener with respect. Gene authored three books and received the Texas Sportscaster-of-the-Year Award several times.

Gene Elston died peacefully at home on September 5, 2015. He was 93. It seems kind of quiet now that I think about it.

CHAIRMAN OF THE BOARDS

Ken Burns once said, "There is always much more drama by what is or what was, than anything our imagination can make up."

He was a freak athletically, who slept in an extra-tall person's bed. He was so big he was worth five electoral votes. He could have been an extra in a *Ben Hur* movie. You need not watch a lot of film to know how good he was at offensive rebounding. He may have had three or four arms depending on who you spoke with. It's funny; he said little and moved slowly, like molasses in the wintertime, until he started sweating. Once he started sweating, it was "go time." He made me wonder if Ivan the Terrible ever played center. He was the kind of player that could make you feel like hyperventilating while standing in the lay-up line. He started out so young, he never stood a chance of getting a razor-blade commercial. The man could be both cruel and kind, and you would never forget the first time you met him. Some said he was kind of backward, but he had manners. He sounded a little slow; he may have thought Hall and Oats was a breakfast cereal.

This fellow may not have been the best-scoring center or jumped the highest or played defense better than all the rest, but what he did do was, for 48 minutes he would not be intimidated or outworked. Ever see the movie "Twister?" At some point, a house will go by flying through the air. That was Moses Malone. The Philadelphia 76ers' system was to give the ball to Julius Erving; and if he was not open, give it to Moses Malone; and if he's not open, give it back to Erving. In 1983, it worked. They became the perfect one-two punch. The word "gamble" means you have a chance. With slot machines and Moses Malone, you had no chance. It was easier to stop a bullet than Moses Malone.

Where do the warriors go? When I mentioned Malone's name to my friend, Coach Willis Wilson, he said that in his opinion, Moses Malone and Artis Gilmore were two of the most underrated centers to ever play in the NBA. Malone left his fingerprints on every other center in the league. At the end of his career, Moses had finished seventh in scoring, third in rebounding, and 24th in blocked shots. His first season in the league he accomplished a double-double, the first of his fifteen. That would be one more than Wilt Chamberlain and three more than Kareem Abdul-Jabbar. All Moses did was deliver wins. The only thing he was no good at, was passing the basketball. Malone became known for his offensive rebounding skills. Some said he may have invented the put-back shot. There is one other category that few talk about: free-throw shooting. Moses Malone made 76% of his foul shots, better than most.

Time flies backward for me now. Growing up in N.C., playing basketball in my driveway on Shawood Drive, I could pretend to be Moses Malone; but when my friends showed up, they sometimes interfered with my destiny. Malone had something a great leader needs; he had 4 o'clock-in-the-morning courage. You could wake him up at 4 o'clock in the morning and he would be as cool as a cucumber. His "thing" was work. No one ever outworked Moses on the basketball court. He remains first all-time, in offensive rebounds (6,731) for his career. By adding his career ABA and NBA statistics together, they will reveal that Moses scored 29,580 points. He pulled down 17,834 rebounds and dished out 1,936 assists. Those numbers are not a misprint, they are real.

Moses Eugene Malone was born on March 23, 1955, in

Petersburg, Virginia. He grew up near a park, where you could find more drugs than kids. He was an only child. One of the biggest fears of a child is being left alone. It remains with us all our lives. It might have remained with him, I fear. Moses was raised by his mother, Mary, who had dropped out of school after the fifth grade. His father was an alcoholic, and his mother kicked his father out of the house when Moses was two years old. His father then moved to Texas. Moses was known for having a slight speech problem where he would seem to mumble, and that caused some people to question his intelligence. He was also a bit shy and did not smile very much, because he was ashamed of having teeth that had not been properly cared for. Moses attended Petersburg High School where he led his team to two undefeated seasons in his last two years. They won 50 straight games and two Virginia state championships.

Moses began to receive letters from colleges all over the country. I'm not sure he could read them, but he did enjoy getting mail. It has been said that Evangelist Oral Roberts himself recruited Moses. He promised Moses that if he came to Tulsa to play basketball for Oral Roberts University that he would cure Malone's mother's ulcers. Some recruiters even slept on their front porch. Moses would lie down on the floor and hide. Moses signed a letter of intent to play for "Lefty" Driesell, Head Basketball Coach at Maryland. The "Terps" spent a lot of time hiding him from other recruiters. One story has Moses with a summer job on the Maryland campus. His job was to turn out the lights at Cole Field House. The funny part was that Cole Field House was closed during the summer. It has been said that Moses spent hours during the day shooting the basketball and then turned the lights out at night. Malone was the kind of player who would laugh out loud as he ran off the court. He never tried to reinvent the jump shot. He just took "his" shot. In 1974, before the college year commenced, the Utah Stars of the American Basketball

Association drafted Moses in the third round. Lefty sat in the living room of Malone's house and tried to convince Moses to stay at Maryland. "Stop jivin' me, coach," said Malone. The Stars offered Moses a five-year deal worth one million dollars. It was too good to pass up. He accepted the offer for the sake of his mother. "His mother was only making like $25 a week," said Lefty. "Moses once said, 'Coach, I've got to tell you a story.' Moses said, 'I wrote in my Bible that I wanted to be the best high-school player in the country by my junior year and I put in the Bible my next goal was to be the first high-school player in the country to go pro.'" Moses Malone accomplished that goal, and became the first ever high-school player to go directly to the pros. He was only 19 years old. It's true that Lefty felt jilted, but they became good friends. In fact Moses and Lefty, now 83, were to have dinner with another friend on the very day Moses died.

Darryl Dawkins, the high-flying center known as "Chocolate Thunder," was the first high-school player to go straight to the NBA when he signed with the 76ers in 1975. Dawkins died on August 27, 2015, at the age of 58.

Moses began his career as a forward because of his slight build. He would eventually bulk up to over 260 pounds. He was named to the ABA All-Star team as a rookie. The Stars went bankrupt after his first year, and Moses was sold to the ABA's Spirits of St. Louis. Malone would spend the 1975-76 season in St. Louis. In his first two seasons, Moses averaged 17.2 points and 12.9 rebounds per game.

The ABA merged with the NBA before the 1975-76 season. Moses would end up in Buffalo for two games during the 1976-77 season, before being traded to the Houston Rockets. In Houston he would be chosen MVP of the league, in 1979 and 1982. In 1979, Moses set the all-time, single-season record with 587 offensive rebounds. On March 11, 1981, Moses scored 51 points against the Golden State Warriors. Moses also began to take Hakeem Olajuwon under his wing and helped make him a Rockets future star. The Rockets would reach the NBA Finals in 1981.

On September 2, 1982, coffee cups stopped in mid-air and radios were turned up. He's going where? Moses Malone had been traded from the Houston Rockets to the Philadelphia 76ers. Moses signed to play for six-years for $13.2 million. "The fans in Philly were incredible," said Moses. "Fathers taught their sons how to moon the opponent's team bus." Moses would join Julius Erving, Moe Cheeks, Andrew Toney, Bobby Jones and others, in Philly. The 76ers were coached by Billy Cunningham. "Dr. J" got to the NBA Finals three times in his first six years in the league, but he did not win a title until Moses Malone joined the 76ers. Gas was 50 cents a gallon the last time Philadelphia had been in the playoffs. The year was 1967. In the 1983 finals, Moses averaged 18 rebounds per game, for a total of 72, and pulled down 27 offensive rebounds. Lakers' stars, Kareem Abdul-Jabbar and "Magic" Johnson, had 30 rebounds total. During the 1984-85 season, Moses scored his 15,000th NBA point on November 28 and grabbed his 10,000th NBA rebound on March 29. On November 15, 1984, he scored 51 points against the Detroit Pistons. The 76ers reached the Eastern Conference Finals in 1985, but lost 4-1 to the Boston Celtics.

Malone was traded to the Washington Bullets, after that season. During the 1985-86 season, he scored 50 points against the New York Nets on April 8th, and his 20,000th NBA point on April 12th against the Detroit Pistons. Malone joined Earl Monroe and Phil Chenier as the only Bullets' players to score 50 points in a single game.

Moses was on the move again before the 1988-89 season. He signed a three-year deal with the Atlanta Hawks. When the Atlanta Hawks starting talking about his contract, they mentioned deferred payments; his response was "'Big Mo' don't do deferred. You need to deal with my agent." During the 1990-91 season, Malone became the NBA career leader in free throws made, with 7,695 and passing Oscar Robertson. On November 21st, Moses scored his 25,000th point, and on March 15, he recorded his 15,000th career rebound against the Dallas Mavericks. Malone also passed Wilt Chamberlain's record of 1,046 games played without fouling out. The Atlanta Hawks made the playoffs, but lost in the first round, to Detroit.

The 1991-92 season would find Moses in Milwaukee with the Bucks. In October of 1992, Moses had surgery for a herniated disc in his back. He played in very few games.

Moses returned to Philadelphia for the 1993-94 season to tutor 7' 6" rookie, Shawn Bradley. Moses played in 55 games, as a backup.

The San Antonio Spurs would be his last stop as he joined superstar David Robinson as a back-up center for the 1994-95 season. During the final game of his career, against the Charlotte Hornets, Moses hit a buzzer-beating three-point shot from the opposing team's free-throw line, some eighty feet away. It was only the eighth three-pointer he had made during his career. Moses played in 17 games for the Spurs, before retiring.

Moses Malone was serious, never smiled, gave short answers; everything about him was defensive and there was something about his eyes. I will never forget the look on teammate Julius Erving's face when Moses Malone, the regular season MVP, was asked by a reporter how the Philadelphia 76er's would fare in the upcoming 1983 NBA playoffs. The 76er's had just clinched the Atlantic Division Championship with a 65-17 win-loss record and were headed for the playoffs against the New York Knicks. Erving, a college graduate from UMASS, had been asked the same question. Erving's answer was professional, well thought-out, astute, and delivered using perfect diction of the English language. Moses, on the other hand, answered as only Moses could. When inclined to speak, Moses was sometimes unintelligible, while mumbling his words. On national television, Malone predicted the 76er's would go "fo fo fo." As Moses was answering, Julius turned to look at Malone with an incredible stunned look on his face. Not only had Moses predicted a sweep, but his pronunciation had been terrible. Erving wanted to thump him on his forehead to see if he was still in there. No one would ever accuse Malone of being very smart, after that. You see, each round of the NBA playoffs was a best-of-seven series, and it would take four wins to advance. Moses wasn't far off, as the 76er's would beat the Knicks four times straight in the Eastern Conference semifinals; beat the Milwaukee Bucks, 4-1 in the conference finals; and then sweep the Los Angeles Lakers, 4-0, to win the NBA Championship. Malone had been off on his prediction by one game. It turned out to be "fo, five, fo." Moses may not have been able to speak very well, but he surely could play basketball. Moses Malone was also named the MVP of the 1983 NBA Finals. He was the first NBA player to make one million dollars a year.

Moses played for 19 seasons in the NBA. He was a three-time MVP (1979, '82, and '83), appeared in 13 All-Star Games, and earned eight All-NBA selections. He led the NBA in total rebounds per season five times, and nine times in offensive rebounds. He also averaged 20.6 points per game. He would earn the moniker, "Chairman of the Boards." He was inducted into the Naismith Basketball Hall of Fame in 2001. In 1996, he was named to the ABA and NBA 50th Anniversary All-Time Teams. His #24 was retired by the Houston Rockets.

Now most of our favorite players are gone, but we can still reach out to them. There are times when you realize that few things are more fleeting than your favorite athletes' immortality. They appear out of the mist of our past-old timers. When you are around greatness, grab hold. You will remember the moments they gave you, the miracles they performed, your hair standing up and feeling "goose bumps" on your goose bumps. His friend and fellow Hall-of-

Famer, Calvin Murphy, said, "At 6' 10" tall and 260 pounds, Moses was not the biggest or strongest, but he played with uncommon intensity and energy." The old saying goes, "When you have a beast, feed the beast." Moses simply wore down his opponents with relentless effort and physical play. At the end of a game, they looked like they had been in an accident. On the Monday after Moses died, Charles Barkley said, "Words can't explain my sadness. I will never know why a Hall-of-Famer took a fat, lazy kid from Auburn and treated him like a son and got him in shape and made him a player. Every time I saw him I called him 'Dad.' I hope he knew how much I appreciated and loved him."

Moses Malone was found dead in his hotel room at the Norfolk Waterside Marriott Hotel before 8 am. He was 60 years old. The date was Sunday, September 13, 2015. He was pronounced dead at the scene. Malone suffered from hypertension and cardiovascular disease but did not smoke, drink or do drugs. His friends said he ate healthy foods while staying away from fried foods and sweets. The Tuesday before he passed away, Moses experienced an irregular heart beat while working out. He visited a doctor but checked out okay. The doctor gave him a heart monitor, to be on the safe side. He was wearing the heart monitor when he was found dead on Sunday. Moses was scheduled to play in a golf tournament that supported single mothers. The tournament was put on by former NBA official, Tony Brothers.

Moses Malone funeral was held on Saturday, September 19, 2015, at Lakewood Church, which turns out to be the same building where Moses played with the Houston Rockets, from 1976-1982. It was then called "The Summit." Behind his casket was a basket and backboard made of flowers with a ball perched on the rim, inviting Moses to tap it in.

Moses lived in Houston. He loved the Dallas Cowboys, playing golf, and speaking engagements. He did not play much basketball in retirement. Moses once said, "When my tee-shot curves, you need three guys and a dog to find my golf ball." Moses was still under a contract with Nike. He also had a 6-year-old son named Micah with whom he spent lots of time. Micah's mother, Leah Nash, was living with Malone at the time of his death. Moses left behind his first wife, Alfreda and two other grown sons, Moses, Jr., and Michael, who both played college sports, and a granddaughter, Mia. Moses and Alfreda had divorced in October, 1992.

Graham Brown once said, "Life is about choices. Some we regret, some we're proud of, some will haunt us forever. The message--we are what we choose to be." As a man, Moses Malone gave us something to look up to. I'm pretty sure I know where the warriors go.

Right Down Kirby

"He's sitting on 714." Most baseball fans believe it's one of the top five calls of all-time. These two guys are forever joined in baseball lore by less than forty words, spoken into a microphone one early evening on April 8, 1974, by Braves' broadcaster Milo Hamilton, forty-one years ago. It was the first game of the new season. The Atlanta Braves were at home against the Los Angeles Dodgers. Here's how the call sounded as Henry Aaron settled into the batter's box.

"He's sitting on 714! Here's the pitch by Downing, swinging, there's a drive into left centerfield, that ball is gonna beee...OUTTA HERE! IT'S GONE! IT'S 715! There's a new home run champion of all-time and it's HENRY AARON!"

It was "pure" Milo Hamilton. For some of us, baseball is life. I still wonder about the places he's been, the players he's interviewed, and the scores of fans he's entertained. For most of us, he's Uncle Milo. He was family; he came into our homes 162 times a year, until these last couple of years. I even listened to his call when I was at the Astros' games. He always stirred my imagination. One of the secrets of baseball is that you play almost every day. Therefore, redemption was only hours away. Milo used the game to help people discover themselves. They could use those discoveries to confront anything in their life. Baseball is a teacher; it reveals your heart and soul, and the game is designed to reveal them to you.

Leland Milo Hamilton was born on September 2, 1927, in

Fairfield, Iowa. He served in the United States Navy during World War II and became a broadcaster for the Armed Forces Radio. When he returned he attended the University of Iowa and graduated in 1949. He began broadcasting the Iowa Hawkeyes' football and basketball games. His first job in Major League baseball started in 1953, with the St. Louis Browns. He has also announced for six other Major League clubs: St. Louis Cardinals, Chicago Cubs, Chicago White Sox, Atlanta Braves, Pittsburgh Pirates and Houston Astros from 1985-2012.

There will never be another like him as far as I'm concerned; I love the old man. As he got older, he began to look tired, frail, and almost sickly until he found his way into the announcer booth or onto the field of play. It was like flipping a switch. A microphone made his eyes light up like lanterns. The game simply turned him on. Milo could sing "Mary Had a Little Lamb," and make you laugh. He walked every day into his radio booth, intoxicated by the promise of that day's game. He didn't like being surprised; he studied and saved his information in a satchel that may have been as old as he was. He loved baseball so much; even his computer wore batting gloves. No one wanted to talk to Milo Hamilton about another announcer or player; they wanted to talk about Milo Hamilton. The longer an announcer stays with the same team, the more the fans identify with that team. Fathers, sons, and sons of sons, we all become a part of his history.

His educated eyes could fill books with the telling of the magic of the grand old game. Most of us know about his calls of eleven no-hitters, the grand slams, and historic home runs. His call of Nolan Ryan's 4,000th strikeout and Craig Biggio's 3,000th hit will always be remembered by the Houston fans. For sixty years, he opened his scorecard and charted baseball history. He taught us how to figure batting averages, told us how players got their nicknames and why. He described routine double-plays, the importance of a bunt single, why stealing third increases the chances of scoring by nine, and the reason so many players are called out looking. He taught us about Uncle Charlie, twin killings, chin music, and frozen ropes. Seeing-eye singles, and "Holy Toledo, what a play!" became his signature calls. Anytime an Astros pitcher burned a strike in there during a critical part of the game, Milo screamed "Right down Kirby," because the street that ran parallel to the pitcher's mound was named Kirby. Every play reminded him of days gone by, when only the player, the city and the circumstances were different. I would love to be able see through his eyes, if only for a moment. Listening to him call a game made me feel like a hundred-dollar bill in a two-dollar wallet. Writer Phil Hirsh once wrote, "Baseball is the only game you can see on the radio." Milo made it easy for all of us. His canyon deep voice was unmistakable. He was always "in" the game. You could never tell by his tone of voice whether his team was behind or ahead. Everybody wanted to be connected, to be a part of him. Let's call that a professional.

Baseball looks so easy to play, from your seat. It is, in fact, the hardest of them all. The game moves at a pace where a grandfather can talk about what's happening on the field, with his grandson. They see and experience virtually the same game. Milo taught me how to score a game, what to look for, how to anticipate a great play. He gave us a history lesson every night and allowed us to dream about what it would be like to play Major League baseball. All words seemed better to me when spoken by Milo Hamilton.

What you saw was what you got with Milo. Not many of us find our true place in life; that does not hold true for Milo Hamilton. I can't imagine him doing anything else. Milo has been a part of the Dennis & Andy's Q & A Session radio show for almost twenty years. Three times every year he joined us on the air, live from Houston, Texas. My partner Dennis Quinn always referred to our interviews as "Milo unplugged." On two different occasions, we took our show on the road to Minute Maid Park, and Milo was nice enough to join us there, in the booth, talking baseball. We talked old school baseball; from "Stan the Man" and "Hammerin' Hank" to "The Ryan Express." We covered everything from the disappearance of the hook slide to the tragedy of steroids, and everything in between. There was never a time I did not learn something. It has been said that the greatest classroom often lies at the feet of the elderly. How true.

Milo was inducted into the Broadcast Wing of the Baseball Hall of Fame in 1992. He was inducted into the National Radio Hall of Fame in 2000. Milo is also a member of four other Halls of Fame. Milo has a street named "Milo Hamilton Way" outside of Minute Maid Park. He had been an announcer for 60 years on television and his favorite, radio. There were several times when Milo visited Corpus Christi and, occasionally, the Corpus Christi Hooks minor league baseball team would set aside a suite for Milo. He always asked us to join him. The conversation was magic, as the years of baseball through his eyes came flooding back. It was as close to baseball Heaven as I will ever get. I once told him how much he was loved, as I was leaving his company. I think it may have surprised him. He didn't know how to respond, but he smiled. I'm absolutely sure he knew he was loved, but did not hear it enough. We are always more appreciative of something we had and have now lost.

Milo last visited Corpus Christi, January 24, 2014, with the Astros' caravan. I couldn't wait to see him. When he walked into the room he was surrounded by the TV guys like Custer at the Little Big Horn. We sat and laughed and talked about the call. He and Hank Aaron still speak with each other quite often. Milo looked good, as he was winning his battle with cancer. I've never met a more giving individual.

There will never be another Milo Hamilton. He not only wrote a nice review for my third book, <u>Greatness</u>

<u>Continued</u>, which I used on the back cover, but he also sent me for Christmas 2013, his scorebook, autographed, that he used to call all the Astros games against the Cincinnati Reds for the last several years. When I opened the gift I said to him, "Milo, are you sure you want me to have this? This scorebook belongs in the Hall of Fame." "It's okay," he said, "I want you to have it."

Milo Hamilton passed away today at 88 years of age. They finally slipped a called third strike past him. He can't argue the call. The date will be recorded as September 17, 2015. I knew he had been placed in hospice care in Houston, but did not know all the circumstances. I called his home twice last week hoping to speak with his son Mark, but never got an answer. Milo lost his wife Arlene several years ago, and Dennis and I took it upon ourselves to call him regularly and check on him. The good Lord may have kissed this guy right on the forehead. This is kind of hard for me as this is not the way I wanted to remember him. For me, Milo will never be gone, he's still here, and he'll always be here.

Reid Ryan, President of the Houston Astros announced before Friday night's game that the Astros would wear a black patch on their uniforms that contained Milo's initials "MH". Reid also told the crowd that the Houston Astros press box at Minute Maid Park will be renamed forevermore the Milo Hamilton Press Box in his honor.

Milo once screamed into his microphone after a dramatic comeback by the Astros for a win, "What a way to finish." I'll say. I could not have said it better myself.

I FEEL STRONGLY BOTH WAYS

No, he probably never said that, but he could have. He has been credited with so many funny and unusual sayings over the years that I don't think anyone really knows what he's said, when he said it or why, including him. He was once quoted as saying, "I don't make them up; they just come out." I have now read six different books written about him and all claim that he said this or that. In fact, one book is entitled <u>I Really Didn't Say Everything I Said!</u> After reading all his quotations, you might begin to think he was retarded, but how untrue. He may have been quoted more than Shakespeare. This guy was Socrates in shin guards. I do know that some of the confusion lies with his St. Louis childhood neighbor, best friend, and fellow baseball player, Joe Garagiola, who became a baseball announcer after a nine-year stint in the Major Leagues. Joe, a better TV and radio personality than ballplayer, not only admired his friend, but championed him with quotations every chance he got. If it sounded like something "Yogi" Berra would have said, the newspaper printed it, whether it was true or not.

Lawrence Peter "Yogi" Berra was born May 12, 1925, in St. Louis, Missouri. It makes me smile just to say his name. Someone once said, "When Yogi was born, God said, 'Yogi, you just breathe, I'll do the rest.'" His father, Pietro, and mother, Paolina, were Italian immigrants from Northern Italy. His father landed at Ellis Island in October 18, 1909. Dad was 23 years of age and went right to work to bring the rest of the family to America. Yogi, John and their sister, Josie, were born here in the States. Yogi grew up on Elizabeth Avenue in St. Louis, across the street from Joe Garagiola, in a section called "The Hill." "My family was very poor, it was embarrassing. When I went bowling, I also had to rent socks," said Berra, about his childhood. They attended St. Mary's High School together, until Yogi left school early. Yogi repeated the fifth grade because he had problems with English and math. He drove teachers crazy. He was once asked by a teacher, "How do you like school?" "Closed," answered Yogi. Imagine that.

"Yogi was always the better player," said Joe Garagiola. "We used to say, 'Wait till you see this kid called "Lawdie."'" Yogi's mother called him Lawdie because she could not pronounce Lawrence. "I lived at 5446 and Yogi lived at 5447, on the same street. I don't remember a day not knowing Yogi," said Joe. "There stood Yogi," said Garagiola, "He was stripped to the waist, barefooted, and kind of leaned back as he stood at the plate." "Joe Garagiola was always funny," Berra said. "When we were young, we played on a team called the Stags." The era in which this guy played and the fact that he had a funny nickname just added to the amusement. He was awkward, a bit clumsy at times, and rigid in his routines; and his looks also added fuel to his fame. Because he was so different, he must have felt like William Travis at the Alamo, constantly surrounded.

Berra had three older brothers who were also ballplayers, Tony, Mike, and John. The two oldest, Tony and Mike, had played against some of the Negro League stars, like Satchel Paige and Josh Gibson. "Tony was a better player than me," Yogi said. Berra played for 18 seasons, participated in 14 World Series, and won 10 World Championships with the Yanks. His stardom grew faster than Napoleon Bonaparte's. He once recorded an unassisted double play at home plate and has been touted as the greatest catcher of all time. Writer Robert Creamer once asked Casey Stengel, "Who's the most natural ballplayer on your team?" Casey pointed at this little short, squatty guy named Berra. My favorite sportswriter, Jim Murray, once said, "Just when you think everything is hopeless, just remember, 'Yogi' Berra." Boy was he worth remembering. No baseball player ever looked like Yogi Berra; he may have been the most recognizable player of all time. This title, "I Feel Strongly Both Ways" is just my feeble attempt at a "Yogi-ism."

At 13 years of age, Berra became an amateur fighter. He represented the Italian-American Club on the Hill, and fought nine different guys from other parts of the neighborhood. He won eight bouts and collected between five to ten dollars for each win. He always took the money home to his mother, who in return would give him back a dollar. His brother, Lefty, finally stopped him from fighting.

At 15 Yogi dropped out of school. He was off to pursue the American Dream with an eighth-grade education. He delivered newspapers, worked on a Coca-Cola truck, in a coal yard, and for Johansson Shoe Company. One of Yogi's newspaper customers was none other than Joe "Ducky" Medwick of the hometown Cardinals. "When Dad came home from work, he wanted a can of beer on that table," said Yogi. "My father knew nothing about baseball, he just said, 'Go play.' That may have been good," said Berra. "We went outside and played until dark." They played park ball, with broom sticks and bottle caps. Yogi Berra went from the Hill to the Hall of Fame and became an American folk hero. Some of us are touched by the baseball gods. "I'd rather be the Yankees' catcher than the President," said Yogi.

Yogi and Joe Garagiola worked at Sears & Roebuck together and both were crazy about the movies. One summer, while they were working at Sears & Roebuck, Joe claims Yogi invented self-service. "They put me in sporting goods and Yogi in hardware," said Joe. "Yogi didn't know a ten-penny nail from a cross-saw. A guy would come in and ask for a hammer, and Yogi would say, 'Just help yourself and then come back and I'll cash you out.'" Their dads also worked together, for a company that made clay pipes.

At the age of 16, Yogi began playing organized baseball on the Stockham Post American Legion team. It was on this team that Yogi received his very first uniform. It is rumored that Yogi also played under an assumed name for a team in Cranston, Rhode Island. In 1942, Yogi's buddy, Garagiola, was signed by Branch Rickey of the St. Louis Cardinals, as a catcher. Joe received a $500 signing bonus. Branch offered Yogi $250, and Yogi turned him down. Rickey then said of Yogi, "He'll never make anything more than a Triple-A ballplayer at best." Rickey tried to explain in his later years that he had already made the decision to leave the Cardinals and join the Brooklyn Dodgers' organization, where he fully intended to sign Berra. Rickey's plan backfired, as Yogi signed with Yankee scout, Leo Browne, of the New York Yankees in 1943, for $90 a month and a $500 signing bonus. Yogi was sent to the Norfolk Tars, a team in the Class-B Piedmont League. In the beginning, he was placed at the catching position, but made so many errors that they sent him to play in left field. While in Norfolk, Yogi was remembered for once recording 23 RBI's in one doubleheader, an astounding feat.

In 1949, Yogi married his sweetheart, Carmen, a waitress at Biggie's restaurant in St. Louis. Together they would raise three boys, Dale, Timmy and Larry. Biggie's was once owned by Stan Musial. Yogi loved the movies, especially westerns, and the Marx Brothers made him laugh. He had a tough time finding clothes that fit because of his stature. He was called names like "ape," "nature boy," and a "troll with a facemask." He attacked his food, had a huge appetite, and ate strange combinations in sandwiches, like banana and mustard. He also loved reading comic books. When his fans found out about this, they sent him hundreds of comics. His Yankee teammates claimed that Yogi's locker was two-thirds full of comic books. He was also really quick, but he didn't run very well. He was a dead-red, left-handed hitter, born to play at Yankee stadium. Left-handed hitting catchers were hard to come by. He was also tight with his money. His teammates always borrowed money from him when they ran out, while on the road. "The last thing Yogi thinks about at night is money," said Manager, Casey Stengel.

Yogi was smart and could talk about all sports. Shy, he was frightened of public speaking, yet he talked all the time on the baseball field. He talked to everyone including the umpire, and most hitters hated it, especially Larry Doby. "I would throw dirt on Minnie Minoso's shoes, and asked Ted Williams when he was gonna go fishing again. Williams was a left-handed hitter like me, but I would have swung at a lot of the pitches he took. He had such a great eye," said Berra. Once when Hank Aaron came to the plate, Yogi said, "You've got your bat upside down. The label should be pointed up." Aaron responded, "I didn't come up here to read." Here is sample of a conversation with "Boog" Powell and Yogi, one afternoon in Baltimore:

Yogi, "Hey Boog, how you doing?"
Boog, "Fine."
"Strike one," said the umpire.
Yogi, "How's your family?"
Boog, "Good."
"Strike two," said the umpire.
Yogi, "What are you doing after the game?"
"Strike three," said the umpire.

He worried constantly, had insomnia, and was referred to as "ugly." At the age of 18, he would serve time in the United States Navy as a Gunner's Mate. Yogi served in North Africa and Italy. On June 6, 1944, Yogi Berra, Seaman 2nd Class, was assigned to a six-man rocket boat known as an LCSS (Landing Craft Support Small). His boat would participate at Normandy in the D-Day Invasion of World War II, by shooting at German gun placements to protect the U.S. troops wading ashore at Utah Beach. He was grazed by bullet from a German machine gun. He had earned a Purple Heart, though to not worry his mother, he never applied for it. He did receive a Distinguished Unit Citation, two battle stars, and a European Theater of Operations ribbon. After the war, Yogi reported to the New York Yankees. Longtime clubhouse manager, Pete Sheehy said, "When Yogi reported to the Yanks' clubhouse still wearing his naval uniform, he didn't even look like a sailor." Berra would be sent by the Yankees to the Newark Bears of the International League for more experience. His roommate was third baseman, Bobby Brown. While in Newark, Yogi played many games against Jackie Robinson, who was with the Montreal Royals.

In 1946, Yogi hit .314 at Newark. Twenty-seven months after D-Day, wearing #38, Yogi was called up by the Yanks at the end of the 1946 season and made his Major League debut on September 22, 1946. Berra went 2 for 4, with two RBI's, and hit his first Major League home run. The next day he hit his second home run. Yogi joined the Yankees at the beginning of the 1947 season as a rookie catcher. He lived in the Edison Hotel in New York. He became a platoon catcher with Aaron Robinson, Charlie Silvera and Gus Niarhos. He played in 83 games in 1947; wearing #35, and then switched to #8 in 1948, the number he would wear for the rest of his career as player and manager. His mentor with the Yankees, Bill Dickey, had also worn #8 and he, too, became a Hall-of-Fame catcher.

When Yogi joined the Yankees, he was introduced to Whitey Ford this way: "Larry Berra, this is Ed Ford." He would be called Larry or Yogi for the first several years, until Yogi stuck. Bob Hoffman, a childhood friend and future New York Giant, gave Yogi his nickname. "I was sitting on the ground with my legs crossed in front of me, and Bob said, 'You look like a Yogi,'" said Berra. Yogi had also never met Joe DiMaggio until he was brought up from the Newark Bears in 1946. When DiMaggio saw Berra for the first time at 5' 7" inches tall and bowlegged, he supposedly said, "What have we here?" Berra ended up playing leftfield next to DiMaggio. "All I knew about DiMaggio was what I read in the papers," said Berra. "He never did anything wrong. I wanted to play with a St. Louis team. DiMaggio was an interesting guy; he always sat in the corner of the clubhouse with his legs crossed. He drank coffee and smoked lots of cigarettes. Oh, he would play 'Hearts' on the train with us; but when we arrived at the next city, he would go off by himself." The Yankees would go on to win the 1947 World Series. Yogi's winning share totaled $5,830, $830 more than he received for the entire season.

On June 15, 1947, Yogi recorded an unassisted double play, rare for a catcher. It occurred during the second game of a doubleheader with the St. Louis Browns. It was the top of the ninth inning, with the Yankees leading 2-1. Jeff Heath of the Browns was on third base and Walt Judnich stood on first. Johnny Berardino was the hitter. Berardino topped the ball in front of home plate in an attempt to squeeze Heath home. Heath was coming hard down the third base line trying to score. Berardino froze in the batter's box while Yogi jumped out and grabbed the ball, then tagged Heath and then Bernardino, for the double play.

On September 28, 1955, the New York Yankees played the Brooklyn Dodgers in the World Series. The baseball gods shined brightly that year on the Dodgers. The Yankees won Game One, but not before the bad blood began to boil over between these two teams. In the sixth inning, Yanks' Billy Martin tried to steal home but was put out by catcher Roy Campanella, with a hard tag to Martin's face. Billy, who had been quoted as saying, "I never throw the first punch, but I will throw the second, third and fourth," jumped up and looked as if he was going to take matters into his own hands, but fisticuffs were averted by the home plate umpire.

In the eighth inning with Brooklyn trailing 6-4 and Jackie Robinson standing on third base, Whitey Ford was caught napping. Jackie broke for home and the ball, and Robinson arrived at home plate about the same time as Yogi put down the tag. To the astonishment of Berra, Robinson was called "safe" by umpire, Bill Summers. Yogi went into hysterics while jumping up and down. To his last breath, Berra insisted Jackie was out and Robinson swore he had scored. Yogi was never able to let it go and was asked about the play on many occasions. He always answered the same way every time, "He was out." Berra also accused Robinson of being a showboat and Jackie responded, "Tell Berra that any time he wants to give me a run, I'll take it."

The date was October 8, 1956. Yogi Berra will forever be remembered for his part in catching Don Larsen's "Perfect Game" in the 1956 World Series against the dreaded Brooklyn Dodgers. The photo of Berra jumping into Larsen's arms after the game said it all. Don Larsen said, I never shook off Berra's pitch selection."

Yankee skipper, Casey Stengel, always referred to Berra as "My man," as in "I never played a ballgame without my man." Stengel said, when asked about Yogi, "He had more understanding than any ballplayer I have ever managed. Yogi instinctively knew what the team needed to do to win, and second, he was lucky. In a game where the pitcher only pitches every five days, and a hitter only comes up to bat three or four times a game, one person cannot impose his will to win consistently, day in and day out. It is truly a team game where players depend on a series of plays by different players, to place them in a position to win."

"We were a happy club," said Yogi. "We had some great players like "Whitey," Mickey, Elston, "Moose," Kubek and Richardson." First time Berra saw Mickey Mantle play, Yogi said, "He's gonna' be a hell of a player. I miss Mickey a lot. He was a good man. When he came up, he did not touch a drink. Most of his drinking came after his playing days."

Yogi continued, "Whitey Ford never threw a spitball to me, never," said Yogi. "He could get any pitch over he wanted." Yogi was allowed to call every pitch, under Stengel. If the pitcher tired, Yogi would rotate his right index finger while squatting behind the dish and Casey would head to the mound to make a pitching change.

Yogi was notorious for being a powerful bad-ball hitter. His forearms were like anvils. He could reach just about anything at the plate and had uncanny bat control. During his career, he had five years where he had more home runs than strikeouts. He could golf out the low pitches for home runs or chop down on high pitches for base hits. The standing joke was that Berra's only hitting weakness was a fastball right down the middle, but I dare you to throw him a good pitch. When asked about swinging at bad pitches, his answer was always, "If I can hit it, it's a good pitch." His batting average was 30 points higher with men on base. He hit more home runs with men on base than with the bases empty, and he was embarrassed when he struck out, so he didn't strike out. He would go three weeks without a strikeout and did not strike out twice in any one game, for over a year. In 1950, Berra struck out only twelve times in 597 at-bats, unheard of in today's game. "I always hit when there were men on base," said Yogi. "When I was a manager, I always told my kids, "If you got men on base, you're not in trouble; the pitcher's in trouble." He was also durable; 177 times during his career, he started as catcher in both games of a doubleheader. What I do know is that Yogi Berra was one heck of a hitter. Yogi played his last game in the Major Leagues on May 9, 1965.

Once while hanging out at Toots Shor's Saloon, Yogi was introduced to Ernest Hemingway by Toots. Toots said, "This is Ernest Hemingway, he's an important writer." Yogi replied, "What paper you with, Ernie?"

You may notice that most of Yogi's words run together, a sign that he didn't like to talk much. There was a time when

Yogi was called "ugly" by an opposing player, he responded, "I don't hit with my face." Once when Yogi failed a test in school, the teacher asked him "Don't you know anything?" He answered, "I don't even suspect anything." Other favorite lines spoken by Berra went like this: "A nickel isn't worth a dime anymore." "You can observe a lot just by watching." "Always go to other people's funerals; otherwise they won't go to yours." "When you come to the fork in the road, take it." "Ninety percent of hitting is mental and the other half, physical." "If the fans don't wanta' come out to the ballpark, nobody's gonna' stop'em." Yogi was also heard saying about a restaurant, "Nobody goes there anymore, it's too crowded." This last quotation made Yogi Berra famous. Yogi was asked by reporters about his 1973 New York Mets team that trailed by 9 ½ games behind the Chicago Cubs, in the National League East. "It ain't over till it's over," said Yogi, and he was right, as the Mets not only caught the Cubs but won the division, on the last day of the season.

The summer of 1964 was the first time I saw Yogi Berra in person; he was the Manager of the New York Yankees. It's funny, he looked old then; but then again, Yogi didn't look like anybody else. This was during the same time I saw Mantle, Richardson, Kubek, Maris, Skowron, and the rest of the Bombers. Elston Howard caught Whitey Ford that day. That's correct, it was a day game. They were playing in "The House that Ruth built." My story entitled "Faster than Electricity," about Mickey Mantle, was written in my first book, In the Company of Greatness. In that story, I describe how big Yankee Stadium seemed to a 13-year-old kid from North Carolina. On the other hand, Yogi looked so small sitting in the dugout, especially from my seat in the second level down the first-base side. He looked like a little kid swinging his feet trying to touch the ground.

Even though he was small in stature, Yogi Berra cut a large path as a manager. In September of 1964, the Yankees lost another game to the White Sox. It was their fourth loss in a row, and the pennant was slipping away. Needless to say, Berra was not happy and neither were the Yanks. On the bus trip to the airport for a flight to Boston, Phil Linz pulled out his newly-purchased Hohner harmonica from his pocket and began to play "Mary Had a Little Lamb." Linz was sitting in the back, as were most of the cut-ups, including Mantle. As Linz played, Berra hollered back, "I said, no joking around." Linz stopped playing and asked, "What did he say?" Mantle answered, "He said, play it louder." Linz should have known better. Berra now furious, stormed to the back of the bus with his arms raised and said, "Shove that harmonica." Linz flipped it towards Berra, and he caught it and fired it back at Linz but missed Phil and hit Joe Pepitone in the knee. By the time the flight landed in Boston, the beat writers traveling with the team had reported the insubordination. Linz apologized to Yogi, even though Berra fined him $250. Not only did the Yankees rally for Berra, but they went on to win 30 of their next 43 games, to catch and pass the White Sox. Linz, on the other hand, received a box full of harmonicas and a $5,000 endorsement check from Hohner. Phil Linz also got his $250 fine back, the next year.

Berra's Yanks won the 1964 pennant but lost to the St. Louis Cardinals in a seven-game World Series, and Yogi was fired. Berra then signed a deal with the New York Mets as a player-coach. Yogi joined Casey Stengel and eventually became the Mets Manager in 1971, after the death of Gil Hodges. As mentioned earlier above, in 1973 Berra led the Mets to the National League pennant. He was dismissed in 1975 and returned to the Yankees as a coach the following year. On December 12, 1984, Steinbrenner fired Billy Martin and hired Yogi to manage the Yankees. George even signed Dale Berra, Yogi's son. It was the first time a father managed his son since Connie Mack managed Earl Mack, from 1910-1914. Yogi was let go 22 games into the

1985 season. Yogi managed a total of seven seasons with the Yankees and the Mets. His win-loss record stands at 484 wins and 444 losses.

I moved to Corpus Christi, Texas, in 1985, and met Yogi a couple of years later. I got his autograph on a baseball after he joined the Houston Astros as a bench coach. I had never met anyone who was so at peace with himself. He made you feel comfortable. I wasn't nervous meeting Yogi. He was never intimidating. Yogi was kind, warm-hearted, funny and always sitting down. I found myself just listening and hoping he would say something magical.

Berra had been fired again by the Yankees' and Astros' owner, John McMullen, who had been a limited partner with George Steinbrenner, and knew how much Yogi was hurting and offered him a job. Yogi Berra was a baseball lifer; he accepted. Berra harbored ill feelings towards Steinbrenner and the Yankees' brass. George had sent someone else to let Berra know he had been fired, instead of telling him himself. This rift between the two men would take 15 years to finally heal. The Astros won their first Division title in Yogi's first season with the Houston club. Yogi remained the bench coach from 1986-1989.

I saw Yogi again in 1990, at a baseball card show in Houston. While there, I heard an interview with Yogi. He told how he had loved working as a coach, with a young catcher named Craig Biggio. Yogi Berra and Astros' coach, Matt Galante, were good friends and spent a lot of time coaching Biggio into a fine player. Biggio made his big league debut in 1988, while Yogi was with the team. He also raved about the hitting of an up-and-coming first baseman named Jeff Bagwell. He mentioned his fondness for Atlanta's catcher, Javy Lopez; once a catcher, always a catcher. Yogi disliked Astroturf and the "designated hitter." He also felt most of today's players wanted to spend more time on hitting than fielding. Yogi said, "We only got five swings in the cage when I played, and that was it." Craig

Biggio would pay tribute to Yogi Berra and Matt Galante in his 2015 Hall-of-Fame acceptance speech in Cooperstown.

He was pleasant to be around and mostly quiet, but smiled continuously when among others. Born an old man who remained young, he was a winner. His ears appeared bigger without a cap, and he now wore glasses. He was once announced at an Old Timers' Game by Michael Kay as having, "One of the best known faces on the planet." He was kind of hard to understand because he had a tendency to mumble. He owned a funny rhythm when he spoke that you may have confused with broken English. I had read where Yogi, like my father, had left school after the eighth grade.

By 1972, Yogi had already been elected to the Baseball Hall of Fame and was well on his way to being independently wealthy. He had started doing Lucky Strike Cigarette commercials in the 1950's and was still at it in 2010. Early on, Yogi decided to take some of his World Series winnings and invest in some swamp land, located in Orlando, Florida. That land was later purchased from Berra by Walt Disney to create Disney World.

My last visit with Yogi occurred during the 1999 Spring Training schedule at Legends Field in St. Petersburg, Florida, the home of the Yankees. A friend, Dave Sullivan, and I had tickets for five straight days to see several teams play. We saw the Yankees play twice, first against Toronto and second against Atlanta. Yogi, Joe Torre and Don Zimmer were all on hand. It made sense for Yogi to be there. I remembered that Joe Torre had once said about Yogi, "He was everybody's good-luck charm." The Yankees usually used a split squad, so we missed seeing Derek Jeter. We did, however, enjoy watching Bernie Williams, Paul O'Neil, Jorge Posada, Chuck Knoblauch, Tino Martinez, Mariano Rivera and several other Yankees' favorites play. We also got to see Greg Maddux, John Smoltz, Javy Lopez, Carlos Delgado, Fred McGriff and a very young Josh Hamilton, with the Tampa Bay Rays.

On Thursday, February 24, 2001, an article appeared in the *New York Times* written by Harvey Araton. It was entitled "It Happens Every Spring: Driving Mr. Yogi." The story was about the relationship between Yogi Berra and Ron Guidry. Guidry, a pretty-fair retired pitcher for the New York Yankees, known as "Gator," made it a point to take care of one of the last remnants of Yankees' royalty from the forties. Yogi, 85 at the time, had come back into the fold. His firing in 1985 by Steinbrenner had driven a stake between the two, but the relationship was mended by 1999, after George made a visit to the Yogi Berra Museum and Learning Center, located at Montclair State University in Little Falls, New Jersey, to apologize. Spring Training is all Yogi Berra had left in the game of baseball. It's what he looked forward to; it was where he felt comfortable. Guidry loved the old man for what they had in common, but refused to treat him as a father. Instead he treated him as a friend. Ron even had a cap made inscribed with "Driving Mr. Yogi." So every Spring Training, Ron picked Yogi up every morning, drove him to the park, and took him to dinner most nights. Guidry even got him to eat some frog legs, a habit for most folks from Louisiana. "It's like I was a valet," said Guidry.

Berra has been called a "Baseball Saint." He was an enormously popular figure. Berra is to baseball like flour is to donuts. He could be considered the first "Mr. October." After Joe DiMaggio died on March 8, 1999, Yogi was crowned the "Greatest living Yankee." Some have suggested that he should have his own wing in the Baseball Hall of Fame. I do know there are two statues at the entrance to the Baseball Hall of Fame: Babe Ruth and Ted Williams. I would not be surprised to see one of Berra in the near future. Yogi was once asked at the beginning of the season, what size cap he wore. Yogi responded, "I don't know. I'm not in shape yet."

There are many firsts in the Yogi Berra story. Berra was the first Major League baseball player to have an agent. His name was Frank Scott. Yogi Berra is believed to be the first catcher to put his index finger outside his catcher's mitt and the first to also use a woman's falsie to pad the center of his mitt. Yogi Berra played in a record 75 games during 14 World Series. He participated in a total of 21 World Series (14 as a player, two as a manager, and five as a coach), and was on 13 winning teams. That's more World Series' rings than John McGraw, Connie Mack, Casey Stengel, Babe Ruth, Joe DiMaggio, and Mickey Mantle combined.

Berra played 18 years with the New York Yankees (1946-1963) and participated in 14 World Series' with the Bombers. As a player, he won so many World Series Championships (10) that he quit getting rings and instead asked for watches and gifts for his wife, Carmen. He once got a gold cigarette box. Berra became an 18-time All-Star, while winning the American League Most-Valuable-Player Award three times (1951, 1954, and 1955). Berra was the first New York Yankee to win back-to-back MVP Awards. He still holds many World Series records including most games by catcher (63), hits (71), and times on the winning team (10). This guy may have invented the Canyon of Heroes. Berra is first in World Series at-bats (259), doubles (10), and singles (49). Yogi is second in World Series runs scored (41) and RBI's (39), and third in home runs hit, with 12. Yogi also became the first player in World Series history to pinch-hit a home run in 1947, off Dodgers' pitcher, Ralph Branca.

During his career, Berra played in 2,120 games and went to bat 7,555 times, while striking out only 414 times. That's one strikeout per eighteen at-bats. He recorded 2,150 hits, 1,430 RBI's while scoring 1,175 runs. He hit 358 home runs (only three less than Joe DiMaggio) and his batting average stood at .285. He is one of a very few managers to have won pennants in both leagues and was elected to the Baseball Hall of Fame Museum in 1972, on his second ballot, with a percentage of 85.6%. Berra is also ranked as he seventh best player during the decade of the 1950's. The first six you will recognize: Mickey Mantle, Stan Musial, Duke Snider, Eddie Mathews, Willie Mays and Ted Williams. No one could call a game like Yogi Berra. He also played in 148 consecutive games, had 950 chances, without committing an error.

Berra and his pal Phil Rizzuto were partners in a bowling alley before Phil passed. It was called Berra-Rizzuto Alleys. Before Rizzuto died he was placed in an assisted-living facility. Yogi would go to visit Phil every day, and the two of them would play cards until Phil started to nod off. Yogi would hold his hand until Rizzuto went to sleep, and then he would leave. He went every day until Phil Rizzuto passed away. That's a teammate. Yogi is also the recipient of the Boy Scouts of America's highest adult award, the "Silver Buffalo." He owned part of the Yahoo soft drink company and appeared in their commercials, as well as AFLAC, Stove Top Stuffing and Miller Lite.

Yogi Berra fell from his front porch on July 16, 2010, and was forced to miss the Old Timers' Day at Yankee Stadium. He returned home from the hospital the following day. As time moved on, Yogi slipped away from the daily news. Yogi lived ninety incredible years. When word got out, comments and condolences poured in from all over the world. There were many stories retold about Yogi by the people he had touched along the way. Here are a few. Johnny Bench said he received a telegram from Yogi after Bench had broken Yogi's home-run record for a catcher. It said, "Congratulations, I knew my record would stand until it was broken." It was pure Yogi Berra. "Yogi was always on time. Once we were at the Bryant Gumbel Golf Tournament and I told him I would meet him downstairs at 5:30 am. I arrived at 5:15 and Yogi was there waiting for me. Yogi said, 'You're late.' I responded, 'I'm 15 minutes early,'" said Joe Garagiola. "Yogi said, 'That's the earliest you've been late.'"

Don Mattingly stated that he loved to hit in the cage, every day. Yogi once told me, "You're going to hit your way right into a slump," said Don. One time, during the 1955 All-Star Game, Yogi was grumbling to Stan Musial about getting tired of catching for 12 innings. Umpire Bill Summers said, "How about me. It's just as tough back here." "Musial said, 'Yeah, I'm tired, too' and promptly hit the next pitch for a game-ending home run and we all went home,'" said Yogi. Ted Williams once said, "Yogi was the toughest clutch hitter the Red Sox ever faced."

Yogi Berra once said about Sandy Koufax, "I can see how he won 25 games. I can't understand how he lost five."

Yogi once commented on the marriage of Joe DiMaggio to Marilyn Monroe. "I don't know if it's good for baseball, but it sure beats the hell out of rooming with Phil Rizzuto."

My favorite story about Yogi Berra was told by his best friend, Joe Garagiola and I don't even know if it's true. It goes like this. One night Berra got three hits in a game, and the next day the paper wrote that Yogi had gone two-for-four. Upset with the official scorer, Yogi said, "How come I only got credited with two hits yesterday? I got three." The scorer said, "That was a typographical error, Yogi. I'm sorry." "Whaddya mean error? Two of them were clean singles to left and the shortstop made a perfect throw on that one I beat out."

Most of the younger fans don't know the Yogi Berra that I knew as a player, because he hasn't played in over fifty years. That is one advantage of being older; I saw him play and most of you only heard about his play. New York Giant Hall of Famer, Mel Ott once said about Yogi, "He seemed to be doing everything wrong, yet everything came out right. He stopped everything behind the plate and hit everything in front of it."

Yogi was known to have written love letters to his wife, Carmen, when the team was on the road. He also carried a picture of his parents in his wallet. He drove a Corvair and made his bed every morning. Berra smoked cigarettes when he played and was a big hockey fan; he enjoyed the handshake at the end. He was also terrible as a left-handed golfer for ten years; then he switched to right-handed and began to shoot scores in the 80's. Yogi also had a special relationship with Derek Jeter. The Captain (Jeter) looked up to Yogi as his mentor.

Yogi was proud to have one of the lowest strike-out averages in the big leagues. In his first eleven seasons, Yogi went to the plate 6,087 times and only struck out 252 times. That is one strike-out for every 24 at-bats.

Yogi and Carmen Berra made their home in Montclair, New Jersey, and had three children. When they moved into their new home, Yogi was quoted as saying, "I don't know if I like it. It's nothing but rooms." The two boys, Dale and Tim both played professional sports. Dale played with the Pittsburgh Pirates, New York Yankees, and Houston Astros. In 1974, Tim played professional football with the Baltimore Colts.

Onetime before Carmen died from complications from a stroke; she asked Yogi if something were to happen, where he would want to be buried. Their families were from St. Louis, Yogi played all those years in New York, and they had lived forever in New Jersey. Yogi told her, "Just surprise me." After 65 years of marriage, Yogi lost his beloved Carmen about 18 months before he died.

In early 2015, Yogi was hospitalized for pneumonia-like symptoms. He was confined to a wheelchair and placed in an assisted-living facility in West Caldwell, New Jersey. He loved watching baseball on television.

Yogi Berra, the cornerstone of the New York Yankees, took his place on the "field of dreams," this morning. Yogi died of natural causes on Tuesday, September 22, 2015. Putting on the Yankee pinstripes was the best thing he ever did. The future will never be the same without him. If you need a role model, this was the guy. He lived a lifetime filled with greatness. Once while looking up at the Old-Timers Day scoreboard which was showing a list of deceased Yankee greats, Hall-of-Fame catcher Yogi Berra said, "Boy, I hope I never see my name up there." He left behind all three sons and eleven grandchildren. I've got to believe that Yogi was watching his Yankees when rookie first baseman, Greg Bird, hit a three-run home run in extra innings to beat the Toronto Blue Jays, the night he died. He is a member of the New Jersey Hall-of-Fame and the St. Louis Walk-of-Fame. Berra was also elected to the 1999 All-Century Team. The Yankees will wear a special #8 patch on their uniform for the rest of their season. On Wednesday night, September 23, 2015, the Empire State Building was lit up in pinstripes to honor Yogi Berra.

I think everyone should have a Yogi Berra in their life. I will end this story with my favorite quotation from Yogi. "To me the beauty of baseball is that it goes all the way back to your childhood. It's a game made for stories. There is nothing more enjoyable than telling old baseball stories. Sometimes it's hard to separate what is real or not real, there are many myths, but that's what makes it fun," said Yogi.

Well said, my friend. Well said.

On November 24, 2015, Willie Mays and Yogi Berra (posthumously) received the Presidential Medal of Freedom from President Barack Obama, the highest honor an American civilian can receive.

PICK A CARD, ANY CARD

He was a master at card tricks and not too shabby with the coins either. He had more tricks than a clown's pocket. His educated hands and long fingers made it possible for him to deceive just about anyone, especially the kids. He loved kids and they loved him right back. He also made magic with his words and they listened. He claimed he had extremely strong hands from shucking corn in the summer and rubbing his mother's painful shoulders when he was a kid. His mom, Kay, had polio.

This fellow would become a fine basketball coach and owned one of the best offensive minds in the game. It didn't hurt that he was fearless and could stare down a rattlesnake. He became known for his extra thick playbooks. He claimed to have at least ten counters for every offensive set. It has been said that he would sit in the stands after telling his team what offensive set to run and, as they crossed half court, he would call out a counter to that set. If you didn't know the counter, you might not be there the next day. He was known for maximizing his players' talents and minimizing their weaknesses. Scouting reports were considered sacred, and you were quizzed before every game. If you didn't know the information about your opponent, again, you might not be there the next day. His mantra was "Get me to the 4th quarter up by two and I'll win it without you." Flip Saunders may have loved basketball, but he was a magician at heart, Harry Houdini in tennis shoes. Pick a card, any card.

Philip Daniel "Flip" Saunders was born February 23, 1955, in Cleveland, Ohio. His middle name should have been "clinic." They say he used his extra long arms to become a prep basketball star at Cuyahoga Heights High School. During his senior year, he led the state in scoring average, with 32 points per game. He was as wholesome as a Boy Scout, and his jump shot was deadly and illegal in three states. He handled a basketball like it was a bubble. Every time he entered the gym it was must see TV. He could perform all kinds of ball-handling tricks and put on an amazing show. Giving this kid a basketball was like handing "Minnesota Fats" a pool cue. From an early age he was different, he was special when it came to basketball. Something incredible was about to happen. The very definition of "game ready" was watching Flip Saunders get off the team bus. He graduated in 1973, after becoming the Class-A Player-of-the-Year, in Ohio.

He received his nickname Flip, from his mother, Kay, after she heard someone use the word at a beauty saloon. After high school, Flip entered the University of Minnesota and became a Golden Gopher. There he completed an excellent team consisting of future Hall-of-Famer Kevin McHale, Ray Williams, Osborne Lockhart and Mychal Thompson. As a senior, Flip helped guide the Gophers to a 24-3 win-loss record.

Just months after graduating from the University of Minnesota, he began his coaching career. Saunders spent 24 years coaching. He started at Golden Valley Lutheran College (1977-1981), a junior college located in Bloomington, Minnesota. While there, he compiled a win-loss record of 92-13, including a 56-0 winning streak at home. Later, he became an assistant coach at the University of Minnesota (1981-1986) and the University of Tulsa (1986-1988). Saunders then served seven seasons (1988-1995) coaching in the Continental Basketball Association (CBA). He coached one year for the Rapid City Thrillers of South Dakota, five years with the La Crosse Catbirds of Wisconsin, and one year with the Sioux Falls Skyforce of South Dakota.

It was with the La Crosse Catbirds that folks began to take notice. Saunders led the Catbirds to two CBA Championships (1990 and 1992), received two CBA Coach-of-the-Year Awards (1989 and 1992), and sent 23 of his CBA players to the NBA. Flip had always claimed it was there in the CBA that he began to understand the work ethic and knowledge it would take to coach in the National Basketball Association. The story goes: He wrote a letter to Glen Taylor, the new owner of the Minnesota Timberwolves, and asked for a job. His letter would be answered and Flip would achieve his dream in 1995. He was hired as an assistant coach to Bill Blair, and his longtime friend and college teammate, Kevin McHale, took over the basketball operations for the Timberwolves. Blair was fired 20 games into the season, and Saunders suddenly became the Head Coach. Up until that point, the Timberwolves had never made the playoffs; all that was about to change.

Flip Saunders made his most-lasting impression in Minnesota where he led this franchise to the first winning season in their history and eight post-season playoffs. He started the process in 1995 with a kid out of high school named Kevin Garnett. Flip Saunders led the Timberwolves to the 2004 NBA Finals, where they were turned away by the Los Angeles Lakers. The Timberwolves were a precision team, the kind of team you beat up and down the court only to get on the bus after the game, heading to the airport realizing you had lost. Despite having won 411 games, while only losing 326 with Minnesota, Saunders was fired during the 2004-2005 season and replaced by Kevin McHale. He replaced Coach Larry Brown on July 21, 2005. He would spend the next three seasons with the Detroit Pistons (2005-2008) and led the Pistons to three consecutive Eastern Conference Finals. Saunders coached the Eastern Conference All-Stars in the 2006 NBA All-Star game played in Houston, Texas. Once again he was let go, on June 3, 2008, and hired by the Washington Wizards on April 14, 2009. Saunders was dismissed from the Wizards on January 24, 2012. Flip joined the Boston Celtics on April 29, 2012, as an advisor.

The Timberwolves had not been very successful since Flip left, so they re-hired Flip as President of Basketball Operations on May 2, 2013. He would be named Head Coach on June 5, 2014. Two of his first personnel moves were to bring back Kevin Garnett and to draft the University of Kentucky star, Karl-Anthony Towns. Saunders would also be diagnosed on August 11, 2015, with Hodgkin's lymphoma. He would begin treatment immediately, but it was not enough.

When I heard the news, I immediately reached out to my friend, Texas A&M Corpus Christi Islanders' Assistant Coach, Mark Dannhoff. I knew Mark had spoken about working with Flip Saunders in the past. I could hear the shock and frustration in his voice as he told me the following. "A year and a half ago I sat at the gate of my connecting flight to Ohio with my friend, GM and former Head Coach of the Minnesota Timberwolves, Flip Saunders. Coach Saunders was heading home to visit his father, and I was going to check out a high-school point guard from the same area. We shared memories of my days working at his basketball camps, his Continental Basketball Association Championship with my hometown team, the La Crosse Catbirds, how our current teams were playing, the profession, and family. I have known Coach for over 25 years," said Coach Mark Dannhoff. "So you can imagine my sadness when I heard about his passing. I knew he had been diagnosed with cancer and was receiving treatment, but in my wildest dreams I did not think the cancer would take his life so soon."

The loss of Coach Saunders hit the NBA hard. Being a

basketball coach was his identity. There were numerous tributes rolled out throughout the league. NBA Commissioner, Adam Silver, and the league gladly allowed the Timberwolves to add a patch to their jerseys to honor Flip.

Thirty-nine-year-old Kevin Garnett, who began his career with Saunders, took the news of his coach's death very hard. Garnett left practice when the news was announced and went out into the parking garage of the Minnesota practice facility and sat down in his coach's empty parking spot. He eventually took a picture of himself sitting there and tweeted out to the world, "Forever in my heart."

Los Angeles Lakers Head Coach Byron Scott said, "He was one of those guys that made you feel like you had known him for awhile, even if it was only 15 minutes."

His close friend, Tom Izzo, Head Coach of the Michigan State Spartans said, "He was a great human being and one of the best offensive minds in basketball. I could talk basketball with him all day and night."

Flip Saunders coached in the NBA for 17 seasons and his win-loss record will be recorded as 654-592, but he won much more than the numbers indicate. He was always a step ahead, and his kindness preceded him wherever he went.

He died on a Sunday, October 25, 2015, from complications from Hodgkin's lymphoma. He was 60 years old. Doctors had called his diagnosis "treatable and curable." He took a leave of absence, but his health failed quickly. Flip and his wife, Debbie, raised four children: Ryan, Mindy, and twin daughters Kim and Rachel. He was very much a family man and seemed to have a real fix on balancing his coaching profession with his home life.

You hear all the time that this coach or that coach was a player's' coach, and we all have a different definition of what that is, depending on our own experience while playing sports. The "word" on Flip from his former players was that he was tough but fair. He talked to his players like a father would talk to his son. "I have a saying I tell my players," Saunders said in 2005. "The game's not black and white; it's played gray." Coach went on to explain: "You've got to make decisions every day, offensively and defensively. I don't believe there's one way to play."

"Flip made practice fun, and he loved to stay after practice and play shooting games with his guys. And in case you didn't know, he could flat out shoot the cover off a basketball," said Mark Dannhoff. "He lived a full life and will be remembered as one of the best offensive minds in the game. I will remember him as a great coach, a wonderful family man, a tremendous person and a Catbird." Thanks Mark, I could not have said it any better myself.

PHI SLAMA JAMA

He could be as tough as rawhide, or as gentle as a grandmother. He was fierce yet kindhearted, cantankerous but reasonable. He remained independent, thoughtful, and hard-fisted all of his life, but was known as completely lovable as a coach-John the Baptist in tennis shoes. He was the kind of guy you didn't mind getting stuck in a submarine with, and the cover of his playbook may have had only one word, "Attack." I guess you could say he was easy to like but hard to know. He succeeded in a profession where even tough guys finish second. Basketball was not only his livelihood, but his life. Loyalty had always been one of his basic tenets. Some said he may have invented recruiting. He owned dark circles that hung like bunting beneath his eyes, and he had been known to chase a referee all the way to the dressing room. If you had the opportunity to visit one of his practices, you would come away with three ingredients for winning: you need good players, who could be physical, and who could push the ball in an up-tempo style of offense. He took his game all around the world, as he visited countries such as China, Germany, Spain, England, Korea, the Philippines, Japan, Brazil and Chile. Yet he always said, "There's nothing like returning home to Houston." My pal, Buck Showalter, Manager of the Baltimore Orioles, once said, "It's not that I like to win so much; I hate seeing somebody else win." That reminded me of basketball coach extraordinaire, Guy V. Lewis. A teacher at heart, he was some kind of basketball coach.

Guy Vernon Lewis, II, was born in Arp, Texas, on March 19, 1922. Arp was a small northeastern town with less than 1,000 inhabitants. Lewis attended Arp High School where he starred in basketball and football. Lewis played on three district championship basketball teams in high school and quarterbacked the football team all three years. Like most other red-blooded American boys, Guy joined the U. S. Army's Air Forces and became a flight instructor during World War II. Upon his return, Lewis enrolled at Rice University. After two years, Lewis decided to leave Rice and then enrolled at the University of Houston, in 1946. As co-captain of the Cougars, Lewis became a part of Houston's inaugural basketball team and not only led the team in scoring, but he helped lead the team to the Lone Star Conference title, in their very first season. During his second season, the Cougars finished with a 15-7 win-loss record and won their second consecutive Lone Star Conference title while Lewis knocked down almost 80 percent of his free-throw shots. Lewis was selected a First-Team honoree during the 1946-47 season. He graduated in 1947 with a bachelor's degree in education, while averaging 21 points per game. In fact, Lewis set the team's scoring record in his first season with 34 points, and then broke his own record in his second season by scoring 38 points. He never scored less than 14 points per game, while at Houston.

In 1953, shortly after graduation, Lewis joined Houston's head coach, Alden Pasche, as his assistant. He would learn from Pasche for three years before taking over the Houston program, in 1956. The Cougars struggled the first several years until 1959, when Lewis put a winning team together. During the next 24 seasons, his teams would win 20 or more games during 14 seasons and 30 or more for three seasons. His familiar sideline apparel of plaid jackets and a polka-dot towel clinched in his fist could be seen regularly on television. His win-loss record for 30 years of work stands at 134-98 during conference play, and 592-279 in overall record.

With star player Elvin Hayes, the University of Houston reached the NCAA Final Four in 1967 and 1968. Hayes would become a #1 pick in the NBA draft and eventually a member of the Naismith Memorial Basketball Hall of Fame. At the 1967 Final Four, Houston lost to U.C.L.A., 73-58 in the semi-finals, and then placed third, with an 84-62 win over fourth place UNC.

Guy Lewis, the architect of the college basketball event that is now known as the "Game of the Century," was inducted into the National Collegiate Basketball Hall of Fame in 2007. This game between #1 U.C.L.A. and #2 University of Houston occurred on January 20, 1968. Over 52,000 fans crowded into the newly-built Astrodome, to see Guy Lewis lead his Cougars to a stunning win over John Wooden's Bruins. The marquee matchup between centers, Elvin Hayes and Lew Alcindor, who later changed his name to Kareem Abdul-Jabbar, was incredible to watch. Millions more watched on television as Houston put an end to U.C.L.A.'s 47-game winning streak (71-69) and got their revenge from a loss the previous year, in the NCAA Final Four. For the rest of his days, Lewis called this win the "greatest thrill" of his career. Houston would fare no better in the 1968 Final Four, where they fell to U.C.L.A. again, 101-69 in the semi-finals. Abdul-Jabbar proved to be too much for the Cougars.

In 1982, *Houston Post* sportswriter, Thomas Bonk, coined the nickname, "Phi Slama Jama," after watching Clyde Drexler and Hakeem Olajuwon run their opponents' teams out of the building with an up-tempo, above-the-rim style that led to thunderous dunks. Dunks had been banned by the NCAA from 1967-1976. With the reintroduction of this high percentage shot, the Cougars made back-to-back-to-back visits to the Final Four in 1982, 1983 and 1984. Again, they fell short of victory on all three occasions.

Guy V. Lewis's accomplishments on the basketball court are exceeded only by his vision to help integrate college basketball in the South by signing the Houston program's first African-American players, Elvin Hayes and Don Cheney. These two were among 30 of his players who moved on to the NBA. Hayes became the university's first No. 1 NBA draft pick, followed by Hakeem Olajuwon.

Guy was a true giant in the game of college basketball. Lewis's accomplishments are many. From 1959-1985, the Cougars of Houston recorded 27 consecutive winning seasons. Of those 27 seasons, the Cougars were selected to play in the postseason 17 times, 14 in the NCAA Tournament, and three times in the (NIT) National Invitational Tournament. His Cougars reached five Final Fours without a national Championship. Lewis is one of seven basketball coaches in NCAA history to compete in nine or more Final Four contests with the same program. John Wooden, Mike Krzyzewski, Dean Smith, Adolph Rupp, Denny Crum and Bobby Knight are the other coaches to accomplish that feat. Lewis was chosen the National Coach of the Year twice, in 1968 and 1983. He was selected Southwest Conference Coach of the Year twice, 1983 and 1984, and four times Texas Coach of the Year, in 1968, '77, '82 and '83. Houston earned six Southwest Conference titles. Lewis coached 15 players who earned All-American honors, including National Players of the Year, Elvin Hayes and Hakeem Olajuwon. Beside Drexler, Hayes and Olajuwon, there are others with names you may recognize that achieved All-American status: Otis Birdsong, Michael Young, Larry Micheaux and Greg Anderson.

Twenty-six of his players scored over 1,000 points during their career. He also provided the NBA with 11 first-round picks. Guy V. Lewis is the only one to be inducted into the University of Houston's Athletic Hall of Fame, as a player in 1971 and as a coach in 1998. In 1995, the University of Houston honored Coach Lewis by naming the court at Hofheinz Pavilion after him. In 2013, the Naismith Memorial Basketball Hall of Fame finally called Guy V.

Lewis a Hall-of-Famer. Broadcaster, Jim Nantz, and many former Cougar players had spent years campaigning for their coach.

In 1985, I moved my family to Corpus Christi, Texas. The company I had joined and worked for at that time, known as Texas Pizza Corporation, had purchased the Pizza Hut franchises in El Paso and Corpus Christi and the surrounding markets. My job as Vice President of Operations was to oversee both markets and return them to profitability. The advertising agency we chose to use to help market our restaurants was known as the Winius-Brandon Agency. They were located in Houston, Texas. This agency was owned and operated by Art Casper. I later found out that Art had another passion, college basketball. For 28 years, Art had been one of the radio broadcasters for the University of Houston Cougars' basketball program. So every year, Art would send me the Cougars' schedule and allow me to pick three or four home games where I would join him in Houston, courtside at the scorers' table. There I would chart rebounds, fouls, turnovers, or whatever Art wanted me to do. It also gave me a chance to meet some of the greatest coaches of the games, along with national broadcasters. Ray Meyer and his son Joey with DePaul, Don Haskins with UTEP, Denny Crum with Louisville, and "Digger" Phelps with Notre Dame were some of the best. Terrific broadcasters like Don Crique, Gary Bender and Cheryl Miller were on hand for nationally televised games.

Being from North Carolina and growing up enjoying Atlantic Coast Conference basketball, I naturally looked for ACC teams coming in to play Houston. On this occasion, the team was the University of North Carolina, coached by Dean Smith. It was a nationally-televised game and I was excited, to say the least. Former basketball coach and Houston legend, Guy Lewis, was in attendance and sat a couple of rows behind the U of H team. Lewis had retired after the 1986 season. I asked Art to introduce me to Lewis before the game. I had no idea that Art would set me up in front of this great coach. As we met, Art said, "Guy, I want you to meet a good friend of mine, Andy Purvis, who knows everything you would ever want to know about ACC basketball." Lewis looked straight at me with disdain and said, "What in the hell would I want to know about ACC basketball?" I was so stunned I almost swallowed my tongue. Then Lewis smiled and stuck out his hand as Art started laughing. Lewis had taken five of his teams to the Final Four but had lost twice to ACC teams: UNC in 1982 and N.C. State in 1983. Those losses still didn't sit very well with him. Art would never let me forget the look on my face that day.

Even though they went to different schools, Guy Lewis met the love of his life, Dena Nelson, while attending a high school dance in the 1930's. They married in 1942 and had three children, Vern, Terry and a daughter Sherry, who died early at the age of 63. Sherry's son, Noah, also survives the family. Dena passed away in June of 2015, five months before Guy. They had been married almost 73 years. Vern Lewis went to junior high school with my pal Ronnie Arrow, but they ended up playing at different high schools, each winning a Texas State title in basketball: Vern Lewis played for Houston's Austin High School whose team won the state title in 1964. Ronnie Arrow played at Houston's Jones, whose team won in 1965.

Guy V. Lewis left us on Thanksgiving morning, Thursday, November 26, 2015. He died of natural causes with his family by his side. Lewis had suffered in recent years from a stroke which occurred in February of 2012. He had been confined to a wheelchair and stayed out of the public spotlight. He was living in a retirement home in Kyle, Texas. Lewis was 93.

Guy V. Lewis's story was a masterpiece as he was much more than a basketball coach. A wise man, Anatola France, once said, "To accomplish great things we must not only act, but also dream, not only plan, but also believe." Lewis had them all, in spades. I'm very glad I got to meet him.

Rainbow Kid

American philosopher William James once wrote, "It is our attitude at the beginning of a difficult task which, more than anything else, will affect its successful outcome."

This guy never complained, never critiqued a teammate. This gym rat was also a genius. He was the kind of guy who did extra credit in school that made all of us look bad. But it was the game of basketball that made him tick. He was big for his day, Paul Bunyan-like; all that was missing was his Blue Ox. In the 1940's, men over 6' 2" tall were rare. Anyone over 6' 4" tall was usually awkward and clumsy as their height had outgrown their coordination. He was so large; going around him was like running around the block. After you made it around, it was halftime and the cheerleaders were on the court. At 6'8" tall, getting up was kind of like parallel parking a car. You just have to ease into your space. It seemed that his arms were so long he could tie his shoes without bending over. Driving against him in the paint was like fighting your way through barbed wire. He would be known in today's terms as a "Planet Guy," as in (there are) only so many guys on the planet that large, that strong, and that good. Not only did he have bushy hair and a wide body, but this guy could shoot a basketball. Every shot you have thought about taking he had already made. He drew more coverage than the White House, and it seemed that every court was his home. Greatness deserves recognition. Some players respond better to pressure than others. They are born with it and it cannot be taught.

The very definition of "game ready" was watching Syracuse Nationals' center, Dolph Schayes, get off the team bus. It was said by his teammates that his two-handed, high-arcing set shots were so high it reminded them of a space satellite, Sputnik. They nicknamed him the "Rainbow Kid."

Adolph "Dolph" Schayes was born in the Bronx, NYC, New York, on May 19, 1928. He was such a good basketball player he didn't need a middle name. Dolph was a son of Jewish immigrants from Romania. Carl, his father, drove a truck for a laundry company and Tina, his mother, was a homemaker. He spent his days playing hoops on the playgrounds in the Bronx. Dolph attended Creston Junior High School #79. "When we played basketball, I did everything. I passed, I dribbled, I played outside," said Schayes, who was 6'5" tall at the age of 11. Dolph later attended and played basketball for DeWitt Clinton High School, coached by Howard Cann. There, his team won a borough championship. Dolph entered New York University (NYU), in 1945. He was 16 years old as a freshman and helped lead his team to the NCAA Finals, against the Oklahoma A&M University Aggies, a game played at Madison Square Garden. Dolph had averaged 13.7 points per game, but it was not enough to beat the Aggies. As a senior, he received All-American mention from the Associated Press. In 1948, he graduated with a degree in aeronautical engineering and received the Haggerty Award. Coach Cann once said of Dolph, "He would sneak in the windows of the gym and practiced every spare minute. We had to chase him out."

In 1948, Schayes was the fourth over-all player drafted and the No. 1 pick of the New York Knicks of the NBA and the Tri-Cities Blackhawks of the NBL. Tri-Cities then traded his rights to the Syracuse Nationals, who offered him a contract worth $7,500 or 50% more than the Knicks. Schayes told the New York Times, "So I figured I might as well take the best offer." He would star as a center and power forward while wearing the #4 and later #55 for the Nationals. Dolph Schayes got progressively better with age. The Knicks regretted there decision to pass on Schayes for years. Dolph would become the "Iron Horse" for the Syracuse. He only missed three games from 1949-1961. In 1952, he had broken his right wrist early in his career and developed a left-handed shot as well. The day after Christmas in 1961, Schayes received a broken cheek bone. He wore a protective mask in the All-Star Game and continued playing.

Schayes led the Syracuse Nationals, coached by Al Cervi, to their only NBA Championship, in 1955, against the Fort Wayne Pistons in seven games. Some of his teammates names may sound familiar: Johnny "Red" Kerr, Earl Lloyd and Paul Seymour. It was also the first year the 24-second shot clock was used in the league. Dolph Schayes was a tremendous free-throw shooter and led the NBA in free-throw percentage, three times: in 1958, 1960 and 1962. Dolph placed a 14 inch basket inside the 18 inch basket to practice free throws. Only Bill Sharman was a better foul shooter than Schayes. The Syracuse Nationals moved to Philadelphia in 1963, and Schayes was named player-coach for the 76ers. With a deadly two-handed, high-arcing set shot, he had led his team into the playoffs 15 times in his 16 seasons. Dolph could also shoot a running one-hander and make shots with either hand.

He retired from playing after the 1963-64 season, but stayed on as the head coach for three more years. He would coach Wilt Chamberlain for three years, while in Philly. As their coach, Schayes took Philadelphia (55-25) to the Eastern Division Finals, but lost to the Boston Celtics when John Havlicek famously stole the inbounds pass in the final seconds, to preserve a 110-109 Celtics victory in Game 7. Schayes was the first NBA player to score over 15,000 points. During 15 NBA seasons and one season in the NBL, Dolph had scored 19,247 points, an average of

18.2 per game. He also pulled down 11,256 rebounds and averaged 12.1 per game. Dolph dished out 3,072 assists during his career and played in more games than anyone else at that time, 1,059. Dolph was a 12-time NBA All-Star who made the All-NBA First Team six times and the All-NBA Second Team six times. He was also named NBA Coach of the Year, in 1966.

From 1966-1970, after coaching the 76ers, Dolph Schayes became the NBA's supervisor of referees. He offered a good friend of mine, Dotson Lewis, a job. "I spent three days with Dolph and we attended a game together. He knew basketball, but I didn't care for the way the game was being called back then. The game had gotten rougher and a fight could break out at any time. I chose not to accept his offer," said Dotson.

In 1970, Schayes became the first head coach for the Buffalo Braves. He resigned one game into his second season. In 1977, Dolph coached the United States team to the gold medal at the Maccabiah Games, the Jewish Olympics, in Israel. After leaving the game for good, Dolph became a real estate developer.

One of the early NBA stars and greatest Jewish player in league history, Dolph Schayes died from cancer at the age of 87. The date will be recorded as December 10, 2015. He had been named to the NBA's 25th and 50th anniversary teams and also enshrined into the Naismith Basketball Hall of Fame, in 1973. He was also a member of the International Jewish Sports Hall of Fame, the U.S. National Jewish Sports Hall of Fame, and the National Jewish-American Sports Hall of Fame. Dolph Schayes of the 1950's was like Joe Montana in the late 1980's, cash money.

In May 2015, Schayes was inducted into the Bronx Walk of Fame, where he received a street named after him. In addition to his son, Danny, who played in the NBA for 18 seasons, he is survived by his wife, Naomi; another son, David; his daughters, Carrie Goettsch and Debra Ferri; and nine grandchildren.

Some wise man once said, "So much of who we are, so much of who we believe we are, is contained in those who came before us, in our history." Sixty-five years ago, Dolph Schayes helped carve out the game of basketball on the professional level. How sweet it is!

Four Guys Named Joe

Groucho Marx once said, "I, not events, have the power to make me happy or unhappy today. I can choose which it shall be. Yesterday is dead, tomorrow hasn't arrived yet. I have just one day, today, and I'm going to be happy in it." Every time this guy stepped on the court it was a "must see." He had one of the most recognizable faces and names in the world. His half-court hook shot was magical, and his behind-the-back bounce passes belonged in a museum. This guy was Ed Sullivan in red-and-white striped basketball shorts; he entertained everyone around the world. He has been called the Clown Prince, the Court Jester, the Ringmaster, Ambassador of Goodwill, and the heart and soul of the Harlem Globetrotters. For almost a quarter-century, the spotlight shown on him and his ability to give people the gift of laughter. He was so funny he could make your pets laugh. He helped words like no-look-pass, fast break, and cross-over-dribble become as common as your mother's cornbread and sweet potato pie. He once said, "Very few knew the score, but everyone knew they were happy." He was everywhere; you could even find him in commercials and kids' animated cartoons. A very gifted basketball player, he would replace Reese "Goose" Tatum in the role of the showman. Wilt Chamberlain said, "He was the most sensational, awesome, incredible player I've ever seen." The players called them "reams," their name for the half-court gags that were used in their basketball circus like routines. One of the most famous reams was when 7-footer,

Wilt Chamberlain, played guard and "Meadowlark" Lemon played center.

Born Meadow Lemon, III, most likely on April 25, 1932, "Meadowlark" was raised in a poor neighborhood in Wilmington, North Carolina. There is some confusion over exactly where and when he was born, and he seemed to like it that way. "The neighborhood was so bad my mother told me if you see a stop sign with bullets holes in it, it means, 'GO,'" said Meadowlark. It was like growing up in a combat zone. By the age of six, his parents had divorced, and he was sent to live with his Aunt Maggie and Uncle Frank. When they moved to South Carolina, he returned to live with his dad, "Peanut" Lemon. His father's real name was Meadow Lemon II and so he had been named Meadow Lemon III. His dad called him "Junior" and his friends called him "Slim." He was tall and narrow like an old phone booth. Peanut was a gambler and known to be good with a knife. "My old man was as tough as they come," said Lemon. "We played football day and night," said Meadowlark. "We had been told that basketball was for sissies."

At the age of 11, Meadowlark paid 25 cents to go to the movie theater in town. The screen was filled with cowboy movies, and black & white newsreels. It was here that Lemon got his first glimpse of the Harlem Globetrotters. "That music from the 'Magic Circle' made me want to dance," said Lemon. "I was hooked. They seemed to make that ball talk. That's mine; this is for me. I was receiving a vision. I was receiving a dream in my heart," said Meadowlark. "I wanted to grow up to be a Globetrotter." The Magic Circle had been fashioned by the Trotters after watching the Negro League teams play pepper in baseball. The music they used to perform was "Sweet Georgia Brown."

Meadowlark would learn how to play basketball at the Boys' Club in town. An older local kid named Earl Jackson had signed a scholarship to play basketball at N. C. State, but had been injured and returned to Wilmington. It was Jackson who taught Meadowlark the hook shot. "I practiced every waking hour," said Meadowlark. He attended Williston Industrial High School during a time of segregation. Williston was the local Negro high school and had an enrollment of about 400 kids. Once they played Laurinburg Industrial High School, who had a star of their own by the name of Sam Jones, a future NBA Hall-of-Fame basketball player for the Boston Celtics.

Lemon averaged 29 points per game in basketball, while he still played wide receiver and cornerback on the football team. He would be chosen All-State in football and basketball. He would receive a scholarship to play basketball at Florida A&M University. He wanted to play football too, but when he arrived on campus the football season had already started and while waiting for the basketball season to start, he was drafted by the Army. He chose to leave Florida A&M and returned to Wilmington and reported to the draft office. While waiting on the Army he received a call from the Globetrotters, who were playing in Raleigh in a couple of weeks. There he met Marques Haynes, who had injured his knee. To Meadowlark's amazement Haynes allowed Lemon to suit up and actually play about one quarter of the game that night. "I was in Heaven," exclaimed Lemon. He returned home sure he had made the right decision to leave college. He would now serve two years in the U. S. Army. While he was in the service, his father was stabbed by his girlfriend and died. His mother remarried.

After his enlistment was up, Lemon joined the Globetrotters in 1955. He was given the #36. He was 6' 3' tall and weighed 190. A teammate, Josh Crider added the "lark' to his first name. Shortly after that, Lemon legally changed his name to Meadowlark Lemon. As Clown Prince, Meadowlark chased referees with buckets of water that were instead filled with confetti. He dribbled the ball way over his head, while taking exaggerated steps. He and his teammates pantomimed a baseball game, while he constantly talked, teased and chattered, the entire time he was on the court. *Los Angeles Times* sportswriter, Jim Murray, once wrote, "Through it all, Lemon became an American institution, like the Washington Monument or the Statue of Liberty, whose uniform will one day hang in the Smithsonian right next to Lindbergh's airplane."

Gordon Purvis was my father. Born on a farm in 1924, he grew up in a time of need. The hardships of the Depression and World War II created tough people who were not afraid of anything, especially hard work. I have often said that my father was everything you would not want to be.

He was short, red-headed, freckles, left-handed, wore glasses, dirt poor and was expelled from school in the eighth grade and never went back. So, he was also uneducated. But you could not outwork him, and he possessed wisdom beyond his years. The important things to him were honesty, effort, and the value of a dollar. He and my mother moved to Raleigh, North Carolina, where my brother and I were born. They sold their car to rent an apartment and then later borrowed some money, and Dad opened a small convenience store, kind of like a 7-11. He would name his store Gordon's Market. It required him to work from 6 AM every morning until 10 PM at night, seven days a week. Therefore, my brother and I rarely spent any time with him, when we were younger. In saying all that, there were two times a year that he made it a point to spend uninterrupted time with us. When the Ringling Brothers Barnum & Bailey Circus came to town, he would take us to watch the animals being unloaded from the train; and when the Harlem Globetrotters played at Dorton Arena in Raleigh N.C., we were there to see the likes of players such as Meadowlark Lemon, Goose Tatum, and Nate "Sweetwater" Clifton. It was at a Globetrotters' game that I vividly remember hearing my father laugh out loud for the first time. He loved the Trotters and they made him laugh, as well as millions of other fans around the globe. That was the real magic of the Harlem Globetrotters. In high school, I became friends with a future Globetrotter by the name of "Twiggy" Sanders, and then met and enjoyed the company of another Globetrotter, Meadowlark Lemon. In fact, I have a signed cancelled check from Meadowlark that was written on his company name, "Four Guys Named Joe." I asked Lemon about the company name, and the story goes like this: Meadowlark was from Wilmington, N.C., and was signed after returning from the Army, by Harlem Globetrotter owner, Abe Saperstein. Abe took Meadowlark to Chicago to introduce him to the press. No one had ever heard of Lemon and when he was introduced, the first reporter asked, "Who the heck is Meadowlark Lemon?" Abe responded, "I can take Meadowlark Lemon and four guys named Joe and beat any team in the country." Meadowlark then told me, "That was the best thing anyone had ever said about me, so I decided that if I ever owned my own business, I would name it 'Four Guys Named Joe.'"

In 2008, I became friends with current Globetrotter, Will "Bull" Bullard, who attended Texas A&M Corpus Christi and played for the Islanders. We are still great friends today. When I told Bull about the story of my father, he smiled and said, "I love that story and that's why I'm a Globetrotter." In an interview, I asked Bull which Globetrotter he wished he could have played with. "Marques Haynes, Goose Tatum, 'Geese' Ausbie, Curly Neal, Meadowlark Lemon," then Bull stopped himself, smiled and said, "All of them."

In 1979, after 26 years with the Harlem Globetrotters, he formed his own basketball team called the Meadowlark Lemon Bucketeers (1980-83). He played and starred for the Shooting Stars from (1984-87) and then formed the Meadowlark Lemon Harlem All-Stars 1988-present). In 1986, he became an ordained minister and a Motivational and Keynote Speaker.

It has been estimated that Meadowlark traveled over 5 million miles and played in well over 100 different countries. The Trotters played for Kings, Queens, Presidents, and Popes, as well as, of course, the masses. He participated in about 16,000 games during his 26 years with the Trotters. Lemon only missed two games in all those years. Meadowlark was also the most well-paid player on the Globetrotters' team. Meadowlark Lemon's awards were many. Meadowlark was inducted into the N.C. Sports Hall of Fame in 1975. In 1997, he was given the Sports Legend Award on *Ebony Magazine's* 50th anniversary. In the year 2000, Lemon received the Lifetime Achievement Award from the Naismith Memorial Basketball Hall of Fame, and also the International Clown Hall of Fame Lifetime-of-Laughter Award. In 2001, he received the Victor Award from the American Academy of Sports. He was enshrined into the Naismith Memorial Basketball Hall of Fame in 2002, as part of the Globetrotters, and became only the second Globetrotter, after Marques Haynes, to become a member of the Naismith Memorial Basketball Hall of Fame, in 2003. In 2006, Lemon received a star on the Celebrate-Wilmington Walk of Fame.

His favorite players were Wilt Chamberlain and Connie Hawkins. Meadowlark always wanted to be a cowboy, so riding horses became one of his hobbies. Meadowlark also loved to sing and did not drink alcohol, smoke or take drugs of any kind.

Over the years, Lemon could be seen on many television shows such as "Ed Sullivan," "Johnny Carson," "The Tonight Show," and "The Late Show" with David Letterman. Additionally, he starred in hundreds of commercials.

This past Sunday, like my father, I lost along with millions of other basketball fans, one of our heroes. Meadowlark Lemon died of natural causes on December 27, 2015. He was living in Scottsdale, Arizona, with his current wife, Cynthia. Meadowlark Lemon was 83. Meadowlark had ten children with three different wives. Wilt Chamberlain once said, "The most fun I ever had playing basketball was when I was with the Globetrotters." I bet that Meadowlark would say the same.

The "Clown Prince" is no more.

WE PLAYED MEAN

He was born hardnosed. Everything he did was fast. He talked fast, ate fast, and rushed the quarterback fast. It was like he had built-in radar. God only makes a few outside rushers on defense. He was what a defensive end should look like: tall and agile, ill tempered and impatient. At 6' 8" tall and 280 pounds, he looked like LeBron James in football gear. There was not much for him to be afraid of, on or off the field. If you saw his footprints in the sand, you'd call 911. When he flew on an airplane, he needed an extra ticket for his helmet. He looked like something that had just walked up from the railroad tracks looking for food. He was the kind of guy from whom you would hide the good china, when he entered your home. A savage competitor with a huge appetite, he owned the temper of gunslinger John Wesley Hardin and could change directions like an antelope. He would dispose of an offensive lineman like swatting a fly. He could spot a sweep coming two plays ahead, and his hands smelled like a quarterback. He was also weather-proof; the worse the conditions, the better he played. While others did wind sprints and jumping jacks, he practiced a forearm shiver to the face and the head slap. Blocking this guy was tougher than curing cancer.

The scariest guys in pro football were the ones who never said a word, no matter how hard you drilled them. For the Chicago Bears, after a whole week of workouts, playing a game was like having a day off. Other teams would rather play the Vikings twice, than the Bears once. The Vikings may beat you on the scoreboard, but the Bears would make you ache. They didn't call them "The Monsters of the Midway" for nothing. It was man-to-man every Sunday, in the National Football League. Each player thought to themselves, I'm going to be better than you at this moment. It's hard to intimidate other players in the NFL. How do you intimidate guys who can bench press a Coke machine? The war in football is not only physical, it contains words as well. This fellow used every last resource to anger his opponent. He would insult your family, your heritage, even your haircut.

Sacking the other team's quarterback is like devastating a city. "I was just doing what I did best, teeing off on the quarterback," exclaimed Atkins. Some years ago I stopped talking about Doug Atkins for the simple reason that I realized that those who had never seen him play didn't believe me. "We played mean," said Doug Atkins. "We knew everybody else had it better than us." He was so good his middle name should have been "Canton."

Douglas Leon Atkins was born in Humboldt, Tennessee, on May 8, 1930. Atkins led his high-school basketball team to 44 consecutive victories. Atkins enrolled at Tennessee on a basketball scholarship, but once the head football coach saw his combination of size and agility, he was persuaded to join the football team. He would become a national champion with the 1951 Tennessee Volunteers, coached by legendary Bob Neyland. The following year, 1952, Atkins was chosen to the NCAA Football All-American squad. He also won the SEC Championship in high jump by clearing 6' 6". Doug Atkins is one of the few players to have his number retired at the University of Tennessee.

Atkins was drafted in the 1953 NFL draft with the 11th pick by the Cleveland Browns. An instant starter, Cleveland won the Eastern Conference Championship, in 1953. In 1954, Atkins helped the Browns win the NFL Title. He would be traded the following year, to the Chicago Bears. Atkins was considered too much trouble for owner and head football coach Paul Brown. "He was not a good practice player," said Brown.

George Halas traded the Bears' 1955 third and sixth draft pick for Atkins. Halas would prove to have vision, as Atkins was selected to eight Pro-Bowls during his 12 seasons with the Bears. He also was selected First Team All-Pro four times (1958, 1960, 1961, 1963). He is a member of the NFL 1960's All-Decade Team. Eventually, he was traded to the New Orleans Saints in 1967, where he would finish his career. Atkins always credited George Allen, the Bears' defensive coordinator, for letting him concentrate on rushing the passer instead of covering short passes, as he had done previously.

There are as many stories about Atkins as there are stars in the sky. Here are a few of the funny ones. Ed O'Bradovich, who played opposite Atkins for the Bears, once recalled the opening day training camp when Atkins showed up 45 minutes late and ran around the practice field wearing shorts, a t-shirt, and a helmet with no chinstrap or facemask. Halas just ignored him. O'Bradovich asked him, "What the hell are you doing? Are you crazy?" "I was breaking in my helmet," responded Atkins.

Doug Atkins owned a pit bull named Rebel who went with him everywhere, even to the bar. There they would sit side by side, as Atkins drowned his sorrows and shared his drink with Rebel. He even brought Rebel to training camp, along with several handguns and shotguns. Very few coaches wanted to do bed check at Atkins room. Defensive tackle, Fred Williams, once recalled a martini-drinking contest in which he and Atkins stopped at 21 each. "But Doug drove me home and carried me in the house, so I always figured he won," said Williams.

"I played against some mean ones," Said Hall-of-Fame lineman, Jim Parker, of the Baltimore Colts, "But I never met anyone meaner than Atkins. After my first meeting him with him, I really wanted to quit pro football." Mike Pyle, a center for Chicago, tells the story of how he was selected the team's player representative for the Bears. Doug stood up and said, "I nominate Mike Pyle 'cause he's from Yale." The rest of the players were asked, "Anybody else?" Atkins then said, "Yeah, I move the nominations be closed."

There was no question that he was the strongest man in football. When he wanted to play, nobody could block him. Atkins knocked out eight quarterbacks during the 1963 season. I mean, they left the field. Bob St. Clair, 49ers offensive tackle said, "Whatever you do, don't hold him; you will only make him mad." Bears' fullback, Rick Casares noted, "We used to hope that somebody would hold Doug. The next play you would see guys flying around like King Kong had gotten a hold of them. I've seen him grab a tackle by the shoulder pads and flip him over like a doll, reach over, grab the quarterback by the shoulder pads and throw him down with one arm." Bears' defensive back, Richie Petitbon once said, "I saw Doug eat 45 pieces of chicken in a single setting." Atkins responded, "I really was never a big eater, now drinking was something else. I think Richie might be confusing chicken for martinis." It has been said that Atkins' shenanigans forced Halas to hire private detectives to track the whereabouts of players.

Doug Atkins played in 205 games (the most at that time for NFL linemen) during 17 seasons, and also intercepted three passes. He only missed 17 games during his career. In 1963, the Chicago Bears set the team record for allowing only 18 touchdowns to be scored, while setting a league low average of giving up 10 points per game. In the title game, played in 8-degree weather in Chicago, Atkins and the defensive line put so much pressure on quarterback Y.A. Tittle of the Giants, that Tittle threw five interceptions. The Bears defeated the New York Giants for the 1963 NFL title, 14-10. Atkins' highest salary was $25,000. It has been said that Atkins once told "Papa Bear" Halas, "You don't pay me enough to practice and play on Sunday." He may have been right.

In 1969, on the final play of his NFL career, 39-year-old Doug Atkins sacked Pittsburgh Steelers quarterback Dick Shiner, securing the New Orleans Saints 27-24 victory.

Atkins was inducted into the Pro-Football Hall of Fame in 1982 and the College Football Hall of Fame in 1985. He was also selected into the Chicagoland Sports Hall of Fame. His collegiate jersey, #91, was retired by the University of Tennessee in 2005. Even though Atkins only played three seasons for the Saints, the club retired his #81. The only other number retired by the Saints belongs to Hall-of-Fame running back, Jim Taylor, the #31. There is no way of telling how many "sacks" Atkins would have recorded as that stat was not tracked until 1982, well after his playing days were though. In retirement, Atkins sold caskets, drove a truck, ran a beer distributorship and worked in the county tax office. His first wife, Joyce, died in 2000.

Doug Atkins died from natural causes at his home in Knoxville, Tennessee, on Wednesday, December 30, 2015. He was 85. He had been ailing for quite a while, as a result of numerous injuries he received during his playing days. Atkins also suffered from Addison's disease and heart problems. He was afraid of having knee surgery, so he resorted to using a cane and, eventually a wheelchair, in his last years. Atkins was survived by three sons, Dalton, Kent and Neil, his wife of 12 years, Sylvia, a brother Royce, four grandchildren, and two great grandchildren.

In 1983, John Facenda described the play of Atkins this way for NFL Films: "Doug Atkins was like a storm blowing over a Kansas farm house. He came from all directions. All you could do was to tie down what you could and hope he didn't take the roof."

I find it funny that a man who caused so much devastation and dominated the league defensively said, near his end, "I never liked the physical nature of the game. I always enjoyed payday best, especially after a game we had won."

ABOUT THE AUTHOR

Andy Purvis is a long time sports enthusiast. He lives in Corpus Christi, Texas, with his wife and two cats. He has four grandchildren and two great grandchildren. They are also in his Hall of Fame! He has been in restaurant management for over 37 years and has recently retired. Andy has always had an acute interest in and knowledge of sports history and has been blessed to meet many of his childhood heroes. Andy writes for the Island Moon Newspaper and The Metro-Leader Magazine. He has also co-hosted a sports talk radio show with a couple of different partners for 20 years and continues on SportsRadioCC 1230 KSIX. He maintains contact with many sports "greats" and other sports friends. Feel free to visit www.purvisbooks.com.

CPSIA information can be obtained
at www.ICGtesting.com
Printed in the USA
LVOW01s2246260416

485475LV00012B/188/P